D0948107

Wang Kuo-wei

HARVARD EAST ASIAN SERIES 101

The Council on East Asian Studies at Harvard University,
through the Fairbank Center for East Asian Research and
the Japan Institute, administers research projects designed to further
scholarly understanding of China, Japan, Korea, Vietnam,
Inner Asia, and adjacent areas.

Wang in later years

Wang Kuo-wei

An Intellectual Biography

Joey Bonner

Harvard University Press
Cambridge, Massachusetts, and London, England
1986

Publication of this book has been aided by
a grant from the Andrew W. Mellon Foundation.

This book is printed on acid-free paper,
and its binding materials have been chosen
for strength and durability.

Library of Congress Cataloging in Publication Data
Bonner, Joey, 1948–
Wang Kuo-wei : An intellectual biography.

(Harvard East Asian series ; 101)
Bibliography: p.
Includes index.
1. Wang, Kuo-wei, 1877–1927—Biography. 2. Authors,
Chinese—Biography. I. Title. II. Series.
PL2732.A5Z59 1986 895.1'8509 [B] 85-14094
ISBN 0-674-94594-8 (alk. paper)

To Wang Kuo-wei,
one of the seminal minds of our century,
and to all those who through the
disciplines of philosophy, literature, and history
seek to humanize the world of men

Contents

Contents

Preface

Alas! Outside the holy continent of China there are other
continents, and after the present generation there will be
future generations. Will there be anyone among [the persons of other continents and future generations] able to
read Mr. Wang Kuo-wei's works? If there is somewhere,
someday such a person, he will profoundly appreciate Mr.
Wang's works and come into close spiritual contact with him.
Such a person will be able not only to visualize Mr. Wang's
personality and the world in which he lived, but also to
understand his extraordinary sorrow and grief.

> —Ch'en Yin-k'o, foreword to the second edition of Wang
> Kuo-wei's collected works, *Hai-ning Wang Ching-an hsien-sheng
> i-shu*

At approximately ten o'clock on the morning of 2 June 1927 a
slight, seemingly aged gentleman dressed in an old-fashioned cloth
gown and cap entered the still, verdant grounds of I-ho Park, located
in the bucolic suburbs of Peking. For a long while he sat by the Marble
Boat, apparently lost in thought. Just moments after spotting him
quietly smoking a cigarette in the Fishes-among-Pondweed Pavilion,
the park gardener heard a loud splash. Wading hurriedly into the
shallow water of K'un-ming Lake, he dragged the stranger to safety.
Barely two minutes had elapsed; the gentleman's inner garments were
not even wet. But one of China's most eminent intellectuals lay dead,
choked by the mud at the bottom of K'un-ming Lake.[1]

The life and concerns of the man who died that early June day
in I-ho Park are the subjects of this study. His was an unusually
productive life, for Wang Kuo-wei (1877–1927) was a scholar of for-
midable abilities who made contributions of the first order to a number
of areas of intellectual inquiry. He is today best remembered for his
articles on German philosophy and philosophical aesthetics; for his
poetry, literary criticism, and aesthetic theory; and for his studies on
Chinese history, particularly of the Shang dynasty (traditionally dated
from 1765 to 1123 B.C.). One of my principal aims in this intellectual
biography of Wang is, accordingly, to provide a critical account of the
evolution of his ideas in, and the substance of his contributions to,
the disciplines of philosophy, literature, and history.

From the moment he first burst into print, Wang Kuo-wei was
preoccupied not with his country's immediate political, economic, and

military problems (these, he seems to have assumed, would somehow resolve themselves), but rather with the enduring, if elusive, questions of higher belief, artistic form, and moral value. In German idealistic and voluntaristic philosophy, the study of which he undertook with enthusiasm at the dawn of the twentieth century and forsook in despair some years later, Wang sought the fundamental truths of the human condition. In his literary and aesthetic pursuits of the period immediately preceding the 1911 Revolution, Wang endeavored to elucidate the character of all that is beautiful. And in the historical and classical texts in which he immersed himself in the postimperial era, Wang saw exemplified the moral principles to which, in his later years, he was fiercely devoted and for which, in the end, he would sacrifice his life. A second aim of this book thus is to relate Wang Kuo-wei's strenuous intellectual search in the fields of philosophy, literature, and history to his very personal quest for truth, beauty, and virtue. Wang's widely and profoundly misunderstood suicide can, in my view, be made intelligible only within the context of his humanistic concerns in general and his extreme commitment in later life to the Confucian ethicoreligious tradition in particular.

Although generally considered the most brilliant and tragic Chinese figure of his day, Wang Kuo-wei has not received the critical treatment that an individual of his stature deserves. While probably due in part to the multifaceted nature of his scholarly achievement, the dearth of critical studies on Wang's life and work is surely due as well to his loyalist orientation in the post-1911 period. Indeed, his loyalism has made Wang an emotionally and politically explosive subject on both Taiwan and the mainland. My third, and final, ambition in this book is critically to describe the actual substance of Wang's conservatism in the years following the 1911 Revolution. By examining the view of late Ch'ing and early Republican developments to which noted loyalists such as Wang Kuo-wei and his intimate friends Lo Chen-yü, Shen Tseng-chih, and K'o Shao-min subscribed, we will, I trust, gain new insight into both the phenomenon of Chinese loyalism in its modern context and the politics of Chinese reformism and revolution.

One cannot read the surviving works of Wang Kuo-wei today without acquiring tremendous respect for him, both as a scholar of wide-ranging intellectual interests and as a gentleman of lofty moral convictions. One need share neither Wang's gloomy assessment of the human predicament nor his thoughtfully pessimistic outlook on life in order to appreciate the profundity of his scholarship, the intensity of his emotional commitments, the clarity of his vision, and the acuity of his observations on the China of his day. Across the barriers of culture and time Wang speaks to us in his books, essays, poems, and letters in words that are insistent, not infrequently self-righteous, at times cynical, but always enlightening.

Because he lived during one of the most tumultuous eras in modern Chinese history, Wang's story, like those of many of his contemporaries, is not a happy one. Indeed, Wang Kuo-wei's youthful image of himself as a lonely, suffering genius, together with his romantic attachment in later years to a way of life he knew to be irretrievably gone, imparts to the tale I am about to tell a peculiar and haunting poignancy.

Acknowledgments

During the course of my research on Wang Kuo-wei, I have sought and received assistance from many quarters. I would like in the first instance to thank the trustees of the five private foundations that provided the bulk of the support for *Wang Kuo-wei:* the Ludwig Vogelstein Foundation, Richard D. Irwin Foundation, Charles M. Ross Trust, John Anson Kittredge Educational Fund, and Earhart Foundation. I am also grateful to the members of Harvard University's Council on East Asian Studies for awarding me, in 1981–82, a John King Fairbank Postdoctoral Fellowship.

On numerous occasions I have asked friends and colleagues for advice regarding this or that aspect of Wang's oeuvre. In three crucial areas it has been my good fortune to consult outstanding authorities. With respect to German philosophy and philosophical aesthetics, I am indebted to Professor Donald Fleming, who has both given me the benefit of his remarkable understanding of these subjects and read critically the chapters of this book that concern them.

No colleague has shown me more personal kindness and offered me more scholarly assistance than Professor James J. Y. Liu. Not only has he patiently answered all my questions regarding Wang Kuo-wei's poetry, literary criticism, and aesthetic theory, but he has as well graciously read three different drafts of the "literary chapters" of this book and offered many valuable suggestions. With respect to Wang's poetry specifically, I would like also to thank Professor Ronald C. Egan and the late Dr. William T. Graham, Jr., for generously sharing with me their critical insights into the poems I have translated and discussed in chapters 10 and 12.

Concerning Wang Kuo-wei's historical pursuits, I have had the pleasure of consulting Professor Chang Kwang-chih on a number of occasions. Both he and Professor David N. Keightley have kindly read and criticized the portion of my intellectual biography dealing with Wang's career as a historian of ancient China.

With respect to this work as a whole, I am indebted to Professors

Benjamin I. Schwartz, Patrick D. Hanan, and Tu Wei-ming for cri-
tiquing my manuscript. I am grateful as well to Professor Loh Wai-
fong for spending countless hours with me reading texts during the
late 1970s. To Mr. Ch'en Yü-p'i (Chinese Academy of Social Sciences)
I owe a very special word of thanks, both for the lively interest he has
taken in my research on Wang Kuo-wei and for the many important
materials that he has brought to my attention over the years.

I am also much obliged to Professor Philip A. Kuhn, with whom
I have had fruitful discussions concerning the nature of Wang's conservative commitments in later life; Professors John K. Fairbank and
Frederic Wakeman, Jr., who have kindly written letter after letter
commending my work to grant-giving agencies; Professor Lo Chi-tsu
(Kirin University), who has graciously shared with me his understanding of Wang Kuo-wei's life in certain controversial particulars and
obligingly furnished the photograph of his grandfather and Wang
reproduced on page 163; and Mrs. Chen Pin Yen (Wang Tung-ming),
who has generously provided the photograph of her father for the
frontispiece. I would like to thank as well the anonymous (to me)
reader engaged by the members of Harvard's Council on East Asian
Studies in the winter of 1980–81 to critique an early version of the
first two-thirds of this book; his comments inspired me to devote an
additional three years to it.

The severest critic of *Wang Kuo-wei* has been my husband, Jeffrey
A. Sheehan, whose herculean efforts over seven years to improve my
manuscript deserve special mention. Despite the demands of his own
career, he has found time to discuss every facet of this work with me;
offer numerous suggestions, both substantive and stylistic, on each of
the five major drafts of the book; review all my grant proposals; and
learn enough Chinese to converse with the visiting scholars I periodically bring home to dinner. He has also good-naturedly forgone
vacations, and most weekends as well, during the years that I have
labored on my intellectual biography of Wang Kuo-wei.

I conceived the ambition, at about age fourteen, of becoming a
Sinologist under the influence of my father, Professor James F. Bonner, a biologist of wide-ranging interests, whom I found one afternoon
in his study reading *Dream of the Red Chamber* (*Hung-lou meng*). My
fate was sealed when not long afterward I was "adopted" by Ambas-
sador and Mrs. James (Chien-hung) Shen, in whose Taipei home I
lived on two occasions (1966, 1968–69). I shall always be grateful for
the encouragement and support that my mother, the late Dr. Harriet
Rees Bonner, provided me during my graduate career at Johns Hopkins and Harvard.

*   *   *

An early version of chapter 6 appeared in *Philosophy East and West* (October 1979) and is used here by permission of the University of Hawaii Press. Excerpts from chapter 13 are included in *Early China* 9. Translated by John C. Y. Wang, the four-line poem quoted on page 86 appears in *Chinese Approaches to Literature from Confucius to Liang Ch'i-ch'ao*, edited by Adele Austin Rickett, copyright © 1978 by Princeton University Press, and is reprinted by permission of Princeton University Press. The passage from *Injustice to Tou O* quoted on page 135 appears in Shih Chung-wen's book of the same title and is reprinted by permission of Cambridge University Press. The passage from *Ch'ien-nü's Soul Leaves Her Body* quoted on page 136 appears in Liu Jung-en's *Six Yüan Plays* and is reprinted by permission of Penguin Books Ltd. Translated by Donald Keene, the passage from *Autumn in the Han Palace* quoted on pages 137–138 appears in the *Anthology of Chinese Literature from Early Times to the Fourteenth Century*, edited by Cyril Birch, and is reprinted by permission of Grove Press. The excerpts from James Legge's *Chinese Classics* quoted on pages 213 and 277 are reprinted by permission of Hong Kong University Press. The characters in chapter 14 were written by Mrs. Diana Wang.

Wang Kuo-wei

Wang's given name was Kuo-wei; his courtesy names, Ching-an and Po-yü; his early sobriquet, Li-t'ang; his later sobriquets, Kuan-t'ang and Yung-kuan; and his posthumous title, Chung-ch'ueh kung. For the reader's convenience, in this book I will always refer to Wang by his given name, except when translating the titles of works either by or about him.

Prologue: The 1890s Generation

With the advantage of hindsight, we can see that the generation of Chinese thinkers who attained intellectual maturity around the time of the Sino-Japanese War (1894–95) constituted the "breakthrough," or "watershed," generation of modern Chinese thinkers. Unlike the younger, more radical, and culturally deracinated members of the May Fourth generation, who would flourish during the second and third decades of the twentieth century, members of the so-called 1890s generation were genuinely products of the old society within the framework of which they had comfortably passed their earliest years. Like their fathers and grandfathers before them, members of this older generation of Chinese intellectuals received a classical literary education, assimilated Confucian moral and political principles, and sought employment in the Ch'ing bureaucracy. Unlike their forefathers, however, they began, after the humiliating denouement of the war with Japan, seriously to doubt certain cardinal features of the Confucian "Way" and seriously to take up the study of Western thought. It was, indeed, members of the 1890s generation who introduced into the intellectual arena all those tendencies whose culmination would be reached in the iconoclastic May Fourth Movement of 1918–1927.

By the mid-1890s the once proud and mighty Celestial Empire had fought and lost wars with both Great Britain and France, as one result of which many literati were at last prepared grudgingly to concede the military superiority of the Western powers. They were, however, by no means prepared to concede the military superiority of Japan, the success of whose modernizing efforts was largely unappreciated in Chinese political and intellectual circles until the traumatic defeat of 1894–95. It was precisely because they had not expected to lose the war with Japan that the tiny literate elite who constituted the vanguard of the Chinese people at the fin de siècle were so profoundly shaken by the 1894–95 debacle.

As one consequence of the disastrous outcome of the Sino-Japanese War, concerned members of the Chinese intelligentsia began a revaluation of values that would lead to the demise of the culture in which they themselves had been raised. After 1895 it was a rare young man who failed to suspect that Chinese civilization could not, after all, provide the answers to his most pressing concerns. The reaction to the war of a worried young man named Lo Chen-yü (1866–1940) was typical: "At that time China's forces had just been defeated and the people's minds were uneasy. I, too, wished to learn a little about foreign affairs, so I borrowed from a friend some books translated into Chinese by the Kiangnan Arsenal and read them."[1] Within months of the humiliating conclusion of the war, this patriotic young man, like many others of his generation, had determined to help the Middle Kingdom become "wealthy and strong" (*fu ch'iang*) by studying the so-called practical knowledge of the West and Japan. Little did he then realize, wrote Lo many years later, that his generation's efforts to promote "self-strengthening" (*tzu-ch'iang*)—that is, technological modernization—were harbingers of the demise of traditional Chinese culture.[2]

The project to bring China technologically into the modern world had in fact been under way for some years before Lo Chen-yü and other members of the 1890s generation first appeared on the national scene. Already in the 1870s and 1880s such leading statesmen as Chang Chih-tung (1837–1909) and Li Hung-chang (1823–1901) had begun painfully to discover that the mere importation of Western military hardware, which the empire's first generation of self-strengtheners had promoted as the panacea for China's military troubles in the years immediately following the Opium War (1840–1842), would not in itself enable the empire to become either prosperous or powerful. Self-strengthening, these scholar-officials realized, would require both the adoption of a whole battery of Western procedures that (as it now appeared to them) were necessarily associated with Western military technology and a systematic attempt to develop industry and commerce. On the happy assumption that the pursuit of national wealth and power would prove compatible with what they considered to be the central values of the Confucian faith, these reformist scholar-officials hopefully established the Middle Kingdom's first industrial enterprises.

It is a salient feature of what might be called the technological approach to China's military and economic woes that its proponents, while seeking Western wisdom in the area of practical knowledge, remained overwhelmingly committed to fundamental Confucian values as the real heart of civilized life. Although leading statesmen of the seventies and eighties were eager to "learn from the West" and even willing to repudiate the traditional Chinese ideal of a subsistence-level agrarian economy, they were by no means prepared to forsake what Chang Chih-tung referred to as the "essential truths" (*t'i*) of the Confucian Way. In his well-known tract, *Exhortation to Learn (Ch'üan-hsueh p'ien)*, Chang is eager not simply to convince his fellow administrators of the necessity of building railways and modern industries in the Middle Kingdom. He is also, and most particularly, concerned to delineate that realm of human endeavor which should properly be regulated by the Confucian values that he cherishes. The essential core of the Confucian faith had, it is true, by this time been reduced to certain basic features of Confucian morality and political theory, but to the preservation of these "ultimate" Confucian values Chang Chih-tung and his colleagues were intensely devoted. However, inasmuch as the "preservation of the faith" (*pao-chiao*) required the "preservation of the state" (*pao-kuo*), and the preservation of the state could now be seen to involve the development of both military technology and native industry and commerce, the latter-day self-strengtheners adopted a policy of "halfway" Westernization whose rationale was aptly epitomized in Chang's famous slogan, "Chinese learning for essential truths; Western learning for practical knowledge."

In the crisis atmosphere of the period immediately following the Sino-Japanese War, some of Chang Chih-tung's younger contemporaries, among them Lo Chen-yü and his friend Liu E (T'ieh-yun, 1857–1909), warmly embraced that gentleman's formula for prosperity and power. Others, however, began to doubt its soundness. The crux of the problem as envisioned by a skeptical scholar named Yen Fu (1853–1921) was whether it was wise to assume that a country's fundamental values can in fact be separated, either in theory or in practice, from its technology and practical skills. Were it indeed the case that Chinese knowledge possesses its own essential truths inextricably linked to its own technology and ways of doing things, Yen Fu boldly suggested, might not the preservation of the Confucian faith prove incompatible with the preservation of the Chinese state?[3]

It is Yen Fu's distinction to have advanced the radical proposition that the preservation of the societal organism known as the state properly takes precedence over commitment to all other values. Whatever their origin, Yen Fu said, all other values ought to be judged by the sole criterion of their ability to contribute to the strengthening of the state. "We must exert our utmost efforts to seek out knowledge. We have no time to ask whether this knowledge is Chinese or Western, whether it is new or old. If one course leads to ignorance and thus to poverty and weakness, even if it originates with our ancestors or is based on the authority of our rulers and teachers, not to speak of persons of a lower order, we must cast it aside. If another course is effective in overcoming ignorance and thus leads to the cure of our poverty and weakness, we must imitate it, even if it proceeds from barbarians and wild beasts, not to speak of persons of a higher order."[4]

His preoccupation with state power led Yen Fu to conclusions about traditional Confucian values that were highly unorthodox within the context of late nineteenth-century Chinese society. The Confucian emphasis on social harmony, on stasis, on the rule of good men, on the renunciation of self, on the rejection of profit as a suitable goal of human activity—all of these Confucian values, Yen Fu opined, had inhibited the development of the wealth and power of the Chinese state. The whole tired self-strengthening movement had amply demonstrated, he maintained, that external reforms in the realms of defense, industry, and commerce, in the absence of internal reforms in the ways men think about their world, cannot take a country very far down the road to wealth and power. What was required was a revolution in Chinese values to supplement and ground the empire's technological revolution. "The faith cannot be preserved," Yen Fu declared categorically.[5]

Like most of his predecessors and contemporaries, Yen Fu was extremely interested in the secrets of the military, political, and economic strength of modern Western nations, but unlike them he was also interested in what Western thinkers themselves have thought about these important matters. Quite early on in his career, therefore, he decided to seek the sources of Western might in the writings of Westerners. Since he knew English, had studied in Great Britain, and regarded that country as the pristine exemplar of wealth and power, Yen Fu was from the first primarily interested in investigating the ideas of certain prominent British intellectuals. In the decade or so following the catastrophic Sino-Japanese War, he wrote several essays on British thinkers as well as some translations of and commentaries on their works. Determined to rouse his fellow literati from their Confucian slumber, the indefatigable Yen Fu assumed the burden of acquainting the Chinese reading public with the heretical (from a Confucian viewpoint) notions of Herbert Spencer, Thomas H. Huxley, John Stuart Mill, Adam Smith, Edward Jenks, and William Stanley Jevons, among others.

Yen Fu's works were nothing less than revolutionary within the context of his time. His basic thesis—that the ultimate source of Western strength lies not simply in weapons and technology, nor even in economic and political institutions, but in an entirely different vision of reality—led him to revaluate values that lay at the root of Chinese culture and to offer his compatriots the striking new view of the world that he had acquired from his British mentors. Yen Fu's heterodox writings caused a stir among members of his generation and had a profound impact on the young. That they did so is attributable to the circumstance that many Chinese in the fin de siècle were, like Yen Fu himself, deeply troubled by the empire's material backwardness and military weakness.

Yen Fu's younger contemporary Wang Kuo-wei represents a fringe element on the contemporary Chinese intellectual scene. Indeed, Wang's significance in the history of late Ch'ing thought lies expressly in the fact that he did not share his compatriots' burning concern with the sources of national strength. On the contrary, Wang was a vehement opponent of what he called "utilitarianism" in both its Chinese and Western guises and disdained Chang Chih-tung and Yen Fu alike. Highly skeptical of the possibility of society's ever achieving a technological solution to the fundamental problems of the human condition, he adopted an attitude toward the project to modernize China that we may fairly summarize with these immortal words of the ultra-Confucian official Wo-jen: "The fundamental effort lies in men's minds, not in techniques."[6]

Unlike Wo-jen, Wang did not believe that Confucianism in any of its schools had adequately satisfied humanity's deepest spiritual and philosophical yearnings. Thus shortly after the turn of the century Wang launched an ambitious project to acquaint his contemporaries in the ranks of the literati with modern German philosophy and philosophical aesthetics. In undertaking this arduous task (all his translations and critical expositions were, like those of Yen Fu, made in elegant classical Chinese), Wang Kuo-wei fervently hoped to impress on his compatriots his profound conviction that their search for the secrets of wealth and power was misguided. The road to human happiness, Wang said, lies in a quite different direction.

Even before he had discovered the writings of Arthur Schopenhauer shortly before the turn of the century, Wang Kuo-wei had begun to brood on the miseries and evils of existence. Deeply sensitive to human suffering, Wang found his first life's calling in the investigation of the sources of man's existential disquiet and in the search for anodynes. In his early works he depicts life as a grim, depressing affair from which temporary refuge may be sought in philosophical reflection and aesthetic appreciation. Wang himself would devote the first half of his adult life to the study of philosophy and literature in the expectation that they would reveal to him the ultimate "truths" (chen-li) of the human situation and provide him with "consolation" (wei-chieh) for the wretchedness of existence.

It is, then, against the background of his predecessors' and contemporaries' overwhelming preoccupation with the secrets of Western strength and within the context of his own relentless, unsparing quest for spiritual moorings in what he considered to be a materialistic age that the cosmopolitan thinker Wang Kuo-wei produced the remarkable, heretical works of his youth.

2

The Early Years

When on 3 December 1877 Wang Kuo-wei was born in Shuang-jen ("doubly virtuous") Lane in the administrative seat of Hai-ning "department," Hangchou prefecture, Chekiang province, the town of his birth was already over fifteen hundred years old. Indeed, we can trace the history of Hai-ning back at least as far as Han times (206 B.C.–A.D. 220), when the area was known as Yen-kuan. Although in the early years of its existence Yen-kuan was just a small village, it prospered and in due course was raised, along with the countryside surrounding it, to the status of a district (*hsien*) and thence to a department (*chou*).[1]

In many respects Yen-kuan must have been an ideal spot in which to make one's home. Located on the northern shore of Hangchou Bay, crisscrossed by canals, and surrounded by gentle hills, this part of Chekiang is one of great scenic beauty. Because of its fertility and its proximity to Hangchou, long a center of intellectual activity in China, Yen-kuan was during the imperial period not only a physically arresting region but also a wealthy and cultured one. The typical pursuits of Yen-kuan's upper crust were, accordingly, the conventional ones of the empire's literate elite—painting, poetry, seal carving, historical scholarship, calligraphy.

Despite the general prosperity of the lower Yangtze delta from Southern Sung times (1127–1279) onward, there was one highly visible drawback to living in northeastern coastal Chekiang. Because the alluvial plain formed by the Yangtze River is elevated only slightly above water level, the towns strung along the coastline of Hangchou Bay were frequently ravaged by the powerful tides of the Pacific Ocean (awesomely high and especially dangerous were the walls of water produced seasonably by the Ch'ien-t'ang bore).[2] During one particularly disastrous period in the late thirteenth and early fourteenth centuries, a long series of floods wreaked almost continual havoc on Yen-kuan. When finally it could be reported to the Dragon Throne that the recalcitrant waters had receded, Emperor Wen-tsung

(r. 1328–1332) was so delighted that he ordered the name of Yen-kuan changed to Hai-ning, meaning "pacified ocean."[3] By this designation the region has been known ever since. But, of course, when Wang Kuo-wei's distant ancestor Wang Hang arrived in Chekiang early in the twelfth century at the behest of Emperor Kao-tsung (r. 1127–1162), all these events still lay in the future and the sea to the south of Yen-kuan was yet far from pacified.

The Wang Family

During the troublous years of the Northern Sung dynasty (960–1126), the Wang family, residents of the capital city of Pien-liang (modern K'ai-feng), Honan, produced more than its share of military heroes. The family seems first to have entered the lists of the famous with the appearance of the dashing Wang Kuei, whose martial exploits are described in the official *History of the Sung Dynasty* (*Sung shih*). One imagines that Wang Kuei thoroughly deserved his sobriquet, "Iron Whip" (T'ieh-pien). This brave and spirited officer distinguished himself in battle against the barbarous Tanguts (Tang-hsiang), who had established themselves in the Northwest, in present-day Kansu province. After many years of sending tribute to the Sung, the Tanguts had finally tired of being subservient to the Chinese. In 1038 they declared their independence and established a separate kingdom known as Hsi Hsia. In 1040 they initiated hostilities against the Chinese. It was during the war of 1040–1044 that Wang Kuei fell in battle near Hao-shui (modern T'ien-shui) River, a martyr to the Sung cause.[4]

With the untimely death of "Iron Whip" Wang, the baton of martial virtue passed to his son, Wang Kuang-tsu. This son appears ably to have carried on the Wang family legacy, for we read of successful expeditions to the Southwest and West to pacify the restless peoples of those regions as well as of excursions to the northern frontier to negotiate with the troublesome Khitan (Ch'i-tan). Wang Kuang-tsu enjoyed a long and prosperous career, and died of natural causes sometime in the 1090s. His patriotic deeds, like those of his father, were duly recorded in the *History of the Sung Dynasty*.[5]

Possibly the greatest sacrifice made by a Wang for the sake of the Northern Sung dynasty was that of Wang Ping. By the time this soldier, Wang Kuang-tsu's son, set out on his military career, the semicivilized Khitan had been replaced as the dominant power in the Northeast by their erstwhile vassals, a powerful people called the Jurched (Ju-chen). In their rise to preeminence in the Northeast, the Jurched had actually been assisted by the Chinese, who realized too late the imprudence of their foreign policy. After the abdication of the chagrined Emperor Hui-tsung (r. 1101–1125), his successor endeavored in vain to buy off the Jurched's newly established Chin dynasty. During the great struggle for North China that subsequently developed, Wang Ping was charged with the defense of T'ai-yuan. Valiantly his troops fought the northeastern barbarians, who invested the city in 1126. When the Jurched war machine proved invincible, the chastened Wang Ping led his son Wang Hsun to the banks of the Fen River, into which both Wangs then nobly cast themselves.[6]

After the fall of T'ai-yuan, the Jurched pushed south in the direction of Honan. Among the prisoners they took in the battle for the Sung capital were the former emperor, Hui-tsung, and the new emperor, Ch'in-tsung (r. 1126), both of whom were to remain in captivity until they expired. Meanwhile, however, a son of the luckless Emperor Hui-tsung had begun to wend his way south, accompanied by at least one guard with the surname Wang. In the region now called Hangchou, Emperor Kao-tsung, as he is known to history, established a "temporary" capital from which the Chao ruling house would thenceforth govern its diminished empire.

Having settled in the new capital city, Emperor Kao-tsung heaped posthumous honors on the martyred Wang Ping and lavished titles, official positions, land, and money on his several surviving sons. Feeling, apparently, that he had not yet adequately expressed the full measure of his appreciation to the family, the emperor also summoned Wang Ping's grandson Wang Hang to court and bestowed on him a mansion in nearby Hai-ning (then still called Yen-kuan). In this way the Wangs entered the local history books (chih) of Hai-ning, in which city they lived ever after.[7]

In the years immediately following their removal to Hai-ning, the Wangs continued to flourish. Wang Hang's son Wang Shu attained in 1163 the coveted literary degree of chin-shih ("presented scholar"), which entitled him to a prestigious and lucrative career in the Chinese civil service. Both Wang Shu's brother, Wang Ch'ien, and his grandson Wang Hui won the same degree thirty years later.[8] Soon thereafter the family fortunes appear to have declined, however, for we read no more of dashing military heroes or distinguished scholars among the Wangs of Hai-ning. Certainly the Wangs can have been no match for the legendary Ch'en family that, while living in Hai-ning from the sixteenth through the nineteenth centuries, produced 31 holders of the third degree (the chin-shih), 103 holders of the second degree, 74 senior licentiates, and approximately 1000 holders of the first degree and students of the Imperial Academy.[9]

Although Wang Kuo-wei's immediate ancestors were not as noted as the illustrious Ch'en family, there was yet an air of scholarly respectability about them. For example, Wang's great-great-grand-father, who held the honorary title of *ch'ao-i ta-fu*, was a student of the Imperial Academy (*chien-sheng*). So were his great-granduncle, great-grandfather, granduncle, and grandfather.[10] Even though Wang Nai-yü, Wang's father, forsook the scholarly way of life during the protracted Taiping Rebellion (1850–1864) in order to engage in busi-ness, he seems later to have returned to the academic fold, for in the 1880s he served as a private secretary (*mu-yu*) to a local magistrate. As secretarial positions in late nineteenth-century China were com-monly awarded to lower-degree graduates, we may safely assume that Wang Nai-yü at some point succeeded in acquiring one of the empire's approximately one million first degrees.[11]

Childhood in Hai-ning

When Wang Kuo-wei was born to Wang Nai-yü and his wife, née Ling, at the close of 1877, the catastrophic Taiping Rebellion had already become an event of the past and life appeared again to be flowing in familiar channels. One is therefore not surprised to find that Wang's parents decided early that their son was to pursue a literary education of the conventional type. If Wang Kuo-wei could pass the civil service examinations, the preparation for which was the raison d'être of the educational system, he would be qualified to enter government service. As there was no more prestigious calling in nine-teenth-century China than government service under the ruling Man-chus, Wang's parents were naturally eager to start their child as soon as possible on the path that would lead from the village school through the civil service examinations to a bureaucratic career. It may well be that Wang Nai-yü, whose own studies had been disrupted during the unsettled years of the Taiping occupation of Chekiang, had high hopes that his son, if given the advantage of a solid, uninterrupted education, might one day receive the higher degrees that seem to have eluded him.

From Wang Kuo-wei's Chinese biographers we are able to obtain scant information on his childhood years. Regarding his earliest re-actions to the course of study set for him by his parents, for example, they are absolutely silent. The biographical accounts (*nien-p'u* and *chuan*) they have left us reveal only that Wang was an unusually bright child. "Mr. Wang was born with a remarkable endowment. He was quick to grasp the meaning of the texts taught to him, and he thereby distinguished himself from other children. Before he was twenty years old he had become known within his hometown for his literary abil-ities."[12]

We do not know who taught Wang how to wield a brush, write his first characters, and memorize such simple texts as the *Primer of One Thousand Characters* (*Ch'ien-tzu wen*). It could not in any event have been his mother, as she died in 1880, when Wang was just a toddler. All we can glean about this period of his life is that after their mother's death Wang Kuo-wei and his elder sister, aged eight, were reared by their paternal grandmother and paternal grandaunts, née Fan, and that Wang Yun-yü found herself baby-sitting her little brother a great deal more than she had hitherto.[13]

Wang Nai-yü was not a wealthy man. His annual income, as his son recalled some quarter of a century later, "was just enough to supply us with food and clothing."[14] One imagines that the elder Wang sacrificed much to put his boy through school, which Wang Kuo-wei began early in 1883, at the age of five. Concerning the scholarly antecedents of Wang's teacher, a gentleman named P'an Shou-ch'ang, we possess no information. Since his name does not appear in any of the books of eminent Ch'ing scholars, it is likely that he was among the usual run of schoolteachers—that is, a former official who had lost his position or a scholar who, having repeatedly failed the examinations, had been obliged to eke out a living instructing young Confucianists.

Education in the neighborhood school near Shuang-jen Lane centered, as it did in most of China at this time, on the Four Books and Five Classics, works that had come to be regarded with a bibliolatry to which history affords few parallels. Since these classical texts, whatever their merits from the point of view of a mature scholar, are not calculated to titillate the imagination of children, it is not surprising that P'an's pupil Wang Kuo-wei found the school curriculum unappealing. As he wrote years later in his "Autobiography" ("Tzu-hsu"), during his childhood he found distasteful both the Classics and their voluminous commentaries, which were also required reading. He could hardly wait to be dismissed from class at nightfall so that he might go home and read something more interesting than classical tomes. "My family possessed five or six boxes of books. With the exception of *The Thirteen Classics with Commentary and Subcommentary* (*Shih-san ching chu-shu*), which as a child I disliked, I perused them all in the evenings after I had returned home from school."[15]

In 1887, at the age of nine, Wang Kuo-wei began to study with the stipendiary student Ch'en Shou-t'ien. About this teacher, too, we know very little, although the fact that he was a junior degree holder on government stipend indicates that he was a scholar of some ability, at least a notch above the ordinary. Despite the change of teachers, Wang's curriculum continued to focus on the memorization of the

Classics. To this task were added several new requirements: becoming intimately familiar with the views on these works held by the great twelfth-century philosopher Chu Hsi, gaining some understanding of tones and rhymes, and learning the art of poetic composition and the weaving of antithetical couplets. Wang was required also to practice answering questions involving passages from the Classics. In this way the boy began to prepare in earnest for the civil service examinations, the heart of which consisted of composing poems on assigned themes using prescribed rhymes and writing essays in a set format on passages selected from the Classics.[16]

From 1887 to 1892 Wang Kuo-wei studied for the examinations. He did not care in the least for the type of study that preparation for these examinations involved, but he seems to have reconciled himself to it, probably with the reflection that the course his parents had set for him was the only one likely to lead to worldly success. Perhaps, too, the dreariness of preparing for the examinations was alleviated somewhat for Wang by the return of his father in 1887 from a job he had held for some time in the neighboring province of Kiangsu. Since Wang Ssu-tuo, Wang Kuo-wei's paternal granduncle, had recently passed away, Wang Nai-yü had been constrained to leave his position as a private secretary in Li-yang district and return home to Hai-ning to observe the mourning rites. During the mourning period father and son passed their evenings together, the elder Wang, who was something of a painter and poet, drilling his boy on his lessons as he pursued his own avocations: seal carving, the study of bronze and stone inscriptions, classical prose, calligraphy, and painting and poetry.[17]

Wang Kuo-wei was evidently a precocious youth. According to his childhood friend Ch'en Shou-ch'ien, even before he had sat for his first examination Wang had become known within the locality as the most talented of "four literary talents" (ssu ts'ai-tzu). From Ch'en, too, we can obtain an interesting glimpse of the adolescent Wang's domestic situation (he had acquired a stepmother, née Yeh, back in 1885 and a half-brother in 1887).

> I was at that time serving as a live-in tutor to the Shen family in the southern part of the city. From there it was barely a third of a mile to Mr. Wang's house. Not a day passed that we did not see each other. On meeting we would talk about all types of literature and history which had been written from ancient times to the present. Sometimes we would correct suspected errors in our texts. Occasionally we would also compose poems and then admire each other's handiwork. We would invariably separate in the late afternoon, as Mr. Wang would always refuse to stay to dinner. I knew that Mr. Wang's stepmother was in charge of meals

in the Wang household and that family members were expected to return home in the late afternoon for dinner. Mr. Wang therefore was obliged to return home to please his stepmother. I usually saw him as far as the main gate.[18]

The Examinations

One day in 1892 the moment for which the Wang family had long been waiting at last arrived. For early one morning in this, his fifteenth year, Wang Kuo-wei finished assembling his "examination basket" and set out in the darkness for the Hai-ning examination hall. Gathering with him in front of the gate of the examination hall were scores of hopeful students from around the department, all intent on passing the so-called youth examinations (t'ung-shih), the first hurdle on the arduous road to bureaucratic success.

In imperial China the system of examinations was divided into two parts: school entrance examinations and civil service examinations proper. This arrangement arose from the circumstance that only men with student status gained through passing an entrance examination for a government school could take the civil service examinations. Thus any aspiring bureaucrat had necessarily to sit for the following examinations: (1) youth examinations, consisting of a district examination, a prefectural examination, and a qualifying examination; (2) the provincial examination (hsiang-shih); (3) the metropolitan examination (hui-shih, or kung-chü); and (4) the palace examination (tien-shih). A candidate's run through this literary gauntlet might easily take up half his life. Simply to sit for the first set of examinations required half a year. Competition for every academic degree—sheng-yuan ("licentiate"), chü-jen ("elevated man"), and chin-shih—was keen, however, particularly in the populous last century of the Ch'ing dynasty, because the civil service examination system comprised the empire's only respectable avenue of upward social mobility.

Wang Kuo-wei was both gifted and lucky. He passed the youth examinations on his first try, in 1892, the year in which he turned fifteen. We can well imagine the feeling of jubilation with which Wang Nai-yü must have greeted the official announcement of his son's success. The young man was now legally a student, entitled to enter the department school and to wear the official uniform of a licentiate, a dark blue gown with black borders and a "sparrow top" cap. As a person of some standing in the local community now, he was expected to refrain from involving himself in unseemly activities, such as political discussions and lawsuits.[19]

Wang's success in the school entrance examination does not appear to have inspired him to devote himself with renewed vigor to his studies. On the contrary, it was just at this time, right after he had been admitted to the department school, that Wang discovered the field of history and certain genres of writing, which were of interest to him personally but irrelevant to preparing for the provincial examination.

> When I was fourteen years old, I saw a friend reading the *History of the Former Han Dynasty* (*Han shu*) and fell in love with it. I thereupon took the ten thousand cash I had saved up of New Year's money and bought the first four dynastic histories [*Records of the Historian* (*Shih chi*), *History of the Former Han Dynasty*, *History of the Later Han Dynasty* (*Hou Han shu*), and *History of the Three Kingdoms* (*San-kuo chih*)] in Hangchou. This was the beginning of a lifetime of study. At that time, however, I was preparing for the civil service examinations. In my spare time, moreover, I was learning how to write parallel prose (*p'ien-wen*) and classical prose (*san-wen*) although, because of lack of concentration, I could master only the superficial forms of these styles, not their spirits.[20]

Despite his avid interest in the field, there was not much future for a career in history in the 1890s. Thus by the beginning of 1893 Wang had enrolled in the Ch'ung-wen ("veneration of literature") Academy in Hangchou, where he continued to prepare for the provincial examination.[21]

Wang Kuo-wei does not seem to have enjoyed his studies at the Ch'ung-wen Academy. He continued to find the curriculum unappetizing since he still could not bring himself to subscribe to Confucian doctrines or to like the Classics and their commentaries. According to his friend Ch'en Shou-ch'ien, "In the matter of scholarly studies, Mr. Wang did not care in the least for trivial sorts of learning [literally, punctuation and annotation]." Too, he found the type of essay that examination candidates were required to write, the so-called eight-legged essay (*pa-ku wen-chang*), repugnant and "especially disdained it."[22] When the special preliminary examination for the 1893 provincial examination was given in March of that year, Wang's growing distaste for the whole examination system erupted.

The special preliminary examination (*k'o-shih*) occupied a sort of intermediate position between the youth examinations and the provincial examination, its purpose being to test the qualifications of licentiates who wished to take the latter and to limit the number of candidates actually admitted to the examination hall. The special preliminary examination, given by the provincial director of studies, was taken very seriously by most licentiates, who realized that missing it or performing badly would jeopardize their careers. Wang Kuo-wei's mind, unlike those of his fellow examinees, must have been on things other than academia when he sat for the special preliminary examination in Hangchou in early 1893, for he never turned in a completed examination paper. As Ch'en Shou-ch'ien laconically puts it, "Although, during the examination of 1893, he entered with all the other examinees, Mr. Wang returned before the examination was over. From this one knew that he had no interest in an official career."[23]

On arriving back in Hai-ning, Wang Kuo-wei must have spent much time pondering his future. While he apparently did not sit for the 1894 provincial examination, things began to look up for him toward the close of that year. As Wang subsequently recalled, "Soon the Sino-Japanese War broke out, and for the first time I came to know that in the world there was such a thing as the New Learning [hsin-hsueh—that is, Western knowledge]." His high hopes were, however, short-lived. Despite his growing hostility toward the examination system and his youthful openness to new currents of thought, Wang was compelled by financial exigency to remain in Hai-ning. "Since my family was poor and unable to give me the money to study outside my hometown, I stayed at home very unhappily and could not concentrate on what I was doing."[24]

In view of his mounting antipathy to the civil service examinations, it is not surprising that Wang could not concentrate on what he was doing since, ironically, he was again in the throes of preparing himself for the provincial examination. For a young man of modest means and conservative academic background, the alternatives were limited. By 1896, moreover, Wang had acquired a wife, the granddaughter of Mo Yin-sheng, a merchant who lived in Ch'un-fu-an hamlet in Hai-ning department. Execrating the conventional avenue of upward social mobility did not, after all, relieve Wang Kuo-wei of the need to build a career and contribute to the support of his family. Thus it was that he came to divide his time between preparing for the next provincial examination, scheduled for 1897, and managing the family school of one Ch'en Ju-chen.

In the fall of 1897 Wang and over ten thousand other Chekiangese descended on Hangchou to take the week-long provincial examination. This time the youth managed to complete his literary assignment. When the names of the successful candidates were posted, however, Wang's was not among them.

On returning to Hai-ning Wang was employed by Shen Kuan-ying as a live-in tutor. There is an old Chinese saying that "in the ink slab fields there are no bad crops," an allusion to the generally accepted theory that the scholarly vocation stands, as it were, on firmer ground than any other. In fact, however, Chinese teachers have often

subsisted in a condition of genteel poverty. It must have been clear
to many in Hai-ning, and to no one more than the young man himself,
that Wang Kuo-wei was going nowhere fast.[25]

The Eastern Language Institute

It was probably the bleakness of his prospects within the conventional
system, his distaste for the kind of study required for the civil service
examinations, his receptivity to new intellectual currents, and a brief
talk with his father that forced Wang's hand one day in 1898. With
Wang Nai-yü's consent, he left Hai-ning early in the year to seek his
fortune in the great treaty port of Shanghai. Being just twenty years
old, Wang Kuo-wei experienced considerable difficulty in finding a
suitable job. When his former classmate Hsu T'ung-lin was suddenly
obliged to leave town on family business, however, events took a seemingly happy turn. Before quitting Shanghai, Hsu thoughtfully entrusted to his unemployed friend his position as clerk and proofreader
for the pioneering journalist Wang K'ang-nien (1860–1911), manager
of the renowned periodical Current Affairs (Shih-wu pao).[26]

When Wang Kuo-wei joined the staff of Current Affairs early in
1898, the paper had been in existence for about two years. Founded
by the well-known reformers Liang Ch'i-ch'ao (1873–1929) and Wang
K'ang-nien, Current Affairs may be described, within the political context of the fin de siècle, as a "progressive" publication. It appeared
every ten days, its pages filled with scathing criticisms of allegedly
deleterious governmental policies as well as daring proposals to abolish the whole civil service examination system and to make other
drastic changes in the body politic. Depending on one's cultural outlook, the periodical appeared to be a harbinger either of China's
eventual salvation through radical social reforms or of the eventual
subversion of the Confucian Way through excessive institutional
tampering. Wang Kuo-wei's future mentor, Lo Chen-yü, was in retrospect an adherent of the latter view.

> After the Sino-Japanese War ended, the Treaty [of Shimonoseki] was
> signed and national prestige declined somewhat. The literati of the coun-
> try anxiously discussed current events in an attempt to effect reform
> and promote self-strengthening. In the year 1896 Mr. Wang K'ang-nien
> of Ch'ien-t'ang, Chekiang, established Current Affairs in Shanghai in order
> to incite the world through literature, and, indeed, the people's hearts
> were moved [by this newspaper]. This was an omen of the calamities
> which were to occur later. However, the leaders in the beginning did
> not yet know that the extent of the calamity would be what it now is.[27]

Wang K'ang-nien's fervid enthusiasm for reform does not seem to have communicated itself to his new amanuensis, Wang Kuo-wei, at this time. Wang's heart simply was not in his work. It was quite obvious to him that he could never make a decent living as a clerk since his salary was very low. His duties, moreover, struck him as excessively dull and tedious. While working at *Current Affairs*, Wang appears to have nursed a feeling that he was undervalued and underutilized. As Lo Chen-yü observed years later about this period of his protégé's life, "It may be remarked that while Mr. Wang was quiet and unassuming, he had a very high opinion of himself. When he worked as a clerk for Mr. Wang K'ang-nien, he merely took care of correspondence and made appointments, as a result of which he was depressed."[28]

Under these circumstances it seems likely that Wang looked forward with anticipation to the opening a little later in the year of the Eastern Language Institute (Tung-wen hsueh-she), a private, modern-style school founded in Shanghai by Lo Chen-yü and Chiang Fu (1866–1911). Already in 1896 these gentlemen, eager to launch a program of agricultural modernization in the Middle Kingdom, had established an Agricultural Society (Hsueh-nung she) in Shanghai. The society's mission, as described by Lo, was to disseminate information on foreign agricultural practices and technical innovations through the translation of European, American, and Japanese materials on agriculture into Chinese. Lo and Chiang had founded as well an *Agricultural Bulletin* (*Nung-hsueh pao*) with the intention of publishing therein these translated works on agriculture.[29]

In this concrete way Lo Chen-yü and his associate hoped to contribute to the general reform movement then being promoted in official circles throughout China. The Agricultural Society lacked, however, a vital ingredient, namely, translators, and it was with a view toward training some that Lo Chen-yü and Chiang Fu had decided to open their own school. As its name was doubtless intended to signify, the Eastern Language Institute, while not slighting Western languages, would take instruction in Japanese (the "Eastern language") as its principal linguistic mission. "China is to Japan what lips are to teeth," the Japanophilic Lo was fond of saying.[30]

Wang appears to have discerned in the Eastern Language Institute, correctly as it transpired, his ticket out of underpayment and underutilization. As soon as the school opened, he began, with Wang K'ang-nien's blessing, to attend classes there for three hours every afternoon. In this way Wang Kuo-wei became one of six students of Lo Chen-yü's good friend Fujita Toyohachi (1869–1929; also known by his pseudonym, Kempō), an authority on classical Chinese litera-

ture who was versed as well in Western learning. Aside from attending
Fujita's lectures, which were delivered in Japanese, Wang apparently
had little leisure in which to pursue his new course of study. His
progress after six months, as he later lamented, was therefore inferior
to that of his fellow students.[31]

Although his academic performance at the institute was initially
unimpressive, Wang Kuo-wei did succeed in obtaining one thing that
few of his fellow students were able to obtain: the patronage of the
wealthy scholar Lo Chen-yü. In a biographical account of Wang
written many years later, Lo recalls how the young man, who was to
form such an intimate relationship with him, first came to his attention.

> When Mr. Wang first came to study at the institute, I did not know him.
> One day, however, I happened to read a quatrain (chueh-chü) on history
> which he had written on a roommate's fan, and I perceived that he
> possessed great literary talent. I then brought him forward from among
> his classmates and assisted him with his family expenses so that he would
> be able to concentrate on his studies without having to worry about his
> family.[32]

The crucial lines of Wang's poem, "Have you ever heard of the gran-
deur of a thousand autumns? / Gaze westward past the Black Sea to
the Roman Empire," are said greatly to have struck Lo.[33]

From the moment that Lo Chen-yü first set eyes on Wang's poem,
he went out of his way to help the young man acquire a modern
education. Wang Kuo-wei seems to have welcomed Lo's attentions
and soon became financially dependent on him. Lo first had occasion
to assist Wang late in 1898, when the latter returned to Shanghai after
an absence of several months. Wang had been compelled to return
to Hai-ning earlier in the year because of a foot ailment, and by the
time he got back to Shanghai the office of *Current Affairs* had been
closed down. At this critical juncture Lo Chen-yü graciously offered
Wang a job doing odds and ends at the Eastern Language Institute
and remitted his tuition.[34]

In the following year, 1899, Lo was even more liberal with Wang.
Since at that time few Chinese schools taught Japanese, the Eastern
Language Institute had become quite popular and the number of
both students and staff had mushroomed. The space available to the
institute being limited in its original location, Lo had found it expedient to move his operation to Kuei-shu Lane, right in front of the
Kiangnan Arsenal. There he made Wang a student proctor, but the
students found the young man so objectionable that he felt constrained to quit. Lo, however, continued to pay Wang his monthly

salary precisely as if he were still on the job. This curious, generous financial arrangement, variations of which were to occur for many years, seems to have been insufficiently appreciated by Wang, according to Lo. "When we became acquainted and I arranged financial assistance for him so that he could complete his studies without the burden of financial worries, Mr. Wang was unmoved. Anyone else would surely have been deeply grateful and assumed that I appreciated his talents. Mr. Wang, however, seems to have believed that I merely benefited him materially but did not really appreciate him."[35]

It was after Wang Kuo-wei had resumed his studies at the Eastern Language Institute in the fall of 1898, after a hiatus of several months, that he first came across the names of Kant and Schopenhauer, whose philosophies were to have so decisive an impact on his intellectual development.

> At that time the professors at the institute were two Japanese gentlemen, Messers. Fujita Toyohachi and Taoka Sayoji, both of whom were college graduates and had studied philosophy. One day I noticed that among Mr. Taoka's essays there were some which contained quotations from Kant's and Schopenhauer's works. Although I enjoyed them immensely, I thought that, because of the language barrier, there would never come a day when I could read the works of these two philosophers.[36]

Taoka Sayoji (1870–1912; also known as Taoka Reiun), a former student of the Marine Products School who had also taken courses on the Confucian Classics at Tokyo University, had been hired by Lo Chen-yü, evidently on the recommendation of his erstwhile classmate Fujita, during the expansion of the institute's student body.[37] He has said of his views in early life, "Pessimism exerted an influence on me in my youth. I was deeply infatuated with the philosophies of Kant and Schopenhauer."[38] It is highly probable that Wang Kuo-wei's own curiosity about the critical philosophy and the philosophy of metaphysical pessimism was piqued by his English teacher, Taoka Sayoji. Although Wang would not formally begin his study of Western thought until 1901–02, his interest had already been aroused while he was a student at the Eastern Language Institute.

After being relieved of the onerous task of earning a living, Wang Kuo-wei apparently became a brilliant student of the New Learning. In addition to mastering Japanese and English, he is said to have acquired a rudimentary understanding of such subjects as chemistry, physics, mathematics, and geography. Years later the eminent Sinologist Kano Naoki (1868–1947) recollected that Fujita Toyohachi had been impressed not only by Wang's linguistic achievements but also by the unconventional bent of his mind.

I first heard the name of Mr. Wang many years ago. It was probably in 1901 [*sic*] or thereabouts, when I was studying in Shanghai. At that time one of my friends, Dr. Fujita (Professor Fujita Toyohachi now of Tokyo University), was teaching Japanese at the Eastern Language Institute, managed by Mr. Lo Chen-yü. Dr. Fujita informed me that among his students was one who was exceptionally bright; whose Japanese was excellent and whose English was good as well; who had, moreover, a profound interest in the study of Western philosophy; and whose future appeared highly promising. Among Chinese youths who at that time were pursuing the New Learning, most were interested in political science or economics. Very rarely did one meet an individual who wanted to study Western philosophy. Dr. Fujita highly prized this student and said many flattering things about him. However, [on this trip] I did not succeed in making the acquaintance of Mr. Wang Kuo-wei, who later on would become very famous indeed.[39]

Although Wang was a gifted adept at the New Learning, he probably viewed the approach of graduation with some misgiving. Chinese conversant with foreign languages and alien modes of thought were not, after all, esteemed by their compatriots in 1900. The great writer Lu Hsun (pen name of Chou Shu-jen; 1881–1936), who, like Wang Kuo-wei, had left northern Chekiang in 1898 to study foreign subjects in a cosmopolitan, modern metropolis, reminds us why. "At that time the proper thing was to study the classics and take the official examinations. Anyone who studied 'foreign subjects' was looked down upon as a fellow good for nothing, who, out of desperation, was forced to sell his soul to foreign devils."[40] Moreover, during Wang's two-and-one-half-year association with the Eastern Language Institute, he had enjoyed a comfortable existence as a fully supported student, thanks to Lo Chen-yü's solicitude. He had little to do, we gather, but study foreign languages and various sciences.

When in the fall of 1900 the institute closed down in response to the Boxer disturbances, graduating its students ahead of schedule, Wang was suddenly cast adrift. Lu Hsun, who graduated from the School of Mines and Railroads in Nanking around the same time, has this to say on how he felt about "coming of age": "Of course, everyone looked forward to graduation, and yet, once it came, I somehow felt as though I had made a mistake . . . as a result of all that [foreign training] I was still without a single, solitary ability."[41] One wonders if Wang Kuo-wei, similarly a graduate of a school of the new type, returned to Hai-ning with a comparable feeling of glumness in the fall of 1900.

3

Wang as Educational Critic

From its inception the late Ch'ing reform movement (1901–1911) was concerned with educational modernization. When, in the aftermath of the Boxer debacle, Empress Dowager Tz'u-hsi (1835–1908) began actively to solicit proposals for reform, education was one of the first subjects on which she urged high officials to memorialize. As part of her general program to "adopt the strong points of foreign countries in order to rectify China's shortcomings,"[1] Tz'u-hsi thus determined to breathe new life into the empire's antiquated educational system.

That the traditional educational system possessed shortcomings was a circumstance which Wang Kuo-wei was by no means the first to lament. As early as the Sung period sensitive members of the literati had begun to voice what by Ch'ing times were familiar complaints: that in their emphasis on formally correct essay writing, the civil service examinations did nothing to encourage real learning; that because the tests were subjectively scored, passing them demonstrated not an examinee's knowledge but his luck; that by inducing men to compete for worldly gain, the examination system prevented them from fixing their gaze on ultimate moral values. Despite the long tradition of protest against it, however, the civil service examination system had, at the time Tz'u-hsi turned her attention to it, a history of over one thousand years as well as great, if declining, prestige. It seems to have been the influence of the West which, in the matter of educational reform, tipped the balance in favor of arguments that were centuries old but had never been persuasive enough, in themselves, drastically to affect the existing institutional arrangements of the Chinese bureaucratic state.[2]

The Educational Reform Movement

By the turn of the century the initiative in formulating domestic policies had passed to the governors-general through the medium of

their memorials. Hence it is not surprising that the bulk of the recommendations for educational reform were made by prominent scholar-
officials, such as Chang Chih-tung, Yuan Shih-k'ai (1859–1916), and
Liu K'un-i (1830–1902). Nor is it surprising that the empire's senior
statesmen took as the theoretical basis for their educational proposals
the slogan made famous by Chang Chih-tung in the late 1890s, "Chinese
learning for essential truths; Western learning for practical knowledge." From an earlier generation of Chinese bureaucrats concerned
with the foreign threat—from Feng Kuei-fen (1809–1874) in particular—Chang and his colleagues had acquired the profound conviction
that in self-defense the Chinese should learn from the West the techniques for making the empire prosperous and powerful. They had
acquired as well the unshakable faith that mastery of Western technology would in no way jeopardize China's "essential truths," undermine Confucian ethics, or subvert the Way of the sages. On the contrary,
Chang and his confrères appear to have imagined that they had found
in Western wisdom a powerful weapon with which to defend the
Confucian Way.

The approach to institutional reform taken by Chang Chih-tung,
China's leading elder statesman in the last years of the Ch'ing dynasty,
was one of balanced inequality. While he sponsored many programs
to modernize the military, industry, and commerce, Chang simultaneously endorsed the view that the Confucian faith, as the spiritual
bedrock of Chinese existence, should be preserved and even nurtured.
The thrust of his reformist proposals in the educational sphere, accordingly, was to urge the gradual widening of the curriculum at
every level of the empire's school system with the aim of introducing
students, once they were versed in the Classics, to the "practical knowledge" of the West.

> Scholars today must, in the first instance, master the Classics so that they
> will understand the purpose of our ancient Chinese sages and teachers
> in establishing the Confucian faith. They must study the Histories so
> that they will be informed about the rise and fall of our empire's suc-
> cessive dynasties and the customs of the land. They must peruse works
> of philosophy and belles lettres so that they will become familiar with
> our Chinese scholarship and literature. After this they may select for
> use those aspects of Western knowledge which can rectify our shortcom-
> ings and select for adoption those Western governmental methods which
> can cure our illness.[3]

Students should under no circumstances, however, be encouraged to
immerse themselves in the study of either Western philosophy or
Western political theory, Chang believed. "While it is not necessary
to seek everything in the Classics, neither is it necessary to contravene

the principles [that they enshrine],"[4] he cautions in a remark which seems to concede that Western knowledge is after all more than simply "practical" knowledge.

Although his earliest schooling had been of the conventional sort that took loyalty and filial piety as the "root" and the study of the Chinese Classics as the "foundation," Wang Kuo-wei had never felt drawn either to Confucianism or to the Classics. Thus by 1898 he had largely abandoned his traditional studies in order to devote himself single-mindedly to the New Learning as a student at the Eastern Language Institute. By 1901–02 Wang would take up the sustained study of foreign thought. In time he would become convinced that Western philosophy could revitalize Chinese intellectual life, solve what he called "the problems of the universe and human life," and provide a sound theoretical basis for China's educational reform program. Under these circumstances, we will not be surprised to discover that Chang Chih-tung's conceptualization of the proper content of a modern school curriculum, which stressed classical learning and ignored foreign philosophy, would vex Wang greatly for some years. One of his biggest complaints when he finally began to speak out publically on educational affairs would concern the exclusion of Western philosophy from the official list of subjects in which young men were henceforth to be instructed.

Not long after the Boxer fiasco, one of whose consequences had been to swing popular opinion from fear of to interest in the New Learning, Tz'u-hsi issued a series of edicts pertaining to educational reform. Although the extent of their actual implementation remains problematic, the drastic measures that the empress dowager announced in the latter part of 1901 were, even on paper, remarkable. The content of the civil service examinations, for example, was ordered revised to the end of testing students not only on the Classics but also on the government and history of China and the government and sciences of foreign countries. That nemesis of many a Chinese scholar, the eight-legged essay, was banned. Provincial authorities were instructed to send promising youths abroad to acquire, at government expense, a foreign education, with the understanding that in due course they would return to China to be granted official degrees and posts. Plans for a national school system with a Sino-Western curriculum were announced, and all existing academies were ordered transformed into three tiers of official schools.[5]

Tz'u-hsi never intended the loosely worded edicts of 1901 to direct for very long the government's vast new educational undertaking. In early 1903, therefore, she appointed Chang Po-hsi (1847–1907) head of a Committee on Educational Affairs and charged him with drawing up formal regulations for the projected national school system. Within a year he and his colleagues Chang Chih-tung and Jung-ch'ing (*chin-shih* of 1886), who were the other members of this committee, produced a comprehensive plan for a new national program of education. Although later modified in several particulars, this plan, which drew heavily on Japanese educational precedents, formed the basis of the Chinese school system in the 1904–1911 period. The purpose of the 1904 *Regulations Governing Education, as Memorialized and Approved* (*Tsou-ting hsueh-t'ang chang-ch'eng*), like that of the edicts of which they were a detailed elaboration, was to train officials through innovative means to deal with the dynasty's unprecedented problems.

With regard to the future course of Chinese education, two noteworthy events took place toward the close of 1905, one of which was the summary abolition of the hoary civil service examination system. Chang Chih-tung, Yuan Shih-k'ai, and other high administrators concerned with pedagogical matters had originally believed that the Western studies they proposed to introduce into the school curriculum could be combined with preparation for the civil service examinations. Subsequently, however, they came to realize that students tended to spend vastly more time studying for the examinations than pursuing Western learning, as a result of which Chang and his colleagues chose in the end to advocate the abolition of the whole examination system. After receiving numerous memorials supporting this view, Tz'u-hsi ordered that the civil service examinations be discontinued permanently.

The other noteworthy educational event to occur in 1905 was the creation of a Ministry of Education (Hsueh pu). The ministry's principal aims in the main reflected the court's aspirations of the previous five years, namely, to develop a modern school system that could instruct young Chinese in the practical wisdom of Westerners yet simultaneously make them knowledgeable about China's own history, culture, and values. There was, however, one radical departure in the overall purpose of education as now envisioned by the empire's leading pedagogues. Influenced by the Western notion that the purpose of education is to train citizens, not bureaucrats, a number of high officials now perceived advantages in promoting a program of universal education (*p'u-chi chiao-yü*). Already in 1902 Liang Ch'i-ch'ao, the most prominent spokesman for Chinese reformism during the last years of the dynasty, had urged the Ch'ing government "to educate the sons of the whole country."[6] In a statement of their educational goals made in 1906, the members of the newly constituted Ministry of Education revealed their intention to take up the gauntlet. "In promoting education today, China properly stresses universal education. We thus order that everyone in the country receive some schooling."[7]

To the end that all Chinese might acquire some schooling, the Ministry of Education drew up a series of regulations concerning primary school education. Of considerable importance was the creation of educational promotion offices (ch'üan-hsueh so) at the county level to oversee all local educational work. Appointed by the county magistrate, the general manager (tsung-tung) of every such office was empowered to select from among the local gentry an educational promotion officer (ch'üan-hsueh yuan) for each of the county's school districts. To these officers devolved the responsibility of establishing and managing the public elementary schools that the Ministry of Education now deemed important.[8]

We need pursue no further the twists and turns in the government's program for educational modernization, for Wang Kuo-wei's mordant critique of the late Ch'ing educational reform movement concerns reforms proposed or inaugurated during the 1901–1907 period only. As will become clear when we examine the substance of his critique, Wang would find himself unable to endorse any aspect of the new educational program. He would not concede, for instance, that officials were encouraging students to study the right subjects (or even the wrong ones for the right reasons), nor that young men should be sent abroad to study, nor that scholars ought to be granted official titles and posts, nor that the Ministry of Education's preoccupation with universal education was well founded.

The theoretical basis for Wang Kuo-wei's critical observations on the contemporary Chinese educational scene is the philosophy of metaphysical pessimism. Of particular relevance to his educational views is Schopenhauer's pedagogical theory. Precisely because of its grounding in certain Schopenhauerian principles, Wang's view of the late Ch'ing educational reform movement is unique in the annals of educational philosophy. Before examining the substance of his critique, however, we must resume our narrative of Wang Kuo-wei's activities in the years immediately following his graduation from the Eastern Language Institute and return to Hai-ning.

In the Entourage of Lo Chen-yü

During the opening years of the twentieth century, Wang Kuo-wei's life became inextricably linked to that of Lo Chen-yü. The young man either lived with Lo in the latter's home in Shanghai or trailed along in his scholarly wake as Lo was posted to one province after another during the last decade of the dynasty's existence. Wang seems to have consulted his mentor on virtually every aspect of his life, from the terms of his acceptance of various job offers (all of which were facilitated by Lo) to what he should do about his poor health.

The precise nature of Wang's dependency on Lo at this time is not easy to ascertain. Although he did not finance Wang's scholarly investigations of the last years of the Ch'ing dynasty, Lo did recommend Wang for jobs or give him work on his educational and agricultural projects. One wonders, however, how congenial Wang Kuo-wei must have found these positions, for he seems to have excelled neither as an educational administrator nor as a schoolteacher.

On the face of it, the two men would appear to have had little in common. Lo Chen-yü's talents as an administrator and expert on educational and agricultural matters presumably made him one of those worldly, "practical" individuals whom Wang Kuo-wei, in his educational and philosophical essays, so roundly condemns. The educational theory of Lo's patron, Chang Chih-tung, Wang furthermore believed, was misguided, and the youth took the liberty repeatedly of saying so in print. There is no evidence that Lo, for his part, exerted a significant influence on either the substance or the course of Wang's scholarship during this early period. That the lives of Wang Kuo-wei and Lo Chen-yü were to become inescapably entwined, however, was apparent by the close of the year 1900.

As a young man trained in the rudiments of Western science and conversant with two foreign languages, Wang Kuo-wei found little to do in Hai-ning on returning there after his graduation from the Eastern Language Institute. He seems to have been content, however, simply to mark time while he resided in his native place. About his brief stay in Hai-ning in the fall of 1900, Wang subsequently recollected:

> The following year [1900] the Boxer Rebellion occurred, and the institute closed down. At that time I had been a student at the Eastern Language Institute for two and one-half years, during one and one-half of which I had studied English. [When the institute closed], I had just finished the third reader, so I bought the fourth and fifth readers and studied them on my own after I had returned home. I completed one or two lessons a day. My goal was to understand them. What I did not understand I put aside.[9]

Wang toiled over his English readers in Hai-ning for only a short while, for Lo Chen-yü summoned him back to Shanghai toward the end of the year. On arriving in the treaty port, Wang moved in with Lo. It is not clear exactly with what Wang Kuo-wei occupied himself during the first few weeks of his stay with Lo. His mentor, it is true, asked him if he would do some translation work for the *Agricultural Bulletin*, but Wang demurred.[10]

Not long after his protégé had returned to Shanghai, Lo Chen-yü received a telegram from the energetic governor-general of Hupei and Hunan, Chang Chih-tung, inviting him to move to Wuchang, the capital of Hupei province, to assist in the management of two agricultural projects the governor-general had under way in that city. That Chang was eager to secure the services of Lo is hardly surprising, for the technological view of modernization to which the latter subscribed was in all its essential features identical to the view so eloquently expressed by the former in *Exhortation to Learn*. Lo had, moreover, an impeccable reputation as an agricultural expert, having promoted agricultural reform for some years by means of the Agricultural Society and the *Agricultural Bulletin*. Noted as well for his achievements in educational administration, Lo Chen-yü was in fact to enjoy, during the dynasty's last decade, a highly successful career as an adviser to the most powerful officials in the land on agricultural and educational matters.

It was, then, against the background of their shared philosophy of modernization as well as Lo's growing reputation as an authority on agricultural and educational reform that Chang Chih-tung decided in the winter of 1900–01 to hire him in his capacity as agricultural expert. On reaching Wuchang, Lo Chen-yü was appointed general manager (*tsung-li*) of the Hupei Agricultural Bureau and director (*chien-tu*) of the Hupei School of Agriculture.[11] It evidently did not take him long to discover that he would need assistants, for in the spring of 1901 Lo sent for Wang Kuo-wei and Fan Ping-ch'ing, the latter of whom had been, like Wang, a student at the Eastern Language Institute. To them Lo entrusted the tasks of teaching translation, helping out with matters pertaining to agricultural materials, and introducing foreign pedagogical theories and educational policies in the *Journal of the Educational World* (*Chiao-yü shih-chieh tsa-chih*), his new publication. In this way Wang Kuo-wei came to work in Wuchang at the School of Agriculture, with which he was affiliated for half a year.[12]

In the fall of 1901 Lo Chen-yü resigned his positions at the Agricultural Bureau and the School of Agriculture since Chang Chih-tung had a new project that required his attention. As part of their contribution toward the late Ch'ing educational reform movement, Chang Chih-tung and Liu K'un-i had decided to establish a Kiangsu-Hupei Translation Bureau. The mission of the bureau, as they envisioned it, would be to translate and publish textbooks. To the Kiangsu-Hupei Translation Bureau, which was in existence until 1910, Chang and Liu appointed Huang Shao-chi, Miao Ch'üan-sun (1844–1919), and Lo Chen-yü. In conjunction with his reorganization of education in Hupei, Chang Chih-tung also sent delegations to Japan to study the Japanese school system. Lo Chen-yü, in his capacity as educational expert, was among the members of a delegation Chang dispatched to Japan in the winter of 1901–02 to buy books and inspect Japanese schools. Thus Lo was probably reunited with Wang Kuo-wei, whom he had sent to Tokyo late in 1901.[13]

During the last decade of the Celestial Empire, the Ch'ing government strongly encouraged young Chinese to study abroad in order to acquire Western knowledge. This governmental policy gradually led to a massive exodus of students from China. For cultural, linguistic, and financial reasons, the majority of these students crossed the Yellow Sea to pursue the New Learning in Japan. Although in 1898 there were only eighteen or so Chinese studying in Japan, by 1903 this number would swell to about one thousand, by the end of 1905 to eight thousand, and by 1906 to thirteen thousand.[14] From an intellectual point of view, Japan must have seemed to these Chinese students an exciting place in which to live, for by the end of the nineteenth century this westward-looking country had translated into Japanese foreign books on virtually every scholarly subject. For a young man such as Wang Kuo-wei, who had already mastered the language, the possibilities must have appeared limitless.

Wang's ostensible purpose in going to Japan seems to have been to acquire precisely one of those "practical" educations that he would later ridicule in his educational and philosophical essays. Through the good offices of Fujita Toyohachi, he entered the Tokyo School of Physics (Butsuri gakkō) and selected a specialty in the sciences (*li-k'o*). It may well be that Wang had little to say about his choice of vocation at this time, inasmuch as Lo Chen-yü had undertaken to finance his trip abroad, and Lo's interests lay in areas far more practical than those of the philosophically inclined Wang Kuo-wei. Wang's routine while living in Tokyo was to study English by day and to attend mathematics classes at the School of Physics by night. One imagines that Wang regretted (indeed, if he had ever liked) his choice of a science major rather quickly, for it is said that by the time he reached geometry he found the going very rough.[15]

It is possible that Wang's lack of aptitude for science, the availability of Western philosophical works in Japanese translation, and his youthful curiosity about, and enthusiasm for, Western thought led him to read some primary or secondary philosophical books while he lived in Japan. Wang himself subsequently recollected that he had begun the study of Western philosophy in 1901–02.[16] It is also likely that Wang Kuo-wei's interest in Nietzsche, whose thought he would later study, was first aroused during his stay in Tokyo. Nietzsche was enormously popular in Japan around the turn of the century, and biographies of him as well as translations of his works were numerous.[17] Although we do not know for a fact that Wang read any books either by or about Nietzsche while he was abroad, it seems probable that at the very least he became acquainted with Nietzsche's name at this time.

One can only conjecture how long Wang Kuo-wei would have kept at his irksome mathematics lessons had he been free to pursue them as long as he wished. As it happened, Wang became ill with beri-beri after he had been in Tokyo for only four or five months. Lo Chen-yü thereupon advised his protégé to return to China.[18]

On arriving back in Shanghai in mid-1902, Wang lived in Lo's house, just as he had done during the winter of 1900–01. He did not have to wait long for a job, as by this time Lo Chen-yü conveniently was serving as director of the Oriental Academy and was thus in a position to offer Wang employment. The Oriental Academy was a newly established branch of the Nan-yang Public Institute, which had been founded in 1896 by the great entrepreneur Sheng Hsuan-huai in order to promote technical education. After Sheng expanded his institute late in 1901 by adding a branch school in the Hung-k'ou section of Shanghai, he had, on the recommendation of the scholar-official Shen Tseng-chih (1850–1922), engaged Lo Chen-yü to manage it for him. When Wang recovered from his illness in the latter part of 1902, accordingly, Lo offered him an administrative position at the Oriental Academy. One gathers that Wang's administrative chores were not particularly onerous, for he was able to find enough spare time to continue his study of English under the supervision of Fujita (like Lo, he had been recommended by Shen Tseng-chih for a job at the Oriental Academy) and edit Lo's two publications, the *Agricultural Bulletin* and the *Journal of the Educational World.*[19]

Before the year was out, however, Lo Chen-yü (and hence Wang Kuo-wei) was making plans to move on, for late in 1902 he received an invitation from Ts'en Ch'un-hsuan, governor-general of Kwang-tung and Kwangsi, to serve as a consultant on the reform of the educational system in those provinces. Casting about for a suitable appointment for his protégé, Lo discovered that the T'ung-chou Normal School in Kiangsu was looking for a teacher of philosophy, psychology, and ethics.[20] This seemed appropriate for Wang, who had been engrossed in the study of Western thought ever since he had come back from Japan in the summer of 1902.[21] Lo therefore recommended Wang for the position. About Wang Kuo-wei's life at

China's first normal school we know, however, very little. His teaching load evidently was not excessively heavy, as he enjoyed sufficient leisure both to pursue his interest in Western philosophy (he was just beginning the *Critique of Pure Reason* in the spring of 1903) and to compose poems.[22]

Because of the vicissitudes of Lo Chen-yü's career, Wang Kuo-wei found himself in 1904 working in yet another city. Tuan-fang (1861–1911), a prominent Ch'ing official who supported Chang Chih-tung's moderate reform policy, had recently been appointed governor of Kiangsu province. On his way through Shanghai to take up his new office, he reportedly stopped to pay a call on Lo Chen-yü. In the course of their conversation, the two friends decided to establish a normal school in Su-chou. When the Kiangsu Normal School opened its doors toward the end of 1904, Lo was appointed its director. Tuan-fang also invited Fujita Toyohachi to work at the school.[23]

Having assumed his position as director of the Kiangsu Normal School, Lo Chen-yü sent for Wang Kuo-wei, who was still off teaching in T'ung-chou. Thus it was that Wang moved to Su-chou, accepted a job lecturing at the Kiangsu Normal School, resumed his studies with Fujita as well as his chats with Taoka (who also had been invited to join the school faculty), continued his reading in Western philosophy, and kept on churning out poems.[24] About his life as an itinerant teacher, Wang has written:

> It was also the case that, in these five or six years, I was unable to devote all of my time to scholarship because in order to make a living I was constrained to work for others. As for the time I had at my disposal for study, it was at least two or three, and at most three or four, hours a day. If I transgressed this limit of between two and four hours a day, I became fatigued and could do nothing but talk with friends or browse through miscellaneous books. I was quite self-disciplined about my studies, however. Although a matter of only two or three hours of reading a day, I rarely missed a day.[25]

Wang Kuo-wei remained in Su-chou lecturing at the Kiangsu Normal School until late 1905. At that time Lo Chen-yü both resigned his position as director of the school and quit Su-chou in order to supervise his father's burial. Wang, too, then resigned his job as a teacher there and returned to Hai-ning, where he lived for the next half-year. Then, in the spring of 1906, Lo moved to Peking, where he had just received the appointment of assistant secretary (*ts'an-shih*) at the newly established Ministry of Education. Wang accompanied Lo and his family on their northward journey and, on reaching the capital, lived in Lo's house. After a short while Wang had to make haste back to Hai-ning, however, for in the summer of 1906 his father, Wang Nai-yü, passed away.[26]

In the spring of 1907 Wang Kuo-wei received word that, on Lo Chen-yü's recommendation, he was to be hired by the minister of education, Jung-ch'ing. On arriving in Peking, Wang was made an attaché in the ministry's Department of General Affairs (Tsung-wu ssu).[27] Here the young man would remain until the Wuchang Uprising, writing the last of his critical articles on the educational reform movement and on Western philosophy, producing two collections of poetry as well as a handful of literary essays and a work on aesthetics and lyric criticism, and publishing all but the last of his studies on Yuan drama. Wang's views on philosophy and literature will be discussed in due course. Here we are concerned exclusively with the substance of his critique of the late Ch'ing educational reform movement, in which, as has just been described, he participated on the margins during the early years of this century.

Wang's Educational Philosophy

The Aims of Education

There are several reasons for the distinctiveness of Wang Kuo-wei's views on educational matters, one of which is his fierce adherence to Schopenhauer's dictum that philosophy is the mother of pedagogy (*chiao-yü-hsueh*).[28] Without a good understanding of philosophy, Wang writes in "Occasional Reflections on Education: Four Items" ("Chiao-yü ou-kan ssu-tse"), one cannot grasp the fundamental principles of pedagogy and related sciences. "Investigating the truths of the universe and human life and establishing the ideals of education are definitely the business of philosophy."[29] These are therefore endeavors that by no means should be left to normal school students or even professional educators to pursue. Examining eternal verities and designing educational programs are properly the activities, Wang avers, of philosophical geniuses alone.

That philosophers should determine the goals of education appeared axiomatic to Wang Kuo-wei. It was equally clear to him that the educational philosophy of only one thinker was impressive enough to serve as the theoretical basis for the Chinese educational reform effort of the early years of this century. That thinker was the great German pessimist, Arthur Schopenhauer.

In 1904, in a lengthy article titled "Schopenhauer's Philosophy and His Pedagogical Theory" ("Shu-pen-hua chih che-hsueh chi ch'i chiao-yü hsueh-shuo"), Wang Kuo-wei laments the European pedagogues' neglect of Schopenhauer.

> While the elaborateness of his arguments may not compare with the elaborateness of the arguments of Herbart, Beneke, and others; as regards the soundness of his premises and the perspicuity of his writing, scarcely anyone has been a match for Schopenhauer since philosophy has existed. Alas! The publication of *The Fourfold Root of the Principle of Sufficient Reason* was already ninety-one years ago, that of *The World as Will and Representation* eighty-seven years ago, and that of *The Two Fundamental Problems of Ethics* sixty-five years ago. Yet no one in the field of education has adopted Schopenhauer's [pedagogical] theory.[30]

Reflecting on the probable reasons for this regrettable state of affairs, Wang eventually arrives at the dubious conclusion that the studied indifference of Schopenhauer's contemporaries to his educational philosophy is largely attributable to Schopenhauer's lack of academic affiliation as well as his misanthropic temperament.

> From the nineteenth century onward, pedagogy has been a prosperous field of study. Its origin may be traced to the high level of development achieved by German philosophy. Already by the end of the eighteenth century, Kant had begun to discourse on pedagogy on the basis of his rigorist theory (*yen-su lun*) of ethics. However, no systematic treatment had yet been undertaken. After Kant, Herbart began to construct a complete theory of education based on his own philosophy. At the same time, famous German philosophers frequently did some research in this area, and each created his own pedagogical theory on the basis of his philosophical system . . . Aside from these philosophers, there were the pedagogues, not a few of whom "borrowed" the doctrines of Schelling and Schleiermacher in order to bolster their theories. On Schopenhauer's philosophy alone did they dare not rely in fashioning their pedagogical theories. This was because Schopenhauer was not a university professor . . . Too, the perversity of his behavior led individuals to regard him as venomous. Thus, all his life he dwelled apart in Frankfurt without a single close friend.

It is also true, Wang acknowledges, that the spirit of Schopenhauer's philosophy was ostensibly opposed to the Zeitgeist of the nineteenth century. For all these reasons, "his attempt to advance contemporary studies through pedagogy was like trying to fit a square handle into a round-ended chisel."[31]

Despite the general neglect of Schopenhauer's pedagogical views, Wang believed that they were significant and worthy of popularization in his own time. Indeed, one of the general purposes of his article on Schopenhauer's philosophy and pedagogical theory is to elucidate the major features of that theory. Presumably Wang hoped to convince readers of the *Journal of the Educational World* that Schopenhauer had something to offer the architects of China's new educational system. That this was one of Wang's aims would seem to be corroborated by the circumstance that in 1905 or thereabouts he published a much-simplified version of "Schopenhauer's Philosophy and His Pedagogical Theory." Collating the remarks on education made in his long, arcane article with the brief, breezy account of Schopenhauer's pedagogical theory presented in "The Purpose of Education" ("Lun chiao-yü chih tsung-chih"), one may derive a general impression of Wang Kuo-wei's view of the proper aim and content of education.

The purpose of education, Wang maintains, is to foster the development of "the whole individual" (*wan-ch'üan chih jen-wu*). By the whole individual, he explains, is meant the totality of a person's abilities. These should be nurtured until they have achieved a complete and harmonious development. An individual's abilities, Wang says, may be divided into outer and inner—that is, physical abilities and mental abilities. A sound theory of education will advocate cultivating the two together.[32]

Wang Kuo-wei's enumeration of the mental abilities to be cultivated is unconventional within the Chinese context. Borrowing from German psychology the tripartite division of mental life into thinking, feeling, and willing, Wang suggests that education may properly be said to have, in its mental aspect, three facets: the intellectual, the aesthetic, and the moral. A truly satisfactory education will embrace all three areas. Education in its intellectual dimension should take for its ideal the realization of truth, in its aesthetic dimension the realization of beauty, and in its moral dimension the realization of goodness.[33]

In his elucidation of the implications of this theory for Chinese education, Wang relies heavily on several principal tenets of Schopenhauer's philosophy. As regards the individual's intellectual education (*chih-yü*), for example, the theoretical crux of the matter is Schopenhauer's theory of perception. According to this theory, all knowledge may be divided into two types, the perceptual and the conceptual, the latter deriving from the former. Explaining Schopenhauer's theory, Wang writes:

> [Schopenhauer] holds that concepts derive their material from perceptions. Thus, the whole world of reflection is based on the world of perception. Depending on the range of a concept, it is more or less removed from the perception [on which it is ultimately based]. However, there is no concept which is not based on a perception. These perceptions provide the [real] content of all reflection, and wherever they are missing we have in our heads mere words, not concepts.[34]

The import of Schopenhauer's perceptual theory for pedagogy is the suggestion that "books cannot take the place of experience," that, in other words, "knowledge derived from books is dead, abstract knowledge, while knowledge derived from perception is living, concrete knowledge." One is tempted to speculate that Wang's many years of laborious memorization of the Four Books and Five Classics, which he heartily disliked as a boy, may have been ultimately responsible for his comment that "incessant reading and study positively ruin the mind." "If a person overutilizes his reading and studying abilities," according to Wang, "his perceptual ability is thereby necessarily weakened, and the natural view is obscured by the light of books."[35] The thrust of Wang's own recommendations with respect to the substance of education in its intellectual dimension is to promote perceptual at the expense of conceptual knowledge.

In 1904–05 Wang Kuo-wei also desired to introduce aesthetic studies into the new curricula of China's educational institutions. Although the importance of both an intellectual and a moral education is universally recognized, Wang opines, the value of an aesthetic education (mei-yü) is appreciated by few. Aesthetic training can, however, develop an individual's feelings as well as provide another means by which to realize the goals of the other two types of education.[36]

Wang was evidently inspired to recommend that aesthetic training be included in China's new curricula in part by his Schopenhauerian bias against scientific knowledge, which displays only concepts, and preference for aesthetic knowledge, which "consists exclusively of perceptual knowledge, containing no admixture of concepts," and in part by his belief, derived from Schopenhauer, in the self-transcending power of art. "Only art causes a man to forget his self-interest and enter a lofty and pristine realm. This is the purest of joys."[37] Wang's view of Schopenhauer's aesthetics will be considered in detail later on.[38] Here we may content ourselves with the observation that Wang Kuo-wei believed that aesthetic studies were important enough to merit inclusion in China's revised curricula.

Why Wang would wish to popularize Schopenhauer's ideas on moral education (te-yü) is unclear. Certainly they were heretical even by European standards; in the staid atmosphere of late Confucian China, they must have appeared positively poisonous. For in the field of ethics, Schopenhauer's major contention is that "virtue cannot be taught." This follows directly from his perceptual theory: nobility of character can come only from perceptual, not conceptual, knowledge. Moreover, according to Schopenhauer, goodness or badness of disposition is innate; although moral training may influence how a man realizes his unalterable character, it cannot affect the nature of the character itself.[39]

Uneasy with what he took to be the implications of this theory, Wang Kuo-wei did his best to reconcile Schopenhauer's view of virtue with conventional wisdom. "In saying that virtue cannot be taught, Schopenhauer does not mean that virtue really is unteachable but only that men cannot be induced through abstract knowledge to be virtuous . . . To lead men by means of perception and thereby to induce them to obtain a genuine knowledge of morality is definitely the business of education."[40] Schopenhauer's views on moral education, Wang brightly concludes, are by no means dangerous.

From this brief exposition of his conception of the aims of education, we can see that Wang Kuo-wei placed great stress on the development of well-rounded curricula. In his opinion an ideal curriculum would include physical education as well as instruction in "intellectual," "aesthetic," and "moral" areas. With these ideas Wang anticipated by some years the pedagogical views of both Lu Hsun and Ts'ai Yuan-p'ei. Wang was, however, unspecific about the exact content of instruction in each of these several realms. We know that, with Schopenhauer, he valued perceptual knowledge over book learning, but what Wang envisioned the actual substance of such knowledge to comprise he never explained in any great detail.

One motif, though, does stand out boldly in the essays considered here. In them Wang Kuo-wei repeatedly emphasizes the importance of philosophy for "investigating the truths of the universe and human life" as well as for "establishing the ideals of education." As one might therefore expect, Wang was a harsh critic of the official Ch'ing educational policy of excluding the discipline of philosophy, as he understood it,[41] from the curricula of both the normal schools and Imperial University.

The Value of Philosophical Training

During the years that Wang Kuo-wei was writing his educational essays, he was deeply immersed in the study of Western philosophy. His enthusiasm for his subject was initially so great that he became convinced that Western thought held the key not only to understanding the existential predicament and revitalizing the Chinese intellectual world generally but also to conceptualizing ideal Chinese curricula. For these reasons Wang was dismayed to learn that the authors of the new normal school and university regulations had made no provision for the inclusion of philosophy in the curricula they had devised.

To exclude the discipline of philosophy from the curriculum of the normal schools was, in Wang's opinion, scandalous. Normal schools, after all, are in the business of producing pedagogues, and philosophy is the mother of pedagogy. It is precisely because the mandate of a normal school is to train future pedagogues that the subject of philosophy cannot be omitted from its curriculum. To ignore the discipline of philosophy in a discussion of pedagogy is, Wang charges, as great a stupidity as to ignore the field of biology in a discussion of medicine or the discipline of physics in a discussion of engineering.[42]

If the omission of philosophy from the curriculum of China's normal schools was ill-advised on purely practical grounds, its omission from the curriculum of Imperial University was ill-advised for other, quite different reasons. Only the very smallest of small-minded men, Wang opines, would look with distrust on a field of intellectual inquiry that holds the key to the solution of basic problems concerning the meaning of existence as well as to an intellectual renaissance in China. Unfortunately, he writes, Chang Chih-tung, coauthor of the 1904 *Regulations Governing Education, as Memorialized and Approved,* is such a man.

After perusing that volume of the *Regulations* which concerns university education, Wang Kuo-wei felt impelled to publish in the *Journal of the Educational World* a lengthy article blistering the plans that Chang Chih-tung, minister of education from late 1907 until his death in 1909, had conceived concerning putative departments of literature and Classics at Imperial University. In Wang's view, the fundamental mistake that Chang Chih-tung had made in drawing up his regulations pertaining to university education was to exclude the study of philosophy from the curricula of these two departments.[43] "In the main [the regulations] follow the Japanese educational system, the one exception being the elimination [in the Chinese case] of the study of philosophy from the university's Literature Department."[44]

It is true, he concedes, that Chang Chih-tung has included the study of neo-Confucianism in the curriculum of the university's Classics Department. Owing, however, to his well-known aversion to "empty talk" (*k'ung-t'an*), a theme on which he expatiates warmly in the *Regulations,* the minister of education has, Wang alleges, pointedly excluded metaphysical subjects from the syllabus of the Classics Department's course on neo-Confucianism. No university student, he charges, will have an opportunity, under Chang Chih-tung's plan, to read such texts as the *Diagram of the Supreme Ultimate Explained* (*T'ai-chi t'u shuo*) and the *Correct Discipline for Beginners* (*Cheng meng*). It is much to be regretted, Wang writes, that Chang's predilection for "real results" (*shih-chien*) has led him to limit the undergraduate student's exposure to Sung philosophy to neo-Confucian ethics.[45]

Even had Chang Chih-tung defined neo-Confucianism broadly enough to include its metaphysical concerns, however, Wang Kuo-wei believed that its inclusion in the curricula of Imperial University's departments of literature and Classics could never compensate for the exclusion of such other important philosophical traditions as those of the Indians and the Europeans.[46] Chang's proposal that, out of the entire range of possible philosophical topics, Chinese college students be permitted to study only neo-Confucian ethics was in fact, in Wang's opinion, tantamount to omitting the study of philosophy altogether from the departments' curricula. A more provincial situation the cosmopolitan young man could not envisage. "The establishment of a department of philosophy within the university did not originate in Japan. In Europe from the Middle Ages onward universities have invariably comprised four departments: medicine, law, philosophy, and theology. German universities today continue to follow this system. There is no university in any other country which has not established a department [of philosophy]."[47]

Why, Wang Kuo-wei asks, just when the Chinese are beginning to promote education, does Chang Chih-tung believe it imperative to prohibit the study of philosophy in the empire's highest institution of learning? "Can it be that he thinks it inappropriate for the average person to participate in discussions about human nature (*hsing*) and the Way of Heaven (*t'ien-tao*), or does [he exclude philosophy because] he fears the spread of heterodox ideas?" If the latter is the case, "we cannot but admire Mr. Chang's policy, which [in proscribing the study of philosophy] is decidedly superior to the policy of European politicians [who tolerate a variety of viewpoints]."[48]

In Wang Kuo-wei's opinion, several circumstances had conspired to make Chang Chih-tung and his colleagues reluctant to introduce Western philosophy into the curricula of Imperial University's literature and Classics departments. In the first place, there was the oppressive weight of intellectual tradition. Explaining the ease with which Buddhism anciently had entered the Middle Kingdom, enthralling emperors and commoners alike, he writes: "Prior to the T'ang and Sung dynasties [A.D. 618–907, 960–1279] the school of Confucius had not yet been established as the only orthodox school of thought, and the doctrine of the transmission of the Way (*tao-t'ung*) had not yet been conceived. Since there was as yet no hierarchical ranking of schools with the Confucian one at the top, [Buddhist] studies flourished easily and [Buddhist] doctrines spread easily." The situation with regard to the introduction of Western thought in the late nine-teenth century was, by contrast, Wang argues, radically different. For centuries Confucianism had been the preeminent intellectual school, and self-satisfied literati had long been in the habit of attacking any new idea as evidence of heretical thinking. "Remarkable theories are always feared by ordinary men. Scholarship generated at the most advanced level is always the butt of mediocre scholars."[49] Seen in this light, Wang Kuo-wei suggests, Chang's conviction that Western phi-losophy is incompatible with Confucian thought is symptomatic of the Chinese literati's cultural outlook in recent decades.

Another reason Chang Chih-tung and his circle have been wary of Western philosophy, Wang opines, lies in their mistaken assump-tion that philosophy and politics are somehow related. "The state suspects that Western thought is the cause of all political distur-bances."[50] This erroneous conviction has in recent years gained so much credence among officials, Wang alleges, that Chang's decision to ex-clude philosophy from the curricula of Imperial University's depart-ments of literature and Classics must be attributed in part to his unwarranted belief that philosophy is a discipline with politically dan-gerous implications.

Chang's antagonism toward philosophy stems also, Wang sug-gests, from his infatuation with "real results" and consequent disdain for disciplines, such as philosophy, which he deems useless (*wu-yung*). As a matter of fact, Wang maintains, while philosophy is indeed use-less, in precisely this feature lies its value to the human species. "Does mankind live by utility alone?" A human being is not merely a bundle of physical wants, the youth declares, but is also, as Schopenhauer has pointed out, a "metaphysical creature" with an irrepressible im-pulse to seek a general interpretation of reality and man's place in it. "This is why, whether we concern ourselves with antiquity or the present day, and whether we concern ourselves with East or West, we can see that once a people's culture has reached a certain level phi-losophy will emerge and 'philosophers' will become popularly es-teemed."[51]

Perhaps, Wang speculates, Chang Chih-tung is simply too obtuse to perceive the benefits to be reaped from something as "useless" as philosophy. However, if he wishes to insist that utility be used as a criterion to determine what should be included in, and what excluded from, the curricula of China's institutions of higher learning, then to be consistent he must, Wang says, forthwith eliminate the two ob-viously useless departments of literature and Classics and content himself with having Imperial University teach only science.[52] On the eminent pedagogue-official Chang Chih-tung, Wang Kuo-wei's mocking verdict is this: "I have heard that Schopenhauer said that philosophy as taught in the university is the enemy of truth and that true philosophy is not to be found in the university but depends, rather, on independent research for its development. This being the case, Mr. Chang's exclusion of this department may conceivably prove to be a blessing in disguise!"[53]

An Aristocratic Educational Policy

One of the principal goals of the late Ch'ing reform movement was the creation of a nationwide network of educational institutions extending from primary schools up through universities. A small number of concerned Chinese, however, doubted the wisdom of committing a country with a vast population but limited intellectual and economic resources to such an ambitious program. Such individuals, of whom Wang Kuo-wei was one, counseled restraint.

In the opening years of the twentieth century, Wang repeatedly informed readers of the *Journal of the Educational World* that, in his opinion, the government's commitment to universal education was premature. The Ministry of Education's decision to establish, through the agency of educational promotion offices, primary schools throughout the land he found especially visionary, ignoring as it did China's obvious dearth of qualified teachers, paucity of school buildings, and insufficiency of funds. Holding the ministry's new regulations concerning elementary school education in very low esteem, Wang Kuo-wei had no difficulty deciding either to send his own children to a private, rather than public, school or to rebuff an offer to become general manager of Hai-ning's educational promotion office.[54]

Although everyone is fond of talking about the paramountcy of primary school education, Wang writes in one of his educational articles, in fact secondary school education is, logically speaking, prior to primary school education. Primary school teachers, after all, obtain their training in secondary schools. Without the establishment and maintenance of a good system of secondary schools, a decent system of primary schools cannot be developed. For this reason Wang Kuo-wei thought the official approach to education was myopic. He dubbed it "topsy-turvy-ism" (*tien-tao chü-i*).[55]

Wang's own approach to education was heavily influenced by Schopenhauer. Particularly pronounced was the influence of the philosopher's intellectual elitism on Wang's pedagogical views.

> Our [educational] doctrine may be called aristocratic. However, this so-called aristocracy is not political but intellectual. That the intellectual endowments of men vary is an obvious, incontrovertible fact. It is the goal [of government officials] to make primary education universal. Partly

from these factors arises the circumstance that, although dull individuals have a right to an education and the government a responsibility to educate them, primary education is a most difficult enterprise.

Wang Kuo-wei's proposal for educational reform was an elitist one that focused on the training of a small group of talented men. Once trained, these men would form a sort of resource pool from which much-needed specialists in various fields could be drawn. They could also serve as primary school teachers.

> If today the middle school students of the country were given an examination, there would be approximately several thousand individuals with superior intellects, some general knowledge, and a familiarity with foreign languages. If, then, [these several thousand students] were given one or two years of intensive preparation and then some training in a specialized area of study, I believe that their record of achievement would definitely be superior to the record of achievement attained by students who go through the sequence of primary, secondary, and college education in foreign countries. The scarcity of human resources is so extreme and the need of the state so urgent that in my opinion no other educational proposal is more apposite than this one. Therefore, at present an aristocratic policy is the most appropriate policy. It also has the additional advantage of being able to provide the basis for the establishment of middle and primary schools.[56]

A Dearth of Real Scholars

Glancing about himself in the earliest years of the twentieth century, Wang Kuo-wei was disheartened to note that few individuals, as it seemed to him, could be called real scholars. This deplorable state of affairs was partly attributable, he thought, to the Chinese educational system, which at its lower levels totally neglected what Wang considered true learning. "In the middle schools and below, youths are taught only the knowledge needed to become citizens. It goes without saying that such knowledge is entirely unrelated to thought." Nor did the training of real scholars appear to be a desideratum of the educational system at its upper levels. "One wonders when the curricula of Imperial University's [various departments] will be [definitely] established. Even if they are eventually established in accordance with Mr. Chang Chih-tung's plan, this will serve merely to produce vulgar Confucians, [not real scholars]."[57] The situation, Wang claimed, was just as desperate in the private institutes as it was in the public schools.[58]

Real scholars might have been trained abroad, of course, had overseas Chinese students been pursuing the proper courses of study. They were, however, in Wang's view, unfortunately not doing so. "Of students who have studied in Europe or America during the T'ung-chih and early Kuang-hsu periods [that is, the latter part of the nineteenth century], the largest group has studied naval manufacture, while the second-largest group has studied law. Only of those who have taken pure science (*ch'un-ts'ui k'o-hsueh*) [that is, philosophy] as their specialty have I not heard." Having pursued practical courses of study during their residence abroad, Chinese experts on naval and legal matters could hardly be expected to engage in real scholarship once they had returned home. "Students who have been abroad in recent years have [as a consequence of their choice of specialties] developed either political ambitions or utilitarian aims. How improbable it is that any one of them will ever be willing to study unpopular, dry intellectual problems which are of no [practical] benefit to the world!" As a result, "one can be certain that there is nobody [in all of China] capable of carrying on the study of the profound and great thoughts of the Europeans, and, even if there were, one can be certain that such persons would not have the ability to communicate [these thoughts to other Chinese]."[59]

Wang Kuo-wei's ruminations on the contemporary Chinese intellectual scene led him to the conclusion that "today nobody in the world delights in learning." The sham and hypocrisy he perceived around him seem to have distressed Wang considerably, as we can see from the following unhappy reflection.

> Someone may say, "Today those above frequently talk about encouraging scholarship, while those below frequently talk about conducting scholarly research. Why, then, do you maintain that such persons do not delight in learning?" One may respond by observing that the reason those above encourage scholarship is either to enhance their own reputations or to utilize later the results [of the scholarship they have encouraged]. How many among them value scholarship for its own sake? As for those below, the reason they conduct scholarly research is also to enhance their own reputations, gain material advantages, or utilize later on the results [of their scholarship]. I suspect that those among them who conduct scholarly research for its own sake number less than one in one thousand.

Almost everywhere he looked, it appears, Wang descried insincere scholars, intellectual opportunists eager to abandon real scholarship for practical benefits whenever and wherever circumstances allowed.

> Thus, as regards scholarship from ancient times to the present, those who have pursued technical learning (*i*) are many, while those who have pursued scholarship (*hsueh*) are few. One wonders, however, how many among these putative scholars have really been able to distinguish between scholarship and technical learning and not regard scholarship as technical learning. Whenever they have been able to capitalize on their

scholarship in such a way as to obtain material advantages or official advancement, they have become complacent and viewed scholarship as a means to material ends. Such persons definitely cannot be said to have an intrinsic interest in scholarship. Thus, it is not surprising that, when they have come halfway [in the journey toward engaging in real scholarship for its own sake], they drop out.[60]

Since he evidently did not wish to make a blanket indictment of Chinese scholars, Wang was willing to concede that there might well be a few exceptions to his generalization that contemporary scholars were opportunistic. These exceptions, he thought, were mostly to be found among the remaining adherents of the Old Learning (chiu-hsueh)—that is, traditional learning of the sort in which Wang himself had been schooled as a boy.

> Today if one wishes to find individuals who truly delight in learning, one must seek them among practitioners of the Old Learning. Whether devotees of the New Learning truly are devoted to scholarship or whether they regard scholarship as a means to material ends is something we cannot easily ascertain. Thus, it is better deeply to study the forsaken Old Learning because [at least] we are able to see that its practitioners really love learning.[61]

What Wang Kuo-wei admired about scholars of the Old Learning at this point in his life was not the substance of their work (of this he apparently did not think very highly) but rather the sincerity with which he presumed they engaged in it. After the official announcement in 1905 of the summary abolition of the civil service examination system, studies of the traditional type were no longer of any practical use in securing a man a job or advancing his career. Anyone pursuing classical studies after that date, therefore, could only be doing so, Wang thought, for his own personal pleasure. Wang's youthful attitude toward the old-style scholar is epitomized in a comment he made shortly after the death of Yü Yueh (1821–1907), the great nineteenth-century philologist and textual critic. "Although Yü definitely did not make any significant contributions to scholarship, his perceptiveness in learning and diligence in writing, which characterized his scholarship up until the very end of his life, should serve as a model for all scholars today."[62]

Scholarship as Its Own Reward

In the earliest years of the twentieth century, it was customary in China to award official titles and posts to successful students. Although the criteria of scholarly success underwent substantial change after the abolition in 1905 of the traditional examination system, the reward for success—namely, employment by the government—remained temporarily unaltered. In the case of certain types of professionals, under certain circumstances, Wang Kuo-wei was willing to concede that the official bestowal of substantive appointments was salutary. When, for example, "professional scholars" (*chih-yeh ti hsueh-wen chia*) such as teachers, politicians, engineers, lawyers, and doctors were given posts in which they could utilize their particular skills, the system of official rewards was, he thought, justified. When, however, such professionals were assigned to official positions with no regard for their special areas of expertise, the system served no better purpose, Wang said, than to deplete the ranks of the professions.[63]

As for "nonprofessional scholars" (*fei chih-yeh ti hsueh-wen chia*)—that is, philosophers and writers—Wang believed that they should under no circumstances receive official titles and posts. "It is my conviction that all scholarship, with the sole exception of philosophy and literature, can be encouraged by profit and remuneration." Because nonprofessional scholars, unlike their professional counterparts, are engaged not in practical, worldly activities but in pure research on questions of the greatest moment to mankind, they cannot be spared for government service. "To encourage [nonprofessional] scholarship by means of official appointments is to destroy [nonprofessional] scholarship."[64]

It was Wang Kuo-wei's contention that scholarship ought to serve as its own reward. That so few scholars, as he believed, engaged in scholarship for its own sake was distressing enough; that the government, by dangling the prospect of a career in government before the eyes of professional and nonprofessional scholars alike, should actively encourage the materialistic and fame-seeking impulses of intellectuals was almost more than Wang could bear. "The majority of gentlemen today," he laments, "love nothing but officialdom."

> The inner significance of this phenomenon is to demonstrate that virtue, scholarship, and enterprise are valueless today. Great indeed is the danger to a country when an official career alone is considered valuable, while virtue, scholarship, and enterprise are considered valueless. Once a society has evinced such an attitude, the situation will probably prove irremediable even if the government exerts itself to the utmost to try to rectify it. [Our government, however, is not simply not trying to remedy the situation]; it is actually aggravating it.[65]

Wang's own recommendation to Ch'ing policy advisers was that they abolish the practice of promising government jobs to students. He even went so far as to urge the authorities to try to make the population understand that scholarship should serve as its own reward. In this way, Wang thought, public opinion might be turned around. "The slightest carelessness, however, will lead to the misconception that seeking an official career is the goal of virtue, scholarship, and enterprise. This is really a case of 'when one makes a minute error in the beginning, one is led many miles away in the end.' "[66]

Wang Kuo-wei's acerbic critique of the late Ch'ing educational reform movement suggests that there was much in the contemporary scholarly world of which he disapproved. There were, of course, numerous difficulties with the educational reform program, both in theory and in practice, and a number of Wang's criticisms are trenchant indeed. More important for our present purposes, however, than the acuity of Wang's observations is the spirit in which he made them; the querulous tone of some of his essays and his stridency in condemning certain features of his country's new educational system serve boldly to underline his disenchantment with the quality of intellectual life in the China of his day.

Wang's view of scholarship, we may furthermore conclude, is both narrow and idealistic. As a young man, Wang Kuo-wei valued scholarship in what is now called the humanities above all other types of intellectual endeavor. He regarded individuals whose expertise lay in technical fields (medicine, law, engineering, and the like) as secondrate, "professional scholars," motivated for the most part by a lust for material gain. Individuals whose area of competence lay in either philosophy or literature, by contrast, Wang considered "nonprofessional scholars" consecrated to the quest for truth and beauty for their own sakes. Contemporary society, which Wang evidently believed to be partially responsible for the moral turpitude of most Chinese scholars, he criticized as being materialistic and pragmatic. Nowhere that he looked within his own world could Wang discover that concern with the plight of the human spirit which so preoccupied him in his early years.

His disillusionment with the sham of Chinese society, one may conjecture, served to stimulate in Wang Kuo-wei a curiosity about Western thought. Western scholars, unlike their Chinese counterparts, Wang seems to have imagined, were both free of the taint of intellectual opportunism and engaged in the study of the questions in life that really matter. It was probably reflections of this sort that led Wang in the opening years of the present century to embark on his celebrated study of European philosophy.

4

Declaration of Principles

The climate of literati opinion had been profoundly altered by the disastrous outcome of the 1894–95 war with Japan. Fearful that the Chinese empire would soon be completely "cut up like a melon" by foreign predators, the dynasty's senior statesmen as well as many members of the 1890s generation of intellectuals were galvanized by the war into a fury of reform activity that would last until the collapse of the Ch'ing in 1912. Although they might argue among themselves over how best to increase China's "wealth and power," many of the educated elite were bound to each other by a common preoccupation with the sources of state power as well as by a common conviction that technological modernization could ameliorate conditions in their backward, powerless country.

The uniqueness of Wang Kuo-wei's position at the dawn of the twentieth century derives principally from the fact that, unlike other sensitive members of his generation, he was not urgently and over-whelmingly concerned with the sources of state power or, despite his involvement in several of Lo Chen-yü's agricultural projects, absorbed in thoughts of technological modernization. The question of how to preserve China from the threat to its integrity posed by the foreign scourge, a question with which many of the best minds in the land were then obsessed, does not appear to have interested Wang in the least. Unlike many of his contemporaries, therefore, Wang was far from being enthusiastic about Yen Fu's investigations into the sources of the military, economic, and political strength of modern Western nation-states. "Mr. Yen Fu advocates merely the British philosophical doctrines of utilitarianism and evolution. His interests lie not in pure philosophy (*ch'un-ts'ui che-hsueh*) but in such subbranches of philosophy as economics, sociology, and so on. These are what he likes best. The animus of Mr. Yen's studies, therefore, is not philosophical but scientific."[1]

In Search of Truth

Wang Kuo-wei was intensely concerned in his twenties not with what he regarded as mundane, practical affairs, but rather with the eternal, elusive question of higher belief, with what he characteristically called "the problems of the universe and human life." The general thrust of the many essays he published in the *Journal of the Educational World* between 1903 and 1907 is the suggestion that man does not, after all, live by bread alone. Even if all our material needs could be satisfied, he thought, doubts concerning the meaning of existence would still remain. For this reason Wang himself chose, as a youth, to devote much of his intellectual energy to the quest for truth.

Wang Kuo-wei seems to have begun wondering about the ultimate nature of the world as early as 1898–99. This is presumably why he found so appealing the quotations from Kant's and Schopenhauer's works that he discovered in Taoka Sayoji's essays. In an autobiographical sketch written in 1907 Wang baldly confesses that, at the turn of the century, "my health was poor and my disposition melancholy. The question of the meaning of life danced before my eyes continually. I therefore decided to devote myself to the study of philosophy." A sickly and unhappy youth, Wang apparently hoped to find in philosophy a congenial *Weltanschauung* that would resolve his doubts about the nature and purpose of existence. In this connection he once remarked, "If a person can explain [even] a part of the problems [of the universe and human life], it is immaterial to me whether he is Chinese or foreign, provided that he satisfies my intellectual needs and gives me consolations to offset the doubts from which I suffer."[2]

His utter lack of interest in Yen Fu's pioneering investigations into the origins of state power, one may suppose, stemmed directly from Wang's own concern with "universal and eternal truth."[3] Votaries of wealth and power, he insists time and again in his early essays, are in no position to shed any light on the problems of the universe and human life, as they can at best satisfy only physical wants. In "pure" philosophy, not in the "subbranches" of philosophy, is the truth of the human situation revealed.

At the dawn of the twentieth century, then, Wang Kuo-wei was urgently seeking an architectonic explanation of the universe, a solution to the riddle of the world. This explanation he expected to find in philosophy, whose mission he took to be the revelation of the fundamental character and significance of existence. Wang thought so highly of philosophy—and also of art, which, he believed, discloses through metaphorical intimation the same truths that philosophy does—

that, in fact, he was emboldened to advance the claim that they are sacrosanct subjects.

"Although they are of no use to contemporary society in its practical aspect," we read in one of Wang's articles, "philosophy and art are the world's most sacred and noble [branches of learning]." Since Wang at no time in his life ever evidenced much interest in the practical arrangements of society, we should doubtless understand his remark on the uselessness of philosophy and art not as a criticism but rather as a further commendation of them. "Who among those the world deems useful is more than a [mere] politician or entrepreneur?"[4] he inquires rhetorically. That the mass of ignorant mankind is incapable of appreciating the sacred status of philosophy and art ought not to vex those noble souls who probe their mysteries.

It is only when philosophers and artists themselves forget their sacred status and attempt to accommodate intellectually to contemporary society, Wang says, that their work becomes valueless. A certain independence of thought and action is, he thinks, one of the prerequisites of a philosopher or an artist. This follows directly from Wang's view of the nature of truth.

> Now, the aim of philosophy and art is truth. Truth is universal and eternal, not mutable, and he who elucidates this truth (the philosopher) or records it (the artist) makes a universal and permanent contribution, not a fleeting one. Precisely because it is universal and eternal, truth cannot be in complete harmony with the interests of any particular country at any given time and occasionally is incompatible with such interests. This is wherein its sacredness lies.[5]

The mission of "real" philosophers and artists, Wang Kuo-wei maintains, is to ascertain the inner significance of reality, thereby satisfying man's yearning to comprehend the ground of his own being.

In an article devoted entirely to a consideration of their high callings, Wang seeks to enumerate the ways in which philosophers and artists are superior to politicians and entrepreneurs. "The intrinsic value of their respective contributions to humanity," for one thing, "is decidedly different," since politicians and entrepreneurs can satisfy only man's baser, animalistic drives, whereas philosophers and artists are able to minister to his spirit. For another thing, the contribution of the former is impermanent, while the contribution of the latter is enduring.

> The contribution of philosophers and artists—that is, providing satisfaction and consolation to the intellects and feelings of humanity, once made, is equally valid [whether we concern ourselves with the present day in one particular country or] whether we speak of a thousand years

hence in some distant corner of the globe—provided, of course, that the truths which philosophy and art elucidate and the signs with which they are communicated still exist. The accomplishments of politicians and entrepreneurs, by contrast, rarely endure for even five or ten generations. There is, then, a difference in the durability [of the achievements of philosophers and artists on the one hand and politicians and entrepreneurs on the other].

And for yet another thing, philosophers and artists derive from their investigations intangible benefits that are unavailable to politicians and entrepreneurs. "If henceforward a man were to devote himself for many months and years to research, there would come a day when suddenly he would grasp through enlightenment the truths of the universe and human life. If one day he were to express the elusive and unseizable verities which he would then cherish in his heart in writing, painting, or sculpture, this would definitely represent the development of his Heaven-bestowed endowment. His happiness at this point he would by no means exchange [even] for that of a king."[6]

China's Lack of a Pure Philosophical Tradition

Since the study of philosophy can bring such joy to the human spirit, the question arises as to why this discipline (in Wang's opinion) has never flourished in China. To answer this question Wang Kuo-wei points to the worldly ambitions of many of the Middle Kingdom's great intellects, reminding us that Confucianism is commonly, and rightly, associated with the notion of public service. In the *Analects* and other Confucian texts, we read that the "superior man's" two great aims are to perfect his own virtue and to seek public office (unless the "times" are out of joint). Given this commitment to public service, which, as Benjamin I. Schwartz has remarked, "forms one of the basic criteria distinguishing the Confucian ideal of self-cultivation from some competing ideals in the Chinese world," it is not surprising that Wang considers Confucian thinkers down through the ages to have harbored political aspirations. "If one glances at the history of Chinese philosophy, one will observe that there has been no philosopher who has not also attempted to become a politician."[7]

Because China's so-called philosophers have characteristically sought to realize themselves in the public sphere, Wang Kuo-wei alleges, they have never regarded philosophy as more than a mere tool of politics. And because they have never valued philosophy for its own sake, they have typically either declined to delve into important, but from their standpoint irrelevant, areas of philosophical inquiry or subordinated them to other, and in Wang's view unimportant, areas of philosophical concern. Consider, for instance, the way in which China's practical-minded thinkers have exploited metaphysics rather than, as real philosophers would have done, pursue it for its own sake. "The metaphysical researches which were carried out during the Chou and Ch'in periods [1122–207 B.C.] as well as during the two Sung periods were no more than attempts to consolidate the foundations of moral philosophy. [The philosophers of these periods] had no intrinsic interest in metaphysics." This deplorable state of affairs has not been confined to metaphysics. "If this has been the case with metaphysics, [which Chinese thinkers traditionally have studied to the extent that they have been able to make use of it], imagine how much worse the situation has been with respect to aesthetics, logic, epistemology, and other unpopular, nonurgent problem [areas]."[8]

The upshot of the tireless quest of Confucius, Mo Tzu, Mencius, Hsun Tzu, Tung Chung-shu, Chang Tsai, Chu Hsi, Lu Chiu-yuan, and the rest for political power is that "our country is without pure philosophy." By pure philosophy Wang seems to have had in mind such areas of philosophical inquiry as metaphysics, aesthetics, logic, and epistemology in contradistinction to moral and political philosophy. In asserting that China lacks what he calls a pure philosophical tradition, Wang thus seems to be claiming that, among other things, Chinese philosophy is without a true metaphysical cast. Now, Confucianism as preached by Confucius himself, as is well known, is primarily concerned with man's place in society, not in the cosmos. It is therefore easy to see why, given his own view of the essence of philosophy, Wang should choose to claim that "at its inception Confucianism did not have a philosophical dimension. Although Confucius lectured men on morality and politics, he said not one word about philosophy. Since not even his most prized disciples, such as Tzu-kung, ever claimed to have heard him discourse on human nature or the Way of Heaven, we may infer that Confucius never spoke on these subjects."[9]

In ancient Confucianism Wang Kuo-wei discerns only faint glimmers of what he regards as the central subject matter of philosophy, namely, metaphysics. "The introduction of philosophy into Confucianism dates from the 'Hsi-tz'u' and 'Shuo-kua' Appendices to the *Book of Changes* (*I-ching*) as well as from the *Doctrine of the Mean* (*Chung-yung*)." The possible contribution that the so-called Changes school might have made to the development of metaphysics in China was, however, vitiated by the literati's general lack of interest in the researches of the school's adherents. "With the exception of Yang Hsiung's *Classic of the Great Mystery* (*T'ai-hsuan ching*) and Shao Yung's *Cosmological Chronology* (*Huang-chi ching-shih*), there have been few scholars in later generations who have carried on the study of the *Book of Changes*. The books written by these few scholars, moreover, have not been much read by others. Therefore, one cannot say that the philosophy of this Confucian school has been very influential."[10]

As intimated above, Wang Kuo-wei perceives in the *Doctrine of the Mean*, too, a hint of metaphysics. This work, one of the Four Books, has traditionally been attributed to Confucius's disciple Tzu-ssu. The question thus naturally arises as to why, if (as Wang claims) Confucius refrained from discussing metaphysical questions, his grandson should choose to do so. Wang, who was never in his life at a loss for theories, presents his in a long review he published of Ku T'ang-sheng's (Hung-ming, 1857–1928) English translation of the *Doctrine of the Mean*. The thrust of his argument is the suggestion that Tzu-ssu dabbled in metaphysics primarily in order to respond successfully to the challenge posed by the flourishing schools of Lao Tzu and Mo Tzu.

According to Wang, Lao Tzu and Mo Tzu, like Confucius, discoursed on morality and politics but, unlike him, appealed to the authority of extramundane entities for confirmation of the correctness of their views. "The theoretical basis of Lao Tzu's moral and political theories can be epitomized in the two words 'empty' (*hsu*) and 'quiescent' (*ching*). If asked why a person should be empty and quiescent, Lao Tzu would no doubt have responded by saying, 'The Way of Heaven is like this, and therefore the Way of man cannot but be like this [as well].' " Mo Tzu, Wang says, would probably have cited the Way of Heaven, too, to give weight to his doctrine that a person should be 'universally loving' (*ai*) and 'pragmatic' (*li*). "While, [therefore], it is true that there are subtle differences between Lao Tzu's derivation of emptiness and quiescence from the nature of Heaven and Mo Tzu's derivation of universal love and pragmatism from the will of Heaven, that which they use to ground their theories [that is, an extramundane entity, Heaven] is identical."[11]

Confucius, by contrast, had no desire to provide his theories with any sort of metaphysical foundation. That is why, Wang says, he intentionally avoided explaining 'human-heartedness' (*jen*) and 'righteousness' (*i*) in terms of extramundane entities. Tzu-ssu, however, could not afford this luxury because he feared that "compared to the theories of other philosophers, his grandfather's teaching was without foundation. He therefore proceeded to discourse on philosophy in order to ground Confucius's moral and political theories."[12] It is because Tzu-ssu wished to provide Confucianism with a metaphysical basis in order to make it competitive with the schools of Lao Tzu and Mo Tzu, Wang suggests, that he related his doctrine of 'sincerity' (*ch'eng*) to the Way of Heaven.

In this manner Wang Kuo-wei explains to his own satisfaction the authorship of an ancient Confucian text with metaphysical pretensions. It was, indeed, precisely because the *Doctrine of the Mean* has a metaphysical cast, Wang says, that it was singled out in Sung times to become one of the pillars of neo-Confucian philosophy.

> Chou Tun-i considered the root of the universe and human life to be the 'supreme ultimate' (*t'ai-chi*), Chang Tsai considered it to be the 'great void' (*t'ai-hsu*), and Ch'eng I and Chu Hsi considered it to be 'principle' (*li*), while [the author of] the *Doctrine of the Mean* considered it to be sincerity. [The Sung philosophers] therefore especially esteemed this book and raised it to the rank of the *Analects* and the *Mencius*. As a result, the *Doctrine of the Mean* not only exemplifies ancient Confucian philosophy, as do the 'Hsi-tz'u' and other Appendices, but also has served as a source of Confucian philosophy down through the ages.[13]

Although the *Doctrine of the Mean* had thus for centuries enjoyed the status of a central Confucian philosophical text, Wang did not believe that its principal metaphysical concept, sincerity, could compare with the principal metaphysical concepts of European thinkers. "Even though the *Doctrine of the Mean* may be considered a philosophical [treatise], and even though it takes sincerity to be the root of the universe and human life, this work is not on a par with recent works of Western philosophy. Tzu-ssu's so-called sincerity can by no means compare with Fichte's Ego, Schelling's Absolute, Hegel's Idea, Schopenhauer's Will, or Hartmann's Unconscious."[14] In fact, Wang alleges, the whole *Doctrine of the Mean* suffers from a certain vagueness and lack of coherency when measured against Western philosophical texts.

From such considerations, Wang Kuo-wei concluded that, despite the existence of a few works which are at least marginally concerned with metaphysical questions, Chinese philosophers down through the ages have slighted metaphysics. In view of the extraordinary emphasis Confucianism places on self-cultivation and public service, he did not, however, find it surprising that the most fully developed aspects of what passed for philosophy in China were "merely" moral philosophy and political philosophy.[15] As a result of his own intense interest in epistemological, aesthetic, logical, and (especially) metaphysical problems, Wang Kuo-wei thus determined, shortly after the turn of the century, to explore the thought of the great philosophers of Europe. He seems to have believed that they, unlike Chinese thinkers, were devoted to the study of philosophy for its own sake, concerned with the areas of philosophical inquiry into which he himself wished to delve, and dedicated to the revelation of the fundamental truths of the human situation.

China's Pursuit of Western Learning

The time to launch a study of European philosophy could not, in Wang's opinion, be more propitious. According to him, Chinese thought had been languishing in a state of stagnation ever since the end of the Sung period, as one result of which intellectual life by the dawn of the twentieth century had become as arid as it had once been during the Han period. It was, Wang writes, because Buddhism made its appearance in China after Chinese thought had become devitalized under the Han that it was able to win so many adherents among the educated elite: "Scholars responded to Buddhism as a starving man does to food or a thirsty man to drink."[16] Today, Wang Kuo-wei opines, when Chinese intellectual life has again degenerated into insipidness, what is needed desperately is an infusion of new ideas, a "second" Buddhism, so to speak. He himself, Wang happily announces, has identified Western scholarship as the second Buddhism.

As a matter of fact, Wang points out, certain areas of Western scholarship had been introduced into China as early as the late Ming period (1368–1644). "At the end of the Ming dynasty mathematics, calendrical studies, and Christianity all entered China and were adopted by the state. However, this sort of scholarship is material (hsing-hsia) and bears not the slightest relation to Chinese thought." Regrettably, the tendency on the part of translators and popularizers of Western thought to seek out works of solely the "material" variety has persisted right up to the present day. "Books translated into Chinese in Shanghai and Tientsin from the Hsien-feng and T'ung-chih reigns [1851–1874] onward are for the most part of this type [that is, material]."[17]

Only one individual, Wang informs us, has dared to depart, however slightly, from this convention of translating books with nothing but practical merits to recommend them. Unlike his predecessors, who sought the sources of the strength of modern Western states in the limited spheres of military technology, industry, and commerce, Yen Fu has concerned himself with the entire complex of ideas that he suspects may lie at the base of Western might. Relating himself in a general, theoretical way to the question of the origins of wealth and power, Yen Fu has, moreover, found occasion to translate and comment on foreign works whose central concepts roam beyond the confines of what Wang considers the purely practical. "It was only with the appearance of Mr. Yen Fu's translation of Huxley's *Evolution and Ethics* seven or eight years ago that the people's intellects were again challenged [literally, that the people's ears and eyes were renewed]. Were one to compare [this work] with one in the Buddhist canon, one could say that [*Evolution and Ethics*] is nearly [as popular as] the

Sutra in Forty-two Sections. From this time forward the names of Darwin and Spencer have been on everybody's lips, and the doctrine of the survival of the fittest has appeared in popular literature."[18]

What Wang Kuo-wei gives with one hand he in some cases takes away with the other. Thus, having praised Yen Fu for his intellectual initiative, Wang proceeds to qualify that praise nearly out of existence. It must be recognized, he declares, that although Yen Fu has made a significant contribution in introducing into China the thought of British economic and political theorists, his contribution nevertheless retains the stigma of practicality. Yen Fu, it must never be forgotten, is interested in simply the "subbranches" of philosophy, not in "pure" philosophy. "This is why he will never be able to influence the Chinese intellectual world [in any serious way]."[19]

Having rebuked Yen Fu for the utilitarian animus of his researches in Western thought, Wang Kuo-wei moves on to criticize his practical-minded contemporary Liang Ch'i-ch'ao, who while in exile in Japan had founded the well-known *Journal of Disinterested Criticism, New Citizen Journal,* and *New Fiction.* Since the turn of the century, the young man notes, all sorts of magazines have sprouted up. Unfortunately, the contributors to these new periodicals seem always to be "either busy-body students or refugee ex-officials." Because these magazines are invariably political in orientation, it should come as no surprise that their editors "have absolutely no conception of what scholarship is." "While occasionally such periodicals do contain scholarly discussions, these discussions are not only plagiarized and crude but also—as, for instance, in the case of [Liang Ch'i-ch'ao's puerile article on] Kant's philosophy in the *New Citizen Journal*—eighty or ninety per cent erroneous."[20]

Wang Kuo-wei's most biting criticism is reserved, however, for the late Ch'ing reformers K'ang Yu-wei (1858–1927) and T'an Ssu-t'ung (1865–1898). These individuals, in Wang's opinion, were guilty of a crime far more heinous than Yen Fu's and Liang Ch'i-ch'ao's, namely, subordinating philosophy to politics. We recall that Wang believed that treating philosophy as a tool of politics is, quite literally, an act of sacrilege. Toward the Philistines K'ang and T'an, he accordingly adopts a posture of utter disgust, declining even to mention the men by name. "Among those who have attempted to reform ancient thought under the influence of foreign doctrines and who have for a period of time occupied influential positions in the Chinese intellectual world are X of Nan-hai, Kwangtung, author of *Confucius as a Reformer* (*K'ung-tzu kai-chih k'ao*) and *Tung Chung-shu's Studies in the "Spring and Autumn Annals"* (*"Ch'un ch'iu" Tung shih hsueh*), and Y of Liu-yang, Hunan, author of *Science of Love* (*Jen-hsueh*)."

About K'ang Yu-wei, Wang has much to say, and all of it is negative.

> X's doctrines . . . smack of pantheism, and his veneration of Confucius is to some extent an imitation of Christianity. In styling himself a prophet, he is simply cherishing the wild ambition of becoming a second Mohammed. That wherein he has stimulated men [literally, excited men's ears and eyes] lies in his throwing off the bonds of several thousand years of thought and replacing them with superstitions that have already been discredited in the West. His scholarly career cannot but end in failure along with his political program. X has no intrinsic interest in scholarship; he merely uses it as a means to political ends.[21]

One may note in passing that from Schopenhauer and Nietzsche Wang Kuo-wei had developed a loathing for religion; from them he understood that Christianity was cant. Probably for this reason he regarded K'ang Yu-wei's efforts to make Confucianism the state religion of China as being atavistic.

T'an Ssu-t'ung fares no better under Wang's acerbic pen; his excursions into metaphysics are ridiculed and his political aspirations are derided.

> Y's theories have their origin in *Ideal Suggestion through Mental Photography,* a book translated by the missionaries in Shanghai. The doctrine of ether (*i-t'ai*) in his metaphysics is half materialistic and half mystical. When a person reads this book [*Science of Love*], his interest is drawn not to this sort of naive metaphysics but, rather, to Y's political views. Y's aim in this book is in fact political rather than philosophical. In this respect he is exactly like X of Nan-hai, Kwangtung.[22]

How can we possibly hope to find value in the jejune works of the politicians K'ang and T'an? Wang demands to know.

In several of the essays he published in the *Journal of the Educational World* during the opening years of the twentieth century, Wang Kuo-wei calls on his fellow literati to acknowledge the independence and universality of learning. Citing Kant's famous maxim, "Regard humanity as an end, not as a means," he suggests that this applies to scholarship as well as to men; repeatedly Wang stresses that "he who desires the development of scholarship must regard scholarship as an end, not as a means . . . When men discuss politics, they ought to discuss only politics. Why they insist on profaning the sacredness of philosophy and literature I cannot understand." Wang even goes so far as to close an article he published on the contemporary Chinese world of scholarship with a peroration exhorting his compatriots both to seek truth in the West as well as in the East and to honor the independence of scholarship.

It is incorrect to imagine that in intellectual matters East is East and West is West because, while everyone has intellectual powers, not everyone is able to explain the problems of the universe and human life . . . Although [Chinese and foreigners] share a universe and human life, their views of the universe and human life differ. Such dissimilarity should by no means, however, be taken as a basis for mutual discrimination. What scholarship disputes is only the difference between right and wrong, between truth and falsehood. Thus, aside from the distinction between truth and falsehood, one may not mix in national, racial, or religious distinctions, for that would entail regarding scholarship as a means, not as an end. There can be no development of scholarship unless it is considered an end [in itself]; the development of scholarship lies solely in its independence. Thus, the contemporary Chinese world of scholarship must, on the one hand, abolish discrimination between East and West and, on the other hand, desist from regarding [scholarship] as a tool of politics. [If these conditions could be secured, Chinese scholarship] might one day develop.[23]

It was with extremely high hopes that he could contribute to what he considered to be an international dialogue on the question of higher belief which absorbed his attention as a young man that Wang Kuo-wei undertook his pioneering study of German philosophy.

5

The Critical Philosophy

Wang Kuo-wei began seriously to study Western thought shortly after the turn of the century. During the period 1901–1907 he read widely in the field of philosophy, publishing prolifically on the philosophies of those thinkers whose ideas he believed to be important. Although scholars writing in the postimperial era often credit Wang with being as great a pioneer as Yen Fu in the introduction of foreign thought into China,[1] it decidedly is not the case that, at their actual time of publication, Wang's essays on philosophy exerted any significant influence on other Chinese intellectuals, as Yen Fu's most demonstrably did. In fact, Wang's philosophical essays seem to have elicited very little interest from his contemporaries during the last years of the Ch'ing.

That the articles on philosophy which he published in the *Journal of the Educational World* failed to arouse much interest was probably due in part to the circumstance that Wang was at the dawn of this century still an obscure young pundit whose writings appeared in a magazine which, if not equally obscure, could not at any rate claim the audience that, for instance, the popular *New Citizen Journal* could. The articles themselves presumed a fair degree of familiarity on the part of the reader with important German philosophical concepts as well as with the names and principal ideas of many major and minor Western thinkers from Greek times onward. Their content, moreover, strongly reflected Wang's overriding concern with the quest of the human spirit for the meaning of its existence. Few of his contemporaries in the ranks of the literati, however, appear to have shared this concern.

Although most of his own generation of intellectuals were preoccupied with the empire's immediate political and economic debilities, Wang's orientation toward universally human problems and fundamental human values was by no means unprecedented. For centuries the exponents of philosophical Buddhism and philosophical Taoism, for instance, had speculated on "the problems of the universe and human life." Wang himself was not impervious to Buddhist and Taoist arguments.[2] Unlike educated Chinese of earlier generations, however, he had available to him not only the traditions of philosophical Buddhism and philosophical Taoism but also the German philosophical tradition; thus, in his eagerness to comprehend the essential truths of the human condition, Wang Kuo-wei decided to study a strand of the New Learning of whose existence he had been made aware through China's so-called encounter with the West.

Wang's Discovery of Kant's Works

As early as 1898 or 1899, while still a student at the Eastern Language Institute, Wang Kuo-wei had become aware of the important position occupied by Kant in the Western philosophical tradition. It was thus only natural that, when he began his investigation of European philosophy, his main objective was to master the thought of Kant. Here, perhaps, he would find the solutions to the questions that troubled him as a young man. Before immersing himself in the critical philosophy, however, Wang wisely did some background reading in Western thought generally.

> He who guided me in my [philosophical] studies during this period was Mr. Fujita. In the spring of the following year [1902], I began to read Fairbanks's *Introduction to Sociology*, Jevons's *Logic*, and Høffding's *Outlines of Psychology*. When I had read part way through Høffding's work, some philosophical books which I had purchased arrived. I thereupon put *Outlines of Psychology* aside and read Paulsen's *Introduction to Philosophy* and Windelband's *History of Philosophy* . . . Fortunately, [in addition to English] I was already able to read Japanese. Referring to some secondary Japanese texts on Western philosophy, I was able to get the gist of what was being said . . . I also occasionally browsed through the works of Locke and Hume.[3]

Having studied, in English, the writings of these Western sages, Wang felt ready by 1903 to tackle the first *Critique*. Unfortunately, it proved to be more than he could handle. "In the spring of 1903 I began to read Kant's *Critique of Pure Reason,* but because I could not understand it, I put it aside after reading only a part of it." Elaborating on his disappointing initial encounter with the first *Critique*, Wang confesses that "when I arrived at the 'Transcendental Analytic,' I found several passages almost totally incomprehensible, so I put the book down and turned to Schopenhauer's *World as Will and Representation*."[4]

After spending a year and a half with Schopenhauer's writings "constantly at my side," Wang returned with renewed courage to the first *Critique*. "This spring [1905] I reread Kant's *Critique of Pure Reason,* and I intend now to devote several years' effort to the study of Kant." On this second reading of Kant's magnum opus, "I did not reexperience the difficulties that I had had on the earlier occasion." Emboldened by his success with the first *Critique,* Wang then went on to study Kant's aesthetics and ethics. In 1906 he took up for the third time the study of the first *Critique.* By 1907 he could report that "this year I undertook a fourth study [of the *Critique of Pure Reason*] and found the difficulties even fewer. I also came to believe that what difficulties remained were probably unsupportable parts of Kant's philosophy."[5]

It is an interesting feature of Wang's study of the critical philosophy that, despite the general understanding of it which he eventually attained, he was not well satisfied with the results of his researches. It seems that the more Wang learned about Kant's thought, the less enamored of it he became. Primarily he was distressed to discover, in the end, that Kant could not provide him with the intellectually appealing and emotionally gratifying *Weltanschauung* that he sought in Western philosophy.

A Phoenix in the Philosophical World

Throughout his life Wang Kuo-wei was a quick study, a scholar who mastered one field of intellectual inquiry after another, conceived the most original (and occasionally audacious) theories on the subject matter at hand, and rapidly went into print with them. That this proclivity was already fully in evidence in his early youth may be seen from the fact that, after studying the first *Critique* for only half a year, Wang felt inspired to write a brief appreciation of Kant's contribution to the world of philosophy. Although this short essay does not purport to be a sophisticated piece of philosophical analysis, it is of interest because it candidly reveals the nature of the initial appeal of the Kantian philosophy for Wang as well as the great enthusiasm with which he began his study of philosophy.

Prior to Kant, Wang informs us in "An Appreciation of Kant" ("Han-te hsiang-tsan"), skepticism had been rampant, and there had been no commonly accepted standard of truth with reference to which men could rectify mistaken ideas. Kant's contribution to philosophy was, through his insights into the nature of human knowledge, to eliminate much of this skepticism. "A sage was born in Königsberg, and his birth brought peace to the philosophical world and pointed out to men the Grand Way (*ta tao*). [Kant holds that] perception entails space externally and time internally. All of his philosophical conclusions are brilliant. The view that results from the aforementioned premises is that the forms of our knowledge of objects lie in the subject rather than in the object. While this is not difficult to assert, it is difficult to prove."[6]

Wang Kuo-wei's remarks suggest that, in the first instance, he was attracted to the so-called Copernican revolution that Kant effected in the field of philosophy. Like Copernicus, Kant put forward a subjective explanation of an apparently objective phenomenon, namely, human knowledge. In doing so he reversed the dependence of intuition on objects to a situation in which objects are dependent on intuition, and he advanced the claim that objects have their properties qua objects dictated by the mind. When Wang says that Kant has shown that "the forms of our knowledge of objects lie in the subject rather than in the object," he doubtless has in mind the following passage from the preface to the second edition of the first *Critique:*

> Hitherto it has been assumed that all our knowledge must conform to objects. But all attempts to extend our knowledge of objects by establishing something in regard to them *a priori*, by means of concepts, have, on this assumption, ended in failure. We must therefore make trial whether we may not have more success in the tasks of metaphysics, if we suppose that objects must conform to our knowledge. This would agree better with what is desired, namely, that it should be possible to have knowledge of objects *a priori*, determining something in regard to them prior to their being given. We should then be proceeding precisely on the lines of Copernicus' primary hypothesis.[7]

Wang seems to have been much excited by Kant's efforts to establish a Ptolemaic, anthropocentric metaphysics.

In view of the nature of his later philosophical ideas and interests, it is also significant that in this, his first published piece on philosophy, Wang discloses his fascination with the Kantian view of the constitution of the faculty of intuition, especially the formal structure thereof, and his fundamental lack of interest in the intellectual faculties, understanding (*Verstand*) and reason (*Vernunft*). On examining space and time, Kant discovered that they cannot be classed with either the data of the senses or the concepts of the understanding. Space and time, in Kant's view, constitute the forms of human sensibility, although considered as characterizing things-in-themselves they are "monstrosities." Over and over again in his philosophical essays we will find Wang lauding Kant's characterization of the nature of space and time.

We will also find him rapturously embracing the Schopenhauerian theory of perception, according to which the true basis of all new knowledge is intuition.

In the early months of his study of the critical philosophy, Wang could not have been more enthusiastic about Kant. The concluding remarks of his short essay on Kant are nothing less than an unstinted encomium to a hero. "With Kant the clouds and mists were dispelled, and men could see clearly the autumn mountains. Kant is like the sun hanging in the sky, illuminating the darkest far corner. He is like a phoenix flying high in the sky, beside which all other birds are shamed into silence."[8]

Wang Kuo-wei's initial adulation of Kant did not last long. Although he would continue to admire the philosopher, he gradually grew more critical of him. There are several reasons for Wang's change of attitude toward Kant, the most important of which is that in the summer of 1903 he undertook a sustained study of Schopenhauer's works. It was from Schopenhauer, the seminal influence on Wang during his philosophical period, that he acquired a thorough understanding of the many "defects" in the critical philosophy.

Most of Wang's observations on the Kantian philosophy are not profound; some are even jejune. However, many of his views on the critical philosophy were acquired directly from Schopenhauer, as Wang Kuo-wei himself once frankly confessed. "That year [1903] I read [*The World as Will and Representation*] through twice from beginning to end. Then I read *On the Fourfold Root of the Principle of Sufficient Reason, On the Will in Nature*, his essays, and other things. In particular, I took his 'Criticism of the Kantian Philosophy,' appended to *The World as Will and Representation*, as the key to the understanding of the Kantian philosophy."[9] Bearing this admission in mind, let us now look at Wang's later view of Kant.

Kant as Schopenhauer's Predecessor

In an article written in 1904, Wang Kuo-wei advances the dubious proposition that, in assessing Kant's contribution to the history of philosophy, it would be more accurate to regard Kant as Schopenhauer's predecessor than to view Schopenhauer as Kant's successor. In Wang's portrayal Kant played a role in the history of philosophy much like that played by Ch'en Sheng and Wu Kuang in Chinese political history. Just as these intrepid souls initiated the disturbances that eventually led to the collapse of the Ch'in (221–207 B.C.) and Liu Pang's establishment of the great Han dynasty, so Kant began a critical review of previous philosophical theories that ended only with Schopenhauer's construction of a "real philosophy" on the charred ground left by the Kantian critique.

> Schopenhauer alone carried on the Kantian tradition in such a way that he was able to correct its errors and thereby construct a complete philosophical system. Kant's philosophy was merely destructive, not constructive. Kant held that metaphysics is impossible and attempted to reduce metaphysics to epistemology. Therefore, his thought may be considered simply a critique of philosophy; it may not be considered real philosophy. Taking Kant's epistemology as his point of departure, Schopenhauer constructed a metaphysics. Furthermore, he gave aesthetics and ethics systematic treatment.[10]

Two things are noteworthy about Wang Kuo-wei's new view of the Kantian philosophy. The first is that if the opinion expressed here appears embarrassingly naive, it is a naiveté shared by Schopenhauer as well, for it is in fact from him that Wang obtained the ideas that, as Schopenhauer puts it, the immediate result of Kant's appearance was "only negative, not positive" and that Kant "did not set up a completely new system."[11] The second point of interest concerns the difference between Kant's and Wang's ambitions in the field of philosophy. Kant was a thoroughgoing deflationary metaphysician whose self-appointed philosophical chore was, as Wang correctly perceived, to provide an epistemological rendering of metaphysics. Wang, by contrast, had embarked on his study of the *Critique of Pure Reason* precisely because he hoped in philosophy to ascertain the metaphysical significance of existence. It seems probable, therefore, that Wang felt cheated by Kant, whose preoccupation with metaphysical questions in writing the first *Critique* he found not nearly as intense as his own in reading it.

That Kant's decisive impact on Wang, as on Schopenhauer, was to tease him with a peek at the impermissible is evident in a number of his comments on the critical philosophy. One of the most interesting concerns Wang Kuo-wei's allegation that Kant, like Hume, must in the final analysis be considered a skeptic.

> [In opposition to the naive realists], Kant alone maintained that in perception we necessarily structure objects in space and time and in accordance with the category of causality. (Although Kant had twelve categories, Schopenhauer selected only this one.) However, space and time are the forms of sensibility and the category of causality is the form of the understanding. These do not exist a posteriori but rather condition our experience. Therefore, in the phenomenal world external objects enter into our forms of sensibility and understanding. They are thus different from things-in-themselves (*wu chih tzu-shen*). Things-in-themselves can be thought but are not knowable. Thus, the objects of

human knowledge are merely phenomena, [according to Kant]. This view differs from Hume's doctrine only in degree, not in kind. Hume thought that the causal principle is derived from experience, possessing neither universality nor necessity. Kant believed that it is a priori and that it has both universality and necessity. However, on the subject of things-in-themselves both philosophers are silent. Thus, if Hume's philosophy is regarded as one of skepticism, Kant's must be labeled one of skepticism as well.[12]

If Kant had not been a skeptic in the manner of Hume, Wang intimates, he would not have insisted that we cannot attain knowledge of noumena.

Luckily, Wang declares, Schopenhauer appeared on the scene to rescue the philosophical world from Kant's pernicious skepticism. Now, although Schopenhauer was willing to concede that the possibility of a certain type of speculative inquiry, namely, transcendent metaphysics, is excluded on Kantian principles, he declined to concede that metaphysics in any sense is impossible. On the contrary, he believed that in human willing he had discovered "the only narrow gateway to truth," and on this foundation he built, so he fancied, a reputable metaphysics. Wang Kuo-wei, for one, agreed with him and even went so far as to claim that it was Schopenhauer's doctrine of the knowability of the noumenon that had saved the critical philosophy from the shoals of skepticism on which it had nearly foundered. Having in one of his essays explained this doctrine, Wang admiringly concludes, "In this fashion Schopenhauer remedied the defect of Kant's *Critique of Pure Reason* and constructed a metaphysics."[13] It thus appears that one of the main reasons Wang became interested in Schopenhauer's philosophy, which he would study for several years, was that it purports to provide a solution to the problem of the relation between phenomena and things-in-themselves.

Unsupportable Elements of the Critical Philosophy

In the end, Wang came to believe that what difficulties he still encountered in his effort to grasp the fundamentals of the Kantian system were in all probability untenable aspects of it. As an example of what he considered an unsupportable element of the Kantian philosophy, we may cite Wang's criticism of one of the most fundamental concepts of that philosophy: reason. Kant, of course, had imagined that his critique of pure reason was one of his signal achievements in the field of philosophy. Wang, however, had his doubts on this score.

According to Wang Kuo-wei, who by the time he wrote the

remarks in question (1904) had adopted Schopenhauer's epistemological standpoint, "Our knowledge may be divided into two types,
perceptual and conceptual. The former is derived from our sensibility
and understanding, while the latter is a product of reason (*li-hsing*).
Perceptual knowledge is that which we have in common with animals,
whereas conceptual knowledge is unique to mankind. This is why the
ancients called man a rational animal." From the time of Plato and
Aristotle all the way down through the time of Locke and Leibniz,
Wang says, it had been standard philosophical practice to refer to this
special power of the human mind as 'reason'. It was Kant's distinction,
Wang charges, to be the first philosopher to use the term 'reason' in
an ambiguous manner, a circumstance that prompts him to comment
wryly, "Although Kant regarded his critique of reason as his greatest
philosophical contribution, his concept of reason is obscure."[14]

Following Schopenhauer, Wang maintains that Kant was ill-
advised to make a distinction between pure and practical reason, according to which pure reason is "the faculty that supplies the principles of a priori knowledge." He also alleges that Kant drew the line
between understanding and reason incorrectly, as a consequence of
which his definition of reason is "self-contradictory."

> Thus, in the "Transcendental Dialectic" he says, "Reason is the faculty
> of inference" (*Critique of Pure Reason*, 5th ed., p. 386), but elsewhere he
> declares, "Mere judging is the business of the understanding" (ibid., p.
> 94). In his "Criticism of the Kantian Philosophy," Schopenhauer com-
> ments on these assertions as follows: "Now by this [Kant] really says that
> judging is the business of the understanding, so long as the ground of
> the judgement is empirical, transcendental, or metalogical . . . but if it is
> logical, and the syllogism consists in this, then . . . reason is here at work."
> Besides the above, there are a variety of additional definitions [of reason],
> each different from the others. The situation is the same as regards the
> understanding. In short, Kant takes what is commonly referred to as
> reason and calls it understanding and gives reason a specialized meaning.
> He says that the ordering of sensations in space and time and our fash-
> ioning therefrom of perceptions is the business of sensibility; the or-
> dering of perceptions and our fashioning therefrom of experience of
> the natural world, the business of the understanding; and the ordering
> of empirical judgements and our fashioning therefrom of metaphysical
> knowledge, the business of reason.[15]

It was only with Schopenhauer's arrival on the philosophical scene,
Wang tells us, that the matter was set right and a bold distinction
made between understanding and reason.

Two things are significant about Wang Kuo-wei's criticism of

Kant's use of the term 'reason'. The first is that he correctly grasps one of the most frustrating problems with the critical philosophy, namely, the looseness with which Kant uses even the most basic of his concepts. In the case of reason, Kant employs the word in no less than three different senses. In its widest sense, reason is used by Kant to designate the source of all a priori elements. As such, it includes what is a priori in sensibility as well as in understanding. In its narrowest sense, reason refers to the faculty that makes the mind unhappy with ordinary and scientific knowledge and leads it to demand an unconditionedness that cannot be found in the empirical sphere. Defined in this way, reason is distinct from understanding, the former having its Ideas and the latter its categories. In a third sense, however, reason is synonymous with understanding. When Kant says that the mind is divided into two faculties, sensibility and spontaneity, he is using reason in this sense. Kant's use of the word 'reason', which Wang Kuo-wei singles out for criticism, is, as Norman Kemp Smith has observed, "an excellent example of the looseness and carelessness with which he employs even the most important and fundamental of his technical terms."[16]

The second point of interest in Wang's résumé of the difficulties involved in Kant's use of the term 'reason' is the faithfulness with which he adheres to Schopenhauer's perceptual theory in making it. Now, while Schopenhauer was quick to criticize Kant's view of perception, his own theory is not without its baffling features. Wang, however, apparently did not discern any inconsistencies in Schopenhauer's position. On the contrary, he found Schopenhauer's epistemology "especially attractive" and used it as the "key" to understanding the critical philosophy. Unlike other aspects of the philosophy of metaphysical pessimism, concerning which he would eventually develop grave doubts, Wang appears never to have ceased giving credence to Schopenhauer's epistemological theories.

It seems clear in retrospect that from Kant Wang Kuo-wei acquired a superficial understanding of the critical philosophy's most fundamental technical concepts as well as a general notion of some basic Kantian doctrines, such as the subjective nature of space and time, the division of the intellectual faculty into two stems, and the disparity between phenomena and noumena. Initially excited by the ambitious project on which he had so hopefully embarked, the mastery of the first *Critique*, Wang rapidly became disenchanted with Kant. He was upset by various things: by the inscrutability—and even "unsupportability"—of parts of the critical philosophy, by the "skeptical" philosopher's prohibition against researches having atavistic metaphysical pretensions, and by the confusing manner in which Kant employed even his most basic philosophical terms. By the summer of 1903 Wang Kuo-wei was thus highly susceptible to the blandishments of that free philosophical spirit, Schopenhauer, whose thought is noticeably less rarified than that of Kant.

6

The Philosophy of Metaphysical Pessimism

Wang Kuo-wei had been struggling with the *Critique of Pure Reason* for several months when he decided to take a look at the works of Schopenhauer. After the intricacies of the first *Critique*, Schopenhauer's writings were a breath of fresh air to him. "Then I read Schopenhauer's works and loved them. From the summer of 1903 through the winter of 1904–05, Schopenhauer's works were constantly at my side."[1] With great enthusiasm he devoured first the philosopher's magnum opus, *The World as Will and Representation,* and then such other works as *The Fourfold Root of the Principle of Sufficient Reason, On the Will in Nature,* and those essays from *Parerga und Paralipomena* that had by then been translated into English.

If Wang's relationship to Kant may be described as a brief flirtation, it is not inappropriate to characterize his relationship to Schopenhauer as an intense love affair. As was the case when he had first begun to study the critical philosophy, Wang was initially so enthusiastic about the philosophy of metaphysical pessimism that his praise for Schopenhauer was unrestrained. "As regards [Schopenhauer's] *Weltanschauung,* the acuity of his observations and the perceptiveness of his theories both delighted me emotionally and appealed to me intellectually." "The content of Schopenhauer's works is profound and his writing clear." "As regards the soundness of his premises and the perspicuity of his writing, scarcely anyone has been a match for Schopenhauer since philosophy has existed."[2]

The world is indebted to Schopenhauer, Wang informs us in his philosophical essays, for having conceived an illustrious, albeit neglected, pedagogical theory; for having saved metaphysics from the ravages of Kant's "skepticism" by disclosing the content of the *Ding an sich;* for having successfully extricated philosophy from the conceptual pit into which it had fallen as a consequence of Kant's "self-contradictory" use of the term 'reason'; and for having infused metaphysics and psychology with a voluntaristic animus. In his assessment of Schopenhauer's place in the history of philosophy, Wang reveals that, in short, he has exchanged his former philosophical hero, Kant, for the even more brilliant Schopenhauer. Indeed, Schopenhauer emerges from Wang Kuo-wei's essays as nothing less than the central figure in Western philosophy.

> At this point we can determine Schopenhauer's place in [the history of] philosophy. In ancient times there was Plato, the Greek, and in modern times there was Kant, the German. During his lifetime Schopenhauer prized them above all others and considered himself the Plato and Kant of his own day. However, the truth that Plato expounds in his philosophy is frequently obscured by mythology. Although the Kantian epistemology represents the highest level that knowledge had achieved up until that time, Kant was . . . destructive, not constructive. He was thus merely like Ch'en Sheng or Wu Kuang . . . When we look at philosophers after the time of Schopenhauer, such as Fechner, Wundt, Hartmann, and others, we see that there is not one who has not been influenced by Schopenhauer's thought. This is true in particular of Nietzsche, who took Schopenhauer's thought as his point of departure, even though he gradually moved in the opposite direction. In a number of places, however, his ideal of the overman is indebted to Schopenhauer's theory of genius.[3]

Because Schopenhauer was not a university professor, "he could not compare with Hegel and Herbart as regards either his place in the contemporary world of scholarship or the number of his disciples." However, his lack of institutional affiliation did, Wang Kuo-wei claims, give Schopenhauer an opportunity to develop his ideas freely, unencumbered by the onerous responsibilities that academic philosophers are constrained to bear. "Schopenhauer alone devoted his life exclusively to researches concerning the universe and human life and to reflections on art . . . Thus, although his philosophy and behavior were often contradictory, he was in fact speaking of himself when he said that one should live *for* philosophy rather than make a living *from* philosophy." It was precisely because he had the leisure to devote himself to what Wang regarded as "serious" philosophical research, in which academic philosophers have scant time to indulge, that Schopenhauer was able to develop his nonpareil philosophical system. The fact that his own contemporaries failed to esteem him simply goes to show that, "just as Schopenhauer himself used to say, the victory of truth must wait until later generations because a brilliant genius will never be appreciated in his own time."[4]

In connection with his study of the philosophy of metaphysical pessimism, Wang published in the *Journal of the Educational World* a number of articles, the most important of which are "Schopenhauer's Philosophy and His Pedagogical Theory," "A Critique of *Dream of the Red Chamber*" ("*Hung-lou meng* p'ing-lun"), "Schopenhauer and Nietzsche" ("Shu-pen-hua yü Ni-ts'ai"), and "My Views on Schopenhauer's 'Hereditary Nature of Qualities' " ("Shu Shu-pen-hua 'I-ch'uan shuo' hou"). From these articles it is apparent that Wang failed fully to grasp the Schopenhauerian doctrines concerning the criminality of life and the denial of the will and, further, that he elected to modify Schopenhauer's positions on suicide and asceticism. In the main, however, Wang Kuo-wei in his writings demonstrates a firm mastery of, and manifests a conspicuous fidelity to, the major theories of Arthur Schopenhauer, the dominant influence on him during his philosophical period (1901–1907).

Wang's View of Schopenhauer's Epistemology

Schopenhauer's *World as Will and Representation* opens with the declaration, "The world is my representation." In other words, it is an object that presupposes a subject. Since the world in which we live exists only as representation—that is, only in reference to that which represents—the reality of the external world must be denied when this is claimed to be independent of the subject. "The whole world of objects is and remains representation, and is for this reason wholly and for ever conditioned by the subject." That the world is representation, says Schopenhauer, is a fact first noted by Plato and the Indians, although it was only with Kant that it was made "a proved and incontestable truth."[5]

Wang Kuo-wei was deeply interested in Schopenhauer's epistemology, which he found "especially attractive," even "profound," and through which he "gained insight into the Kantian philosophy."[6] There are several reasons for Wang's interest, one of which is Schopenhauer's philosophical demonstration of the illusory status of the external world. On beginning his study of the critical philosophy, we recall, Wang had been drawn to Kant's so-called Copernican revolution—that is, his hypothesis of a subjective explanation of a seemingly objective phenomenon, human knowledge. Now, while Schopenhauer made some drastic departures from the Kantian legacy, he did on the whole uphold the central features of Kantian epistemology. Wang seems to have been much attracted to the Kantian notion of subjectivity, which Schopenhauer accepted and embroidered in his own fashion.

It is possible that Wang was attracted to Schopenhauer's doctrine of the illusory status of the phenomenal world not only by its apparent gross similarity to Kant's theory but also by the obvious affinities between Schopenhauer's doctrine and certain fundamental tenets of the Upanishads and Buddhist scriptures, especially those of the Mahāyāna school, with which, in their Chinese form, he was familiar. Schopenhauer himself admired the great Indian religions, and in his works he often describes his doctrine of the world as representation as broadly corresponding to the Upanishadic contention that phenomenal reality is ultimately illusion (*māyā*). Indeed, when speaking of the illusory status of the phenomenal world, he uses "veil of *māyā*" as a virtual synonym for "realm of appearance." The notion that the world as we ordinarily perceive it is in some fundamental sense unreal is not lacking in certain schools of Chinese Buddhism. One is therefore tempted to speculate that Wang became interested in Schopenhauer's theory of the world as representation not only as a result of his sketchy knowledge of Kantian epistemology but also as a consequence of his familiarity with particular strands of Buddhist thought.

In his exposition of Schopenhauer's epistemology, Wang Kuo-wei devotes a great deal of attention to the philosopher's theory of perception. In "Schopenhauer's Philosophy and His Pedagogical Theory," the theoretical underpinning of which is the Schopenhauerian proposition that perception is the true basis of all new knowledge, Wang propounds the view that perception (*chih-kuan*) provides the only adequate foundation for "real" philosophy. Unfortunately, he finds, no philosopher prior to Schopenhauer had grasped this important truth, as a consequence of which pre-Schopenhauerian philosophical systems by and large had been spun out of mere concepts (*kai-nien*). "Philosophers historically have usually based their doctrines on concepts. Even Kant, not to mention the minor philosophers, was no exception."[7]

It was only with the appearance of Schopenhauer, Wang informs us, that the world was treated to a philosophy that is based on the perceptual knowledge acquired by its creator over the course of a lifetime.

> Schopenhauer was different [from Kant and the others]. His metaphysical system truly is based on the results of a lifetime's perception . . . Thus, he says that philosophy deposits its results in concepts but does not start from them as that which is given. Accordingly, he recorded the results of his researches in writing (conceptual signs) but did not take concepts as his point of departure. This is the source of the superiority of Schopenhauer's philosophy over the philosophies of others from antiquity to the present day.

In short, "the most important characteristic of Schopenhauer's philosophy as a whole is the fact that Schopenhauer's point of departure is perception (or intuition), not concepts."[8]

Schopenhauer's theory of perception, Wang discovers, has ramifications throughout his philosophy. It is, for example, the basis of the philosopher's dicta about education as well as one reason he prefers art to science.[9] His perceptual theory is also the grounds on which Schopenhauer denounces the Euclidean method in mathematics, Wang observes.

> If we turn with this conviction [that perception is the source of all truth] to mathematics as conceived by Euclid and followed for two thousand years, we cannot help pronouncing it strange and perverse. We seek the reduction of logical proofs to those of perception. Mathematics definitely involves no more than the intuitions of space and time, and these are not a posteriori but a priori intuitions. They are, in other words, not empirical perceptions but pure intuitions. Accordingly, mathematics rests on intuitions which do not require proof and are, in fact, incapable of proof. In mathematics to reject the certain evidence of perception in order to substitute for it logical evidence is like a man who cuts off his own legs in order to travel by carriage.[10]

Wang Kuo-wei's exposition of Schopenhauer's theory of perception in the main does not go beyond recapitulating its principal features and implications. While his comments do reveal Wang's flair for collating and synthesizing Schopenhauer's scattered remarks on a given subject, they also disclose his unwillingness or inability to perceive even the most flagrant difficulties with this theory.[11] It may well be that Schopenhauer's epistemological doctrines always appeared thoroughly credible to Wang. If this was indeed the case, it was in marked contrast to Wang's experience with Schopenhauer's metaphysics, concerning which he developed, in the course of his philosophical investigations, some serious reservations.

Wang's View of Schopenhauer's Metaphysics

It is an interesting feature of Schopenhauer's approach to philosophy that, while he professed wholehearted allegiance to the major implications of Kant's antispeculative theses, he was not eager to accept the drastic curtailment of the scope of philosophical inquiry that such allegiance would seem to entail. On the contrary, Schopenhauer was bent on rescuing philosophy from what he considered the "despair" of the Kantian critique. The fascination of Schopenhauer's relation to Kant arises from the fact that, although Schopenhauer claimed to have accepted Kant's view that knowledge is confined to phenomena, his entire philosophy rests on the disclosure of the *Ding an sich* and dogmatic assertions about its content.

Schopenhauer reveals the thing-in-itself to be a single cosmic will. This 'will', also called the 'will to live', objectifies itself in the natural world in both inanimate and animate objects. One of the principal characteristics of the will is that it is always at variance with itself, and this conflict which the will experiences with itself is reflected in nature through all its grades. It appears most clearly in man, where it manifests itself as egoism, desire, hatred, and strife. The life history of every human being, reflecting as it must the inner nature of the will of which he is an objectification, is thus by definition a history of suffering and pain. No one, says Schopenhauer, would ever care to live his life twice.

Wang Kuo-wei was mesmerized for some time by Schopenhauer's depiction of the world as will. He seems to have had no difficulty whatsoever accepting the philosopher's doctrine of the knowability of the noumenon as well as his portrayal of the universe and human life as mere manifestations of the surging, striving first principle. He was firmly convinced, initially, that Schopenhauer had made a sterling contribution to mankind by identifying the will as the *Ding an sich,* thereby revealing the metaphysical reason for the bleakness of phenomenal reality.

It is conceivable that, in addition to the element of personal taste, Wang was drawn to Schopenhauer's metaphysics by his perception of similarities between certain of the philosopher's ideas and specific tenets of Indian religion. For example, Schopenhauer's distinction between phenomenal and noumenal reality, the former envisioned as comprising a multiplicity of objects in contrast to the unitary thing-in-itself, is akin to the Indian juxtaposition of the veil of *māyā*, conceived as embracing a plethora of beings, with *Brahman,* the unitary source out of which the plurality of individual things emerges and eventually returns. Again, Schopenhauer's conviction that life is an inferno of seething misery from which we require deliverance, which is the leitmotiv of his entire philosophy, bears affinity to the Upanishadic and Buddhist characterization of human existence as being enmeshed in suffering and as needing liberation from the constricting ties of egoism and from the desires to which as phenomenal creatures we are subject.

In the essays he published on the philosophy of metaphysical pessimism, Wang Kuo-wei devotes considerable space to Schopenhauer's *idée maîtresse*, the concept of the will. Much of his exposition of this concept, however, is nothing more than a recapitulation of the relevant passages from *The World as Will and Representation.* Consider, for example, Wang's presentation of Schopenhauer's philosophical demonstration of the inevitable wretchedness of life. Following his German mentor, Wang depicts the essence of existence as ceaseless striving and, therefore, as interminable suffering. Man, the most necessitous of beings, is a concretion of a thousand cravings. If the satisfaction of a craving is impeded, he suffers, but if satisfaction is attained too easily, he becomes bored. Human life, consequently, "swings like a pendulum to and fro between pain and boredom,"[12] its ultimate constituents, and lasting satisfaction is a chimera. With Schopenhauer, Wang defines happiness negatively as the mere absence of suffering and ennui.

Although craving, and hence suffering, are thus inescapable features of the human condition, man regards life as a great desideratum and clings convulsively to it. Since the degree of his suffering is directly proportional to the intensity of his cravings, Wang suggests, it follows that man suffers most from the desire to love, which is the strongest of his myriad cravings. Why, when it causes such pain, human beings have continued to love is a question that has baffled philosophers and poets for centuries. The answer to this query, Wang brightly informs us, has at last been supplied by Schopenhauer in the chapter of *The World as Will and Representation* titled "The Metaphysics of Love."[13]

Wang Kuo-wei's account of the reasons for the importunity of the sexual impulse, like his discussion of the essentiality of suffering to life, follows that of Schopenhauer to the letter. The sexual impulse, Wang maintains, is the most insistent of all human urges, surpassing in strength even the desire for nourishment, because it is the core of the will. While it is true that the will manifests itself in the first instance as an effort to maintain the individual, Wang holds with Schopenhauer that this represents simply a stage in the will's larger and more important attempt to preserve the species. With only an incidental interest in the individual, the will nevertheless finds its expedient to appeal to the individual's egoism in order to accomplish its species-oriented goal.[14]

This Schopenhauerian interpretation of the nature of the will's operations is reminiscent of Hegel's "cunning of reason," whereby the individual's petty aims are utilized by reason to achieve its own exalted purposes. However, in the case of the will's manipulation of human beings one cannot speak of the unitary principle's having any preselected final aim in mind, unless life itself is designated an aim, for the will wills only life. Thus, on Schopenhauer-Wang's view of the matter, we find that sex ensnares us in cosmic designs of which we are completely ignorant and that egosim lies at the base of all sexual passion.

In his depiction of the relation of suffering to life and in his exposition of the metaphysics of love, Wang gives faithful summaries of Schopenhauer's doctrines. Concerning one doctrine of his German mentor, however, he has serious doubts. It is unclear why Wang Kuo-wei singles out Schopenhauer's theory of the metaphysics of heredity to criticize when he is able to accept other dubious doctrines of the philosopher with apparent ease. It is certainly true, however, that Schopenhauer's theory of heredity, according to which a person's will is inherited from his father and his intellect from his mother, is one of the most questionable of his innumerable theories.

Schopenhauer assumes, Wang argues, that his theory of heredity follows from the principal tenets of his philosophical system and that it can be confirmed by personal observation and the study of history. He is wrong. In the first place, Wang points out, it is obvious that in advancing the view that character is inherited from the father and intelligence from the mother, Schopenhauer has contradicted one of his own philosophical claims, namely, that the will is the primary element in all phenomena, the intellect being merely a special faculty that has been produced by the will out of its own resources. This being the case, Wang charges, it is theoretically inconceivable that the one can be inherited from the father and the other from the mother. The proper conclusion for Schopenhauer to have reached, says Wang, is the one that accords with his own philosophical principles, to wit, that character and intelligence are inherited equally from both parents and not wholly from either.[15]

Schopenhauer is also in error, Wang maintains, in thinking that he can find confirmation of his theory of heredity in personal observation and the study of history. He has evidently forgotten his own epistemological conviction that experience possesses neither universality nor necessity. It is therefore inadmissible for him to make sweeping statements on the basis simply of what he has seen and what he has read. Moreover, the facts of history, such as we know them, do not support Schopenhauer's theory of heredity. The cases of the great Chinese historians Ssu-ma Ch'ien (145?–90? B.C.) and Pan Ku (A.D. 32–92), for instance, demonstrate beyond a shadow of a doubt that a father's intelligence can be passed on to his offspring. Having demolished to his own satisfaction Schopenhauer's theory of heredity, Wang then proceeds, curiously, to devote sixteen pages to a translation of "The Hereditary Nature of Qualities," a chapter of *The World as Will and Representation*. He evidently hoped to gain support for his own view of the nature of heredity by permitting readers of the *Journal of the Educational World* to see for themselves how untenable Schopenhauer's position on the matter really is.[16]

While in his analysis of Schopenhauer's theory of heredity Wang demonstrates a fair degree of critical acumen, in general he accepts without reservation the major features and ramifications of the philosopher's doctrine of the will. To many of the obvious weaknesses of this doctrine Wang was, it seems, completely blind. It is difficult, for example, to see how he can readily accede to Schopenhauer's thesis that an irrational will can objectify itself in intellect, since this appears to make the will incommensurable with its effect. If the world is not the mirror, but rather the effect, of an irrational will, the question arises as to how phenomenal reason can possibly issue from it. But if the world *is* the mirror of the will, the fact that we find reason in the world must mean that the ultimate principle is not irrational.

It is also hard to see how Wang Kuo-wei can embrace Schopenhauer's view that our awareness of the will operating within us can provide us with an intuitive confirmation of the thesis that all is will.[17] Even if we concede that the will is primary in man, it is still questionable whether this same will can be attributed to all other objects, animate and inanimate, as Schopenhauer claims on the basis of analogical arguments. It is, however, difficult to comprehend how the thing-in-itself *can* be intuitively knowable since, on Schopenhauer's epistemological principles, our knowledge of our will is necessarily confined to its phenomenal aspect. We can, in other words, have no direct access to the noumenal ground of our phenomenal being, this having already been ruled out by the philosopher himself. Given what Schopenhauer says about cognition, our will ought to be considered as belonging to the phenomenal order in such a way that self-reflection is of no more assistance in attaining knowledge of the thing-in-itself than sense perception.[18] Therefore no basis whatsoever exists for Schopenhauer's thesis that there is a cosmic will lying behind individual wills, much less for a characterization of it.

Despite his burning interest in metaphysics, Wang Kuo-wei cannot be said fully to have appreciated the strictly metaphysical nature of the Schopenhauerian will. Instead, in his philosophical essays he evinces a marked tendency to run together Schopenhauer's metaphysical concept of will and Nietzsche's empirical notion of will, claiming, for example, that the two philosophers share the conviction that "the will (*i-chih*) is the root of human nature" and differ only with respect to their ethical doctrines.[19] The pronounced empirical flavor that, in Wang's hands, some of Schopenhauer's doctrines possess can be seen in the young man's elucidation of the philosopher's doctrine that life is a crime.

Although Schopenhauer sometimes speaks as if man himself were responsible for his existence, it is difficult to see how this could be the case in a universe dominated by the will. If the world is merely the objectification of the will, as Schopenhauer repeatedly declares it to be, then everything must be the way it is because the will so wills it. On Schopenhauer's principles it would thus seem that the will, not the world, bears the responsibility for the world's existence and nature.[20] The will first commits the crime of existence and then pays the penalty by suffering in and through us.

Wang's version of the Schopenhauerian doctrine that life is a crime contains ambiguities. Occasionally he appears to suggest that the will has committed the crime of existence, although neither he nor Schopenhauer ever explains how a will which is free only in that it is self-determined and acts under no external constraint can commit a crime or be guilty.[21] Occasionally he seems further to suggest that the will's crime is expiated by human suffering. Wang even speaks, with Schopenhauer, of the realization of "eternal justice," apparently overlooking the fact that if man is phenomenal, his suffering must be phenomenal as well and can by no means affect the will as thing-in-itself.[22]

More frequently, however, Wang Kuo-wei appears to claim that man himself is responsible for his own existence. "The lamentations of poets, speculations of philosophers, and the legends of the various peoples of antiquity" all bear testimony to the truth that "the existence of the world and human life is the result of the onetime error of our remote ancestors."[23] As both "Genesis" and *Dream of the Red Chamber* make abundantly clear, our own forebears must shoulder responsibility for our existence, since it was they who committed the crime of desiring life. On balance, Wang seems not to construe Schopenhauer's thesis concerning the criminality of life in the metaphysical light that a strict adherence to the philosopher's principles would appear to require.

Wang's View of Schopenhauer's Aesthetics

The key concept in Schopenhauer's aesthetics is that of the Idea (*Idée*), which is the immediate objectification of the will at a definite grade.[24] The Idea differs from the Kantian thing-in-itself in that it assumes the most basic of all the forms that adhere to knowledge as such, that of being-object-for-a-subject. Standing halfway between noumena and phenomena, the Idea is related to the individual thing as its eternal form or prototype. The elucidation of the Ideas is the common aim of all the arts, which Schopenhauer arranges in a hierarchy according to the grades of objectification of the will that they express. The hierarchy culminates with those arts that express human beauty, which is the fullest objectification of the will at the highest grade at which it is knowable, namely, the Idea of man in general.

One who possesses the ability to apprehend the Ideas and express them in artistic works Schopenhauer calls a genius.[25] In such an individual there is a superfluity of intellect, more than is required for the service of the will. As a result of this accident of birth, the genius is able periodically to cease thinking in terms of the principle of sufficient reason, which ordinarily governs our knowledge of particular objects, and become a "pure will-less subject of knowledge" resting in disinterested contemplation of phenomena. In the more or less lengthy intervals when he is not exercising his special cognitive capacity, however, the artistic genius is subject to all the deficiencies of ordinary people.

Wang Kuo-wei was deeply fascinated by Schopenhauer's philosophical aesthetics, the influence of which would remain with him for some years. The reason for this is not difficult to fathom. As E. Joan Smythe has observed, "Schopenhauer was the artist's philosopher of the nineteenth century, and Wang was himself a writer of tz'u [lyrics] of considerable note. Schopenhauer thus provided a convenient bridge between the two main interests of Wang's early life, philosophy and literature."[26]

Many aspects of the theory of art that Wang Kuo-wei expounds in his youthful essays are faithful reiterations of the major points of Schopenhauer's theory as developed in the "third book" of The World as Will and Representation. Following Schopenhauer, Wang claims, for instance, that science involves merely knowledge of the relations between things, whereas art involves knowing things independently of the principle of sufficient reason. Following Schopenhauer, he defines genius as the ability to contemplate objects apart from this principle, to grasp their Ideas (shih-nien), and to reproduce these Ideas in art.[27] Wang appears initially not to have wondered how a blindly striving, self-tortured impulse to live can objectify itself immediately in Platonic Ideas, or how, without contradicting his own epistemological convictions, Schopenhauer can ascribe to the genius a cognitive capacity that transcends all ordinary forms of knowledge.[28]

To Schopenhauer's Romantic conception of creative genius Wang Kuo-wei was especially attracted, as it fitted in nicely with his view of himself. The very idea of genius is enough to make him feel a sharp stab of pathos.

> Alas! Heaven acts disgracefully in producing geniuses (t'ien-ts'ai), and he who is born one is unlucky indeed. Ordinary men eat when they are hungry, drink when they are thirsty, and raise children once they have

matured. They thereby fulfill their will to live (*sheng-huo chih yü*), and that is all [there is to their lives]. Their sufferings are merely the ordinary sufferings of life, their joys merely the ordinary joys of life. Beyond this, even if they do [occasionally] develop grave doubts and grave concerns, they never become disturbed by them. It is assuredly their good fortune and a boon from Heaven that they are able eternally to maintain this ignorant state of mind. A genius's deficiencies are the same as other men's, but he alone is clearly aware of these deficiencies. He lives as ordinary men live, but he alone doubts why he lives. In other words, he is like others in possessing life but unlike others in regarding life as a problem, like others in having been born into the world but unlike others in regarding the world as a problem ... The law of causality and the forms of space and time imprison him cognitively. The innumerable laws which inform our natures both individually and collectively as products of will oppress him practically. Moreover, his intellect and will are not like others' intellects and wills, for [the genius] knows what others are unable to know and desires what others do not dare to desire. However, like others he is imprisoned and oppressed [by the aforementioned factors].

Preoccupied in his twenties with "the problems of the universe and human life," the temperamentally pessimistic Wang Kuo-wei seems to have embraced wholeheartedly Schopenhauer's claim that great mental abilities are invariably associated with a vehement will and that, furthermore, the genius's "higher intellectual power" makes him "susceptible to much greater sufferings than duller men can ever feel."[29]

Wang's View of Schopenhauer's Ethics

The summum bonum in Schopenhauer's moral philosophy is denial of the will, the possibility of which exists because of man's ability to penetrate the principle of individuation, the veil of *māyā*, to a lesser or greater degree. He who has penetrated the veil to the extent that he grasps the fundamental identity of all phenomena and the essentiality of suffering to life Schopenhauer calls a morally good man. The knowledge of the world's inner nature that such a man possesses leads him deeply to sympathize with the miseries of others and to do all in his power to alleviate them. Consistently identifying himself with others and placing their troubles on a par with his own, the virtuous man is made acutely aware of the vanity of life. By this means is he placed squarely on the path to salvation.

The final and complete expression of the penetration of the *principium individuationis* is found not in the practice of the moral virtues, however, but in asceticism—that is, in celibacy, voluntary poverty, and holy indifference. It sometimes occurs, Schopenhauer says, that the virtuous man has so keen an appreciation of the horrible truth that this is the worst of all possible worlds that, in him, the will actually turns round and permanently silences itself. While Schopenhauer seems occasionally to imply that a man may, through his own conscious volition, renounce his former way of life and all that he previously held dear, in fact the philosopher by no means wishes to suggest that self-denial in the first instance issues from a deliberate act of choice. The complete transformation of a man's personality that takes place when the will denies its own nature in him is more accurately described as something that "happens" to him, although it is inseparable from the attainment of that profound insight into the real nature of existence which characterizes the virtuous soul.

From his philosophical essays we can see that Wang Kuo-wei had a number of objections, reservations, and doubts concerning Schopenhauer's doctrine of the denial of the will. The notion of universal love, for instance, by which the philosopher puts so much store in effecting the transition from affirmation to denial of the will, Wang finds logically incompatible with the elitism of his aesthetics.

> In conformity with his metaphysical tenets, Schopenhauer declares all inanimate and animate objects, including ourselves, to be manifestations of the unitary will. Accordingly, he extends his ethical theory of universal love to animals and plants. With regard to the intellect, however, [in Schopenhauer's view] not only are men different from animals but also geniuses from the masses and men from women. Between these there are insurmountable barriers.

It is because in his aesthetics Schopenhauer espouses a doctrine of intellectual aristocracy, according to which geniuses are "great" while the populace at large is knavish, that "although in his ethics he commends the practice of humility, in his aesthetics he excoriates modesty."[30]

Although he finds Schopenhauer's emphasis in his ethics on the endlessly charitable personality to be incompatible with his stress in his aesthetics on the strongly individualistic genius, Wang shares the philosopher's lofty view of asceticism. Like Schopenhauer, Wang believes that our lives are better served by our woe than our welfare, since only through personal suffering and the observation of the suffering of others are we steered, through a process of purification and sanctification, into the safe harbor of resignation.[31] Wang seems not to have grasped, however, that in Schopenhauer's view the "transcendental change" that sometimes develops in the personality of an individual who has attained knowledge of the real nature of the world occurs, in the first instance, not as the result of a conscious choice but rather as something that, as it were, "flies in from outside." We find him, accordingly, declaring categorically that denial of the will proceeds from an assertion of will.[32]

All the world's great religions, such as Brahmanism, Buddhism, and Christianity, and all the world's great philosophers, such as Plato and Schopenhauer, Wang informs us, regard release from this mortal vale as the highest moral ideal. He himself does as well. Can release, however, in fact be achieved? "Schopenhauer maintains that our essence is the will to live, but then whence arises the putative denial of the will to live?"[33] Although the philosopher claims that the possibility of man's denial of the will constitutes the single exception to the rule that his conduct is determined, it is unclear how, if man is nothing more than the objectification of the will, the will can be denied in man. If the will denies itself in man, it is patently more than the will to live, while if man denies the will, he is patently more than the will to live.

Nor, says Wang, can Schopenhauer claim, without contradiction, both that all phenomena are identical in their metaphysical essence and that individual phenomena can achieve permanent liberation from the tyrannous will. If the will is the unitary principle at work throughout creation, as Schopenhauer repeatedly declares it to be, how, he inquires, can attempts by particular individuals to deny it be successful unless all other beings in the world simultaneously "cross over" with them into complete will-lessness? Although he seems to accept the philosopher's contention that the will is present, whole and undivided, in each of its objectifications, Wang Kuo-wei insists that it follows from this, not that the whole world would vanish if even a single being could be entirely annihilated, but, on the contrary, that the annihilation of the world must logically precede that of any individual being.[34]

Schopenhauer himself, according to Wang, both sensed this difficulty with his doctrine of the denial of the will and tried to solve it by advancing, toward the end of "book four" of his major work, the following claims: first, that the human race would entirely die out if all its members were to deny the sexual impulse, which is the core of the will; second, that the animal kingdom, as a "weaker reflection" of the will than mankind, would disappear if the human race were to disappear; and third, that the world itself would vanish if both man and the animals were to vanish, as there can be no object without a subject. This line of reasoning, says Wang, is completely fallacious. In the centuries that have passed since Shakyamuni pointed out the route to nirvana and Christ died on the cross, human suffering has been mitigated not a whit, mankind's will to live diminished not a mite. Thus it is crystal clear that Schopenhauer's claim that "the good man draws all things up to God" has no basis whatsoever in reality and even leads one to wonder whether Shakyamuni and Christ themselves truly succeeded in escaping from the thraldom of the will.[35]

His criticisms of the doctrine of the denial of the will suggest that Wang Kuo-wei took strong exception to Schopenhauer's sudden and arbitrary introduction of an almost Calvinistic notion of election into an ethical theory supposedly grounded in the metaphysical doctrine of the unitary will. Schopenhauer's dilemma in *The World as Will and Representation* arises from the circumstance that he wishes both to maintain that the entire world is nothing but the objectification of the indestructible first principle and to claim that this seemingly irresistible, indivisible principle can be denied. These conflicting aims lead him to advance at the end of his major work an ad hoc explanation of how such denial is possible, the flaws in which Wang and others were not slow to discern. In the final analysis, Wang declares, Schopenhauer's doctrine of the denial of the will must be said to be "theoretically unsound." "Whether or not the will can be extinguished," he pensively concludes, "must remain an unsolvable problem."[36]

7

Analysis of
Dream of the Red Chamber

By the close of the nineteenth century, Ts'ao Chan's (Hsueh-ch'in, 1715?–1763) literary masterpiece, *Dream of the Red Chamber,* had become immensely popular with Chinese cognoscenti. Many were the efforts of these early "redologists" (*hung-hsueh chia*) to elucidate the famous novel's grand design. Some, supposing the work's account of the adolescent hero to be based on the life of the Manchu poet Singde (Na-lan Hsing-te, 1655–1685), declared *Dream of the Red Chamber* to be a roman à clef, while others, anticipating the view of such twentieth-century scholars as Hu Shih and Yü P'ing-po, believed it to contain a description of the author's own life. Wang Kuo-wei, who had no use for either of these interpretations, advanced his own in 1904 in an article titled "A Critique of *Dream of the Red Chamber.*"[1] For all its simplifications, this article is, as C. T. Hsia has observed, "a remarkably brilliant study of the novel" made from the standpoint of the philosophy of metaphysical pessimism.[2]

"Dream" and Schopenhauerian Metaphysics

As a very young man Wang Kuo-wei was deeply influenced by Schopenhauer's vision of the world as a ceaseless, destructive "struggle for existence." He was attracted to many aspects of the philosopher's metaphysics, including the doctrine that life is a crime, although Wang seems not to have understood that doctrine in the metaphysical light which a strict conformity to Schopenhauer's principles would appear to require. In his writings he usually speaks, in fact, as if he believed that man himself, rather than the cosmic will, were responsible for the existence and nature of human life.[3] One is therefore not surprised to find Wang claiming, in his study of *Dream of the Red Chamber,* that no work of imaginative literature expresses more artistically than

81

Ts'ao's the philosophical truth that life is a crime committed by free moral agents.[4]

According to Wang, the truth that humanity must bear the responsibility for its own existence is conveyed in *Dream of the Red Chamber* by means of the mythological tale with which the novel opens. A magical Stone, the only one of a large number of building blocks not to have been used by the goddess Nü-wa to repair the sky, lies unhappily at the foot of Greensickness Peak in the Great Fable Mountains, wishing for life, until at length a mangy Buddhist monk and a lame Taoist priest agree to arrange for its incarnation as Chia Pao-yü. "This Stone," Wang comments, "was lucky not to have been used [for heavenly repairs]."[5] Why, then, instead of contenting itself with roaming the Void, does it crave existence? Had the Stone not desired to sojourn in the world of men, he says, it would have been spared the lifetime of suffering that, as a mortal, will necessarily be its lot.

The author of *Dream of the Red Chamber*, Wang Kuo-wei thus suggests, has placed his novel in an allegorical framework in order to convey the message that life, by its very nature, involves willing, and hence suffering. It is no coincidence, therefore, that "there is no character in this book who affirms the will to live without suffering."[6] In the end, however, several characters attain that profound insight into "the genuine nature of the universe and human life" that will place them, he says, on the path to emancipation.[7]

"Dream" and Schopenhauerian Aesthetics

Schopenhauer considers tragedy the highest of all the written forms of art that reveal the Idea of man because, in its depiction of life's terrible side, it starkly lays bare the will's perpetual and destructive conflict with itself, which is the fundamental truth of existence. The essence of tragedy, according to Schopenhauer, lies in the "conversion" experienced by those who have seen through the veil of *māyā* to the extent that direct knowledge of the true character of the world is present in them in the highest possible degree of clarity. This knowledge, without which "transcendental changes" in personality cannot occur, is ordinarily acquired through grave personal suffering, although in really saintly individuals it can be acquired through mere observation of the suffering of others.

The only essential of tragedy, therefore, according to Schopenhauer, is the presentation of a catastrophe that, by enabling the hero completely to penetrate the *principium individuationis,* makes him ripe for conversion. The necessary misfortune may occur through the exceptional wickedness of a character, a colossal accident or error, or "the mere attitude of the persons to one another through their relations." The third kind of tragedy, in which characters "are so situated with regard to one another that their position forces them, knowingly and with their eyes open, to do one another the greatest injury without any one of them being entirely in the wrong," is preferable to the other two since it shows the reader that disaster can, and often does, arise out of the ordinary circumstances of everyday life.[8]

"A tragedy from beginning to end," *Dream of the Red Chamber* contains, according to Wang Kuo-wei, both characters who obtain release through observation of others' suffering and one character who achieves it through personal travail. The accomplishment of Hsi-ch'un and Tzu-chuan, he says, following Schopenhauer, is "one hundred times greater and one hundred times more difficult" than that of Pao-yü since it is predicated on a merely theoretical understanding of the genuine nature of existence. The emancipation of Pao-yü, however, which occurs only after a lifetime of suffering, is potentially more edifying. "This is why the protagonist of *Dream of the Red Chamber* is not Hsi-ch'un or Tzu-chuan but Pao-yü."[9]

Although the sensitive Pao-yü suffers considerably in the early portion of the novel, his will is actually broken only with the death of Tai-yü and his marriage to Pao-ch'ai, Wang says. Since the author of *Dream of the Red Chamber* has employed the exemplary third method for engineering a tragic catastrophe, the disastrous marriage comes about, precisely as Schopenhauer recommends that it should, as the consequence of the very ordinary attitudes and wishes of various members of the Chia family.

Grandmother Chia, for instance, wants to wed Pao-ch'ai to Pao-yü, Wang Kuo-wei observes, because she prefers the girl's agreeableness to Tai-yü's aloofness, believes that "gold and jade" are destined for one another, and hopes that marriage to Pao-ch'ai will cure her grandson of his illness. Lady Wang naturally favors her own niece over Tai-yü; Hsi-feng, fearing that her own exalted position in the family will be jeopardized if the intellectually gifted Tai-yü marries Pao-yü, also is partial to Pao-ch'ai; and Hsi-jen, misunderstanding Tai-yü's remark about the "east wind" and the "west wind," throws in her lot with Hsi-feng. Although Pao-yü himself loves Tai-yü, he is prevented by contemporary moral standards from informing his relatives, even his beloved grandmother, of his intense feelings for his cousin. "For these various reasons, the marriage of 'gold and jade' and [simultaneous] separation of 'wood and stone' occur not through the exceptional wickedness of a character or through a colossal accident, but through the mere [play of] ordinary moral [principles], ordinary human sentiments, and ordinary life situations. From this perspective, *Dream of the Red Chamber* may be regarded as the tragedy of tragedies."[10]

"Dream" and Schopenhauerian Ethics

According to Schopenhauer, denial of the will in man must take the form of asceticism rather than suicide. Although suicide is, in his view, by no means a crime or a sin, it *is* a mistake since it substitutes for the highest moral good, genuine release from the world, one that is simply apparent. By killing himself, says Schopenhauer, the suicide admittedly destroys his existence as an empirical individual, but it does not follow that he thereby destroys his metaphysical essence because the will as thing-in-itself cannot be affected by acts undertaken against the merely phenomenal objectification of its nature. The suicide, in any event, unlike the ascetic, has not wearied of life itself but only of the terms on which it has come to him. "Far from being denial of the will, suicide is a phenomenon of the will's strong affirmation."[11]

Voluntary death arising from extreme asceticism is the one type of suicide that Schopenhauer concedes is compatible with denial of the will. In the ascetic, denial of the will may proceed to the point where even the will to sustain life withers away. This kind of suicide occurs, therefore, not as the result of the will to live, but from a cessation of willing altogether. While Schopenhauer suggests that there may be various intermediate types between the extreme ascetic's death by starvation and the common suicide, he does not venture to describe any of them.

Following Schopenhauer, Wang maintains that "release takes the form of asceticism, not suicide." Since the arbitrary destruction of an individual phenomenon cannot affect the will as thing-in-itself, the suicide cannot obtain genuine release from his suffering, says Wang, who, like Schopenhauer, appears to overlook the possibility that a man might take his own life precisely in order to destroy that empirical consciousness through which he is made familiar with his suffering, regardless of whether or not he will persist after death in an unconscious and impersonal fashion. He who commits suicide, declares Wang, "affirms the will to live and is dissatisfied merely with [the conditions of] his present life." The suicides Chin-chuan, Ssu-ch'i, Yu San-chieh, and P'an Yu-an in *Dream of the Red Chamber* illustrate this truth. "[None of them] will obtain release; they simply have sought to satisfy their desires and, being unable to do so, [decided to take their own lives]." There can be no doubt whatsoever, Wang says, that "they will life vehemently" and have ceased living only because they have been unable to cease willing.[12]

While common suicide thus constitutes, in both Schopenhauer's view and his own, a strong affirmation of the will to live, Wang Kuo-wei identifies one kind of suicide that is compatible with its denial. The kind of suicide he has in mind, however, is not voluntary death arising from extreme asceticism, although it has in common with that type of death the complete will-lessness of those who expire in this way. According to Wang, there are actually persons in the world who have no will to live but who are prevented by circumstances from becoming ascetics. Persons who, like Yuan-yang in *Dream of the Red Chamber,* commit suicide under these conditions will obtain release.[13]

Wang usually speaks as if he believes, with Schopenhauer, that the ascetic is one who has gained the deepest possible understanding of the true nature of existence, as a result of which the will in him is silenced forever. As previously pointed out, self-denial is something over which Schopenhauer says a man can have no conscious control; it simply "happens" to him. Wang, however, insists that denial of the will in an individual occurs through a deliberate act of choice.[14]

In light of his interpretation of the Schopenhauerian doctrine of the denial of the will, it is not difficult to understand why Wang, in his analysis of *Dream of the Red Chamber,* suggests that, after Tai-yü's death and his marriage to Pao-ch'ai, Pao-yü attains so profound an insight into the genuine character of life that he *chooses* to renounce it. "On hearing the monk's words, he realizes that his unfortunate life has arisen as a consequence of his own will [to live] and, further, that his denial of [the will to live] will have also to issue from his own self. This is why he wants to return the jade. The so-called jade is nothing more than a symbol representing the will to live."[15] Wang maintains that Hsi-ch'un and Tzu-chuan as well choose completely to change their dispositions. All three of these young ascetics will obtain release because, perceiving the essentiality of suffering to life, each has "sought" (*ch'iu*) successfully to deny the will.[16] With Schopenhauer, Wang seems to hold that the will exists in the ascetic in greatly attenuated form and to imagine that, at his death, it actually is extinguished along with his phenomenal identity. It is difficult to see, though, why the ascetic's inner nature, however weak, should not at his death be reabsorbed into the metaphysical will, as the suicide's is.

Denial of the will, which in man takes the form of asceticism, constitutes the highest moral good, according to both Schopenhauer and Wang. Were the existence of the world and human life to have a rational basis, Wang concedes, the ordinary morality of the Three Major Relationships (*san-kang*) would have to be considered absolute, and those who "seek" to deny the will to live, therefore, would have to be regarded as both disloyal and unfilial. "Does, however, the existence of the world and human life have a rational basis, or have [the world and human life] been produced by blind striving and have no significance, apart from this?"[17] It is precisely because existence is a crime committed by our ancestors that persons who, like *Dream of the Red Chamber*'s adolescent hero, embrace the ascetic life may be considered, from the perspective of a higher morality, truly filial; wanting to correct the error of our forefathers in willing life, they cease themselves to will.[18]

In a curious departure from Schopenhauer's view of the matter, Wang Kuo-wei maintains that there is a kind of asceticism that is incompatible with denial of the will. This kind of asceticism, like common suicide, is characterized by strong affirmation of the will. "If the will to live exists [in a person], release will not be obtained even through asceticism."[19] The characters Liu Hsiang-lien and Fang-kuan in *Dream of the Red Chamber*, he says, exemplify this thesis. Liu Hsiang-lien's beloved, like P'an Yu-an's, commits suicide, and Fang-kuan, like Chin-chuan, is ignominiously expulsed from the Chia household. P'an Yu-an and Chin-chuan thereupon kill themselves, while Liu Hsiang-lien and Fang-kuan choose to become ascetics. There is no essential difference among the four unhappy youths, however. They all, Wang declares, will life and are merely dissatisfied with the conditions on which it has come to them. Like P'an and Chin-chuan, therefore, Liu and Fang-kuan will fail to achieve liberation from the miserable pressure of the will.

Wang's Analysis in Historical Perspective

Stripped of its distinctively Schopenhauerian trappings, Wang Kuo-wei's interpretation of *Dream of the Red Chamber* is astonishingly reminiscent of that of the early commentators, Red Inkstone and his associates. As John C. Y. Wang has observed in his study of the remarks they wrote in the margins of Ts'ao Chan's manuscript, Red Inkstone and his colleagues were all convinced that *Dream of the Red Chamber*'s overarching theme is that phenomenal reality is ultimately illusion, that life is brief and mutable, and that, therefore, genuine peace of mind can be obtained only through repudiation of all earthly entanglements.

Why such hard running around in this fleeting life of ours?
Sumptuous feasts and gorgeous banquets must all dissolve in the end.
Sorrow and joy, like a myriad other things, are illusory and unreal;
Past and present are but a dream in their complete grotesqueness,

they write in a poem appended to the general remarks that precede the first chapter of the novel.[20]

Like Wang Kuo-wei, the early commentators lay much stress on the opening chapter of *Dream of the Red Chamber* because in it, they believe, Ts'ao Chan adumbrates the moral to the story that he will spell out in the rest of the novel. That the first part of Ts'ao's "dream" is taken up with the delineation more of joy than of sorrow, they imply, should not blind us to the fact that a tragic denouement is lying in the wings and will be revealed in due course. Fully aware of the author's artistic intentions, Red Inkstone and his associates are not at all surprised to read of the eventual discovery of a purse with obscene embroidery on it in the hitherto-unsullied Grand View Garden, which serves as the Land of Illusion for Pao-yü and his young female companions. On the contrary, they relish this development, for they see that it will propel the story line forward to the novel's tragic ending.[21]

The similarities between Wang Kuo-wei's and the early commentators' interpretations of *Dream of the Red Chamber* are undoubtedly attributable to the pronounced affinities between the philosophy of metaphysical pessimism, with reference to which Wang analyzes the novel, and philosophical Buddhism and Taoism, in the light of which the commentators explain it. As noted earlier, Schopenhauer's thought shares with Mahāyāna Buddhism the belief that the world as we ordinarily perceive it is in some fundamental sense illusory; the view that desire, and hence suffering, are essential features of the human condition; and the conviction that genuine release from this vale of tears can be obtained only through self-abnegation. Even though he had never heard of Red Inkstone, therefore, Wang was led by the Schopenhauerian principles in the light of which he studied the novel to conclusions quite similar in spirit to those of his insightful predecessor.[22]

The author of *Dream of the Red Chamber*, Wang Kuo-wei suggests in his critique of the novel, is, like Schopenhauer, engaged in a relentless search for the meaning of existence. In his fiction he endeavors to express artistically the philosophical truths that life is deeply steeped in suffering and that only through renunciation can one achieve true equanimity. Existence must be regarded at base as a bad dream, to awaken from which is the greatest good. In *Dream of the Red Chamber* this view of the world is conveyed, Wang says, through the depiction of Pao-yü's spiritual ordeal, in which the implicit sense of tragedy is so overpowering that we see clearly the inexorable logic that leads the young hero eventually to repudiate his former way of life and all worldly entanglements. Disappearing with the mangy Buddhist monk and the lame Taoist priest into the transmundane whiteness of the falling snow, Pao-yü, the incarnate Stone, reverts to type. The price of personal liberation has proved to be insensibility. The lesson that the Stone, lying once again at the foot of Greensickness Peak in the Great Fable Mountains, has at last learned is that it should never have left.

8

Disillusionment with Philosophy

The contradictions that, over time, Wang Kuo-wei discovered in the philosophy of metaphysical pessimism troubled him considerably and were undoubtedly the proximate cause of his eventual conclusion that Schopenhauer did not, as he had originally supposed, base his philosophical system on his own penetrating perceptual knowledge. By the winter of 1904–05, in fact, Wang had already come to realize that, on the contrary, "Schopenhauer's doctrines have their origin partly in his subjective character and bear no relation to objective knowledge."[1] This realization brought him no joy.

Final Estimation of Schopenhauer

The grave doubts concerning Schopenhauer's thought that he developed during the course of his philosophical investigations drove Wang in the end to conclude that the philosopher had been motivated to develop his system, in the first instance, not by a consuming ambition to identify the fundamental truths of the human condition, but by a vain desire to console himself for the wretchedness of existence. According to Wang's new view of Schopenhauer, the philosopher was a suffering genius of extraordinary intellect and passionate will who, unable to find comfort in the paltry pleasures of common people, chose to "amuse himself" (*tzu-yü*) by speculating on the metaphysical source of human suffering as well as on the possibility of man's escaping from his earthly fetters either temporarily or permanently. While the philosophical system that he fashioned in connection with his introspective quest for consolation no doubt became for Schopenhauer a sort of refuge from the pettiness and ugliness of everyday life, it should be understood, Wang declares in an article written toward the end of 1904, that this system is sadly out of tune with reality in a number of places.[2]

Wang Kuo-wei believed that he could account for most of the nettlesome features of Schopenhauer's thought in the light of his new understanding of the philosopher's basic animus. In one of his philosophical essays he suggests, for instance, that the contradiction between the egalitarian tendency of Schopenhauer's metaphysics and ethics and the aristocratic tendency of his aesthetics is just the sort of thing we should expect to find in a philosophy whose creator values consolation over truth and even over logical consistency. Since Schopenhauer adamantly maintains that individual wills are identical in their essential nature, should he not, to be consistent, hold that individual intellects are fundamentally identical as well? According to Wang, the reason the philosopher goes against the grain of his own metaphysics and ethics to espouse a theory of intellectual aristocracy in his aesthetics is that, had he not done so, his aesthetics "would have been a source of shame, rather than glory, and of suffering, rather than consolation, to him."[3]

The hypothesis that Schopenhauer's principal concern in developing his philosophical system was to console himself, rather than to seek truth, is also useful, according to Wang Kuo-wei, in explaining the origin of the philosopher's *idée maîtresse,* the concept of the will. Schopenhauer invented this concept, Wang now claims, because it enabled him "to regard himself as a second Atlas, shouldering the earth, and as a second Brahma, giving birth to the universe." In his metaphysics Schopenhauer both sought and found "enough consolation to last a lifetime."[4]

Schopenhauer's moral philosophy as well, Wang writes, is most appropriately viewed, at least in part, as an expression of his deep antipathy toward life and persistent search for a means of escape from it. That the philosopher's doctrine of the denial of the will presents many theoretical difficulties Wang now finds less significant than that it reflects aspects of Schopenhauer's personal character and world view. "Although he speaks about extinguishing [the will, Schopenhauer] does not genuinely wish [the will] to be extinguished. He is merely dissatisfied with the present world," and his dissatisfaction has led him to seize on the conceit of the silenced will.[5]

Wang Kuo-wei himself, we recall, had launched his pioneering study of German philosophy in 1901–02 because he was overwhelmingly preoccupied with the enduring question of higher belief. Ill, depressed, and troubled by "the problems of the universe and human life," he had tackled the critical philosophy with the dangerously high expectation that it would reveal to him the fundamental truths of the human condition. From Kant, whom Wang had initially approached with unbounded enthusiasm, he obtained, however, not even an inkling of an answer to the problems that haunted him as a young man, for the German sage had declined ever to comment on things-in-themselves.

There can be little doubt that the tremendous fascination of the philosophy of metaphysical pessimism lay for Wang, in the first instance, in Schopenhauer's reluctance to observe the Kantian prohibition against metaphysics as traditionally conceived. Schopenhauer's metaphysics, in particular his concept of the will, on which all the other aspects of his philosophy pivot and from which in the final analysis they derive their interest, both "delighted" Wang emotionally and "appealed" to him intellectually for some length of time. As his study of philosophy progressed, however, he gradually grew more critical of Schopenhauer's thought, which is not without its baffling features, paradoxes, inconsistencies, and contradictions.

In the end, the difficulties that he discovered in the philosophy of metaphysical pessimism seem to have strained Wang Kuo-wei's credulity to the breaking point, as a result of which he gradually tired of the discipline of philosophy altogether. But before he did so, Wang delved briefly into the thought of Nietzsche.

Nietzsche as Schopenhauer's Successor

It is probable that the late Ch'ing political theorist Liang Ch'i-ch'ao was the first Chinese intellectual to introduce Nietzsche's name into the Celestial Empire. In an essay written in 1902 on the English social philosopher Benjamin Kidd, Liang advances the dubious view, acquired in all likelihood from the Japanese among whom he was then living, that Marx and Nietzsche represent the two principal tendencies in nineteenth-century German philosophy.[6] Already in the 1890s the works of Nietzsche had become popular in Japan, the vanguard nation in introducing Western thought into the Orient, and by the turn of the century Nietzsche was actually beginning to enjoy a great vogue among Japanese savants. Like two slightly younger contemporaries who in 1902 were also sojourning in Japan, Lu Hsun and Wang Kuo-wei, Liang Ch'i-ch'ao seems from the Japanese both to have become familiar with Nietzsche's name and to have obtained an inflated sense of his importance in the Western philosophical tradition.[7]

The distinction of being the first Chinese to write substantively on Nietzsche's thought belongs to Wang Kuo-wei. In an article titled "Schopenhauer and Nietzsche," written toward the end of 1904, Wang propounds the interesting thesis that the German Way (*tao*) has been transmitted from Kant, through Schopenhauer, to Nietzsche. Since his whole argument hinges on the demonstration that the philosophies

of Schopenhauer and Nietzsche are alike in essential respects, Wang
feels obliged in this article both to describe the similarities between
the philosophers' respective conceptions of will and to explain how a
philosophy advocating universal love and denial of the will can be
said to have affinities with a philosophy championing absolute egoism
and assertion of will. He has no difficulty executing either assignment.

From the way in which Wang speaks about the 'will to live' and
the 'will to power', it is difficult not to conclude that, in his view, they
enjoy the same ontological status.

> In the German philosophical world of the mid-nineteenth century, there
> were two great men, Schopenhauer and Nietzsche. They were alike in
> using their unparalleled literary talent to propagate their thought. They
> were also alike in overwhelming the world and yet receiving as much
> criticism as praise. With respect to their theories, too, they were alike in
> considering the will to be the root of human nature.[8]

Now, Wang Kuo-wei seems from the outset to have grasped that
Nietzsche, who was a vehement critic of all theories that posit a distinction between phenomenal reality and a transcendent reality that
alone is really "real," meant his theory of the will to power to be
understood, not as an a priori metaphysical thesis about the ultimate
reality lying behind the visible world, but as a sweeping empirical
hypothesis. If, therefore, as he seems repeatedly to imply, Wang considers the Schopenhauerian will to be identical in nature to the
Nietzschean will, it is probably because he has assimilated the former
to the latter. We recall that Wang's elucidation of the Schopenhauerian
doctrine of the criminality of life possesses a decidedly empirical flavor
and, further, that his interpretation of Schopenhauer's doctrine of
the denial of the will, according to which denial of the will proceeds
from an actual assertion of will, is Nietzschean in spirit.[9]

While the Nietzschean overman, Wang Kuo-wei concedes, has
little in common with his ostensible Schopenhauerian analogue, the
holy ascetic, it should by no means be imagined that the concept of
the overman has sprung full-blown from Nietzsche's mind. On the
contrary, he argues, this concept represents merely an extension of
Schopenhauer's theory of genius into the realm of ethics.

> Nietzsche extends [Schopenhauer's theory of genius] into the area of
> praxis, with the result that the relationship between the laws of morality
> and the overman (ch'ao-jen) is identical to that between the principle of
> sufficient reason and the genius. According to Schopenhauer, the prin-
> ciple of sufficient reason is not simply of no benefit to the genius; that
> which makes him a genius lies precisely in his [ability to] contemplate

objects apart from this principle. According to Nietzsche, the laws of morality are not simply of no benefit to the overman; to act without regard for morality is the overman's distinguishing feature. According to Schopenhauer, the highest knowledge lies in transcending the laws of [ordinary] knowledge. According to Nietzsche, the highest morality lies in transcending the laws of [conventional] morality. Being a genius consists of knowing without restriction, while being an overman consists of willing without restriction. What restricts our intellect is the principle of sufficient reason, while what restricts our will are the laws of morality. Thus, beginning with Schopenhauer's doctrine of knowing without restriction, Nietzsche winds up advocating his doctrine of willing without restriction.[10]

Although one may justifiably wonder whether there is not a world of difference between "casting aside the principle of sufficient reason" in order to reflect on Platonic Ideas and "casting aside morality" in order fully to realize oneself, it is obvious that Wang has chosen to advance the claim that "the Nietzschean overman is modelled on the Schopenhauerian genius" in order to bolster his argument that the two men's philosophies are not so far apart as has been commonly supposed. "Even if the doctrines of [Nietzsche's] last period appear to be in opposition to Schopenhauer's philosophy, in essence they do not go beyond taking Schopenhauer's aesthetic theory of genius and applying it to ethics."[11]

According to Wang Kuo-wei, the elitist tendency of Nietzsche's moral philosophy represents nothing more than the logical extension into the ethical realm of the dominant tendency of Schopenhauer's aesthetics. Schopenhauer, Wang reminds us, fully subscribes to the view that, as he puts it in his major work,

> in regard to the intellect nature is extremely *aristocratic*. The differences she has established in this respect are greater than those made in any country by birth, rank, wealth, and caste distinction. However, in nature's aristocracy as in others, there are many thousands of plebians to one nobleman, many millions to one prince, and the great multitude are mere populace, mob, rabble, *la canaille*.

The philosopher in fact has a decided weakness, Wang says, for "great" artistic geniuses, whose intellect and even whose behavior he is forever contrasting with the intellect and behavior of "small" and "modest" men, mere "knaves and wretches." Despite, however, the fact that he espouses a doctrine of intellectual aristocracy in his aesthetics, Schopenhauer is prevented by "his false theory of the unitary will" from espousing a doctrine of moral aristocracy in his ethics.[12]

"Although [Nietzsche] had Schopenhauer's genius," Wang tells us, "he lacked his faith in metaphysics," and he "despised modesty."

For these reasons Nietzsche had no reservations whatsoever about extending Schopenhauer's doctrine of intellectual aristocracy into the area of ethics, with the predictable result that we find him in his works denying Schopenhauer's suggestion of a subsisting moral relationship between the higher class of individual and the mass of humanity. "Nietzsche says [instead] that the intellect and the morality of this [higher] class are both absolute, as a result of which they cannot be harmonized [with the intellect and morality of the herd]." In *Thus Spoke Zarathustra,* Wang says, he positively rages against small, "tame" men of modest virtue. What Nietzsche esteems are "absolute individualists" who dare to transcend the morality of the "far-too-many" in order to create their own values.[13]

In light of his thesis that much of Nietzsche's thought is based on Schopenhauer's, Wang Kuo-wei also thinks it significant that the Schopenhauerian genius and the Nietzschean overman share a childlike quality. In the chapter titled "On Genius" in his magnum opus, he notes, Schopenhauer speaks of "a certain resemblance between genius and the age of childhood." Nietzsche's view of the child as depicted in his doctrine of the three metamorphoses, Wang believes, is indebted to Schopenhauer's notion of the childlike genius.[14]

On the basis of these and other considerations, Wang concludes in "Schopenhauer and Nietzsche" that the philosophies of these two German thinkers are as complementary as can be. "[Their philosophies] are like a tree: Schopenhauer's doctrines are the gnarled roots at its base, while Nietzsche's doctrines are its leaves and branches stretching up into the blue sky. Nietzsche's philosophy may be likened to T'ai-hua mountain's three highest peaks, which rise high into the heavens, while Schopenhauer's philosophy may be likened to the stones at its base." This being the case, Wang Kuo-wei suggests, "it is more satisfactory to regard Nietzsche as Schopenhauer's successor than to regard him as Schopenhauer's opponent."[15]

The similarities between Schopenhauer and Nietzsche do not stop with their philosophies, Wang informs us. "From ancient times to the present day, never have the characters of two philosophers been as similar as theirs." Each man, says Wang, citing Paulsen and Windelband as his authorities, suffered from an inner antagonism of his own nature arising from a Dionysian–Apollonian disjunction between his sensual self and his spiritual self. Both Schopenhauer and Nietzsche possessed, moreover, strong wills and remarkable intellects. "With their vehement wills and towering intellects, they travelled so far in the realm of the spirit that, had the First Emperor of Ch'in or Emperor Wu of Han been alive, he would have prostrated himself on the ground [to acknowledge fealty], and, had Chinggis Khan or Napoleon been alive, he would have turned and fled [in fright]. Thirty thousand miles of land and six thousand years of culture were not enough to suppress their exceedingly vehement wills." Thinking the unthinkable and daring to desire what others did not dare to desire, these extraordinary geniuses "aspired to destroy the old culture and create a new culture."[16]

By the time he wrote "Schopenhauer and Nietzsche," at the end of 1904, Wang had already concluded that his former philosophical hero, Schopenhauer, pursued his calling less in order to find truth than to obtain consolation. Even though he considered Nietzsche's thought, on the whole, more internally consistent than Schopenhauer's, he believed that the former, like the latter, conceived his major doctrines principally to console himself for the miseries of existence. Because he did not consider metaphysics a serious subject of scholarly inquiry, Wang Kuo-wei informs us, Nietzsche had no use for Schopenhauer's metaphysical thesis concerning the ultimate reality lying behind phenomenal reality, or his conception of genius as the ability to grasp and reproduce Platonic Ideas, or his doctrine that in self-abnegation lies the highest moral good. However, in his own empirical hypothesis of a ubiquitous will to power as well as in his doctrines of the overman and the revaluation of values, Nietzsche was able "to let loose his rebellious spirit without any compunctions" and thereby "to console himself."[17]

From German Voluntarism to Aesthetics

By the winter of 1904–05 Wang had thus begun to grope toward the view of philosophy that he would fully articulate only in 1907. In an autobiographical sketch written at that later date, he frankly explains why he has gradually lost interest in philosophy.

> In general those philosophical theories that can be loved cannot be believed, and those that can be believed cannot be loved. I seek truth and yet I love mistaken forms of it. Great metaphysics, rigorist ethics, and pure aesthetics—of these we are inordinately fond. However, in searching for what is believable, we turn instead to the positivistic theory of truth, the hedonistic theory of ethics, and the empiricist theory of aesthetics. I know the latter are believable but I cannot love them, and I know the former are lovable but I cannot believe them. This has caused me great distress during the last two or three years.[18]

There can be very little doubt that Wang's new view of philosophy was inspired primarily by his disappointment with Schopenhauer's thought, with which at one time he had been totally enraptured. In the articles concerning Schopenhauer that he had published in the

Journal of the Educational World, Wang had repeatedly extolled the philosopher's "great metaphysics," commended his ascetic ethics, and lauded his characterization of aesthetic consciousness.[19] As his study of philosophy progressed, however, he gradually became convinced that Schopenhauer's "lovable" ideas were not always "believable."

It is highly probable that Wang was awakened from his Schopenhauerian slumber not only by the difficulties that he perceived in the philosophy of metaphysical pessimism, but also by Nietzsche and Høffding, from whom he learned that Schopenhauer's brand of philosophizing had by the latter part of the nineteenth century become discredited. "Because Nietzsche was an advocate of positivism, he was impatient with idle metaphysical speculation" of the sort in which Schopenhauer indulged, Wang tells us, and in later life he even took a perverse pleasure in railing against his former master's pretensions in this area.[20] Although Wang's description of Nietzsche as a positivist is open to question on a number of counts, it nevertheless seems likely that the philosopher helped to draw the young man's attention to the positivistic and empiricist tendencies of much of late nineteenth-century Western philosophy.

As for Høffding, we recall that Wang Kuo-wei had begun his study of philosophy in 1901–02 with, among other works, *Outlines of Psychology* (1881). While he put this book aside after reading only part way through it, Wang must have taken it up again a few years later, for in 1907 he published a complete translation of it.[21] Since Wang was intimately familiar with *Outlines of Psychology*, it is hardly likely that the positivistic animus of the work would have escaped his notice. Concerning metaphysics, for example, Høffding has the following deflationary remarks to make:

> The human spirit will never let itself be debarred from brooding over the ultimate principles of that universal system of which it is a member. It will always seek to build its view of the universe on certain highest definitive ideas. But what it must learn, and should have already learnt, is this—that speculation may not mix itself up with the every-day affairs of experiential knowledge, may not anticipate the solution of purely experiential problems. It is not meant that speculation should wait until experience is exhausted; for that it never will be. But the really wise metaphysician is he who lets his ideas move in the direction already indicated by the leading features of experiential knowledge. He thus expresses only the thoughts which, more or less unconsciously, lie at the basis of experientially determined research, and carries them to their legitimate conclusions. He seeks an ultimate, definitive hypothesis, but the foundation is common to him and to the empiricist.[22]

Although by 1907 he had long since concluded that not all aspects of Schopenhauer's thought are credible, Wang was still deeply attached emotionally to "great metaphysics, rigorist ethics, and pure aesthetics." It is thus not surprising that he found himself totally unable to develop an interest in what passed for philosophy in the fin de siècle.

> Since Hartmann, no one in the contemporary philosophical world has dared to establish a school or system. Anyone living today who desires to establish a new system or create a new philosophy is [taken to be] either stupid or mad. Philosophers of the last twenty years, such as Wundt in Germany and Spencer in England, have merely gathered together the findings of science or the theories of the ancients and simply synthesized or revised them. They are all second-rate writers, those who can be believed but cannot be loved. The rest of the so-called philosophers are in reality only historians of philosophy.[23]

Since Wang was firmly convinced that, even when all conceivable scientific questions have been answered, "the problems of the universe and human life" will still not even have been broached, it is hardly to be wondered that in 1907 we find him deploring the emergence of thinkers who imagine that they can approach "truth" through empirical science. And since, as Wang himself tells us, he has neither the inclination to become a mere historian of philosophy nor the talent to become a first-rate philosopher in his own right, it is also hardly to be wondered that by 1907 his interests had already shifted decisively from philosophy to literature.[24]

9

The Aesthetic Education of Man

Wang Kuo-wei's interest in aesthetic philosophy was probably first aroused by Schopenhauer, whose theory of art and description of aesthetic awareness he had enthusiastically introduced to his compatriots in 1904 via the *Journal of the Educational World*. Although he gradually became disillusioned with specific tenets of Schopenhauer's thought, particularly in the areas of metaphysics and ethics, Wang would continue for some time to be fascinated by certain of the philosopher's aesthetic concepts and, indeed, by aesthetics—"the German science"—generally. From Schiller, Nietzsche, and Kant, in addition of course to Schopenhauer, he acquired the novel ideas that inform the view of art he propounds in his literary essays of 1906–07: "A Study of Man's Pastimes" ("Jen-chien shih-hao chih yen-chiu"), "On Extirpating the Poison" ("Ch'ü-tu p'ien"), "The Place of the Elegant in Aesthetics" ("Ku-ya chih tsai mei-hsueh shang chih wei-chih"), "Comments on Literature" ("Wen-hsueh hsiao-yen"), and "The Spirit of Ch'ü Yuan's Poetry" ("Ch'ü-tzu wen-hsueh chih ching-shen").

Taken collectively, his literary essays of 1906–07 provide an overview of Wang's own philosophical aesthetics in the crucial period of his transition from philosophical to literary studies. They form, as it were, a prolegomenon to *Remarks on Lyrics in the World of Men* (*Jen-chien tz'u-hua*), which Wang would publish in 1908–09. Because *Remarks on Lyrics in the World of Men* is written in the aphoristic style characteristic of "remarks on poetry" (*shih-hua* and *tz'u-hua*), even its most basic concepts are developed unsystematically and often cryptically. His literary essays of 1906–07, fortunately for us, shed considerable light on the lines of reflection from which Wang would later produce the aphoristic distillates which comprise that famous work.

The Origin and Nature of the Aesthetic Impulse

While in 1906–07 Wang Kuo-wei still considered "pure aesthetics" to be "lovable," he seems to have become convinced that only the "empiricist theory of aesthetics" can be taken seriously by modern men. By pure aesthetics, he probably had in mind Schopenhauer's metaphysical theory of art, according to which "pure will-less subjects of knowledge" can in disinterested reflection on Platonic Ideas escape temporarily from the tyrannous clutches of the will. By the empiricist theory of aesthetics, Wang appears to have had in mind Schiller's and Nietzsche's aesthetic philosophies, according to which the aesthetic impulse is rooted not in the genius's uncanny ability to contemplate and reproduce Ideas, but in certain facts of human physiology and psychology.

"Schiller," Wang writes in an essay expressing his new view of the matter, "once said that the play of children consists of their utilization of excess energy (*sheng-yü chih shih-li*). Since literature and art represent nothing more than the mental play of adults, there can be no doubt that their origin lies in excess energy as well." Elaborating on his new view of the origin of the aesthetic impulse, Wang declares:

> Literature is an occupation of play. What energies remain to a man over and above those expended on the struggle for existence are directed toward play. Now, the treasured child has his parents to clothe, feed, and care for him, and thus there is nothing for which he must struggle. Since his energies have no other outlet, he engages in many types of play. As the day approaches when he will have to struggle for his own existence, he ceases to play. Only when a man has great mental energies and is not constrained to worry about his livelihood can he preserve until death his playful nature. After he has attained maturity, however, a person cannot be satisfied with a child's notions of play. Instead, he writes or sings about his own emotions and observations in order to give vent to his accumulated energies. If, therefore, the development of a people's culture has not reached a certain level, literature will be unable to develop. Men who struggle unceasingly for their existence by no means possess the prerequisites for becoming writers.[1]

Wang Kuo-wei's theory that the aesthetic feeling has grown out of the instincts that lead to the preservation of the individual and the race has its roots in Schiller's neo-Kantian view of art and beauty as the medium through which man advances from a sensuous to a rational, and thus truly human, stage of existence. The subject of animality is pervasive in German idealistic philosophy, and no one was more concerned than Schiller with the animal–human polarity and with the significance of man's transition from being an animal to being human. His view that man only fully realizes his humanity when engaged in the aesthetic vocation is developed in several poems and essays, and principally in his *Letters on the Aesthetic Education of Man* (1793–1795).

Schiller's distinctive philosophical contribution is his identification of three basic human drives, two of which are the sensuous drive (*Stofftrieb*) and the formal drive (*Formtrieb*). These drives he synthesizes and elevates through the agency of what he calls the play drive (*Spieltrieb*). The play drive may be defined approximately as the impulse to apply form on matter for the sake of beauty alone with no regard for utility. The essence of play, according to Schiller, is that one feels no constraint while playing. Since constraint is an inescapable feature of the realm of organic necessity, the only perfect expression of the play drive is the creation of works of art; in artistic creation, Schiller maintains, constraint vanishes entirely as all is sacrificed to form. Art alone heals the breach between sensual abandon and intellectual aridity, making man whole and revealing both sides of his nature at once.[2]

Wang Kuo-wei was familiar with Schiller's ideas through, among other works, Høffding's *Outlines of Psychology,* a Chinese translation of which he was just finishing at the time he wrote the literary essays here under consideration. It is thus not altogether surprising to discover Wang, like Schiller, dilating on excess energy and lauding art as the medium through which man realizes his own humanity. What *is* somewhat surprising is to find him welding the Schopenhauerian notion of boredom and the Nietzschean concept of a ubiquitous will to power to his account of the origin and nature of the aesthetic impulse.

Those who have fully satisfied their material needs, Wang Kuo-wei tells us, have vast amounts of excess energy that they must dissipate in one fashion or another in order to forestall boredom (*chüan-yen, yen-chüan, k'ung-hsu ti k'u-t'ung*). Boredom, in Wang Kuo-wei's view, is a baleful phenomenon that emerges precisely when an individual has gained all that he needs to ensure his own survival and appears, therefore, to be free from both want and care. Almost anything, including work, which he characterizes as "positively painful," is preferable to the "negative pain" that ennui induces because "positive pain is yet a type of mental activity. From it, therefore, a certain kind of satisfaction can be derived. From boredom, however, not even this kind [of positively painful satisfaction] can be derived. It is better to have an unfortunate life than to have an uneventful life. It is better to engage in hateful activity than to engage in no activity at all. These are two incontrovertible principles of physiology and psychology."[3]

The many types of "pastimes" (*shih-hao*) that we find in the world, Wang suggests, have been conceived by man as outlets for his surplus energies, "methods 'to kill time,' as the Westerners say, or 'to pass time,' as we Chinese say." The divertissements in which human beings indulge vary greatly as regards quality, some being exceedingly vulgar and others remarkably genteel. Through all of them, however, individuals strive to assert their will to power (*shih-li chih yü*)—that is, their will "to become superior to others in both the material and the mental aspects of their existence."[4]

Like Nietzsche, Wang Kuo-wei finds the will to power operating everywhere he looks. Gambling, horseback riding, and dancing are all, he says, avocations through which individuals endeavor to assert their will to power. So are antiquarianism and bibliophilism. The antiquarian's love of antiquities, Wang points out, "does not necessarily spring from a love of the beauty and elegance of their forms," nor does the bibliophile's love of books "necessarily spring from a love of the truths they contain." The truth is, he declares, that often the antiquarian's motive is simply "to show off the size of his collection, its high quality, and the fact that his objects are rare and not easily acquired," and just as often the bibliophile's motive is merely "to show off the breadth of his knowledge." "In other words," Wang declares, "such persons strive only to display the fact that they are more powerful than others."[5] Individuals who have a passion for beautiful dwellings, handsome conveyances, and fine clothing, he adds, share their animus.

"Even the noblest pastimes, such as literature and art," Wang Kuo-wei continues, "are nothing more than manifestations of the will to power." Both the creation and the appreciation of literary and artistic works are, according to him, based on the will to power. In an interesting account of literary creation that seems to incorporate Nietzsche's concept of sublimation, according to which passions, or instinctual energies, are discharged not as passions but as something else into which they have evolved in order to become socially acceptable, Wang suggests that "ordinarily our inner thoughts and emotions cannot be expressed to others or cannot be expressed in socially acceptable terms. In literature, however, because of its lack of a definite relationship between the author and the reader, the former is able to pour out his thoughts and emotions. In other words, the energies that we are unable to express in real life can be expressed in play."[6]

To corroborate the theory that the appreciation of literary works involves considerations of power, Wang says, one need do no more than point to the nature of mankind's love of drama. Power is surely at the root of our fondness for comedy.

> He who is able to laugh at others is invariably more powerful than he who is being laughed at. Laughter, therefore, is truly one type of manifestation of power. In actual life, however, one does not dare to laugh even if one encounters a laughable situation unless the object of one's

laughter is an intimate of one or well below one on the social scale. Only in comedy, due to its fictional character, do we not only encounter laughable situations but also dare to laugh at them. Herein lies the pleasure of comedy.

Tragedy as well is appealing because of the element of power.

> Horace once remarked that from the viewpoint of a spectator life is a comedy, but that from the viewpoint of a participant it is a tragedy. On reflection we cannot but concede that human life is indeed a tragedy. However, when men enact this tragedy, they either suffer silently or calmly accept their lot. If a man were to act like a hero in a tragedy, who expresses the pain that he feels through acting and singing, who would listen to or commiserate with him? That the characters in a tragedy have no power of which to speak goes without saying. However, regarding the extent of a person's power, there is certainly a distinction to be made between those who dare to cry out about their pain and those who do not dare to cry out about their pain. In real life there are no monologues, but in plays it is possible because of this convention [for the hero] to express long-repressed energies. Even those who do not appreciate artistic virtuosity attain in this way a type of satisfaction deriving from [considerations of] power.[7]

Without a theory such as his, Wang claims, the average person's pastime of theater-going would be inexplicable. In the light of it, however, we can see this pastime for what it really is: a vicarious outlet for the theatergoer's repressed drives.

Wang Kuo-wei discerns the will to power at work not only in literature and art but also in philosophy and science and, indeed, in every sort of intellectual endeavor. "Bacon once said that knowledge is power. It would even be permissible to say that the desire for all kinds of knowledge arises from the will to power." Thus Wang, like Nietzsche, who also explains the pleasure associated with the acquisition of knowledge in terms of power, discovers this irrepressible force at every turn. Although individuals may choose different arenas in which to strive to overwhelm their neighbors, they are alike in aspiring through their pastimes to attain "eternal power" over others.[8]

The Role of Art in Society

Although by 1906–07 he had become disenchanted with various aspects of the philosophy of metaphysical pessimism, Wang Kuo-wei continued fiercely to subscribe to Schopenhauer's view that human life "swings like a pendulum between pain and boredom." It is probably in the light of his Schopenhauerian conviction that existence is a tragedy that we should understand the preeminent position which Wang, like the philosopher himself, accords aesthetic consciousness in the realm of experience. Art emerges from his literary essays of 1906–07 as nothing less than "the religion of the upper classes of society."[9]

There is no pastime in all of China, Wang declares, that is more sinister than opium smoking, and it is as an alternative to that repellent habit that he proposes the lower classes turn to religion and the upper classes to art. While he admits that the present shabby state of the government and the lack of universal education are partly to blame for the empire's opium problem, Wang insists that the Chinese people are addicted to the drug principally because they suffer from pain and boredom. Lacking other diversions, they have taken to smoking opium.

What is required, Wang Kuo-wei believes, is the substitution of new pastimes for the old. "Aside from reforming the government and greatly increasing education so as to elevate the level of the people's knowledge and morality, close attention must be paid to the people's feelings. This can be done through religion and art, the former of which is appropriate for the lower classes of society and the latter of which is appropriate for the upper classes of society." Although the literati regard it as nothing more than superstitious nonsense, and although it is admittedly unsatisfying from an intellectual point of view, religion, Wang maintains, can play a positive and important role in the emotional life of the average man. A belief in God and the immortality of the soul, he says, enables a person "to think that a brilliant and eternal life is awaiting him beyond the present dark and confining one," and this, in turn, makes it possible for him "to replace his present despair with hope for the future and to console himself in his pain on this shore with thoughts of the happiness which will be his on the opposite shore."[10]

While he offers religion to the lower classes as an ersatz opiate, Wang does not believe that religion can lighten the emotional burden of the upper classes. "Since the knowledge of members of the upper classes of society is broad and their hopes, therefore, likewise greater in number, religion is unable to exert the influence over them that it does over the lower classes of society." At the same time, however, it must be acknowledged that "the feelings of pain experienced by [members of the upper classes] are identical [in number and intensity] to those experienced by members of the lower classes of society, while the former's feelings of boredom actually exceed [in number and intensity] those of the latter."[11]

According to Wang, members of the upper classes are afflicted by an emotional illness that can be cured by "giving their minds something on which to focus during their spare moments, something whereby they will thereafter be able to pass the time." Art he recommends as the perfect avocation for members of the upper crust, as it is a "lofty pastime" appropriate for persons of their station. Wang speaks more highly of literature than of sculpture, painting, music, and other kinds of art since books are easy to obtain, and they provide, moreover, "the greatest consolation which can be derived from art." For these reasons, among others, he urges governmental officials to incorporate the study of literature into China's new curricula. "Although [through studying literature in school] no artistic geniuses can be cultivated, much good will yet be done if those who have the ability to understand literature and love the pastime of literature are enabled in their sufferings from boredom to console themselves and are thereby prevented from succumbing to baser pastimes."[12]

While Wang Kuo-wei thus assigns to literature a leading role in the emotional life of China's literati, he does not wish to suggest that all types of literature are equally worthy. The sad fact is, according to him, that much more literature has been written to serve extraliterary ends of one disreputable sort or another than to achieve purely artistic purposes. Works that have been produced for any reason other than the sake of beauty alone necessarily represent incomplete expressions of the play drive and, as such, cannot provide the emotional satisfaction that we seek in aesthetic contemplation.

Among those who are debasing literature by putting it to practical uses, Wang alleges, are "professional writers." Unlike "expert writers," who write for the sheer joy of writing, professional writers actually earn their living by writing, as a consequence of which their works can never be taken seriously as art. "When one makes one's living by writing, one produces only literature that caters to contemporary fashions. A professional writer makes his living *by* writing, but an expert writer lives *for* writing."[13] In view of Wang's long-standing conviction that literature is properly an end in itself rather than a means to other ends, it is not hard to see why in 1906–07 he reacted negatively to the new type of commercial writer who, availing himself of the immensely popular literary magazines that were proliferating in China's treaty ports during the last years of the Ch'ing dynasty, was beginning to establish a profession in a sphere of life in which Wang believed professionalism had no place.

Particularly repugnant to Wang Kuo-wei is the thesis, first put forward around the turn of the century by Yen Fu and Liang Ch'i-ch'ao, that fiction has a major role to play as an instrument of national regeneration. Worried about China's lack of "wealth and power," influenced by the Japanese vogue for the political novel, and committed to the view that works of imaginative literature have an educative function to perform, Yen and Liang had no reservations about promoting fiction as a vehicle for political and social reform. To Wang, however, both the utilitarian view of literature that these men espoused and the kind of satiric and castigatory novel that, through their efforts, became the staple of late Ch'ing fiction are anathema. "I would far rather listen to traditional poetry [literally, poems that describe soldiers away on campaign and the ladies at home who pine for them] than have the sound of this sort of literature dinned into my ears."[14]

Also unpalatable to Wang is the traditional Chinese conception of literature as a means to achieve moral aims. "Alas!" he cries. "Art has enjoyed no independent value for a long while. It is therefore not strange that many among the successive generations of poets have relied on the principles of loyalty to one's lord, love of one's country, exhortation to goodness, and warning against evil in order to avoid [not being taken seriously by others]." It is deplorable, Wang says, that "plays and novels as well often possess a didactic thrust."[15]

In his own view, literature worthy of the name expresses universal human emotions. The essence of literature, according to Wang Kuo-wei, "lies in describing human life. By human life is meant not the solitary life of an individual, but rather the life of a clan, nation, or society." A truly great writer, he says, "regards the emotions of all mankind as his own personal emotions. He is so full of energy that he is unable to restrain himself. Not satisfied therefore with expressing his own emotions, he endeavors to express the emotions of all mankind. His works constitute in fact the voice of all mankind, and in them the reader hears the sound of his [own] pain and joy, his [own] weeping and laughing."[16]

His conception of the writer as the "universal man," which is reminiscent of Schopenhauer's view of the artist as the "mirror of mankind," suggests that in 1906–07 Wang Kuo-wei still believes, with his former philosophical hero, that good literature "reflects the inner nature of the whole of mankind."[17] It is true that he no longer subscribes to Schopenhauer's metaphysical thesis that mankind's inner nature is nothing but will. However, Wang seems still to share both the philosopher's conviction that suffering and ennui are essential features of the human condition and his belief that art provides a partial escape from the oppressiveness of everyday life.

Types of Beauty Found in Art

While hailing Burke's *Philosophical Inquiry into the Origins of Our Ideas of the Sublime and the Beautiful* (1756) as a pioneering work, Kant thought that its treatment of aesthetic experience still left something to be desired. What was needed, he believed, was a "transcendental exposition" of aesthetic judgments to supplement Burke's "purely empirical" and "physiological" one. The *Critique of Judgment* (1790) represents Kant's effort to provide just such an exposition.

In the third *Critique*, Kant offers four complementary elucidations of the meaning of the term 'beautiful'. The thrust of the first definition is the suggestion that aesthetic experience is entirely disinterested. The judgment of taste, according to Kant, is contemplative in the sense that it does not involve an interest in the object—that is, contemplation of it produces satisfaction with no reference to appetite or desire. The beautiful, then, is that which "merely *pleases.*"[18]

From a second perspective, Kant says, the beautiful may be defined as "that which pleases universally without [requiring] a concept."[19] Because all considerations of private interest have been factored out, the object is, or should be, the object of universal satisfaction. This judgment is not, however, directed toward, or based on, concepts.

In a third definition, Kant suggests that the beautiful may be described as "the form of the *purposiveness* of an object, so far as this is perceived in it *without any representation of a purpose.*"[20] The satisfaction that is the determining ground of the judgment of taste is the feeling that the object is "perfect," that it embodies a purpose, although no purpose is represented or conceived. According to Kant, beauty may be attributed to an object only on account of its form. What pleases by means of its form, not what gratifies in sensation, is crucial for taste. A judgment of taste can never rest on the representation of an object's utility.

According to Kant's fourth, and final, definition, beauty constitutes "that which without any concept is cognized as the object of a *necessary* satisfaction." It is a peculiarity of a judgment of taste that, although it has merely a subjective validity, it claims the assent of all subjects. This type of necessity is neither a theoretical objective necessity nor a practical necessity, but what Kant calls an "exemplary" necessity—that is, "a necessity of the assent of *all* to a judgment which is regarded as the example of a universal rule that we cannot state."[21]

His reflections on the nature of aesthetic experience lead Kant to conclude that the judgment of taste is a priori. A person arrives at a judgment of taste without needing to consult the views of others or to become acquainted with received opinions of the object. To explain this feature of aesthetic experience Kant posits the existence in man of a *sensus communis,* or common sense—that is, a faculty of judgment that takes account a priori of the mode of representation of all other persons in thought.

Following Burke, Kant distinguishes between two types of beauty, the beautiful and the sublime. Although they both please in themselves, the beautiful produces a pleasure that may be described as a positive joy, prolonged through quiet contemplation, whereas the sublime causes a negative pleasure that may be characterized as admiration or respect. The experience of the sublime, unlike that of the beautiful, is associated in Kant's view with emotion in the sense of a temporary cessation and a consequent more powerful outflow of what he calls the "vital powers."

Wang Kuo-wei's views on the nature of artistic awareness seem to have been decisively influenced by Kant, whose *Critique of Judgment* he may well have been studying at the time he wrote the literary essays in which he developed them. In one of his own definitions of beauty, for instance, Wang advances the Kantian claim that the beautiful is that which simply pleases, with no intrinsic reference to utility. "The essential feature of beauty, in a word, is that it is something which can be appreciated but cannot be utilized. Although occasionally we can utilize a beautiful object, a person by no means takes its useful features into consideration while engaged in aesthetic contemplation of it."[22]

Wang also holds, with Kant, that beauty may be ascribed to an object solely on account of its form.

> All beauty is beauty of form. Considered from the standpoint of beauty qua beauty, everything that is beautiful (*yu-mei*) may be said to derive its beauty from the symmetry, variation, and harmony of its form. With respect to objects which are sublime (*hung-chuang*), it is true that Kant says that they are formless. However, since they are able by means of this type of formless form to evoke feelings of the sublime, they may yet be said to possess a type of form. Considered from the standpoint of types of fine art, the beauty [we find in] architecture, sculpture, and music, it goes without saying, derives from their forms, while the beauty [we find in] paintings, poems, and songs derives from the content of their subject matter. Since, however, this subject matter can evoke feelings of beauty, it too may be regarded as a type of form.

Following Kant, Wang believes as well that judgments of taste possess an exemplary necessity. "That judgments of the beautiful and the sublime are a priori judgments is a thesis which has rarely been contested since the publication of Kant's *Critique of Judgment.* Since this sort of judgment is a priori, it possesses universality and necessity. In other words, what one artist regards as beautiful all other artists necessarily also regard as beautiful. That is why in his aesthetics Kant presupposes a common sense (*kung-kung chih kan-kuan*)."[23]

In 1904 Wang Kuo-wei had rapturously embraced Schopenhauer's metaphysical theory of art, according to which aesthetic knowledge constitutes knowledge of eternal Ideas that can be apprehended only by the person whose intellect has achieved temporary mastery over his will. It is thus not to be wondered that the explanations of the beautiful and the sublime that he had offered in articles written at that early date are Schopenhauerian. "Both the beautiful and the sublime cause us to turn away from the will to live and become pure subjects of knowing." "The feeling of the beautiful arises when an object leads a person to forget his personal interest in it and to take a prolonged, disinterested pleasure in it, while the feeling of the sublime arises when an object that has a directly hostile relation to our will confronts us and, violently tearing the will away [from consciousness], gives us knowledge of its Idea." Both of these species of beauty Wang, following Schopenhauer, had contrasted with the merely "charming" (*hsuan-huo*), "which draws us down from pure contemplation, causing us once again to become subjects of willing."[24]

By 1906–07 Wang Kuo-wei appears to have lost all interest in Schopenhauer's concepts of a cosmic will and Platonic Ideas. Now his elucidation of the character of the beautiful and the sublime is more Kantian than Schopenhauerian.

> Summarily speaking, [the feeling of the beautiful] arises when the form of an object is [seen as] unrelated to our personal interest and causes us . . . wholeheartedly to merge with it. The most common type of beauty found in both nature and art is of this variety. [The feeling of the sublime] arises when the form of an object exceeds our intellect's ability to comprehend it or greatly threatens us and we feel that it is not something which can be resisted with human strength, when, therefore, our instinct for self-preservation and our thoughts of personal interest are transcended and we reach a level at which we are able to contemplate disinterestedly the form of the object. Examples of such objects in nature are high mountains, great rivers, strong winds, and thunder showers.[25]

His new description of the sublime suggests that Wang was familiar both with the distinction Kant draws between the mathematically and the dynamically sublime and with the examples he cites of natural objects that excite in us a feeling of the sublime.

To the beautiful and the sublime Wang Kuo-wei adds a third type of beauty. "That art is the product of genius is a proposition which has been regarded as axiomatic by scholars since the time of Kant one hundred years ago. However, among the things in the world are those that are by no means real works of art but that are by no means useful objects. The creators [of such things], moreover, are by no means necessarily geniuses, but when we examine [their creations] we find that they are indistinguishable from artistic works produced by geniuses. Not knowing how to describe the character of this sort of beauty, I refer to it as 'the elegant' (ku-ya)."[26] While the concept of elegance, or refinement, is not a new one in Chinese aesthetics, Wang claims to be the first both to provide a systematic exposition of it and to determine the status of the elegant as an aesthetic judgment.

Having asserted that all beauty is, at base, beauty of form, Wang observes that "all beauty of form must express itself in another form." It is this second kind of form that he has in mind when he speaks of the elegant.

> The essence of the elegant lies in conscious artistry (i-shu) rather than in nature. With nature one merely passes through the first form, but with conscious artistry one necessarily expresses in a second form either a particular given form of nature or a new form which one has created oneself. The expressions of a given form, accordingly, all differ one from the other. The performances of a given piece of music differ, depending on the performers. The imitations of a given piece of sculpture or painting differ greatly from the original. In poetry and singing it is the same.

Even if the form of an object is of neither a beautiful nor a sublime character, Wang says, "it can attain a certain independent value through this second form." Therefore, the elegant may be called "the beauty of the form of the beauty of the form."[27]

To elucidate his view of the nature of the elegant, Wang Kuo-wei invites us to examine specific lines of poetry. In poetry, he explains, that which is elegant (or not) is the verbal structures through which a poet depicts a mood, or world. Knowing this, we can easily see why Tu Fu's lines, "When the night deepens, a candle is lit; / We look at one another and wonder whether we are not in a dream," are superior to Yen Chi-tao's lines, "Tonight, let the light of the silver lamp shine on you fully, / For I'm still afraid that we are meeting in a dream," and we can just as easily see why the Book of Poetry's lines, "Longingly I think of my husband, / Till my heart is weary, and my head aches," are superior to Ou-yang Hsiu's lines, "My sash is getting looser and looser; still I don't regret: / For her sake, it's worthwhile pining away!"[28]

According to Wang, the underlying sentiment—what he calls the first form—of Tu Fu's and Yen Chi-tao's lines is the same, as is that of the lines he has quoted from the Book of Poetry and Ou-yang Hsiu.

The verbal structures in which these sentiments are encased—what Wang calls the second form—are, however, markedly different, the former of each pair of couplets attaining in his view a certain formal beauty that is lacking in the latter. "It is in this way that the putative distinction between elegance (ya) and vulgarity (su) has arisen." No matter how beautiful or sublime a sentiment may be, Wang says, it must be expressed elegantly "if its intrinsic value is to be observable."[29]

Wang Kuo-wei describes the position of the elegant as "being equidistant from the beautiful and the sublime and partaking of both." The elegant may be considered a sort of junior version of the beautiful because "a beautiful form causes our mind to be at peace, while an elegant form causes our mind to be at rest." At the same time, the elegant may be regarded as a kind of low-level version of the sublime since "a sublime form invariably calls forth from our confrontation with its irresistible force a feeling of respect, while an elegant form, as something to which our ordinary senses are unaccustomed, awakens in us a certain astonishment, which is the beginning of the feeling of respect."[30]

Despite these commonalities, the elegant differs from the beautiful and the sublime, Wang suggests, in three respects. First, as we have seen, it does not exist in nature but is achieved through conscious artistry. Second, the judgment of the elegant, unlike other judgments of taste, is not a priori but a posteriori. "What we judge to be elegant in fact depends for its determination on our being situated in the present. There is no ancient artifact which we do not regard as more elegant than a modern product, and there is no ancient literary work, however clumsy or crude, which on reading we do not regard as elegant." Such judgments, according to Wang, spring from the circumstance that, as moderns, our contemplation of relics of antiquity "involuntarily gives rise to a sense of bygone ages." Since the ancients themselves obviously could not have felt as we do about these same objects, the judgment of the elegant may justifiably be characterized as "a posteriori and experiential as well as particularistic and contingent."[31]

And third, unlike beautiful or sublime works, which can be created and appreciated only by artistic geniuses, works that are elegant can be created and appreciated by the merely talented. "Since the essence of the elegant does not lie in nature, and since the judgment of it arises simply from experience, elegance in artistic works . . . can be achieved and grasped through human effort (jen-li)."[32] For this reason Wang commends literature that is elegant to those who suffer from boredom but are of average or even below-average intelligence.

The Character of Artistic Genius

While he stresses that works which are elegant can be produced through sheer hard work and application, Wang Kuo-wei does not wish to suggest that works which are either beautiful or sublime can be produced completely without human effort, through divine inspiration alone. It is true that Wang fully subscribes to the view of Schopenhauer, Wang Fu-chih (1619–1692), and others that the distinction between the man of mere talent and the man of artistic genius is absolute. Since, however, he insists that genius is a necessary but not sufficient condition for the creation of truly great art, Wang dwells in his literary essays not only on the remarkable endowment of the genius but also on the training that he must undergo in order to realize his artistic "potential."

That genius must be cultivated (*hsiu-yang*) is a proposition to which Wang is firmly committed. Cultivation, in his view, is a process both lengthy and demanding, although ultimately rewarding.

> Those who from antiquity to the present have accomplished great deeds or attained great knowledge have invariably gone through three stages. The first stage may be described by the lines, "Last night the west wind withered the green trees. / Alone I mounted the lofty tower / To gaze at the roads, as far as the world's end (from Yen Shu's lyric to the tune 'Butterflies Lingering over Flowers' ['Tieh lien hua'])." The second stage may be described by the lines, "My sash is getting looser and looser; still I don't regret: / For her sake, it's worthwhile pining away (from Ou-yang Hsiu's lyric to the tune 'Butterflies Lingering over Flowers')!" The third stage may be described by the lines, "In the crowd I looked for her a thousand and one times; / And all at once, as I turned my head, / I was startled to find her / Among the lanterns where candles were growing dim (from Hsin Ch'i-chi's lyric to the tune 'Green Jade Cup' ['Ch'ing yü an'])." No one has ever been able to leap over into the third stage without having passed through the other two. This generalization applies to literature, too, which is why literary geniuses must cultivate [their inborn talent] extensively.[33]

From this description we can see that Wang believes that gradual cultivation (*chien-hsiu*) is not merely compatible with, but is actually a sine qua non for, sudden illumination (*tun-wu*). Like other intuitionalist critics such as Yen Yü (fl. 1180–1235) and Wang Shih-chen (1634–1711), he thinks that only those who have been engaged in training are in any position to grasp intuitively and "all at once" the art of poetry. As for the kind of training that Wang Kuo-wei has in mind, it evidently involves both book learning and moral cultivation. "A genius may appear once every few decades or once every few centuries, but even he must be versed in scholarship and guided by virtue if he is to produce really great literature."[34]

According to Wang, the genius will emerge from the rigors of the training program without having lost the childlike character (*ch'ih-tzu chih hsin*) that is his hallmark. The notion that genius possesses a childlike quality is one that, we recall, Wang had acquired from Schopenhauer as early as 1904.[35] This notion he subsequently developed, as we have seen, under the influence of Schiller. "[Literature] is solely the business of the genius at play," we find him declaring in one of his literary essays.[36] Novelists, dramatists, and all other kinds of artists as well are, in Wang's view (as in Schiller's), individuals who have undertaken to play on behalf of the human race.

Geniuses, Wang maintains, are distinguished not only by the profundity of their knowledge, the loftiness of their character, and the playfulness of their disposition, but also by the originality of their work. Ch'ü Yuan (343?–278 B.C.), for instance, wrote excellent poetry because in it he "expressed his own feelings in a style which was also his own." T'ao Ch'ien (A.D. 365?–427) was the greatest literary talent in the centuries following Ch'ü Yuan's death because he, too, produced poems that were original in both content and form. And Su Shih (1037–1101) achieved his reputation as a brilliant writer because in his poetry he, like Ch'ü Yuan and T'ao Ch'ien, "expressed his own feelings in a style which was also his own." Wang in general condemns imitation in poetry since most imitators, lacking the imaginative power and technical virtuosity of the geniuses whose works they seek to copy, manage merely to become the Tung Shihs of the literary world.[37]

At the same time that he was expounding in his literary essays critical ideas that he had acquired from his German sages, Wang Kuo-wei was writing poetry himself, evaluating the poetry of others, and beginning to jot down the terse sayings that would comprise *Remarks on Lyrics in the World of Men*. We will thus not be surprised to discover many points of intellectual affinity between Wang's literary essays of 1906–07 and his literary criticism and mature aesthetic theory.

10

Wang's Lyrics, Lyric Criticism, and Mature Aesthetic Theory

As a young man Wang Kuo-wei had a conspicuous weakness for poetry, of which over the years he wrote a great deal. It was, we recall, on account of a particularly fine quatrain that he had written on a roommate's fan at the Eastern Language Institute that Wang had originally come to the attention of his future mentor, Lo Chen-yü. During all the years he studied Western philosophy, Wang never ceased to compose poems in his spare time. He evidently thought very highly of his early efforts, which were mainly poems of the "regular" type (*shih*), for in 1905 he published a number of specimens as a supplement to his anthology of philosophical articles titled *Essays by Ching-an (Ching-an wen-chi).*[1]

Wang's Lyrics

In 1905 Wang decided to try his hand at a poetic genre entirely different from those in which he had until then been composing. Between 1905 and 1909 he wrote over one hundred lyrics (*tz'u*), most of which were published in 1906 and 1907 as *Lyrics in the World of Men, Part One (Jen-chien tz'u chia-kao)* and *Lyrics in the World of Men, Part Two (Jen-chien tz'u i-kao).* The excessive sensibility of his lyrics is attributable in part to Wang Kuo-wei's own melancholic temperament and in part to the terrible personal losses—the deaths of his father, wife, and stepmother—that he sustained in the years 1906–1908.[2]

From the standpoint of content, the distinctive feature of Wang's lyrics is the philosophical thrust he often gives them. Consider, for example, the following lyric, written to the tune "Sand of Silk-washing Stream" ("Huan hsi sha"):

A mountain temple, indistinct, silhouetted against the setting sun.
Birds do not fly as far as halfway up the mountain, now that the
    sky is darkening.

Above, a solitary chime arrests the drifting clouds.

I climb the highest peak to glimpse the bright moon.
Happening to become enlightened, I turn my gaze toward the
    Red Dust:
Oh! What a pity that I am no different from the men below.[3]

In this joyless lyric, Wang provides a novel twist to a conventional theme. Having climbed midway up the mountain, the speaker has long since left the world of men, and even birds, far behind. As he stands before the temple, his only companions are the clouds that graze his head as they drift by (they are so near that they can hear the chime). On ascending the mountain's loftiest peak, the speaker attains a panoramic view of mankind, although, ironically, he gains no sense of liberation from his contemplation of the grand prospect spread out before him. The lyric ends on a paradoxical note: even though he is able to see life from a transcendent point of view, the climber is unable to escape his own humanity. Indeed, his insight into the nature of the human condition is precisely that man cannot escape his own humanity.

A lyric written to the tune "Song of Picking Mulberry" ("Ts'ai-sang tzu") is likewise pessimistic in tone.

On the high city wall the drums stir; the lampwick has burnt to
    ashes.
Unable to lose myself in sleep,
Unable to lose myself in wine—
Suddenly I hear a solitary goose cry two or three times.

Life may be likened to catkins buffeted by the wind.
Joy in fragments,
Sadness in fragments—
All turn to dots of duckweed on the Lien River.[4]

This poem reveals Wang's continuing belief in the illusory nature of human life. The poet is spending a restless, sleepless evening brooding on the character of existence (the wild goose crying in the distance symbolizes his loneliness and bewilderment). It is already very nearly dawn, as suggested by the beating of the drums and the burnt-out lampwick. Life, he reflects unhappily, is as fragile, fleeting, and mutable as willow catkins which, as he thinks, turn into duckweed when they fall in water.

Other lyrics express Wang Kuo-wei's conviction that doubting, uncertainty, longing, and parting are unfortunate but inescapable features of human existence. In a lyric written to the tune "Partridge Sky" ("Che-ku t'ien"), Wang assumes the intellectual posture of a Cartesian.

On the high road around the palace the wind rustles banners
    fifty feet long,
And storied buildings rise as high as the clouds.
In vain the bright moon shines on weeds by the water,
Failing to illuminate the red blossoms falling into the well.

Incessant groping and stumbling—
Of all the palace doors, which is the right one?
In the world of men there is always something to doubt;
Only the existence of doubt itself may not be doubted.[5]

The first stanza of this lyric possibly concerns the flight of Empress
Dowager Tz'u-hsi and Emperor Te-tsung (r. 1875–1908) to Sian,
where the First Emperor of Ch'in built the fabulous palace to which
the opening line twice refers, and the tragic demise of the so-called
Pearl Concubine (Chen fei), who met her end in a well.[6] In the second
stanza the poet advances the existentialist thesis that all of our actions
are predicated on choices, choices for which, in the last analysis, there
are no rational grounds. No propositions, therefore, may be considered indubitably true—except for the proposition that no propositions may be considered indubitably true.

In a similar philosophical spirit, Wang suggests in a lyric written
to the tune "Immortal at the Magpie Bridge" ("Ch'ueh-ch'iao hsien")
that there is nothing dependable in life except the fact of undepend-
ableness itself.

Ch'en ch'en beat the drums in the garrison;
Hsiao hsiao neigh the horses in the stable.
On rising I see that frost covers the entire ground,
And suddenly I recall the day we parted—
The weather was just the same as it is today in this lodge.

My carriage transports me northward,
While my dreams transport me back southward.
My movements cannot be planned.
In the world of men nothing is reliable,
Except the fact of unreliability itself.[7]

When the speaker left his love in the South, he anticipated a quick
return to her side, but his itinerary now calls for him to travel farther
and farther north. He is passing a sleepless night, as suggested by the
beating of the drums and the neighing horses, contemplating his
unhappy situation. The speaker's gloominess is symbolized by the
unwelcome frost outside his bedroom window, which indicates that
the desolate and melancholy season of autumn has arrived. His Sar-
trian insight into the radical contingency of human existence only
increases his anguish.

The theme of longing is one frequently found in traditional Chinese poetry, and Wang has written several lyrics on it. One of them, composed to the tune "Butterflies Lingering over Flowers," reads as follows:

> How much sorrow there was in last night's dream!
> A thin horse, a fragrant carriage—
> We two approached one another.
> Facing each other, you seemed to pity my wasted frame;
> Disregarding the others, you raised the curtain to inquire about
>   my health.
>
> I listened to the muffled rumbling of carriage wheels.
> Since in my dream it was difficult to follow you,
> How, after awakening, will I obtain news of you?
> The candle's tears on my windowsill stand an inch deep;
> In the world of men yearning is our lot.[8]

Like a candle devoured by its own heat, the lovesick poet is being consumed by his own unfulfilled passion. Even his dreams are so grim that they afford him no vicarious satisfaction.

Another of Wang's lyrics on the theme of longing, also written to the tune "Butterflies Lingering over Flowers," runs:

> As evening approaches, suddenly I feel distressed.
> While the new moon rises,
> Silently I lament our separation.
> This evening's limpid moonlight reminds me of another night—
> I do not hesitate to lower a heavy curtain.
>
> What is it that brings sorrow or joy to the wine cup?
> I have already lost my former love;
> There is nothing on which to rely for a rendezvous in some
>   future year.
> How many times has the candle blossomed and faded!
> In the world of men it must be understood that one's
>   expectations are often dashed.[9]

When his day's work is completed, the jilted poet can no longer ignore the sadness that gnaws relentlessly at his heart. So intense is his sorrow and so vivid his memories, in fact, that he cannot bear even to look at the moon—the moon that reminds him of past romantic moments. Many years have passed since the poet's beloved forsook him (the candle's blooming and fading here represent the arrival and departure of spring), but he continues to indulge in reminiscence. As he sips a glass of wine, his mood darkens from regret to cynicism. Not much, the poet thinks, should be expected from life.

The bitterness of parting sorrow is another stock theme in traditional Chinese poetry, and Wang, as we can see from this lyric to the tune "Butterflies Lingering over Flowers," wrote movingly on it.

> The entire ground is covered with frost as thick as snow.
> We speak in the west wind;
> A lean horse neighs under the waning moon.
> Before the departure song has been completed,
> The sound of the carriage blends with the sound of singing.
>
> Completely changed is the color of the fragrant grass which
>   stretches as far as the horizon.
> Deep, deep in the road
> Are the wheel tracks of years past.
> About our evanescent life little can be said;
> In the world of men parting is the hardest thing to do.[10]

The first stanza portrays a woman saying farewell to a loved one at dawn on an autumn's day. The landscape, like her feelings, is bleak, as suggested by the thick frost, west wind, lean horse, and waning moon. The second stanza shows the heroine still to be suffering the pangs of separation the following spring. Rooted to the spot where her beloved took leave of her and gazing at the wheel ruts in the road, she muses on the innumerable women whose hearts must have been broken as savagely as hers by separations in months and years gone by.

In another lyric, written to the tune "Butterflies Lingering over Flowers," Wang Kuo-wei evinces a sentimental poet's preoccupation with the irretrievable passage of time.

> Having experienced all the pain of separation in faraway places,
> Unexpectedly I return
> To find the flowers fallen like this.
> Underneath the flowers we gaze at each other silently.
> Through the green window spring vanishes with the day.
>
> Soon by the candlelight we shall speak of our longing for one
>   another—
> One thread of new happiness for
> Thousands and thousands of threads of old regret.
> Those things in the world of men which can never be stopped
>   are
> Youth's bloom leaving the mirror and flowers leaving the trees.[11]

Although the poet's reunion with his love has brought him a modicum of pleasure, it has awakened many painful memories. His seemingly naive surprise at discovering that during his prolonged absence both he and his love have aged leads him to regret that he has been away so long that they have been unable to share the precious years of their youth.

While most of Wang's lyrics are melancholy in tone, some are actually shrill. In the latter category is this unstintingly pessimistic lyric, written to the tune "Sand of Silk-washing Stream":

> Black clouds on the horizon press in from all directions.
> A lone goose which has lost its way flies into the wind;
> Amidst desolate rivers and lakes, where will you find a home?
>
> Holding metal pellets on the path, the hunter watches as your
>   feathers fall.
> Delicate hands from the women's quarters blend you into a soup;
> Tonight's feast will be happier than ever before.[12]

The note of terrible irony on which this lyric ends gives its highly conventional theme a bizarre and macabre twist.

An experienced reader of lyrics, taking Wang Kuo-wei's collection of lyrics as a whole, would probably not mistake his work for that of a Sung lyricist; too many of his lyrics express ideas, explore worlds, and contain stylistic features that are distinctively Wang's own and "un-Sung."[13] Some individual lyrics, however, are very similar to those of Ou-yang Hsiu (1007–1072) and Ch'in Kuan (1049–1100), as Wang's close friend Fan Ping-ch'ing has pointed out. "From antiquity to the present, no one has excelled more than Ou-yang Hsiu at the expression of ideas (*i*) and no one more than Ch'in Kuan at the description of worlds (*ching*) . . . Mr. Wang's lyrics in the main express ideas that are more profound even than Ou-yang's and describe worlds that are inferior only to Ch'in's."[14] We may suppose that Wang wrote movingly about such things as romantic yearning, parting sorrow, and the passage of time because these themes were, in a sense, his themes. That is to say, Wang was probably no stranger to the emotions that he explores so sensitively in those of his lyrics which are written on the traditional topics of Chinese poetry.

The originality of those of his lyrics which express abstract, philosophical ideas obviously arises from the circumstance that, during the years Wang was writing most of his lyrics (1905–1907), he was still strongly influenced by certain Western thinkers. Although he seems by this time to have lost his former obsession with the "problem of the universe," Wang was still vitally concerned about the "problem of human life." There can be very little doubt that he intended the words "in the world of men" (*jen-chien*), which occur thirty-eight times in his 115 lyrics and form part of the titles of three different works (his two volumes of lyrics and *Remarks on Lyrics in the World of Men*), to signify his intense concern with humanistic matters. From this perspective, we may regard Wang's lyrics containing philosophical reflections as simply another medium through which he endeavored, with the help of his Western sages, to identify the fundamental features of the human condition.[15]

Fan Ping-ch'ing has characterized Wang Kuo-wei's lyrics as "straightforward," yet "sophisticated" and even "subtle." In them Wang observes nature with a keen eye for detail and explores the human world with great sensitivity. Indeed, Fan says, his friend's lyrics possess such emotional depth that they positively resound with Wang's "secret grief, which moves the heart."[16] They are, in sum, superior to the lyrics of almost every other lyricist who has ever put brush to paper. "Although I have not yet written even one hundred lyrics," Wang himself declares in 1907, "I am convinced that from Southern Sung times onward there has been, with the exception of one or two lyricists, no one who can compare with me. While I confess that I am inferior to the great lyricists of the Five Dynasties and Northern Sung periods [907–1126] in some respects, I believe that these lyricists cannot compare with me in other respects." Wang's lyrics, rhapsodizes Fan, "soar to the ends of the earth, and they will elevate the human mind for a thousand years to come."[17]

Wang's View of Other Lyricists

At the same time that he was composing lyrics, Wang was also earnestly studying the lyrics of earlier masters. By 1906 he had already developed decided preferences and prejudices as a critic and had begun to express his opinions in print through his friend Fan Ping-ch'ing, who describes Wang's views in the foreword he wrote to *Lyrics in the World of Men, Part One*. This foreword, along with the foreword to *Lyrics in the World of Men, Part Two*, which also reflects Wang's ideas, and *Remarks on Lyrics in the World of Men*, constitute our three sources of information on Wang Kuo-wei's views as a critic of lyric poetry.

From his lyric criticism we can see that Wang prefers the lyrics of Li Yü (better known as Li Hou-chu, or "Li the Last Ruler," 937–978) to those of any other lyricist of the late T'ang and Five Dynasties periods, although he also esteems the lyrics of Feng Yen-ssu (903–960). His favorite Northern Sung lyricists are Ou-yang Hsiu, Ch'in Kuan, Su Shih, and Chou Pang-yen (1056–1121). While he has some good things to say about Chiang K'uei (c. 1155–1221), Wang believes that Hsin Ch'i-chi (1140–1207) is the only truly outstanding lyricist of the Southern Sung dynasty. And he finds that, aside from himself, the only great lyricist to emerge in the centuries following the collapse of the Southern Sung is Singde.

It was with Li Yü, Wang Kuo-wei observes, that the lyric as a poetic genre "began to broaden in scope and to achieve greater depth in the expression of human emotions." Departing from the tradition of the lyricists of the Hua-chien school (named after the anthology *Hua-chien chi* [Among the Flowers], which contains lyrics dating from the years 836–940), Li Yü wrote lyrics on themes more serious than those of his predecessors, and he imbued them with an unheard-of intensity of feeling. This is why, Wang says, Li Yü's lyrics are superior in spirit (*shen*) to those of the leading Hua-chien lyricists, Wen T'ing-yun and Wei Chuang.[18]

In Wang Kuo-wei's portrayal, Li Yü was an unworldly man "whose birth, which occurred deep in the palace, and whose upbringing, which was entrusted to women, proved disadvantageous to [him] as a ruler but advantageous to him as a lyricist." His "childlike character" may have cost Li Yü his kingdom (the Southern T'ang), Wang declares, but it enabled him to write poetry that is conspicuous for its utter lack of reserve, artifice, and guile. His lyrics, which frankly and sincerely give vent to his grief and despair over the loss of his kingdom, may most appropriately be described as a corpus with Nietzsche's words, "written with his blood." They pierce one to the heart, rive one's soul with pangs of anguish, because they succeed fully in expressing universal human emotions, not just the poet's own personal emotions. "Like Shakyamuni and Jesus Christ, Li Yü seems to have borne the guilt of all mankind."[19]

In view of the exceedingly high regard in which he holds Li Yü, we are not surprised to find that Wang Kuo-wei disagrees violently with the nineteenth-century critic Chou Chi, who ranked his lyrics below those of both Wen T'ing-yun and Wei Chuang. Consider, Wang suggests, Li Yü's lines, "Human life is ever full of grief; / Rivers ever flow to the east" and "The water flows, the blossoms fall, the glory of spring is gone / In nature's domain and in the world of men." Are there, he demands to know, any lines in Wen's *Golden Iris* (*Chin-ch'üan*) or Wei's *Washed Flower* (*Huan-hua*) that can compare with these in mood?[20]

Since, in the opinion of many literary critics, the lyric attained its full florescence during the eleventh and early twelfth centuries, it is perhaps not to be wondered that four of Wang's favorite lyricists lived during the Northern Sung dynasty. Ou-yang Hsiu's lyrics he admires for their abstract conceptual meaning. Those of Ch'in Kuan he believes excel at blending inner experience with the external environment to form concrete poetic worlds. Su Shih's lyrics Wang praises for their amazing breadth of vision as well as their elegant diction; he seems particularly to feel drawn to those of Su's lyrics which explore worlds that are sublime and transcendental, tragic and heroic.[21]

As for Chou Pang-yen, Wang rejects the view of many traditional Chinese critics, including Chou Chi, that he was the greatest poet in the lyric genre. "Regrettably, he had much talent for developing new tunes but little talent for developing new ideas." From a literary point of view, Wang maintains, Chou Pang-yen must be considered inferior to both Ou-yang Hsiu and Ch'in Kuan. "He is, however, extremely adept at expressing emotions and capturing the essence of things, as a result of which he may still be regarded as a writer of the first rank."[22]

Unlike some Chinese scholars, Wang Kuo-wei believes not that the lyric reached its peak of development during the Southern Sung dynasty, but that it in fact began just at this time to lose its creative vitality. Accordingly, he has, on the whole, a positive aversion to Southern Sung lyricists. Particularly distasteful to Wang are Wu Wen-ying (c. 1200–1260), because of the extravagant ornamentation of his lyrics, and Chang Yen (1248–1320?), because of the verbosity of his. "Wu Wen-ying places word upon word, while Chang Yen piles line upon line." The long decline of the lyric actually began, in Wang's view, with Wu and Chang, whom posterity has honored for their diction but whose lyrics he thinks are lacking in depth and vitality. Ridiculing them by punning on their courtesy names (Meng-ch'uang, or "Dream Window," and Yü-t'ien, or "Jade Fields"), Wang offers the following assessment of their poetry: "I may characterize Wu Wen-ying's lyrics as a corpus with a line from one of them—'shadows in green disarray falling on the dream window.' I may likewise characterize Chang Yen's lyrics as a corpus with a line from one of them—'jade grown old and fields gone to waste.' "[23]

Of the Southern Sung lyricist Chou Mi (1232–1308), Wang Kuo-wei also entertains a very low opinion. Like Chang Yen, Chou Mi was more interested in quantity than in quality. As a result, he produced lyrics concerning which Chu Hsi's words that "one hundred of them can be turned out in a day" are apt. Even Chiang K'uei, whom Wang considers the supreme master of the lyric from a purely stylistic point of view and whose lyrics he praises for their elegance and robustness, cannot compare with the great Northern Sung lyricists either in the realm of ideas or in the description of worlds.[24]

The only truly outstanding lyricist of the Southern Sung period, according to Wang, is Hsin Ch'i-chi, whose most representative lyrics are, as James J. Y. Liu has observed, "those which give vent to his frustrated ambitions to help recover North China from the invaders [the Jurched], or reflect his calmer moods of quiet enjoyment of Nature and stoic resignation to his lot in life." Hsin Ch'i-chi's lyrics, like those of Su Shih, are, Wang says, characterized by breadth of vision and elegant diction. They reflect Hsin's own personality, are written in a powerful style, and transport us into special worlds.[25]

The early Ch'ing lyricist Singde was, in Wang Kuo-wei's view, "a hero who emerged after [the lyric genre had been in decline for] one hundred generations." Singde's remarkable success as a lyricist Wang attributes in part to his "Heaven-bestowed talent" and in part to his ethnic origin; as a Sinicized Manchu, he was able to write more freely and naturally than the tradition-bound Chinese. Shunning ornamentation and artifice, Singde composed lyrics that, according to Wang, are notable not only for their naturalness but also for their sincerity, qualities that he claims had not been seen in lyrics for centuries. Singde thus ranks high above such other Ch'ing lyricists as Chu I-tsun, founder of the Che-hsi school of lyric composition and criticism; Ch'en Wei-sung, leader of the Yang-hsien school; Chiang Ch'un-lin; and Hsiang Hung-tso.[26]

As a critic of lyrics, Wang Kuo-wei is clearly not very original. In the main his views of various lyricists follow those of Chou Chi, although, as we have seen, he disagrees strongly with the latter as regards Li Yü. The apotheosis of Li Yü seems, in fact, to constitute Wang's distinctive contribution to lyric criticism. Previous critics had, of course, eulogized Li Yü, but none had ever compared that luckless soul to Shakyamuni and Christ.

Although his lyric criticism is not highly original, Wang does depart in it from the most influential schools of lyric composition and criticism of the Ch'ing period. He heartily dislikes both the Che-hsi school, which championed the sort of poetic elegance and refinement found in the lyrics of Chiang K'uei and Chang Yen, and the popular Ch'ang-chou school, whose proponents had a weakness for interpreting lyrics allegorically. Indeed, Wang Kuo-wei appears to have been one of the very few (perhaps the only) lyricist-critics to have escaped the enveloping influence of the Ch'ang-chou school during the late Ch'ing dynasty.[27]

Wang's Mature Aesthetic Theory

As a refinement and distillation of the views set forth in his literary essays of 1906–07 as well as in the forewords to his two volumes of lyrics, *Remarks on Lyrics in the World of Men* may be considered the capstone of Wang Kuo-wei's work in the field of aesthetics. Like his literary essays, *Remarks on Lyrics in the World of Men* is dotted with concepts and terms that Wang had acquired from Kant, Schiller, Schopenhauer, and Nietzsche. The voices of these German sages are now, however, muted. Nor are the ideas of one foreign thinker any longer easily distinguishable from those of another, or even from those of certain Chinese critics. Significantly influenced by, but not completely beholden to, his German mentors, Wang has boldly recast in this work his favorite foreign concepts, often going so far as to fuse them with specific Chinese ideas to form new theoretical amalgams. The aesthetic theory he propounds in *Remarks on Lyrics in the World of Men* is thus one that embodies a synthesis of foreign and native ideas.

When it was first serialized in the *National Essence Journal* (*Kuo-ts'ui hsueh-pao*) during the last weeks of 1908 and the first weeks of 1909, *Remarks on Lyrics in the World of Men* comprised sixty-four "remarks" (*tse*—literally, items). From Wang Kuo-wei's hand-written draft manuscript, which is still extant, subsequent editors of the work have retrieved many remarks omitted from the 1908–09 text. These "expunged" remarks, as well as miscellaneous observations on literature jotted down by Wang over the years in the margins of his books and elsewhere, have been published alongside the "original" remarks in all modern editions of *Remarks on Lyrics in the World of Men*. While emphasizing those items which Wang himself saw fit to print, we shall not hesitate in our discussion of his mature aesthetic theory to draw on both the expunged remarks and the miscellaneous observations wherever it seems profitable to do so.[28]

Wang Kuo-wei's basic conception of poetry must be deduced from a handful of concise and rather opaque remarks strung together in the casual manner typical of "remarks on poetry" (*shih-hua* and *tz'u-hua*). The remarks in question are all designed to elucidate Wang's theory of 'worlds' (*ching-chieh*, or simply *ching*) in poetry. This theory, which has exerted considerable influence on modern Chinese criticism, is the principal innovation of *Remarks on Lyrics in the World of Men*.[29]

Wang Kuo-wei states, to begin with, that the term 'world' "does not refer to scenes and objects alone; joy, anger, sadness, and happiness also form a world in the human heart. Therefore, poetry that describes true scenes and true emotions may be said to embody a world; otherwise, it may be said not to embody a world." He also states: "When persons of former times discussed poetry, they made a distinction between 'scene' and 'emotion', not realizing that all descriptions of scenes are also descriptions of emotions."[30] From these remarks we can see that, from one perspective, a 'world' involves a fusion of inner and outer experience.

The concept of 'world' itself Wang seems to have derived from Wang Fu-chih's notion of 'emotion' and 'scene' (*ch'ing ching*). " 'Emotion' and 'scene'," says Wang Fu-chih, "are nominally two entities but are inseparable in reality. Those who work miracles in poetry can subtly unite them, leaving no boundary line, while those who are ingenious can reveal an emotion in a scene and a scene in an emotion." As early as 1906–07 Wang Kuo-wei himself had suggested, in a similar vein, that "literature contains two basic elements, 'scene' and 'emotion', the former of which refers to the depiction of the facts of nature and human life and the latter of which refers to our mental attitude toward these facts."[31] He had, furthermore, suggested that superior poetry perfectly blends the external environment with the poet's feelings. From the idea that poetry fuses scenes and emotions it appears to have been, for Wang, but a short step to the idea that, in fusing scenes and emotions, poetry creates 'worlds'.

In Wang's view, the best kind of poetry not only "describes true scenes and true emotions" but also captures the spirit, or essence, of things as filtered through an individual sensibility. From a second perspective, then, a 'world' refers to an ineffable, miraculous quality that may be likened to "sound in the air, color in appearances, the moon in water, or images in a mirror," to borrow the words of Yen Yü. Like Yen Yü, Wang Kuo-wei emphasizes intuitive apprehension of reality as well as intuitive artistry. "The 'world' is of paramount importance in lyrics. If [a lyric] embodies a world, it will naturally possess a lofty style and naturally have striking lines."[32]

To Wang Kuo-wei, poems that capture the essence of true emotions and true scenes have a quality of immediacy or transparency, which he calls 'not veiled' (*pu-ko*). "In expressing emotions, the works of great masters necessarily pierce one to the heart, and in describing scenes, they necessarily bring them right before one's ears and eyes. Their words come out naturally, without affectation or artificiality, because their observations are genuine and their knowledge profound." The works of mediocre poets, by contrast, have an opaque or 'veiled' (*ko*) quality that arises from their excessive reliance on allusions, quotations, substitute words (*tai-tzu*), and other kinds of literary devices. When one reads a poem that is 'not veiled', Wang says, "every word comes alive before one's eyes," but when one reads a poem whose mode of expression is oblique, it is like "gazing at flowers through a mist."[33]

A 'world', Wang suggests in another elucidation of his conception of poetry, may be either beautiful or sublime, depending on whether it 'lacks a self' or 'has a self'. A 'world that lacks a self' (*wu-wo chih ching*) is attained when "the mind is in repose." In this kind of world, "it is as if one object were observing another object, as a consequence of which self and object are indistinguishable." As examples of a 'world that lacks a self', Wang adduces T'ao Ch'ien's lines, "I pluck chrysanthemums under the east hedge, / Easily the south mountain comes into sight," and Yuan Hao-wen's lines, "Lightly, lightly arise the chilly waves, / Slowly, slowly descends the white bird."[34]

A 'world that has a self' (*yu-wo chih ching*), by contrast, is attained when "movement is checked." In this type of world, "the self observes an object, as a consequence of which the perceived object is infused with the self's subjective disposition." Examples are Ou-yang Hsiu's lines, "Tearful eyes ask the flowers; the flowers do not speak. / A riot of red whirls away past the garden swing," and Ch'in Kuan's lines, "How, in the lonely hostel, with its doors closed, / Is one to bear the chill of spring? / Amidst the cries of the cuckoo, the sun sets."[35]

The notion of 'worlds that lack a self' and 'worlds that have a self' is obviously related to Kant's conception of the beautiful and the sublime, although Wang is now referring, not to the reader's contemplation of poetry, but to the speaker's interaction with the world. A 'world that lacks a self' may be said to achieve a tranquil sort of beauty, in Wang's view, because in it the speaker has quietly transcended personal emotions (his "mind is in repose"). A 'world that has a self' is characterized, by contrast, by an awe-inspiring kind of beauty since in it the speaker is fully immersed in emotion, particularly all-engrossing sorrow. A 'world that lacks a self', therefore, is a world that transcends personal emotions, whereas a 'world that has a self' is a world in which nature is colored by some dominant human emotion.

From another perspective, Wang Kuo-wei suggests, 'worlds' may be divided into those which, because of the profundity of the ideas they embody, can be appreciated only by geniuses and those which, because of the ordinariness of theirs, can be understood by persons of average intelligence.

> There are two kinds of worlds: 'worlds of poets' (*shih-jen chih ching-chieh*) and 'worlds of ordinary men' (*ch'ang-jen chih ching-chieh*). 'Worlds of poets' can be experienced and described only by poets. Thus, those who read their poems also are raised to lofty heights, admire that which is distant, and soar beyond the confines of the world. However, there are those who can enter [into the 'worlds of poets'] and there are those who cannot enter. Moreover, those who can enter do so with different degrees of insight. But in the case of sadness, happiness, separation, reunion, con-

stant travelling, and going off to war—these are themes which all ordinary men can grasp, although only poets can write about them. This is why a poet who writes for a popular audience has a profound influence on men and is extremely well received by them.

It is clear from this remark that Wang still believes, with Schopenhauer, that there is a great difference between the achievement of genius, which "transcends not only others' capacity of achievement, but also their capacity of apprehension," and the achievement of talent, which transcends others' capacity of achievement, but not their capacity of apprehension.[36]

The classic exemplar of the poet who writes about the experiences and feelings of the average person, Wang suggests, is Chou Pang-yen. Although his lyrics express ideas that, in Wang's view, are neither novel nor profound, Chou proved highly influential as a lyricist because he chose, in general, to describe the 'worlds of ordinary men'. His works, accordingly, went through many editions, and "everyone from gentlemen on down to women and girls knew the name of Chou Pang-yen."[37]

While the term that, following James J. Y. Liu, I have translated as 'world', *ching-chieh,* had been used casually over the centuries by Chinese critics, Wang was the first to give it anything even remotely resembling a definition. As we have seen, Wang defined a 'world' in poetry as consisting of 'emotion' and 'scene'. To this basic idea, which he had acquired from Wang Fu-chih, Wang Kuo-wei added elements of Wang Shih-chen's theory of 'spirit and tone' (*shen yun*) and Yen Yü's theory of 'inspired gusto' (*hsing-ch'ü*), as well as certain German notions regarding the character of beauty and genius. In Wang Kuo-wei's own opinion, however, the theory of 'worlds' should be considered superior to the theories of earlier critics because, unlike them, it truly "probes the fundamentals [of the art of poetry]."[38]

In the spring of 1907 Lo Chen-yü had recommended Wang Kuo-wei for a position in the Ministry of Education, then headed by the Mongol bannerman Jung-ch'ing. Wang had barely assumed his new duties in Peking, however, when he felt compelled to rush back to Hai-ning, where his wife lay gravely ill; she died shortly after Wang arrived, in the summer of 1907, leaving her husband with three small children (Ch'ien-ming, born in 1899; Kao-ming, born in 1902; and Chen-ming, born in 1905). Returning disconsolately to the capital, Wang worked uneventfully at the Ministry of Education for the next half-year. Early in 1908, however, he was constrained again to hasten back to Hai-ning on family business of the most somber sort, as his stepmother had just passed away. For his own sake as well as for the sake of his children, Wang Kuo-wei's relatives, including his mother-in-law, Mrs. Mo, all urged him on this occasion to take a second wife; on the first of March he was duly wed to the daughter of P'an Tsu-i, a licentiate whose family had been a scholarly one for generations.[39]

Involved as he thus was, in the early months of 1908, with both a funeral and a wedding, Wang probably had little time for scholarly research until he and his family had safely reached Peking and comfortably settled themselves in a new home in Hsin lien-tzu Lane, inside the Hsuan-wu Gate. By the fall of 1908, however, Wang must have completed *Remarks on Lyrics in the World of Men,* since it was published in the *National Essence Journal* (nos. 47, 49, and 50) in the last weeks of 1908 and first weeks of 1909. By the fall of 1908 he had also completed "On the Origins of Drama" ("Hsi-ch'ü k'ao-yuan"), which appeared in the *National Essence Journal* (nos. 48 and 50) at the same time as *Remarks on Lyrics in the World of Men,* as well as a draft of *Catalogue of Plays (Ch'ü lu).*[40] By the latter part of 1908, in short, Wang Kuo-wei's interests had begun to shift from lyrics to drama.

11

Critique of Yuan Drama

During the last five years of the Ch'ing dynasty, Wang Kuo-wei worked in the Ministry of Education's Department of General Affairs. For some time he served as a compiler and translator in the Book Compilation and Translation Office (Pien-i t'u-shu chü), where, among other things, he translated Jevons's widely used textbook *Elementary Lessons in Logic* (1870). The chore of rendering this work into Chinese, we may suppose, was not very difficult for Wang, as he had become by now an accomplished translator of English writings and was familiar with Jevons's thought, which he had studied in 1901–02 during the course of his background reading in Western philosophy. After 1909 Wang served as a compiler on the ministry's Committee for the Compilation of Technical Terms (Pien-ting ming-tz'u kuan), headed by Yen Fu.[1]

During the years that Wang Kuo-wei spent in Peking (1907–1911), Lo Chen-yü spared no effort to advance his protégé's career. When, for example, Lo was made chairman of the Department of Agriculture at Imperial University on the recommendation of Chang Chih-tung, he lost no time proposing to the chancellor of the university that Wang be given a professorial position in the Literature Department. Although Chancellor Liu T'ing-ch'en rejected this proposal, Lo was later able to secure Wang an administrative appointment in the Department of Agriculture.[2]

In addition to recommending Wang for positions, Lo seems to have taken great pains to introduce his protégé to other scholars in the capital. Through Lo Chen-yü, he met at this time the noted bibliophile Miao Ch'üan-sun, whose last post under the empire was that of director of the Metropolitan Library, and the eminent poet-historian K'o Shao-min (1850–1933), chairman of the Classics Department of Imperial University and at one point its acting chancellor. During the last years of the Ch'ing, Wang also came to know the bibliophiles Liu Shih-heng and Wu Ch'ang-shou, both of whom shared his budding interest in drama and helped him to compile *Catalogue of Plays.* He apparently saw a good deal of Chiang Fu, remained on excellent terms with the ubiquitous Fujita Toyohachi (now a professor in Imperial University's Department of Agriculture), and became acquainted with the well-known writer Sun Hsiung (1866–1935), chairman of the Literature Department of Imperial University.[3]

From Lyrics to Drama

Although Wang Kuo-wei was thus employed as an editor, a translator, and an administrator during the closing years of the dynasty, he does not appear to have been overburdened by his responsibilities at the Ministry of Education and Imperial University. On the contrary, they seem to have afforded him ample leisure in which to pursue his own scholarly interests. The most conspicuous corroboration of this comes from Wang himself, who between 1908 and 1911 produced no fewer than seven studies on the latest subject of his intellectual affections, Chinese drama: "On the Origins of Drama," *Catalogue of Plays,* "Anecdotes about Actors" ("Yu yü-lu"), "On the Great Melodies of the Sung" ("Sung ta-ch'ü k'ao"), "Table of the Origins and Evolution of the Modes Used in Drama" ("Ch'ü-tiao yuan-liu piao"), "Miscellaneous Observations on Drama" ("Lu-ch'ü yü-t'an"), and "On the Role System Used in Ancient Drama" ("Ku-chü chiao-se k'ao").[4] According to Kano Naoki, who visited Peking in 1910 as part of a delegation of Kyoto University professors, Wang's enthusiasm for drama at this time was positively infectious.[5]

Most of Wang Kuo-wei's works on drama, like *Remarks on Lyrics in the World of Men,* were published in the *National Essence Journal,* a publication of the Society for the Protection of National Studies (Kuo-hsueh pao-ts'un hui). The aim of this society was to preserve Chinese culture through a variety of means, one of which was the celebration of the empire's literary heritage. While Wang by no means shared the radical political sentiments of the society's leading members, he seems to have been sympathetic to their efforts to keep Han culture alive; no sooner had he finished one of his studies than he would dispatch it to Teng Shih for publication in the *National Essence Journal.*[6]

For some time before he decided to research the early history of Chinese drama, Wang Kuo-wei had contemplated becoming a playwright himself. From Schopenhauer he had acquired, very early on, an extremely high opinion of drama, especially of the tragic variety, "both as regards the greatness of the effect and the difficulty of the achievement," as the philosopher puts it. In one of his literary essays of 1906–07 Wang had suggested, in a Schopenhauerian spirit, that plays can be written only by geniuses who have, in addition, much leisure. According to him, "this explains why the number of poets is so great as to be uncountable, while there is not even one writer of narrative literature for every hundred of them."[7]

Having been made aware, through his reading in German philosophy and aesthetics, of the esteem in which fiction and drama are held in the modern West, Wang had been moved to compare the state of the art of writing plays in China with what he knew about its state abroad. The results had been disastrous for China. "As regards literature of a narrative sort (such as historical poems, drama, and so on, but not prose writing)," Wang had claimed in 1906, "our country is still in a state of infancy . . . Not one of the most excellent pieces of literature in this Far Eastern country with a long literary tradition can compare with the literature of the West. To make it do so is a task for future writers."[8]

During this period Wang Kuo-wei had apparently thought of himself as one of these "future writers," for in 1907 he had declared:

> Because of my success in writing lyrics, I have developed ambitions in the area of drama; this has recently become a great aspiration of mine. However, lyrics (tz'u) are lyrical, whereas drama (hsi-ch'ü) is narrative. They differ, moreover, not only in nature but also in difficulty of execution. How, then, can I dare, on the strength of my success with the former, suddenly hope to succeed with the latter? I do, though, have another, more specific reason for developing ambitions in the field of drama, namely, the fact that drama is the most underdeveloped branch of Chinese literature . . . Even though writers of the present dynasty have on the whole made some progress, their works are immeasurably inferior to famous Western plays. This is why I have disregarded my lack of talent in this area and am single-mindedly contemplating going on to drama.

Despite his avowed interest in writing plays, Wang had, however, entertained serious doubts as to whether he could ever become a successful playwright. "My ambition is greater than my ability, a common failing among men. Thus, I dare not profess to know whether or not I will be able one day to write plays. Even less do I profess to know whether or not, if I do write them, I will be able to do so successfully."[9]

As it happened, Wang Kuo-wei did not become a playwright, successful or otherwise. Instead, he undertook "to study vernacular literature of the Sung and Yuan periods [960–1368] and to gather historical data pertaining to drama," as Wang's future student Wu Ch'i-ch'ang has pointed out.[10] Wang probably did begin his reading of Chinese plays with the idea of writing one himself that would "compare with the literature of the West." But as he started studying the old plays that were still extant, he seems to have discovered his distinctive bent for bibliographical and historical research. Wang's doubts about the extent of his artistic potential in all likelihood served simply to facilitate this discovery.

This view of the process whereby he relinquished his youthful dream of becoming a playwright in favor of conducting bibliographical and historical research on Chinese drama has been partially confirmed by Wang Kuo-wei himself. In the draft preface to *Catalogue of Plays*, dated September 1908, he frankly tells us that he has been prompted to put brush to paper by his concern over the tremendous loss since Ming times of plays and materials pertaining to them.[11] The polished preface, written in June of the following year, voices this concern most explicitly: "I love music and poetry and have some general ideas concerning their development. Distressed that a little of our legacy is being lost every day and fearing that future generations will have no materials on drama, I have extensively investigated ancient documents and compiled this general catalogue." Elsewhere in the same preface he exclaims, "The loss [of plays and catalogues of them] has thus been great indeed; herein lies my reason for undertaking the present compilation."[12]

Hand in hand with bibliographical research went historical research, Wang informs us in a retrospective account of his work on drama written in the winter of 1912–13. "Some time ago I read a number of Yuan plays . . . Immediately I decided to investigate their origins and explain their evolution. I believed that this could be done only by going through the literature of the T'ang, Sung, Liao, and Chin dynasties. I thereupon wrote *Catalogue of Plays* in six chapters (*chüan*), 'On the Origins of Drama' in one chapter, 'On the Great Melodies of the Sung' in one chapter, 'Anecdotes about Actors' in two chapters, 'On the Role System Used in Ancient Drama' in one chapter, and 'Table of the Origins and Evolution of the Modes Used in Drama' in one chapter."[13] Investigating the origins and explaining the evolution of Chinese drama appear to have absorbed much of Wang's attention during the years 1908–1911.

While he was avidly interested in the origins and evolution of Chinese drama, Wang Kuo-wei was by no means oblivious to the style and content of the plays whose history he was studying. On the contrary, he was a critic with strong preferences and prejudices, as we can see from *Sung and Yuan Drama* (*Sung Yuan hsi-ch'ü k'ao*), his last and most important work on drama. Although Wang is said to have written a draft of this book before the Wuchang Uprising, he completed it only in 1912–13. Concerning its genesis Wang has remarked: "One day I realized that there were many things that had not yet been treated either in the works of earlier scholars or in my own work. My notes and ideas, furthermore, were increasing daily. Toward the end of 1912, when in my temporary lodgings [in Kyoto] I had some spare time, I wrote this book in three months."[14] Whether because he wished in the work he knew would be his last on drama to treat things that he had not yet treated or because he had never lost his love of great poetry, Wang offers in *Sung and Yuan Drama*, alone of his many works on drama, a literary critique of the genre.

The Description of Emotions and Scenes in Drama

Like his Ming predecessor Tsang Mao-hsun, Wang Kuo-wei was an aficionado of Yuan plays who looked with disdain on dramatic forms developed in later periods. In *Sung and Yuan Drama,* accordingly, he extols the Yuan dynasty as the golden age of drama. "Yuan drama is the most exquisite creation of its era." "In the case of Yuan literature, there is definitely no genre which can surpass the song form (*ch'ü*) [nondramatic songs (*san-ch'ü*) as well as dramatic ones]." "As regards the song form, Heaven was generous with Yuan writers." "There had been nothing like [Yuan plays] previously, and no one has been able successfully to imitate them since."[15]

Plays written after the Yuan period, by contrast, held no interest for Wang. He declined to attend the theater of his own day, presumably because Yuan plays were no longer enacted, and once tried to dissuade Aoki Masaru (1887–1964) from writing *A History of Chinese Drama in Modern Times* (*Shina kinsei gikyoku shi*) with these words: "There is nothing worth studying from the Ming period onward. Yuan drama is a living literature, while Ming and Ch'ing drama is a dead literature."[16]

The basic thesis of those chapters of *Sung and Yuan Drama* that deal with drama from a strictly literary perspective is that the particular excellence of Yuan plays is to be found not in their plots, which are clumsy and jejune, but in the beauty of the language of their songs, or arias. Now, there is nothing extraordinary about this view from a historical standpoint; many Yuan and Ming critics, such as Chou Te-ch'ing, Chu Ch'üan, Wang Chi-te, Shen Te-fu, and Tsang Mao-hsun, had reached similar conclusions many years before Wang Kuo-wei arrived on the scene. His critical assessment of the literary merits and demerits of Yuan drama is quite surprising, however, when placed within the context of Wang's own earlier pronouncements on the subject.

In earlier years Wang had repeatedly declared that Chinese plays are inferior to Western ones because of their inability to portray human character, develop a plot, structure a story, and convey sophisticated ideas. The only decent thing about Chinese drama, he had said in 1906, is its language, a feature that did not then strike him as important. "Although the language of Yuan drama is aesthetically pleasing, Yuan playwrights do not know how to describe human character. *The Peach Blossom Fan* (*T'ao-hua shan*), written in the present dynasty, does, it is true, contain good character delineations, but this certainly cannot be said of other plays. Chinese plays are, in short, nothing more than slightly structured lyrics which have, however, lost the character of lyrics." In 1907 he had remarked in a similar spirit: "There are today still extant one hundred Yuan and Ming plays. While their language is occasionally superb, their ideas and structure are undeniably naive and clumsy."[17] It was, indeed, precisely the "undeniably naive and clumsy" nature of Chinese plays that had kindled in Wang the desire to become a playwright himself.

In 1912–13, however, we find Wang in *Sung and Yuan Drama* casually dismissing as minor flaws the same elements of Yuan drama that he had previously regarded as damning defects. "The clumsiness of the plots of Yuan plays will not concern us here," he announces offhandedly. "Such clumsiness arose from the fact that in those days this aspect of drama was not stressed. [Playwrights] therefore often modeled themselves on one another or simply wrote sketchily." Wang now maintains that the language of Yuan drama is, after all, its best as well as its most important aspect. "The most excellent feature of Yuan drama is neither its ideas nor its structure but its language."[18]

Wang Kuo-wei's dramatic volte-face was probably inspired by his growing appreciation, during his years of reading and writing lyrics, of the formal features of poetry. In 1907, we recall, he had in fact devoted an entire essay to the subject of elegance of style, as distinct from beauty of content, in literary works. In this essay Wang had even gone so far as to claim that, regardless of content, a work of literature may attain through careful craftsmanship a certain formal beauty that has its own independent value and that may be admired for its own sake. It is thus entirely possible that his interest in what he referred to as "the beauty of the form of the beauty of the form" of Sung lyrics, the direct ancestor of Yuan songs, eventually led him to see the language of Yuan plays in a new light.[19]

Wherein does the particular excellence of the language of Yuan drama lie? Wang inquires. "It lies, in a word, in its naturalness (*tzu-jan*)." Warming to his subject, he declares:

> All great literature is superior because of its naturalness, and nowhere is this more evident than in the case of Yuan songs. The Yuan playwrights

were none of them of high social standing or even greatly learned; their purpose in writing plays was not to store them in famous mountains for posterity. They simply wrote as the spirit moved them in order to amuse themselves and others. They did not think about the clumsiness of their plots, did not avoid expressing vulgar ideas, and did not pay attention to the contradictions they created in their characters. They merely copied down the emotions in their breasts and recorded the circumstances of the age, with the result that frequently genuine truths and an elegant style can be found in their works. Yuan songs may thus be called China's most natural literature. Naturalness of language was a necessary result or concomitant of these characteristics of Yuan playwrights and their method of composition.[20]

The erstwhile weaknesses of Yuan drama, which Wang had previously execrated unmercifully, have in this new account become actual strengths of a sort in that they result "necessarily" in a natural kind of language.

According to Wang Kuo-wei, both northern drama (tsa-chü) and southern drama (nan-hsi, hsi-wen) of the Yuan period are distinguished by the naturalness of their language. "In describing emotions they pierce one to the heart, in describing scenes they bring them right before one's ears and eyes, and in narrating events they make one think that the actual personages themselves are speaking." The "only" difference between northern and southern drama is that the former is "tragic, sublime, profound, and vigorous," whereas the latter is "fresh, gentle, intricate, and sophisticated."[21]

That Yuan drama excels at the description of emotions and scenes as well as at the narration of events Wang Kuo-wei attributes to certain stylistic innovations introduced into the genre in its earliest stages of development. The most important of these, in his view, was the use of colloquial expressions in the arias of plays. "In ancient literature the classical language (ku-yü) was generally used to describe things; the colloquial language (su-yü) was by no means ever used. The number of characters used in a piece of ancient literature, moreover, was never very great; only in Yuan songs, because of the permissibility of using nonmetric words (ch'en-tzu), was it suddenly possible to describe things with many colloquial words and natural sounds. This is something which had never occurred in ancient literature."[22]

Since 1905, as we know, Wang had been captivated by lyrics (tz'u), which, with their lines of unequal length and limited use of colloquial language elements, had introduced into poetry an air of naturalness absent, as a rule, from regular poems (shih). With the song (ch'ü), the irregularity of line length and the use of colloquial expressions were further extended by the insertion of nonmetric words. The new metrical structure devised by the Yuan playwrights, critics agree, imparts to their arias a heightened sense of vitality, freedom, and naturalness. Wang Kuo-wei, for one, was so enthusiastic about the stylistic innovations made by Yuan dramatists that he went so far as to suggest that "as regards Yuan drama, truly a new language was freely employed in a new genre. This has occurred only three times in our country's literary history: with the poetry of Ch'u, with the Buddhist scriptures, and with [Yuan drama]."[23]

In *Sung and Yuan Drama* Wang Kuo-wei offers us many examples of describing emotions so movingly that one is pierced to the heart, describing scenes so vividly that one imagines one had seen them oneself, and narrating events with such verisimilitude that one believes the actual personages themselves to be speaking. To illustrate excellence in the expression of emotions and narration of events, Wang cites, for instance, the eloquent passage from act 2 of *Injustice to Tou O* (*Tou O yuan*) in which Tou O advises her mother-in-law to forget Old Chang (who has mistakenly been poisoned by his own son).

> It's no use grieving; you really have no understanding.
> Birth and death are part of transmigration.
> Some fall sick, some encounter hard times,
> Some catch a chill, some suffer rheumatic fever,
> Some die of hunger, overeating, or overwork;
> Each knows his own lot.
> Human life is ruled by Heaven and Earth;
> How can one substitute years for another person?
> Our life-span is not determined in this world.
> You and he were together only for a few days;
> What is there to speak of in terms of one family?
> Besides, there is neither sheep, wine, silk, money, nor other
>   wedding gifts.
> Clenching our hands, we work and go on,
> Letting loose the hand, it is the end of life.
> It is not that I am contrary; only I fear what others may say.
> It is better to heed my advice and regard the whole thing as poor
>   luck.
> Sacrifice for him a coffin and secure several pieces of cotton and
>   silk;
> Get him out of our house and send him to his grave.
> This one is not a marriage contracted from your young age;
> I really do not care and cannot shed half a drop of tear.
> Do not be so overcome with grief,
> Sigh or wail like this![24]

"This song is so colloquial in style," Wang marvels, "that it leads one to forget that it is indeed a song. Most of the so-called authentic dramatists (*tang-hang chia*) of the early Yuan period wrote in this manner. From the middle of the dynasty onward, however, dramatists seldom wrote like this." In a passage such as the above, written by the gifted playwright Kuan Han-ch'ing (c. 1220–1300) during the heyday of Yuan drama, "every word is as clear as a picture, and the language contains limitless meanings beyond the words themselves."[25]

No one, in Wang Kuo-wei's view, has ever been able to describe the feelings of separated lovers more movingly than Cheng Kuang-tsu (c. 1280–1330). As an example of Cheng's virtuosity, he cites passages from act 3 of *Ch'ien-nü's Soul Leaves Her Body* (*Ch'ien-nü li-hun*) that reveal the heroine's ennui and lovesickness.

> When I lie down I cannot sleep;
> Of food and drink I cannot tell the taste,
> No use the medicines I take,
> There is no cure.
> I know this secret sickness,
> When it began.
> If I am to be well again,
> It will not be till I see him.
> One moment I am floating,
> Bereft of my soul,
> The next all is clear,
> And I am myself—
> Then all is confusion again,
> And I cannot tell Heaven from Earth.
> . . . .
> The days grow long, and longer my sorrows;
> The blossoms grow scarce, and scarcer his letters.
> . . . .
> Suddenly spring has come and gone and you have not returned.
> . . . .
> Though I say we are parted scores of years,
> Though separated ten thousand miles,
> To count the days till his return
> I have made marks in the bamboo grove on every emerald
>   stalk.[26]

According to Wang, these lines are so perfect that no further refinement is desirable or even possible; they are perfectly natural and thus naturally perfect. "Later writers, however, were unable to attain the level of such predecessors [as Cheng Kuang-tsu]. Of southern plays, only the *Moon Prayer Pavilion* (*Pai-yueh t'ing*) and the *Lute* (*P'i-p'a chi*) come close."[27]

Because Wang Kuo-wei, like many earlier drama critics, believes the *Lute* to be superior to the *Moon Prayer Pavilion*, he has little to say about the latter. His main objection to the *Moon Prayer Pavilion* is that it is too imitative, its best parts being "largely adapted from Kuan Han-ch'ing's play" of the same name. Nevertheless, it is not, in Wang's view, without moving, intricate, and elaborate scenes. "The emotions evoked and the language used to evoke them," he even suggests, "are so well fused (*hsieh*) that only a playwright of the Yuan period could have produced this work. Thus, even if the *Moon Prayer Pavilion* was not written by Shih Hui, it must have been written by another talented hand of Yuan times."[28]

In Wang's estimation, the best examples of excellence in the expression of emotion and depiction of events to be found in southern drama are contained in the *Lute*, a play that he praises for its originality in the area of phraseology. The highlight of the play, he suggests, is the scene titled "Eating Husks." This scene is so wrenching that the story had long circulated that, when Kao Ming wrote it, the candles by whose flickering light the playwright labored were so moved that their flames merged into one another. This apocryphal anecdote demonstrates, Wang says, that "from very early on this scene has been considered to have been divinely inspired. Places which approximate this one are not lacking in this play. Unfortunately, playwrights from the Ming period onward could not reach the level of this sort of writing. Therefore, although a distinction is made between northern and southern drama, both belong to the Yuan period."[29]

In the absence of elaborate scenery, much stage-setting in Yuan drama was accomplished through descriptions given by the actors in song. To illustrate excellence in the description of scenes Wang Kuo-wei cites the following passage from act 3 of Ma Chih-yuan's (c. 1250–1323) *Autumn in the Han Palace* (*Han kung ch'iu*):

> Before me lie the bleak and ravaged plains,
> The grass has yellowed, stricken by the frost,
> The mottled coats of dogs grow gray and shaggy.
> Men raise their tassled lances in the chase,
> And horses struggle under heavy loads.
> Wagons bear provisions for the journey,
> And all is ready for the hunt to start.
> She, yes, she brokenhearted said good-bye;
> I, yes, I took her hand and climbed the bridge.
> She and her train ride into the desert;
> I in my carriage return now to the palace.
> I return now to the palace and pass the wall,

I pass the wall and follow a twisting lane,
A twisting lane that leads close to her room,
Close to her room where the moon grows dusky;
The moon grows dusky and the night turns cold,
The night turns cold and the cicadas weep.
The cicadas weep by green-curtained windows,
By green-curtained windows that feel nothing.
To feel nothing! Only a man of steel
Could feel nothing. No! Even a man of steel
In grief would shed a thousand trickling tears.
Tonight I'll hang her portrait in the palace
And have a service chanted for her there.
Then I'll lift high the silver candlestick
And let the light fall on her painted form.

. . . .

I must make some excuse, tell my council
I cannot meet them. They will want to prate
Of state affairs. I cannot bear to talk.
Without her here in flower-like loveliness
What solace do my palace gardens offer?
No doubt she often pauses, paces to and fro,
Irresolute; then suddenly she hears
Caw! Caw! the cries of southward-flying geese:
But all that fills my eyes is sheep and kine,
The sound I heard was but the creaking wheels
Of the felt-covered cart bearing its load
Of sorrow up the slopes of northern hills.[30]

After giving up his favorite consort, Lady Chao-chün, to the Tartar (Hsiung-nu) chief, the grief-stricken emperor returns to his empty palace. We may speculate that Wang Kuo-wei admires this passage because its images deftly combine the functions of description of scenery and expression of emotion: they disclose the emperor's sense of despondency and desolation while simultaneously indicating the season—early autumn, when the nights turn cold and the geese fly south. As he had suggested in *Remarks on Lyrics in the World of Men*, "all descriptions of scenes are also descriptions of emotions" in poetry of the highest order.[31]

It is not surprising that Wang Kuo-wei chooses to cite as exemplifications of excellence in the description of emotions, scenes, and events passages from *Injustice to Tou O, Ch'ien-nü's Soul Leaves Her Body,* and *Autumn in the Han Palace* since Kuan Han-ch'ing, Cheng Kuang-tsu, and Ma Chih-yuan are three of his four favorite dramatists (the fourth is Po P'u, 1226–1313?). He thinks most highly of Kuan: "[Kuan

Han-ch'ing's] language minutely describes human emotions and every word is genuine (*pen-se*); he may therefore be regarded as the greatest dramatist of the Yuan period." The plays of Po P'u and Ma Chih-yuan Wang describes as "elegant and powerful; their emotions are profound and their language lucid." About Cheng he observes: "Cheng Kuang-tsu's style is beautiful and his sentiments romantic. His works have their own distinctive flavor He is equally qualified to rank in the first class of dramatists." It is Wang Kuo-wei's firm conviction that "the works of all other dramatists never went beyond those of these four individuals."[32]

Wang's conception of poetry, we may conclude, did not undergo any appreciable change between the time he wrote *Remarks on Lyrics in the World of Men* and the time he wrote *On Sung and Yuan Drama.* In the latter work, as in the former, Wang commends language that is 'natural', 'genuine', and 'not veiled' (from the reader). He also praises poetry that describes true emotions and true scenes. From this per-spective, we may regard *On Sung and Yuan Drama* as a sort of pendant to Wang Kuo-wei's earlier writings on literature.

Tragedy in Chinese Drama

Although by 1912–13 he had outgrown many of the ideas he had acquired from Schopenhauer, Wang still believed, following the phi-losopher, that tragedy represents the highest possible poetic achieve-ment. In *The World as Will and Representation,* we recall, Schopenhauer insists that art performs no greater service than to suggest, by de-picting life's terrible side, that men renounce the world. Wang had been so enthralled with this view of literature that already in 1904 he had attempted to evaluate some Chinese plays on the basis of Scho-penhauer's aesthetic principles.

In his "Critique of *Dream of the Red Chamber,*" written in 1904, Wang had paused long enough in his analysis of the novel to make some observations on Chinese drama. The thrust of his remarks on that occasion had been the suggestion that Chinese drama, unlike its Western counterpart, lacks a tragic dimension. This fatal flaw he had attributed to the damnable optimism of the Chinese people them-selves. "The spirit of our people is this-worldly and optimistic. Plays and novels of ancient times that exemplify this spirit are, without exception, all infused with this optimism; they begin sadly but end happily, begin with separation but end with reunion, begin with hard-ship but end with good fortune. Unless he writes according to this [formula, a Chinese writer] finds it difficult to satisfy his readers' cravings."[33]

The most conspicuous examples of this proclivity of Chinese dramatists to write plays according to the happily-ever-after formula, Wang had suggested, are *Peony Pavilion* (*Mu-tan t'ing*) and *The Palace of Eternal Life* (*Ch'ang-sheng tien*), in both of which love defies death itself. *The Romance of the Western Chamber* (*Hsi-hsiang chi*) also ends on entirely too cheery a note, he had said. While maintaining that the last part of Wang Shih-fu's (fl. 1295–1307) great work, the so-called Continuation, was written by another hand, Wang Kuo-wei had not thought it likely that the original author could have conceived an ending any better than the one we now have. "If this work had been completed [by Wang Shih-fu himself], I wonder whether his ending would not have been as superficial and vulgar as the 'Continuation' to *The Romance of the Western Chamber*."[34]

Using Schopenhauer's criteria, Wang had been hard pressed in 1904 to find any real tragedies among Chinese plays. The only play that he had regarded as approximating a tragedy is *The Peach Blossom Fan*, written by the early Ch'ing playwright K'ung Shang-jen (1648–1718). "In all our literature, only *The Peach Blossom Fan* and *Dream of the Red Chamber* are imbued with a spirit of pessimism and emancipation." The former work cannot, however, in the last analysis be considered a genuine tragedy, Wang had said.

> The emancipation depicted in *The Peach Blossom Fan* is not true emancipation. Despite all the changes that he either witnessed or experienced, [Hou Fang-yü] was unable to attain enlightenment on his own, and yet he became enlightened on hearing Chang the Taoist utter one sentence. That [Hou] should suddenly give up [Li Hsiang-chün] because of one sentence from Chang the Taoist after he has, for her sake, willingly undergone the rigors of hundreds of miles of travel, taken unpredictable risks, and even landed in jail strains the credulity of all but a small child. Therefore, whereas the emancipation depicted in *Dream of the Red Chamber* is convincing, the emancipation depicted in *The Peach Blossom Fan* is implausible.[35]

Of particular interest to us in this assessment of K'ung Shang-jen's play is the Schopenhauerian standpoint from which it is made. We recall that, according to Schopenhauer, the essence of tragedy lies in the conversion of the hero's will induced by either personal suffering or, in the case of truly saintly persons, the mere observation of the suffering of others. From his comments on *The Peach Blossom Fan* it is clear that, in 1904, Wang Kuo-wei had fully subscribed to the Schopenhauerian proposition that spiritual conversion is a necessary requirement—indeed, the supreme achievement—of tragedy; what is at stake in these comments is not the necessity of K'ung's inducing resignation in Hou Fang-yü but merely the plausibility of the way in which he achieves the required effect.

We have dwelled at some length on Wang Kuo-wei's earliest views on Chinese drama because it is not until 1908–09 that, in *Remarks on Lyrics in the World of Men,* he again says anything about plays, and what he says is very little. "Po P'u's play *Rain on the Wu-t'ung Trees (Wu-t'ung yü)* is profound, vigorous, tragic, and sublime. It represents the supreme achievement of Yuan drama." In 1910, in his "Miscellaneous Observations on Drama," he is slightly more expansive. "I may mention here three great masterpieces of Yuan drama: Ma Chih-yuan's *Autumn in the Han Palace,* Po P'u's *Rain on the Wu-t'ung Trees,* and Cheng Kuang-tsu's *Ch'ien-nü's Soul Leaves Her Body.* Ma's play is vigorous and strong, Po's is tragic and sublime, and Cheng's is delicate and romantic. They are all timeless works of great excellence. If we were to place these two [*sic*] plays on the right side of a scale and all other works of Yuan literature on the left side, I suspect that the scale would tilt toward the right." By 1912–13, in *Sung and Yuan Drama,* he is almost effusive.

> Although from Ming times onward all plays (*ch'uan-ch'i*) have been comedies, the Yuan dynasty produced some tragedies. As regards those which are still extant, plays such as *Autumn in the Han Palace, Rain on the Wu-t'ung Trees, Dream of Western Shu (Hsi Shu meng), Minister Chieh Tzu-t'ui (Chieh Tzu-t'ui),* and *Killing the Wife of a Sworn Brother (T'i sha ch'i)* are not written according to [the conventional formula of] beginning with separation but ending with reunion, beginning with hardship but ending with good fortune. Those plays most imbued with the tragic spirit are Kuan Han-ch'ing's *Injustice to Tou O* and Chi Chün-hsiang's *Chao Family Orphan (Chao shih ku-erh).* While these plays contain scheming villains, courageous acts are still performed through the heroes' assertion of will. They may be ranked among the world's great tragedies.[36]

It is from the foregoing remarks that we are constrained to deduce Wang Kuo-wei's view of tragedy in the 1908–1913 period. To begin with, we may observe that in the winter of 1912–13 Wang has no difficulty identifying a whole handful of tragic plays, even though in 1904 he had found not a single one worthy of the designation. We may note as well that in thus discovering some Chinese plays that "may be ranked among the world's great tragedies," he is far more charitable as a critic in 1912–13 than in previous years, when he had insisted that no works by native playwrights could "compare with the literature of the West." By what criteria, one may justifiably wonder, has Wang arrived at the conclusion, in 1912–13, that China possesses no fewer than seven plays fully informed with the tragic spirit?

While in Western aesthetics there are, of course, many different conceptions of tragedy, it seems safe to assume that Wang Kuo-wei was intimately familiar only with Schopenhauer's. In the earliest years of this century, we recall, he had acquired a good grasp of the philosopher's theory of tragedy, he had admired it greatly, and he had analyzed China's most famous novel (as well as the ending of a popular Ch'ing play) in terms of it. If we are able to find any theoretical underpinning to Wang's view of tragedy in the years 1908–1913, it will probably be Schopenhauerian in inspiration.

Despite the titillating comment about "the heroes' assertion of will," anyone familiar with the seven plays in question will have to conclude that by the time he wrote *On Sung and Yuan Drama* Wang had cast a large part of Schopenhauer's theory to the winds. Although he appears still to put much stock in suffering, Wang no longer insists that suffering must have the "purpose" of inducing resignation in the hero. In all of the seven plays that Wang considers tragedies, the protagonists suffer mightily, but their suffering typically leads merely to more suffering, or to their deaths; only the loyal but unappreciated minister Chieh Tzu-t'ui, who ends his days as a recluse on Mount Mien, might be said to have attained enlightenment in the Schopenhauerian sense.

Calling these seven plays tragedies even by some other, non-Schopenhauerian conception of tragedy is problematic, as Ch'ien Chung-shu pointed out some decades ago.[37] It is obvious that in 1912–13 Wang Kuo-wei is able to discover so many "tragic" Yuan plays only because he has widened his own Schopenhauerian definition of tragedy to include any play that contains a sense of injustice or ends on a note of despair. Thus, for instance, the titular heroine of *Injustice to Tou O,* although vindicated posthumously, is put to death for a murder she did not commit. In *Killing the Wife of a Sworn Brother* the famous Judge Pao, in an act of uncharacteristic harshness, sentences the butcher Chang Ch'ien to death because, in order to save the life of a close friend, he has been forced to take that of his friend's wife (she had intended to murder her spouse). While *The Chao Family Orphan* ends on an upbeat note, most of the play concerns the villainous minister Tu-an Ku, who unjustly puts three hundred members of the Chao lineage to the sword, and the honorable men who sacrifice their own lives for the sake of the orphan. The emperors in *Autumn in the Han Palace* and *Rain on the Wu-t'ung Trees,* who have lost their consorts through political circumstances beyond their control, pass their days in deep despair and aching remorse, and Liu Pei in *Dream of Western Shu* grieves day and night for his two sworn brothers, Chang Fei and Kuan Yü, who have died on the battlefield.

Wang's definition of tragedy, we may conclude, by 1912–13 was considerably broader than it had been in earlier years. However, he continued to maintain that tragedy, broadly construed, represents the highest achievement of the human spirit. We may thus assume that, when he wrote *On Sung and Yuan Drama*, Wang still subscribed to the Schopenhauerian belief that writers who place their protagonists in difficult, unhappy situations and impossible impasses have aimed at a truth more meaningful philosophically as well as more gratifying aesthetically than have those who offer their characters a way out of their problems, allowing them to live happily ever after.

Of *Sung and Yuan Drama* Wang Kuo-wei had a very high opinion. "All of the materials [used in this work] have been collected by me, and the theories advanced in it for the most part have also been conceived by me. The world's study of this subject [Chinese drama] has begun with me, and the greatest contribution to this subject has been this work." Unlike his predecessors and older contemporaries, who (as he said) "all despised drama and would not discuss it," Wang was enabled by his study of Western philosophy and philosophical aesthetics to free himself from the traditionally contemptuous Chinese view of drama.[38] Well over a decade before Hu Shih, Ku Chieh-kang, and Yü P'ing-po set out to raise the status of vernacular literature, accordingly, he had begun to proclaim the dignity of traditional literary works that either are written in a vernacular style, such as novels, or contain vernacular elements, such as lyrics and plays. By doing so, Wang Kuo-wei unwittingly began that reappraisal of the Chinese literary heritage that would reach its culmination in the Literary Revolution of the late teens and early twenties.

12

Conservative Commitments

"Conservatism" is a richly ambiguous word that, with reference to modern China, one is well advised to use in the plural. We may discriminate, for example, as Benjamin I. Schwartz has done, between sociopolitical conservatism and cultural conservatism, and between happy and unhappy modes of conservatism.[1] Because the conservatism of one Chinese intellectual may thus have little in common with that of another, it is essential to a discussion of any variety of Chinese conservatism to specify the ideas and tendencies with which it is associated, the period in which it flourished, and the persons in whom it is chiefly exemplified.

The kind of conservatism with which the name of Wang Kuo-wei is identified after 1911 rests on a romantic attachment to the past that is, however, closely linked to scholarly concerns and by no means based on an uncritical acceptance of traditional assumptions and values. Unlike most Chinese conservatisms, which typically affirm certain aspects of the cultural tradition but rarely evidence any serious commitment to the traditional political order, this type of conservatism embraces all three orientations in the Confucian project: Confucianism as a way of life, Confucianism as a mode of scholarship, and Confucianism as a political ideology. Conservatism of this sort is at bottom an enlightened effort to conserve both the ideals and the literature (the two are intimately related) of the past.[2]

Despite its affirmation of the past in toto, the mode of conservatism with which we are concerned is nevertheless a conservatism of despair. Emerging in dialectical reaction to the 1911 Revolution, it flourished for two decades in a "revolutionary" milieu hostile to traditional ideals. Intellectuals such as Wang Kuo-wei, his friends Shen Tseng-chih and K'o Shao-min, and his mentor Lo Chen-yü, who exemplify this distinctive strain of conservatism, are genuinely committed to the culture of the past—indeed, single-mindedly devoted to preserving it and presenting the best possible defense of it—but dubious about the power of the culture of the past to influence contemporary society. Theirs is thus an unhappy mode of conservatism distinguished by its belief in the worthfulness, but not the efficacy, of traditional values.

Reformulation of Principles

Although he had reportedly completed a draft of *Sung and Yuan Drama* in 1911, Wang Kuo-wei had no opportunity to revise his manuscript later in that year owing to the turmoil into which Peking was thrown by the Wuchang Uprising. It would be difficult to overstate the effect that the political developments of late 1911–early 1912, in particular the Hsuan-t'ung Emperor's abdication, were to have on Wang: as time would show, they were decisively to influence the entire spectrum of both his personal and his scholarly commitments. Of crucial relevance as well to the subsequent direction of his life was Lo Chen-yü, whose own values, interests, and aspirations began at this time to be clearly reflected in those of his protégé.

Wang's initial reaction to the Wuchang Uprising, as recalled many years later by Lo Chen-yü, was the same as his own, namely, to remain in Peking at all costs. "When the Wuchang Uprising occurred, residents of the capital became fearful. At that time my late friend Mr. Wang Kuo-wei was also at the Ministry of Education. We each pledged to store grain and salt and vowed not to quit Peking. If by any chance anything untoward were to happen, we swore that we would die." Yuan Shih-k'ai's reentry into Ch'ing politics, however, seems rapidly to have diminished their enthusiasm for this particular plan. "When Yuan Shih-k'ai again appeared on the scene," Lo subsequently recollected, "men became somewhat calmer. I, however, realized that the situation had actually become more critical than before."[3] Wang, too, seems to have entertained no illusions about Yuan's intentions.[4]

Finding the political situation unbearable after Yuan Shih-k'ai's recall to power, Lo Chen-yü was pleased to receive one fall day a visit from a monk belonging to the Nishi Honganji Temple in Japan.

> This monk said that his religious master [Ōtani Kōzui, the Chief Abbot] wished to advise me to go abroad and to offer me and my family the use of his house in Sumiyoshi eki. Although I was not acquainted with Count Ōtani, I was moved by his generosity. Before I had given him my response, however, I received letters from my old friends at Kyoto University—Professors Naitō Torajirō, Kano Naoki, and Tomioka Kenzo— inviting me to come to Kyoto. My private library, being large, could be sent to the university library, they suggested. They also said that they would get a house ready for me. I thereupon discussed the matter with my late friend Mr. Fujita, who recommended that I accept the invitation

of the professors. The Nishi Honganji Temple could assume responsibility for the shipping of my books and artifacts to Kyoto; I could be reimbursed for the shipping costs when I reached Kyoto. Mr. Fujita moreover proposed that he precede me to Japan in order to get everything ready for my arrival. Thus it was decided.[5]

Bundling up his own family, as well as those of his protégé, Wang Kuo-wei, and his son-in-law, Liu Ta-shen (the son of his late friend Liu E), Lo Chen-yü and his sizable party set sail for Japan in November.[6]

Lo Chen-yü had, it seemed to him, eminently good reason to hurl himself and his loved ones into exile in November 1911. By conviction his sympathies had always lain with the empire's Manchu overlords, to the restoration of whose rule he would in later years, with Japanese accomplices, sedulously devote himself. As a conservative modernizer working either for or alongside Chang Chih-tung during the twilight years of the dynasty, Lo had been as firmly wedded to the "Chinese values–foreign techniques" (t'i-yung) approach to reform as had been the author of Exhortation to Learn. This approach involved, we recall, a simultaneous commitment to basic Confucian moral and political principles and to the rectification of China's shortcomings in the "practical" sphere through the selective importation of foreign agricultural, educational, commercial, and military methods. Like other conservative reformers of his day, Lo Chen-yü had sought to graft a modest number of technological innovations onto a fundamentally Confucian society, the continued vitality of whose values he had always been at pains to reaffirm.

It is not difficult, therefore, to imagine the revulsion with which Lo, as a champion of the most cherished ideals of traditional Chinese culture, including the monarchic constitution of the state, had met the burgeoning revolutionary group's persistent demands for a Western-style republic. Filled with disquiet over the prospects for China's future, he had, as a matter of fact, even before the Wuchang Uprising, lost his zeal for modernization and had begun instead to devote an increasing amount of his time to the acquisition and examination of antiquities.[7] The military and political developments of late 1911, the news that his friend Tuan-fang had been assassinated, and the collapse of the Ch'ing early in 1912 appear, in retrospect, to have had the collective effect of intensifying Lo's political commitments; from the bleak winter of 1911–12 onward, he would regard himself, as Confucian tradition demanded, as a loyal minister of the defunct dynasty.[8]

His inveterate disgust with politics and politicians constrains us to infer Wang Kuo-wei's youthful political outlook from the substance of his views on, and the fact of his personal involvement in, the government-sponsored reform program of 1901–1911. It nevertheless seems safe to suggest that Lo Chen-yü's protégé had tacitly placed himself, like his mentor, in the reformist camp of Chang Chih-tung. Concerning the educational program that the governor-general and his confrères had devised in the opening years of this century, Wang had, it is true, entertained serious reservations—reservations that he had not refrained from airing publicly in articles published over several years. Wang's had been, however, the voice of what might be called the loyal opposition; there is no evidence to suggest that he had ever rejected Chang's program in principle. On the contrary, Wang, who had been for an entire decade involved in agricultural and educational projects conceived by conservative modernizers, seems from the first to have embraced the reformers' premise that what China required was cautious, piecemeal change directed from above, not a violent overthrow of the empire's political system from below. That aspect of Chang's program of which Wang had been critical was not its underlying rationale, which as an intellectual elitist deeply imbued with Confucian political culture he seems never to have questioned, but rather its content, which he had endeavored to persuade the governor-general to modify in certain particulars.[9]

As was the case with Lo Chen-yü, the 1911 Revolution appears to have had the effect on Wang Kuo-wei of clarifying and intensifying ideas he had in all likelihood developed prior to it but had never committed to paper. There can be no doubt that Wang, from early youth a rigorist, was deeply troubled by the unprincipled behavior of many of his compatriots in the chaotic months immediately preceding the Hsuan-t'ung Emperor's abdication. Grieved by the publication of what he felt to be calumnies on the integrity of Empress Dowager Lung-yü (about whom he would later compose a long poem to vindicate posthumously that lady's fair name), Wang was also appalled by Yuan Shih-k'ai's treasonable betrayal of his dynasty's interests during the last months of its existence.[10] Disturbing to him as well was the brazen murder of Tuan-fang by his own mutinous troops at the height of the anti-Ch'ing revolution. Of Tuan-fang himself, a conservative modernizer who fully subscribed to Chang Chih-tung's reform philosophy, Wang entertained a high opinion, regarding that gentleman as both cultured and honorable. The renegade character of Tuan-fang's men, their macabre dismemberment of his corpse, and their brutal slaying of Tuan-fang's brother (who had attempted to rescue him), as one can well imagine, filled Wang with profound unease. For months afterward he brooded over the tragic incident, thinking the distressing thoughts he would record for posterity the following year in a lengthy poem titled "The Road to Shu Is Hard" ("Shu tao nan").[11]

In the months immediately preceding and following the Hsuan-t'ung Emperor's abdication, Wang seems to have been much concerned with what might be called the ethical implications of the revolution for an upright individual such as himself. It must have been around the time of Tuan-fang's death, as he helplessly watched his world crumbling around him, that Wang Kuo-wei committed himself irrevocably to the nobly motivated eremitism of the unyielding man of principle.

His decision to embrace Po-i's ideal of purity did not, however, represent a wholly new departure in Wang's thinking but was rather a natural extension of certain moral orientations that he had developed prior to the revolution.[12] Years before the demise of the dynasty Wang had revealed himself to be deeply enamored of the lofty and austere moral philosophies of Kant and Schopenhauer, and from his early classical training he was, moreover, intimately familiar with the moral principles that had actuated the ancient martyrs whose deeds are applauded in the Four Books. Wang was also, as we have seen, much attracted to works of popular literature that, like *Injustice to Tou O* and *The Chao Family Orphan,* praise the moral courage of persons who, at the cost of their lives, refuse to compromise their principles or that, like *Dream of the Red Chamber* and *Minister Chieh Tzu-t'ui,* commend the eremitic ideal. It is, then, perhaps not to be wondered that, when he felt himself challenged by the revolution to clarify and articulate his own moral code, Wang vowed henceforward, come what may, to walk the path of integrity, honor, propriety, and righteousness. To his friend Kano Naoki he confided with satisfaction in mid-1912, just months after he had resolved his future course of conduct:

> I, too, for half my life drifted aimlessly;
> All kinds of opinions and positions I adopted whimsically.
> Not until I had experienced many sorrows and seen many places
> Did I realize that this Way is as lofty as Mounts Heng and
>   Sung.[13]

In view of Wang's subsequent suicidal thoughts and eventual suicide, we may here remind ourselves that Confucianism, despite its affirmation of life, concedes that under extraordinary circumstances it may be necessary, even laudable, to sacrifice life. When a gentleman is constrained, for example, to choose between life and virtue, he may, declare Confucius and Mencius, honorably opt for the latter. Although his uncompromising adherence after 1911 to the tenets of

Confucian morality would commit him for many years only to that life of intense scholarship typical of the Confucian eremite, it is thus understandable that Wang's determination to act in accordance with what he considered to be fundamental principles would, in the end, lead him to commit suicide. It is, indeed, precisely because of his intense devotion, during his last fifteen years, to traditional moral notions that his friend Aoki Masaru has viewed this phase of Wang's life, in its ethical dimension, as a seamless whole. Wang Kuo-wei's journey to K'un-ming Lake, into whose chilly waters he would cast himself in 1927, thus actually began, in Aoki's opinion, in the winter of 1911–12, when he set his moral compass and composed the poem "I-ho Park" ("I-ho yuan tz'u").[14]

A Threnody for the Ch'ing

"I-ho Park," which Wang wrote shortly after landing in Japan, is at once a threnody for the Ch'ing dynasty and an elaborate eulogy to Empress Dowager Tz'u-hsi. From an overview of political developments during the Hsien-feng and T'ung-chih periods (1851–1874), which witnessed Tz'u-hsi's rise to power, the poem drifts into a detailed description of the empress dowager's summer retreat and thence to an extended depiction of her involvement in, and direction of, governmental affairs during the turbulent half-century she was destined to guide the foundering Chinese ship of state. Like the account of Tz'u-hsi written by Chang Erh-t'ien (1874–1945), a prominent Ch'ing loyalist and subsequently an intimate friend of Wang Kuo-wei, "I-ho Park" attempts to refute the libels of the empress dowager that K'ang Yu-wei, Liang Ch'i-ch'ao, and their sympathizers had found it expedient to publish after the failure of the Hundred Days' Reform.[15]

In view of the site of Wang's eventual suicide, it is undoubtedly significant that already in 1912 he has developed an intense emotional attachment to I-ho Park (especially K'un-ming Lake and Wan-shou Hill), which he associates with Tz'u-hsi in particular and her dynasty in general. It is also undoubtedly significant, in view of Wang's friendship with noted Ch'ing loyalists during the teens and his own service at "court" during the twenties, that "I-ho Park" celebrates the neo-Confucian concept of loyalty (*chung*), which demands as a moral duty that all public servants withdraw into lifelong retirement on the collapse of the dynasty that employed them. Wang's lengthy account of the tragedy that overtook the Ch'ing dynasty is suffused with his own sense of gratitude (*hou-en*) to the woman under whose rule he had himself been born and raised and frankly discloses both his fierce determination to do his duty by her successor and his bitter resentment of moral reprobates like Yuan Shih-k'ai who shamelessly "eat the grain of Chou."[16]

That he himself was the scion of a family renowned in Sung times for its Confucian martyrs was a circumstance of which Wang was, of course, well aware and one of which he seems to have grown increasingly proud as the years went by.[17] It is not inconceivable, therefore, either that Wang Kuo-wei's view of the extent of his moral obligations in the post-Ch'ing period was influenced somewhat by the lofty example set him by his ancestors or that his own last desperate act would be made, so to speak, in the family spirit.

In the seventh generation[18] the imperial house was confronted
    with disaster,
As wind-blown dust[19] swirled up and darkened all the land.
In the south the lakes were the site of a rebellion,[20]
While in the north the keys to the gates flew away.[21]

Suddenly the Lord of a Myriad Chariots[22] fled to Chin-wei;[23]
Once it had left, the imperial carriage never returned.[24]
Then the heir to the throne[25] was installed to restore peace to the
    realm;
Henceforward state affairs were conducted in the women's
    apartments.[26]

The Eastern Empress Dowager, farsighted and trustworthy, had
    no match;
The Western Empress Dowager, with her ability and
    statesmanship, was peerless.[27]
Their grace and favor by no means extended to their relatives;[28]
Government policies were often formulated in their private
    quarters.[29]

The prince of the blood, who assisted the government, was the
    best of men;[30]
The generals, granted special authority, speedily reported their
    victories.[31]
Quickly the comets[32] were swept away and the sun and moon[33]
    returned,
As the empire again experienced a restoration.[34]

In close succession Fang-shu and Hu of Shao were elevated to
    senior positions at court,[35]
And control of the north gate was entrusted entirely to Hsi-
    p'ing.[36]
Then [Tz'u-hsi] built the storied boat and dug a Han lake;[37]
She also constructed terraces and pools to recreate [the late
    Emperor's] exquisite park.[38]

West of Hsi-chih Gate[39] the willows are green;
Below Yü-ch'üan Hill[40] the waters flow clear.
The newly named hill is called Wan-shou;
The formerly dredged lake is known as K'un-ming.[41]

Amidst the beautiful vistas of K'un-ming and Wan-shou,
Palaces and halls rise up to the clouds.[42]
The winding walkway[43] along the water's edge extends for one
    thousand steps;
On the peak of the hill is a magnificent pavilion three stories
    high.[44]

The path up the hill twists and turns up to the purple mists;
The Buddhist building on the crest of the hill[45] is a second Hall
    for Praying for a Bountiful Year.[46]
On the scaffolds she had erected, a thousand blossoms opened,[47]
And innumerable glowing pearls[48] hung down through the night.

At that time both court and people prospered;
Every year in the third moon the imperial carriage arrived [at I-
    ho Park].
The Ch'ang-lo Palace's deep seclusion and austerity sapped the
    spirit,
But the Kan-ch'üan Palace's altitude made it cool in summer.[49]

In the clear autumn, amid breeze and sun, [Tz'u-hsi] would
    celebrate the Double Ninth;[50]
On an auspicious day, once the yin had formed, she would
    reopen the Wei-yang Palace.[51]
On the cinnabar steps[52] there would be a great array of imperial
    musicians;
[Tz'u-hsi] would personally raise her jade goblet in response to
    [Te-tsung's] proffered ten-thousand-year toast.[53]

The Emperor, in wishing her longevity, would refer to himself as
    Her Majesty's servant-son;
The present dynasty's house rules are incomparably strict.[54]
To her child,[55] when he came to pay his respects, she never
    granted sitting privileges;
With her retinue, while enjoying leisure moments, she seldom
    observed family etiquette.[56]

The young daughter of Tung-p'ing received the utmost imperial
    grace;[57]
Married afar, she returned to serve the Purple Chambers.[58]
Waking and sleeping, [Tz'u-hsi] was always with Princess Jung-
    shou;
Her favorite court painter was Lady Miao.[59]

Her titles, like pearls in a string, amounted to sixteen
    characters.[60]

The imperial chef provided her food according to historical
    precedent.
[Tz'u-hsi] separately opened an Agate Forest[61] to store
    unexpended tax monies,
And reestablished a Jade Bureau[62] to collect treasures and
    rarities.

Moon halls and cloud steps rose up to the upper regions;
In the palace she sat in meditation and burned incense at night.[63]
[Tz'u-hsi] prayed only that the times might be peaceful and the
    borders quiet,[64]
So that after a thousand autumns and ten thousand years the
    dynasty might still not come to an end.[65]

For fifty years she was the mother of all under Heaven;
She has no equal among either successors or predecessors.
When in leisure moments one reflects on her life—
How can one bear to recall her myriad troubles?

I remember that, long ago, during the late Emperor's tour of the
    North,[66]
His Majesty showed [Tz'u-hsi] favor beyond measure.
Together they wrote comments [on memorials] in Ch'ing-shu
    Hall;[67]
The small seal bore the freshly inscribed characters *t'ung-tao
    t'ang*.[68]

Unexpectedly, however, while casting a tripod, [Emperor Wen-
    tsung] caused a dragon to descend;
Because its whiskers broke off, [His Majesty's] wives and
    concubines were prevented from accompanying him.[69]
How could the Child of God bear her grief on the northern
    bank?[70]
In addition she encountered the wrath of outer court ministers.[71]

Single-handedly [Tz'u-hsi] eliminated Tuan-hua and Su-shun and
    returned to the capital,[72]
Always bearing in mind that the child emperor[73] was not yet
    capable of governing;
Thus she appointed Confucian officials to teach him well
And sought ladies from good families to run the women's
    apartments.

What a shame the sun speeds so quickly across the sky!
In a twinkling twelve years of [Tz'u-hsi's] kind and conscientious
    [rule][74] had passed like flowing water.
Because, however, there was in the First Lodge no Grandson
    Who is the Heir by the Principal Wife,
Nor in the imperial harem any son of a gifted concubine,[75]

[Tz'u-hsi] raised up a nephew[76] and gave him the empire;
Her toil thereafter was similar to that of the early T'ung-chih
    era.[77]
Again she gave audiences in the throne room leaning on a jade
    table;
Once more she directed affairs beneath the martial canopy
    dressed in a pearl jacket.[78]

The realm during this period was in constant turmoil;
Recent events remind one of the shame of Huai-lai.[79]
Making her way with difficulty across the grasslands in a cart
    with shortened hubs,[80]
[Tz'u-hsi] consumed Wu-lou gruel thrown together at a post
    station.[81]

Her highest minister remained in the capital and set up the
    imperial standard,[82]
While the generals in the Southeast supported the royal house.[83]
Without much effort [Tz'u-hsi] caused auspicious vapors to rise
    up in the imperial palace;[84]
On her return journey residents of the capital gazed on the
    imperial banners.[85]

From of old the loyal and the good have been able to save the
    realm;
Thus mother and child could again eat off jade.[86]
In the nine ancestral temples bells and drums again were
    heard;[87]
The detached palace's terraces and pools remained unchanged.[88]

Since the Emperor had repeatedly been indisposed,[89]
[Tz'u-hsi] entertained little hope of eating sweets and fondling
    grandchildren in her last years.[90]
When she looked at herself, she could see that she was still
    physically robust;[91]
One would never have guessed that grief had already left its
    mark [on her soul].[92]

The Two Palaces[93] one day lay both on the brink of death;
Who would have imagined that the Heavenly Pillar would
    collapse before the Earthly Support?[94]
How many descendants of Emperors Kao and Wu were there?[95]
The line of succession under Emperors Ai and P'ing was broken
    three times.[96]

At that time, even as she lay dying,
In pain [Tz'u-hsi] was still planning for the good of the dynasty.
She installed Po Ch'in to inherit the throne
And selected the Duke of Chou to oversee the lords.[97]

[Tz'u-hsi] moreover permitted important ministers to ascend to
    the imperial couch,[98]
And assigned elder statesmen to the Grand Council:
An-shih's loyalty and diligence were enduring,
While Pen-ch'u's ability and vigor were especially soaring.[99]

These men simultaneously received [Tz'u-hsi's] instructions,[100]
And the prince Liu Tse truly proved worthy of his royal title.[101]
Alone [Prince Ch'ing] was to oversee the myriad officials and
    serve as prime minister;
Together [he and the others] were to support the young prince[102]
    through trials and crises.

Since the altars of the soil and grain had divine efficacy and the
    empire a ruler,
[Tz'u-hsi] could then report in the other world to Wen-tsu.[103]
One could only sit back and watch as the cloud-blocker was
    placed in a jade coffin;[104]
All that remained was her last testament, lying in the Repository
    of Covenants.

The portrait in her shrine is as solemn as a deity's;
Her mirrors and other personal effects still appear new.
Who would have thought the ruler of the new dynasty
Would be the minister to whom [Tz'u-hsi] had entrusted her
    dying words?[105]

The detached palace, once closed, has remained closed now for
    three years.
The green waters and azure hill have not changed.
Rain washes the dark moss; the stone animals are deserted.
The wind rattles the vermilion doors, whose bronze knobs are
    still intact.

Neither official nor banquet music has been heard for a long
    time;
Both elegant draperies and beaded curtains have been falling one
    by one.[106]
Who would have imagined that the Ch'u palace[107] built under a
    former dynasty
Would today compel us to grieve over the imprisonment [of
    Yao] at Yao-ch'eng?[108]

The dying words [of Tz'u-hsi] still ring in one's ears;
By a solemn oath [Yuan Shih-k'ai] vowed forever to be loyal [to
    her dynasty].
It is easy to cheat widows and orphans;[109]
Praise or censure—which will he ultimately receive?[110]

Deep in the palace mother and child[111] are lonely and sorrowful;

Their situation is reminiscent [of Tz'u-hsi and Mu-tsung's] the
    year the latter made an excursion to Luan-yang.[112]
In the earlier case, however, the boy emperor was nourished and
    protected by the entire world,
While today he barely receives a leper's pity.[113]

Tigers, rats, dragons, and fish have no fixed form;[114]
The marquis who served under Yao is now in a privileged
    position in the court of Shun.[115]
Just let me say, "Please, scion of the imperial house, take loving
    care of yourself;
May you live, unharmed, to the age of yellowing hair!"[116]

At Ting-ling[117] pines and cypresses grow luxuriantly;
Reflecting on the rise and fall [of the Ch'ing dynasty] makes one
    cry out with grief.
Yet I recall that every year on the Cold Food Festival
The Marquis Chu personally offers sacrifice at the Thirteen
    Imperial Tombs.[118]

As "I-ho Park" and his subsequent actions make clear, Wang Kuo-wei was a sincere adherent of the monarchic principle who looked on usurpation with revulsion. The position that he, a legitimist, would take vis-à-vis the fallen dynasty was to be, as the poem suggests, the precise opposite of that of the traitorous Yuan Shih-k'ai, whom he bitterly denounces again and again in words that even today sting one's ears. As a concrete token of his "convictions, integrity, and resentment," to use Aoki Masaru's phrase, Wang, like other conservative intellectuals with outlooks similar to his own, declined ever to alter his hairstyle; he would go to his watery grave with a long queue, the symbol of Ch'ing authority par excellence, dangling down his back.[119]

As "I-ho Park" also makes clear, in the months following the 1911 Revolution Wang took a charitable view of Tz'u-hsi's long and checkered career. Like many other twentieth-century loyalists, such as Chang Erh-t'ien and Ku T'ang-sheng, Wang Kuo-wei was inclined in retrospect to overlook the empress dowager's shortcomings, put the best possible construction on her actions, and regard with indifference the plight of the luckless Emperor Te-tsung (1871–1908). Wang's tolerant judgment of Tz'u-hsi may well have stemmed from his apparent conviction that she had resolutely endeavored over the years, against increasing odds, to hold the empire together and to preserve the traditional fabric of Chinese life.

Like his mentor, Lo Chen-yü, who was inclined in retrospect to anathematize both radical reformers and revolutionaries for their cultural subversiveness, Wang Kuo-wei seems in 1912 painfully to have realized that, in the world of ideas, the republican principle would necessarily be identified with cultural iconoclasm, the monarchic principle with intellectual traditionalism. It is not a coincidence that Wang's own decision to embrace Confucianism (itself an "early thing" and a "glorifier of early things," as Joseph R. Levenson once put it) and to join the ranks of the Ch'ing loyalists would be accompanied by a bitter repudiation of his youthful excursions in German philosophy and aesthetics and a fierce determination henceforward to devote his scholarly energies entirely to the Old Learning.[120]

While Wang's particular brand of loyalism was, then, in part a matter of values (moral, political, and intellectual), it was also in part a matter of sentiment. Having just witnessed the collapse of the most ancient monarchy on earth, Wang was not disposed in 1912 to quibble over fine points, such as the undesirability, in the orthodox Confucian view, of extended female regencies. On the contrary, his manifest nostalgia for the ancien régime, which suffuses "I-ho Park," appears to have led him to regard as benign virtually anything out of the vanishing Chinese past, just because it was "past." With his wistful and idealized view of times gone by, Wang was, in fact, the quintessential Chinese loyalist, for a distinguishing feature of loyalism has always been a sentimental and backward-looking state of mind.

A poem whose resonant beauty strikes one forcefully, "I-ho Park" was much admired by Wang Kuo-wei's circle of friends in Japan. Suzuki Torao (1878–1963), in particular, himself the author of a "Lament for the Ch'ing" ("Ai Ch'ing fu"), esteemed it highly, saying that "I-ho Park" reminded him of, but was superior to, the poetry written by Wu Wei-yeh (1609–1672) after the collapse of the Ming dynasty. Lo Chen-yü, an ardent monarchist, was also enthusiastic about "I-ho Park," whose conservative political tone he must surely have found most agreeable. In view of his own conservative commitments in the latter part of his life, it is undoubtedly significant that Wang himself treasured "I-ho Park." Of all the many poems he had composed over the years, Wang Kuo-wei once remarked, the only ones he prized in later life were the three that deal with late Ch'ing personages and developments—that is, the lament for Tuan-fang, the dirge to Lung-yü, and the eulogy to Tz'u-hsi.[121]

From Drama to History

After 1911 the major catalyst in Wang Kuo-wei's scholarly life, as in his personal life, was the cultural crisis into which China, as we can see in retrospect, was thrown by the revolution. Influential as well was Lo Chen-yü, whose friendship with Wang appears to have been intenser during the period of their residence abroad than at any time either prior or subsequent to it.

When Lo and Wang sent themselves into exile that fall day in 1911, they had known each other for fourteen years. During those years of increasingly intimate association, Lo had helped finance his protégé's studies both in China and abroad; secured jobs for him through timely recommendations to influential scholar-officials; introduced him to prominent Chinese, Japanese, and Western Sinologists; and proffered advice on a number of private matters. The only area of Wang's life on which, it seems, Lo exerted little influence prior to the 1911 Revolution was his scholarship, which circumstance would change dramatically once they had settled down in Japan.

When they first arrived in Kyoto, the Lo, Wang, and Liu families all lived together, an arrangement that in the case of Lo and Wang appears to have further deepened their friendship. The two were actually inseparable, their mutual friend Kano Naoki later recalled. "During the years Mr. Wang lived in Kyoto, he was day and night in close contact with Mr. Lo Chen-yü," Kano writes, either studying with his mentor or strolling over to the university with him to put Lo's vast library in order, an activity the older man found "rather grueling."[122]

It must have been around this time, shortly after the two friends had set up housekeeping together in Kyoto, that Lo Chen-yü took Wang Kuo-wei aside one day and earnestly exhorted him to renounce the philosophical and literary researches with which he had been overwhelmingly preoccupied during the previous ten years. By the dark winter of 1911–12 Lo himself had resolved to dedicate what remained of his life to the preservation of China's cultural heritage, which he considered to be "hanging by a thread." For some time he had been growing increasingly distraught by the skeptical, even iconoclastic, spirit that he discerned in the works of an alarming number of Ch'ing scholars, among whom, because of his former philosophical investigations, he frankly counted his own protégé. Now that the dynasty, as it seemed to Lo, was actually collapsing as one result of this pernicious skepticism and the insidious influence of Western ideas, he wished to waste no time apprising Wang of the scholarly obligations of all men of integrity fated to live in the present degenerate age.[123]

In keeping with his own vow henceforward to devote his scholarly energies to the preservation of China's literary legacy, Lo Chen-yü felt impelled one day, so he later recollected, emotionally to harangue his protégé in the hope of securing the latter's cooperation in the great task that lay ahead.

> Discussing the strengths and weaknesses of scholarship with Mr. Wang, I said: "Traditional Confucian scholars had faith in the ancient (*hsin ku*), but contemporary men have faith in the new and doubt the ancient (*i ku*). Scholars of the present dynasty have doubted the authenticity of the ancient text of the *Book of Documents* (*Shang shu*), K'ung An-kuo's *Commentary on the "Book of Documents"* ("*Shang shu*" K'ung chu), and the *Family Sayings of Confucius* (*K'ung-tzu chia-yü*); their doubts are certainly justifiable. Mr. Ts'ui Shu of Ta-ming, Chihli, however, in his *Record of Beliefs Investigated* (*K'ao-hsin lu*) has grave doubts about what need not be doubted. Recently the situation has become worse, some persons even going so far as to suggest that all the Classics are forgeries. Many of the theories of Western philosophers are similar to those of the philosophers of the Chou and Ch'in periods. The doctrines of philosophers such as Nietzsche, for example, disparage benevolence and righteousness, hold modesty in low esteem, and have no use for self-restraint. Such philosophers wish to create a new culture to replace the old, and problems are multiplying as a result. Today such doctrines are becoming ever more fallacious. Although the teaching of three thousand years has not yet been completely eliminated, it is being preserved by only a small number of scholars. If we do not remedy this situation, we will be unable to return to the Classics. A scholar living today can do little about the general course of events. If, however, he wishes to rectify the abnormal situation [which I have just described], he has but one choice: to return to the Classics and have faith in the ancient. You, [Mr. Wang], are just now at the peak of your manhood, and I am not yet old. Let us exhort each other to preserve the tradition and to await later transmitters."[124]

Lo Chen-yü concluded this hortatory talk by advising Wang Kuo-wei to devote himself to "Sinology" (*kuo-hsueh*—that is, the Old Learning), taking traditional linguistics and philology as his points of departure.[125]

According to Lo, whose account of this conversation is the only one that has come down to us, his words were a revelation to Wang. "When Mr. Wang heard this, he trembled. Aghast at the thought that his previous studies might have been immature, he took over one hundred copies of *Essays by Ching-an* out of his traveling trunk and burned them all . . . Such was his courage to reform and pursue virtue."[126]

Whether or not Wang Kuo-wei really set fire to his anthology of philosophical essays (Lo's writing style is sometimes hyperbolic) we do not know, although it is certainly conceivable that at age thirty-four he found the extremely candid views set forth in *Essays by Ching-an* indecorous and eminently burnable. Nor do we know for certain whether or not other factors besides Lo's stern admonition entered into Wang's decision "to reform and pursue virtue." It is surely possible, however, that Lo's words concerning cultural subversion struck deeply at the emotions of the young man who personally had introduced the heretical thought of putative German geniuses who, in his own characterization, "aspired to destroy the old culture and create a new culture." It is also possible that Lo's opinion on the proper relationship between the upright scholar and China's cultural heritage fit in nicely with Wang's own evolving views on how to conduct himself, and with what to concern himself, in the postimperial period.

There was, in any event, no great incompatibility between Wang Kuo-wei's scholarly interests in the years immediately preceding the revolution and those following it. In the first place, Wang had recently been engaged in a type of scholarship, "empirical scholarship" (k'ao-cheng), that could as easily be applied to the historical problems with which Lo wished Wang henceforward to concern himself as to the literary researches that had absorbed the young man in the past few years. In the second place, the end to which Lo now proposed he devote his intellectual energies, namely, the preservation of China's cultural heritage, was one to which Wang had been committed for several years already. Had he not, after all, launched his pioneering study of Yuan drama precisely because he had been distressed that "a little of our legacy is being lost every day"? For a man with "national essence" sympathies, there is by no means a great divide between preserving the literary legacy as it manifests itself in belles lettres and preserving the literary legacy as it manifests itself in the Classics and Histories.

And in the third place, by 1911 Wang had accomplished virtually all that he had set out to accomplish in the literary arena and had already begun to cast longing glances in the direction of the discipline that had fired his imagination as a teenager. Even before the collapse of the dynasty, he had actually become involved in one of Lo Chen-yü's historical projects, published "A Note on 'Reproductions of Military Tallies of the Sui and T'ang Periods' " (" 'Sui T'ang ping-fu t'u-lu' fu-shuo"), and begun to study bronze and stone inscriptions in his spare time.[127]

Although one can thus discern, in retrospect, certain strands of filiation between his scholarly concerns in the years immediately preceding the 1911 Revolution and those following it, there can be no doubt that Wang's decision to become a historian took his own contemporaries by surprise. Many of his Japanese colleagues, in particular, were dismayed and puzzled to discover that this former student of Western philosophy and authority on Chinese vernacular literature was now, in the winter of 1911–12, determined completely to abandon his earlier studies in order to plunge into the field of history. Kano Naoki, for instance, later recollected that

> from the moment he arrived in Kyoto, the direction of Mr. Wang's scholarship seemed to change. More specifically, he seemed to wish to revitalize classical scholarship and to establish a new approach to it. Whenever during a conversation I mentioned Western philosophy, Mr. Wang would always smile bitterly and say that he did not understand the subject. When later he extended his research on Yuan drama [backward in time to include the drama of the Sung period], he wrote *The History of Sung and Yuan Drama*. To Mr. Wang, however, this was simply a work that he produced on the side. It was just as he would always say, *"The History of Sung and Yuan Drama* will be my last work on drama. When I finish it, I will not study the subject anymore." By that time the focus of Mr. Wang's scholarly research had already shifted.[128]

Aoki Masaru, who had hoped to study Chinese drama under Wang Kuo-wei's tutelage, was sorely disappointed to learn in early 1912 that the great pioneer in the field had decided to turn his scholarly attention to other things.

> In March 1912 I paid my first visit to Mr. Wang . . . Having in the previous year written "Researches in Yuan Drama" ("Genkyoku kenkyū") in order to complete my college studies, I had great ambitions just at that time to continue my research on drama and was eager to receive instruction from Mr. Wang. Mr. Wang, however, only loved to read plays; he disliked going to the theater. Even less did he concern himself with the music used in Chinese drama. Mr. Wang's scholarship was, moreover, at that time shifting toward the subjects of bronze and stone inscriptions and high antiquity as he grew tired of lyrics and songs. Being young and proud, I unwisely considered Mr. Wang a pedant and stopped visiting him after one or two interviews. Thus, I did not inquire further into his knowledge, a fact that I regret to this day.[129]

Suzuki Torao and Naitō Torajirō (Konan, 1866–1934), as well, noticed that Wang Kuo-wei's interests were shifting away from drama and toward the Histories and Classics, several chapters of whose commentaries and subcommentaries had by now become his standard daily diet.[130]

Recollections of the foregoing type by those Japanese scholars who knew Wang well during this period confirm our general impression that, as Lo Chen-yü maintained, "while he lived abroad, Mr. Wang totally renounced his former studies and deeply immersed himself in the works of empirical scholarship that I had given him on an earlier occasion . . . What he had written prior to the age of thirty-four he discarded as being worthless . . . The direction of Mr. Wang's scholarship after his study abroad was thus completely different from that [of his work] in earlier years."[131]

"On an earlier occasion" (sometime between 1901 and 1907) Lo Chen-yü had found his protégé reading Chiang Fan's *Lineage of the Present Dynasty's School of Han Learning* (*Kuo-ch'ao Han-hsueh shih-ch'eng chi*, 1818), whose ideas the older man believed to be "biased and self-contradictory." He therefore had urged Wang Kuo-wei to study instead the thought of his own favorite Ch'ing scholars—Ku Yen-wu, Tai Chen, Ch'eng I-ch'ou, Ch'ien Ta-hsin, Wang Chung, Tuan Yü-ts'ai, Wang Nien-sun, and Wang Yin-chih—and had presented his protégé with copies of their works. "Although he glanced at them," Lo subsequently recalled, "Mr. Wang was just then studying foreign scholarship and lacked the leisure to devote himself exclusively to them."[132]

By 1912, however, Wang Kuo-wei had, as a result of his own intellectual evolution and Lo's exhortations, the interest and, as a result of Lo's wealth, the wherewithal (Lo supported Wang and his large family while they lived in Japan) to study carefully these and other books of interest to intellectuals working in the tradition of the school of empirical research. As further incentive, Lo Chen-yü made available to Wang "for his own researches" five hundred thousand *chüan* from his private library, the Great Cloud Library (Ta-yun shu-k'u), several thousand rubbings of inscriptions on ancient artifacts, and over one thousand ancient vessels and other types of antiquities. Thus began Wang's apprenticeship in the Old Learning.[133]

Wang's decision to plunge into the study of Chinese history, we may suppose, was facilitated by the access he was granted, in a day of few public libraries and historical museums, to his mentor's fabulous collection of books, relics of antiquity, records on bone and shell, and rubbings of inscriptions on bronze, stone, and clay. The sheer novelty of many of the artifacts housed in the Great Cloud Library may also have been a consideration, for Wang's enterprising spirit had on more than one occasion in the past led him into great uncharted regions of scholarship. Crucial as well, however, must have been Lo Chen-yü himself, whose dedication to, and enthusiasm for, his subject proved so infectious that his brother Chen-ch'ang and his sons Fu-ch'eng, Fu-ch'ang, and Fu-i, in addition to his protégé, developed a taste for antiquarian pursuits during this period.[134]

According to Lo Chen-yü, Wang Kuo-wei was grateful that his mentor had chosen to share with him his view of the proper vocation for scholars living in their day. After he had counseled Wang to pursue true learning and devote himself to the preservation of China's historical record, Lo later recollected, "Mr. Wang appears to have concluded that I really appreciated him and to have believed that the way in which he could repay me would be to establish principles, behave in an exemplary fashion, and live in accordance with what he had learned in order not to disappoint his friend."[135] The principles that Wang chose at this time to embrace were, as we know, those associated with the idealistic pole of Confucianism. A gentleman of intrepid virtue, traditionally defined, he would cleave for the next fifteen years to a moral code so lofty that by the time of his demise he would fully deserve the epithets "loyal and upright" (*chung ch'ueh*), which comprise the posthumous name conferred on him by the deposed Hsuan-t'ung Emperor (P'u-i, 1906–1967).

As for his scholarly aims, from 1912 onward Wang would dedicate himself, just as Lo had advised, to combatting the "pernicious" drift toward skepticism that had been gaining momentum in the historical field ever since Ts'ui Shu, the patron saint of the May Fourth "antiquity doubters" (*i-ku p'ai*), had begun back in the eighteenth century his rigorous investigations into the authenticity of certain passages in, and even whole works belonging to, the classical canon. For the next fifteen years Wang Kuo-wei's overriding ambition would be to supplement, emend, and (most especially) to confirm, on the basis of newly discovered written records, the accounts of Chinese antiquity contained in a wide variety of traditional texts whose veracity had been called into question by skeptical scholars. It would, indeed, become a matter of some bitterness to him that, as he once sardonically observed: "With respect to the ancients' social institutions, cultural artifacts, and doctrines, there is not one whose authenticity has not been doubted by contemporary scholars. The only things that these scholars have been unwilling to doubt are the bases for their own statements." "From these words of Mr. Wang," Lo Chen-yü subsequently remarked, "one can discern the reason for the change of direction in his scholarship."[136]

Wang Kuo-wei and Lo Chen-yü in Kyoto (1916), aged thirty-eight and forty-nine, respectively

13

Archaeological Enthusiasms

That Wang Kuo-wei was able, as Kano Naoki put it, "to revitalize classical scholarship and to establish a new approach to it" in the postimperial period was due in no small measure to his willingness to make extensive use of written records that were discovered at various sites in China during the earliest years of the twentieth century. The best known of Wang's many works in the historical field are, accordingly, based not only on meticulous examination of a wide spectrum of traditional textual sources but also on painstaking analysis of these newly discovered materials—in particular, the documents on wood found by M. Aurel Stein along the foot of the Great Wall and elsewhere during his first two Central Asian expeditions (1900–01, 1906–1908), the paper manuscripts obtained by Stein (1906) as well as by Paul Pelliot (1907) from a Taoist monk in Tun-huang, and the records on bone and shell whose historical significance was first perceived by Wang I-jung (1845–1900) and Liu E in 1899. The story of Wang Kuo-wei's career as a historian is thus intimately bound up with the story of both the discovery of these important literary relics and the dissemination in China of information about them.

One of the most celebrated feats that Lo Chen-yü ever performed was, on two separate occasions (1909 and 1922), to rescue the Ch'ing archives from destruction.[1] Equally noteworthy, however, were his herculean efforts over four decades to collect, catalogue, and reproduce (often at his own expense) incalculable quantities of rare or previously unpublished documents, among them recently discovered documents on wood, paper manuscripts, records on bone and shell, and inscriptions on bronze, stone, and clay. It is probably fair to say that no one man has ever done more than Lo Chen-yü to transmit, in the literal sense of the word, the written record of China's past.[2] To him belongs the distinction of acquainting the Chinese scholarly world in general, and Wang Kuo-wei in particular, with every type of historical material that was brought out of the ground in China by foreign explorers, Chinese antiquaries, and others during the opening decades of the twentieth century.

Wang's First Historical Works

Wang Kuo-wei had first become aware of Stein's and Pelliot's discovery of ancient wooden documents (*mu-chien*) and paper manuscripts in 1909. In the fall of that year Pelliot himself, during the course of a visit to Peking, had met with Lo Chen-yü, Tuan-fang, Wang Kuo-wei, and others to show them specimens of his Tun-huang finds and to discuss with them plans for preserving those of the ancient manuscript rolls which still lay unclaimed in Tun-huang's Cave of the Thousand Buddhas. Pelliot must also have spoken to his Chinese colleagues about the ambitious project on which Edouard Chavannes was then engaged, namely, the decipherment and interpretation of the wooden documents discovered by Stein in Northwest China in 1900–01 and 1906–1908, for Lo Chen-yü had initiated a correspondence with Stein's French collaborator shortly after Pelliot's visit.[3]

Electrified by his meeting with Pelliot, Lo Chen-yü had determined to do all in his power to prevent the remaining Tun-huang manuscripts from falling into foreign hands. It was, in fact, principally as a result of his efforts that in 1910 the Ministry of Education had finally requisitioned the unclaimed documents from the Taoist priest in whose custody they had been until that time.[4] From the manuscripts that Pelliot had carried with him to Peking in 1909, as well as from facsimile editions that the Frenchman subsequently sent him, Lo also had published during the last years of the Ch'ing a number of anthologies of Tun-huang manuscripts. In the compilation of the first of these, *Lost Manuscripts from the Stone Chamber in Tun-huang* (*Tun-huang shih-shih i-shu*), published by Tung K'ang in 1909, Lo Chen-yü had been materially assisted by Wang Kuo-wei, who also had translated for inclusion in the anthology's appendix the second half of a talk that Stein had delivered on 8 March 1909 to the Royal Geographical Society on the subject of his second Central Asian expedition.[5]

Although prior to the 1911 Revolution he had thus been marginally involved in Lo Chen-yü's efforts to disseminate information about Stein's and Pelliot's archaeological finds and to make those finds available to the Chinese by publishing them in facsimile editions, Wang Kuo-wei did not become seriously interested in the foreigners' discoveries until 1912, the year in which he wrote "On Bamboo and Wooden Documents and the Methods of Packaging and Addressing Them" ("Chien-tu chien-shu k'ao"), his first historical monograph.

While in this treatise on ancient Chinese stationery Wang relies primarily on traditional textual evidence, his penchant is already noticeable for supplementing, emending, and confirming with the evidence of newly unearthed written records, wherever possible, assertions made in the Classics and Histories.

It is not known when the technique of making bamboo and wooden "books"—that is, sets of notched bamboo or wooden slips fastened together by silk, leather, or hemp cords—was invented, Wang writes, but both traditional texts and inscriptions on bone and bronze suggest that the system dates from high antiquity. Although literary evidence seems to indicate that the use of silk as a writing material had originated by middle antiquity, it would be a mistake, he warns, to imagine that bamboo and wooden documents were quickly supplanted by silk ones. In fact, Wang says, the use of bamboo and wood as "stationery" overlapped for many centuries with that of silk, and even for several centuries with that of paper, which was invented in A.D. 105 by Ts'ai Lun. Bamboo and wood were abandoned as writing materials only during the Chin period (A.D. 265–419), when paper finally achieved widespread popularity as a medium for writing.[6]

The purpose of "Bamboo and Wooden Documents and the Methods of Packaging and Addressing Them" is to describe, on the basis of the literary and archaeological evidence available to its author, the technical features of records written on bamboo and wood—that is, the kinds and sizes of such records, the number of columns they contained per slip or tablet, their styles of writing, and the methods of packaging, sealing, and addressing them. Both bamboo and wooden stationery, Wang reports, came in varying sizes, depending on the sort of document that was to be written on it. The general rule of thumb for both kinds of stationery was that the more important the document, the longer the slips that would be used to write it.

The Six Classics of the Han period, for instance, and other important works, such as statutes and ordinances, are said by traditional literary sources to have been written on slips of bamboo measuring two feet four inches (according to the Han measure) in length. Some noncannonical books, like the *Book of Filial Piety* (*Hsiao ching*), as well as administrative documents are said to have been written on bamboo slips one foot two inches long, while other noncannonical books, such as the *Analects* and *Tradition of Tso* (*Tso chuan*), are said to have been written on bamboo slips eight inches long. Minor documents, such as identification tallies, were apparently written on bamboo slips only six inches long.[7]

The standard lengths for wooden documents of the Han period ranged, Wang Kuo-wei informs us, from two feet to five inches (according to the Han measure). According to him, official summonses (*hsi*) were written on wooden slips two feet long;[8] the special passports (*sheng-chuan chih hsin*) carried by persons specially summoned to the capital on wooden slips one and one-half feet long; private correspondence (*tu*) on wooden slips one foot long, which was the standard length for wooden stationery for ordinary use by ordinary men;[9] and the regular passports (*t'ung-hsing chih hsin*) carried by those traveling through China's guarded passes on wooden slips five inches long. That bamboo documents were represented by fractions of twenty-four inches while wooden documents were represented by multiples of five inches Wang attributes to the circumstance that the number six (and its multiples) was the standard unit used in the late Chou and Ch'in periods, whereas five was used during the Han dynasty.[10]

The standard widths for bamboo and wooden documents are not precisely indicated in the literary record, Wang Kuo-wei observes. It seems, however, that by Han times there were two types of wooden slips, a wide type that could accommodate up to five columns of characters and a narrow type that carried only one or two columns. Most of the wooden slips discovered by Stein and by Tachibana Zuichō during the course of their respective explorations in Northwest China, Wang notes, are of the latter sort and measure approximately one-half (Han) inch in width.[11]

The individual bamboo or wooden slips making up a text usually carried one or two columns of characters, Wang Kuo-wei says, and from eight to forty characters, depending on their length. Although for most kinds of documents the number of characters per column appears not to have been fixed, lexicographical texts typically contained about sixty characters per paragraph. The reason they did so, he explains, is that they were written on wooden prisms (*ku*) possessing as many as six or eight writing surfaces; for the reader's convenience, each prism was designed to carry one paragraph of the text, with eight or ten characters in a single column on each of its six or eight sides.[12]

Different writing styles were used on bamboo and wooden documents, Wang points out, depending not only on the period in which the documents were produced but also on their relative importance. In the Han-Chin period, for instance, important documents were written in the ancient seal style (*chuan-shu*) on bamboo, while minor matters were recorded in the popular clerical style (*li-shu*) on wood; as late as the sixth century A.D., he says, some official appointments were still written in the seal style according to the Han-Chin convention. As for wooden documents, they were written in the seal style until the end of the Ch'in period, after which they were written in the clerical style. In the middle of the first century B.C., however, there arose a new style of writing known as *chang-ts'ao,* which thereafter was also used in writing both bamboo and wooden documents.[13]

Whatever the particular style of writing, Han-era documents on bamboo and wood were in fact written, Wang Kuo-wei maintains, rather than engraved, as some early scholars had inferred from the frequent references in the literature to several kinds of knives (*tao, hsueh,* and *shu-tao*) in connection with writing. According to Wang, such knives served during the Han period not as "pens" for engraving characters, but as "erasers" for deleting errors. The technique of writing documents with a brush and black ink, known to the people of the Shang and Western Chou dynasties, probably replaced the practice of engraving them with a knife during the Warring States period (463–222 B.C.).[14]

To prevent unauthorized personnel from seeing the contents of an individual wooden document, Wang writes, a separate piece of wood called a sealing board (*chien*) was bound with cords (held in place by grooves, usually three in number, engraved for this purpose) over its face. A special type of clay was then placed over that section of the cords which passed through a square socket (the so-called sealing teeth) cut on the outside surface of the sealing board. Once the seal of the sender had been impressed in the clay, it became impossible to separate the document from its "envelope" without either breaking the seal or cutting the cords. Usually the name of the addressee, together with a brief description of the document's contents, were noted alongside the seal on the outside surface of the sealing board. Stein, Wang remarks, recovered specimens of such sealing boards in Northwest China.[15]

Because the sealing board could be used only with individual documents, the secrecy and authenticity of a group of documents was guaranteed, Wang Kuo-wei reports, by sealing and "mailing" them in a square bag (*nang*) with seamless ends. Made of cloth or silk, such bags might be green, black, or some other color, depending on the importance of their contents (green, for instance, was used for imperial edicts). Once a bag had been filled with documents through the opening in its center, its two ends were folded to cover the seam in the middle and wrapped with cords. Attached to its outside was an address label as well as an impression of the sender's seal.[16]

We have discussed, in a general way, the contents of Wang's monograph "On Bamboo and Wooden Documents and the Methods of Packaging and Addressing Them" because it was his first major work in the field of history. From its date of composition, 1912, we may confidently conclude that the months immediately following the collapse of the Ch'ing, months during which he produced both his last work in the literary field (*On Sung and Yuan Drama*) and his first work in the historical field, were from an intellectual point of view transitional ones for Wang Kuo-wei. From the content of "Bamboo and Wooden Documents and the Methods of Packaging and Addressing Them," we may further conclude that by 1912 Wang was well on his way toward acquiring that vast knowledge of textual sources which would help to make him, in time, one of the world's foremost authorities on ancient Chinese history; as his future intimate Shen Tseng-chih once observed, "Although a short article . . . [' On Bamboo and Wooden Documents and the Methods of Packaging and Addressing Them '] could not have been written by anyone who was not thoroughly familiar with the Classics and Histories."[17]

Toward the close of 1913, Lo Chen-yü received from Chavannes a copy of the latter's monumental work, *Les documents Chinois découverts par Aurel Stein dans les sables du Turkestan Oriental*. Both because they wished to make the results of Chavannes's research available to those of their compatriots who did not read French and because they were dissatisfied with a number of the French Sinologist's transcriptions and critical remarks, Lo and Wang decided to publish, on the basis of 588 documents reproduced in Chavannes's plates, their own study of Stein's Chinese finds. The result was their well-known treatise, *Wooden Slips Buried in Drift-Sand* (*Liu-sha chui-chien*), completed in early 1914. In this work, edited and hand-copied for publication by Wang Kuo-wei, Lo Chen-yü concentrates on all that concerns the philological interest of these ancient records, while his protégé seeks to establish the historical identities of the sites at which Stein made his memorable discoveries, to reconstruct the Han defense line, and to clarify the details of the administrative routine and military organization of the garrisons stationed along the base of the extreme western portion of the Great Wall during the heyday of ancient Chinese expansionism.[18]

In addition to his works on bamboo and wooden stationery and Han military operations along the Northwest frontier, Wang Kuo-wei published monographs during the 1912–1915 period on a variety of other specialized topics, including the probable spatial configuration of the ancient Chinese sacred hall known in Chou times as *ming-t'ang*, the total number of commanderies (*chün*) in the empire during the Ch'in and Han dynasties, and the different lengths of the foot measure (*ch'ih*) over the centuries.[19] He also began earnestly to study bronze inscriptions (*chin-wen*) and shell and bone inscriptions (*chia-ku-wen*) under the tutelage of Lo Chen-yü. At his mentor's urging, Wang produced two catalogues of bronzes, undertook his pioneering study of Wang Hai, and wrote a foreword and postface for Lo's *Critical Study of Inscriptions from the Ruins of Yin (Yin-hsu shu-ch'i k'ao-shih)*.[20] During the four years he lived in Japan, Wang also wrote "On the Kuei-fang, Hun-i, or Hsien-yun" ("Kuei-fang Hun-i Hsien-yun k'ao") and "A Brief Account of the Geography [of China] during the Three Dynasties Period" ("San-tai ti-li hsiao-chi"), the first of his own pathbreaking works on the Shang.[21]

Lo Chen-yü and Bone Inscriptions

Although he did not begin to study "oracle bones" in earnest until after the 1911 Revolution, Wang Kuo-wei had probably learned from his mentor of their existence some years earlier.[22] As for Lo Chen-yü, he had seen his first inscribed plastron and scapula fragments in 1901, when his good friend Liu E had shown him his own sizable collection. Quick to grasp their significance for philological study, Lo had immediately assigned to himself the tasks of collecting, deciphering, and reproducing oracle-bone inscriptions. By the time of the Wuchang Uprising, when his fellow-collector Tuan-fang was murdered, he had amassed twenty to thirty thousand inscribed fragments, had published "On Divinatory Inscriptions of the Yin-Shang Period" ("Yin-Shang chen-pu wen-tzu k'ao"), and had both assisted Liu E with the publication of *Turtle Shells in the Collection of Liu E* (*T'ieh-yun ts'ang-kuei*) and published a small portion of his own collection of inscribed oracle-bone fragments. By this time Lo Chen-yü had also managed to discover the provenance of the oracle bones.[23]

While in the years immediately preceding and following the 1911 Revolution foreign interest in bone materials was considerable, after the deaths of Sun I-jang, Liu E, and Tuan-fang (1908, 1909, and 1911, respectively) there was only a single Chinese scholar, Lo Chen-yü, seriously collecting and studying bone inscriptions.[24] Since during the teens he published thousands of rubbings of bone inscriptions in his collection and wrote an important monograph on them (*A Critical Study of Inscriptions from the Ruins of Yin*), it is not surprising that the name of Lo Chen-yü came, in the minds of his compatriots, to be synonymous with shell and bone texts.[25] And in view of the skepticism with which cautious scholars initially greeted the publication of *Turtle Shells in the Collection of Liu E,* and in view of the prevalence of forged inscriptions in the years immediately following the discovery of inscribed shells and bones, it is perhaps not surprising that the name of Lo Chen-yü came also, in certain quarters, to be synonymous with forgery.

"When the oracle bones, with their amazing inscriptions, were first made known to the world," Herrlee G. Creel observed in 1935, "it was natural that many cautious scholars, Chinese and foreign, should declare that they were faked." Some of those scholars, like Hayashi Taisuke (1854–1922), revised their opinion after personally examining genuine bone inscriptions and even began collecting and studying bone materials themselves. Others, however, felt encouraged by the abundance of forgeries to cling to the view that all the bone inscriptions were spurious.[26]

Among Lo Chen-yü's contemporaries, there was no scholar more skeptical of shell and bone inscriptions than the prominent epigraphist Chang Ping-lin (1868–1936). Over the course of many years, Chang strenuously, stubbornly, and vociferously objected to the use of bone materials as historical documents on the grounds that (1) the earliest collectors of them were untrustworthy (according to Ku Chieh-kang, Chang Ping-lin at one time believed the bone inscriptions to be forgeries from the hand of Liu E), (2) bone inscriptions are not mentioned in classical books, (3) shells and bones could not have been preserved in the ground for over three millennia, and (4) bone inscriptions are easily faked (at another point Chang is said to have regarded shell and bone documents as Northern Sung forgeries).

In the best known of his philological works, *A Balanced Assessment of the National Heritage* (*Kuo-ku lun-heng*, 1919), accordingly, Chang Ping-lin denounces the bone inscriptions as fakes and insists that Lo Chen-yü, who has promoted the study of them, is an intellectually dishonest scholar with the instincts of a merchant. "Such skepticism," David N. Keightley has remarked, "still influenced Marcel Granet, who could write in 1929 (the date of the French edition of his book [*La civilisation Chinoise*]) that 'it would perhaps be an abuse of scepticism to refuse to trust in such labours as the learned M. Lo Chen-yu has consecrated to the bones, which he has, no doubt, good reason to declare authentic.' It is clear from the context that Granet felt the 'good reason' to be partly commercial."[27]

Because the committed monarchist and Japanophile Lo Chen-yü was instrumental in setting up the Ch'ing scion as the chief executive of Manchoukuo in the early 1930s, it is understandable that certain anti-Japanese nationalists should continue to take a dim view of his moral character even after the oracle bones themselves had been universally accepted as authentic documents of the late Shang dynasty. Thus, for instance, at the close of the "second" Sino-Japanese War (1937–1945) we find Fu Ssu-nien claiming in his foreword to Tung Tso-pin's *Yin Calendar* (*Yin-li-p'u*, 1945) that Lo Chen-yü was so crooked, and even incompetent, a scholar that in the winter of 1914–15 he had paid Wang Kuo-wei five hundred (Chinese) dollars for his *Critical Study of Inscriptions from the Ruins of Yin,* which he (Lo) then passed off as his own work. Fu Ssu-nien's allegation was reiterated by Kuo Mo-jo not long afterward in his well-known essay "Lu Hsun and Wang Kuo-wei" ("Lu Hsun yü Wang Kuo-wei," 1946), although, in Kuo's telling, Wang offered his monograph to his mentor out of gratitude for all that he had done for him rather than for money. It was also reiterated by the Ch'ing scion in the memoirs he wrote in later life.[28]

That Lo Chen-yü really *was* given to fraudulent business practices and that it really *was* Wang Kuo-wei, not his mentor, who wrote *A Critical Study of Inscriptions from the Ruins of Yin* are rumors that today seem to enjoy the status of something approximating established facts in the minds of many. Benjamin A. Elman, for example, confidently states that "Lo was known as a forger, and is suspected of taking credit for some of Wang's research," while Li Chi unhesitatingly declares that "in the early Republican era, some scholars were definitely of the opinion that Lo Chen-yü's main works, such as *Yin-hsu shu-ch'i k'ao-shih* (Interpretation of the Oracle Inscriptions at 'Deserted' Yin), were actually authored by Wang Kuo-wei."[29] From the context it is clear that Li Chi not only believes these unnamed scholars to be correct in their opinion that all of Lo's "main works" (he does not specify the number or, aside from the monograph he calls *Interpretation of the Oracle Inscriptions at "Deserted" Yin,* the titles of the "main works" involved) were written by his protégé, but also regards Lo as a plagiarist of long standing.[30]

Despite the credence that many contemporary scholars have given to the allegations of Chang Ping-lin, Fu Ssu-nien, Kuo Mo-jo, and P'u-i, there are solid grounds for thinking that *A Critical Study of Inscriptions from the Ruins of Yin* is just what it purports to be: a report by Lo Chen-yü of his discoveries to date in the field of oracle-bone inscriptions, based on ten years of study of them as well as on a lifetime's study of bronze and stone inscriptions.[31]

There can, of course, be no doubt that Wang Kuo-wei hand-copied *A Critical Study of Inscriptions from the Ruins of Yin* for publication. In his postface to the work, which is dated "winter of 1914–15," Wang declares that "the history of traditional linguistics in the past three hundred years of the present dynasty began with Mr. Ku Yen-wu and has now reached its culmination with Mr. Lo Chen-yü" and describes his role in the production of *A Critical Study of Inscriptions from the Ruins of Yin* as being identical to the role that Chang Shao played in the production of Ku Yen-wu's *Five Books on Phonetics* (*Yin-hsueh wu-shu,* 1667)—that is, he proofread and fair-copied it for its author, his mentor.[32] Since, during the years he lived abroad, Wang edited, proof-read, fair-copied, and wrote forewords and postfaces for many of Lo's books,[33] there was nothing unusual in this arrangement. According not only to Lo but also to Wang—the latter of whom in every study he ever published that draws on *A Critical Study of Inscriptions from the Ruins of Yin* refers to it as his mentor's work—the monograph in question was written by Lo but hand-copied for publication by Wang.

With regard to the monograph itself, we may observe that taking it to be by Wang Kuo-wei, rather than by Lo Chen-yü, makes *A Critical Study of Inscriptions from the Ruins of Yin* a very strange sort of work indeed. Consider, for instance, its opening section ("Capitals"), the principal purpose of which is to demonstrate that Wu I (traditionally regarded as the twenty-seventh Shang king) moved the dynasty's capital to present-day Anyang (= Yin, Yin-hsu) and, further, that Ti I (the twenty-ninth sovereign) moved it from there to Chao-ko (= Mei).

The Cheng-i commentary on *Shih chi* ("Yin pen-chi") quotes the ancient text of *Chu-shu chi-nien* as saying, "During the 275 years that elapsed between P'an Keng's move to Yin and the downfall of Chou [Ti Hsin, the thirtieth (and last) Shang king], there was no further transfer of the capital." *Shih chi* ("Yin pen-chi") itself, however, states that "after Wu I ascended the throne, the Yin again left Po and moved north of the River [the Yellow River]." ("San-tai shih-piao" says that it was Keng Ting who moved north of the River.) The modern text of *Chu-shu chi-nien,* moreover, relates that in the third year of his reign Wu I moved from Yin to [a place] north of the River and, further, that in the fifteenth year of his reign he moved from [the place] north of the River to Mei. In his *"Shih" ti-li k'ao,* Wang Ying-lin quotes *Ti-wang shih-chi* as saying that Ti I . . . moved the capital to Chao-ko . . . Thus we see that there were, in fact, further transfers [of the capital] in the period following P'an Keng and extending through the last reign [Ti Hsin's].

While the texts [cited above] agree that [Wu I] moved to [a place] north of the River, they do not give its name. *Shih chi* ("Hsiang Yü pen-chi"), however, says, "Hsiang Yü arranged a meeting with [Chang Han] at Yin-hsu, south of the Huan River." [Apropos of this passage] the Chi-chieh commentary on *Shih chi* quotes Ying Shao as stating, "The Huan River is within the boundary of T'ang-yin." (This is present-day Anyang. In Han times T'ang-yin *hsien* included the Anyang area.) [Ying-shao also states that] "Yin-hsu was anciently a Yin capital." [The Chi-chieh commentary then notes that], "according to Hsieh Tsan, the Huan River lies to the north of present-day Anyang *hsien* and is 150 li away from the Yin capital of Chao-ko." Thus we know that this Yin-hsu may not be identified with Chao-ko.

Now, the Cheng-i commentary on *Shih chi* ("Yin pen-chi") quotes *Kua-ti chih* as stating: "Anyang, Hsiang chou, was originally [the site of]

P'an Keng's capital. It may be identified with Pei-chung, to the south of Yin-hsu and 148 li away from the city of Chao-ko." [The Cheng-i commentary also quotes] the ancient text of *Chu-shu chi-nien* as saying that "P'an Keng moved from Yen to Pei-chung, which was called Yin-hsu, forty li to the south of Yeh." (The character *hsu* is a gloss.) This, [according to the Cheng-i commentary], was the old capital. [The Cheng-i commentary says further that] "thirty li to the southwest of the city [of Yeh] is the city of Anyang, and to the west of it is the city named Yin-hsu, which is what was called Pei-chung." According to the *"Shui ching" chu* ("Huan shui"), "the Huan River originates east of the mountains and flows past Yin-hsu on the north." It says too that the Huan River flows from the east of Yeh past the city of Anyang on the north, and it quotes *Wei-t'u ti-chi* as saying that "forty li south of the city of Yeh is the city of Anyang, north of which is the eastward-flowing Huan River."

The texts [cited above] agree in locating Yin-hsu south of the Huan River. Wu I's move must therefore have been to this [spot]. We may reject as erroneous the Cheng-i commentary's statements that Anyang was [anciently] P'an Keng's capital and that the Yin-hsu near Anyang may be identified with Pei-chung (in his *"Chu-shu chi-nien" t'ung-chien*, Hsu Wen-ching has already noted these [errors]) . . . Now that turtle shells and animal bones are in fact being unearthed in Hsiao-t'un, five li "to the west of [the city of Anyang in] Anyang *hsien*" and "south of the Huan River" (which the local people call the Anyang River), just as described in the foregoing accounts, we know that Wu I's move was indeed to this place . . .

The statement in the modern text of *Chu-shu chi-nien* to the effect that in the fifteenth year of his reign Wu I moved to Mei is incompatible with *Ti-wang shih-chi*'s statement that it was Ti I who moved to Mei [= Chao-ko]. Since Wu I is the last king to be mentioned by name in divinatory inscriptions, we know that the move to Mei must have been made in the time of Ti I. On this point the modern text of *Chu-shu chi-nien* is wrong, while *Ti-wang shih-chi*'s account is correct.[34]

Three things are noteworthy about the argument advanced in that section of *A Critical Study of Inscriptions from the Ruins of Yin* which concerns Shang capital removals, most of the text of which has just been quoted.[35] First, the argument has been advanced by someone who accepts the statements made on this subject by the authors of *Shih chi*, the modern text of *Chu-shu chi-nien*, and *Ti-wang shih-chi* but who rejects as erroneous the conflicting testimony of the Cheng-i commentary on *Shih chi* and the ancient text of *Chu-shu chi-nien*. In that portion of "A Brief Account of the Geography [of China] during the Three Dynasties Period" that is now known as "On Yin" ("Shuo Yin"), a work published in the same year as *A Critical Study of Inscriptions from the Ruins of Yin* (1915), Wang Kuo-wei casts doubt on the reliability of the statements concerning capital removals that appear in the first two sources mentioned above but takes seriously the testimony of the last two.[36]

Second, the argument itself—that the Shang moved to present-day Anyang (= Yin, Yin-hsu) in the time of Wu I and abandoned the city in the time of Ti I—is diametrically opposed to the argument that Wang Kuo-wei advances in his 1915 study of the subject. On the basis of various kinds of textual evidence, Wang argues that the Shang moved to present-day Anyang (= Yin, Yin-hsu) in the time of P'an Keng and, on the basis of inscriptional evidence, he argues further that they were still residing there in the time of Ti I.[37] And third, the text of the argument consists of an almost verbatim reproduction of the section on Shang capitals in Lo Chen-yü's 1910 essay, "On Divinatory Inscriptions of the Yin-Shang Period."

Or, to take another example, consider the contents of the second section of *A Critical Study of Inscriptions from the Ruins of Yin*. Titled "Kings," it quotes Wang Kuo-wei at considerable length on the identities of Wang Hai and Wang Heng but draws heavily on Lo's "Divinatory Inscriptions of the Yin-Shang Period" in its transcriptions of and remarks concerning archaic graphs denoting the names of other Shang predynastic lords, specifically Shih Jen and Shih Kuei, and a number of Shang kings, in particular Ta I, Ta Keng, and Wen Wu Ting.[38] Because of the nature of its substantive comments as well as its mode of presentation, *A Critical Study of Inscriptions from the Ruins of Yin* can be regarded as having been authored by Wang Kuo-wei only if it is assumed that he actually ghostwrote the work, relying principally on his mentor's research findings to date, suppressing his own ideas wherever they happened to conflict with those of Lo, but quoting himself on subjects concerning which his mentor had no opinion.

The hypothesis that Wang Kuo-wei ghostwrote *A Critical Study of Inscriptions from the Ruins of Yin* strikes one today as highly implausible, presuming as it does that (1) Lo Chen-yü was not a bright enough scholar to write the work himself, even though it draws heavily on, and even quotes copiously from, his own earlier study, "On Divinatory Inscriptions of the Yin-Shang Period"; (2) by the winter of 1914–15 Wang had moved so far beyond his tutor, Lo, in his understanding of bone and bronze inscriptions that he was in a position to write the entire monograph for Lo; (3) despite the fact that many of the most prominent Chinese, Western, and Japanese Sinologists of his day took him very seriously as a scholar ("a first-rate authority" on bronze inscriptions, declared Bernhard Karlgren; "a famous authority in the fields of traditional linguistics and epigraphy," said Kano Naoki), Lo was at bottom so intellectually insecure that he was willing, in the event, to pass his protégé's research off as his own; (4) the scholarly relationship between Lo and Wang during the teens was not a mutually productive one, but an exploitative one. These presuppositions do not square with the large body of evidence currently available concerning both the texture of Lo and Wang's personal relationship and the nature of their professional association during the years in question.[39]

14

Wang as Shang Genealogist

Wang Kuo-wei has said that his attention was first drawn to the subject of the Shang kings' distant ancestors by Lo Chen-yü, who in the winter of 1914–15 mentioned to him that he had discovered the name of one Wang Hai on oracle bones in his collection. "I then read *Shan-hai ching* and *Chu-shu chi-nien*," Wang subsequently recollected, "whereupon I realized that Wang Hai was a former lord (*hsien-kung*) of the Yin and, further, that [the names Wang Hai 王亥], Hai 胲 (*Shih pen,* 'Tso'), Ho 核 (*Ta-Tai li-chi,* 'Ti-hsi'), Kai 該 (*Ch'u tz'u,* 'T'ien wen'), Wang Ping 王氷 (*Lü-shih ch'un-ch'iu,* 'Wu kung'), Chen 振 (*Shih chi,* 'Yin pen-chi' and 'San-tai shih-piao'), and Kai 垓 (*Han shu,* 'Ku-chin jen-piao') all in fact refer to the same individual." Pursuing the matter further, he also succeeded in identifying the name of Wang Heng, who is said to have been Wang Hai's brother (*Ch'u tz'u,* "T'ien wen"), in bone inscriptions.[1]

Lo Chen-yü, to whom Wang Kuo-wei reported his exciting discoveries, was the first to describe them in print; he devoted three pages of *Critical Study of Inscriptions from the Ruins of Yin,* published in early 1915, to recounting his protégé's findings. Naitō Torajirō, to whom Wang also reported his discoveries, was the second to mention them in print; in 1916 he published an essay, "Wang Hai" ("Ōi"), based on Wang's ideas.[2] As for Wang Kuo-wei himself, he apparently continued his investigations into the names of the Shang kings' forebears in a desultory fashion during his last year in Kyoto (1915) and his first year in Shanghai (1916). At the same time he published prolifically on sources that can be used for the study of Shang China. After conferring with both Lo and Naitō during the course of a trip to Japan in early 1917, Wang returned to Shanghai and wrote his path-breaking articles "Former Lords and Former Kings of the Yin [Whose Names] Appear in Divinatory Inscriptions" ("Yin pu-tz'u chung so-chien hsien-kung hsien-wang k'ao") and "Further Information on Former Lords and Former Kings of the Yin [Whose Names] Appear in Divinatory Inscriptions" ("Yin pu-tz'u chung so-chien hsien-kung hsien-wang hsu-k'ao").[3]

Early Ancestors of the Shang Sovereigns

By comparing the names of Shang royalty as given in oracle-bone inscriptions with the names of the Shang kings and their forebears as recorded in *Shih chi* ("Yin pen-chi"), Lo Chen-yü had been able, in *A Critical Study of Inscriptions from the Ruins of Yin*, to confirm much of the Historian's data on the royal lineage. Specifically, Lo had used inscriptional evidence to corroborate, and in some cases to emend, the names of twenty-two of the thirty Shang sovereigns, as well as six of the fourteen predynastic lords, recorded by Ssu-ma Ch'ien in his genealogical list.[4] By increasing the scope of textual inquiry to include the systematic study of bone inscriptions in relation to many traditional texts, some of them generally considered to be of doubtful reliability, Wang Kuo-wei believed that he could shed additional light on the six Shang forebears whose names Lo Chen-yü had already deciphered as well as verify and elucidate the names of four other predynastic ancestors given by the Historian in his list. He also thought that he could identify in the inscriptions the name of the father of the first of Ssu-ma Ch'ien's fourteen lords.

Wang's identifications of specific Shang graphs with the names of specific Shang forebears as recorded in the transmitted literature are based on numerous bits and pieces of textual as well as phonetic and graphic evidence, each of which, in itself, is far from conclusive. The rare distinction of his researches on the Shang royal lineage lies in the care with which Wang Kuo-wei marshals so many bits and pieces of evidence that, taken collectively, they make his identifications seem highly plausible. Consider, for instance, the grounds on which he identifies K'uei (following Wang's transcription of 夔 and 夔 as *k'uei* 夔), a Shang progenitor mentioned in bone inscriptions, with K'u, a Shang progenitor mentioned in a number of literary texts.[5]

Wang observes, to begin with, that K'uei must have been an especially important ancestral figure since he is referred to in bone inscriptions as "illustrious ancestor (*kao-tsu*) K'uei."[6] Of all the remote Shang forebears whose names are given in textual sources, he finds that there is only one, Emperor (*ti*) K'u, who is particularly prominent and who has, moreover, a name that anciently was phonetically similar to K'uei's. This makes it seem likely, Wang says, that K'uei is the same individual as K'u 嚳, whom literary texts (some of which give his name as Kao 告, Kao 誥, or Kao 俈) describe as the father of Hsieh, founder of the House of Tzu.[7]

In the transmitted literature, Wang Kuo-wei observes, the name K'u is sometimes associated, directly or indirectly, with the name Chün 夋 . According to Huang-fu Mi, K'u's given name was in fact Chün 夋 , or Ch'ün 逡 , or Chi 岌 . (The first character is given by *Ti-wang shih-chi* as quoted in the So-yin commentary on *Shih chi*, "Wu-ti pen-chi," as well as in *Ch'u-hsueh chi*, 9; the second is given in that same source as quoted in *T'ai-p'ing yü-lan*, 80; and the third is given in *Ti-wang shih-chi* as quoted in the Cheng-i commentary on *Shih chi*, "Wu-ti pen-chi.") *Ch'ün* 逡 , Wang remarks, is a variant of *chün* 夋 , while *chi* 岌 is a mistake for it.[8]

In *Shan-hai ching*, Wang Kuo-wei points out, repeated reference is made to an Emperor Chün 俊 , who in at least one passage appears to be identical with Shun[9] but in others seems to be identical with K'u. The book states, for example, that Chün had "eight sons" ("Hai-nei ching"), that one of these sons was named Chung-jung 仲容 ("Ta-huang tung-ching"), and that another of them was called Chi-li 季釐 ("Ta-huang nan-ching"). In *Tso chuan* ("Wen 18") we find the assertion that Kao Hsin Shih, whom *Shih chi* ("Wu-ti pen-chi") and *Ch'u tz'u* ("Li sao" and "T'ien wen"), among other texts, identify with K'u, had "eight talented sons," two of whom were named Chung-hsiung 仲熊 and Chi-li 季貍 . In the passages from *Shan-hai ching* cited above, therefore, Chün must be the same person as K'u, Wang says.[10]

Nor is this all. According to another passage in *Shan-hai ching* ("Ta-huang hsi-ching"), Chün was the father of Hou Chi, founding ancestor of the House of Chi. Since elsewhere (for instance, in *Shih ching*, "Sheng min"), Hou Chi's mother is said to have been Chiang-yuan, whose husband (according to the Mao commentary on *Shih ching*, "Sheng min," and other sources) was K'u, clearly Chün here is also the same person as K'u. In yet another passage in *Shan-hai ching* ("Ta-huang hsi-ching"), we read that Chün had a consort named Ch'ang-hsi 常羲 , who gave birth to twelve moons. This woman Wang Kuo-wei identifies with Ch'ang-i 常儀 , whom other literary texts list as the fourth of K'u's four wives and the mother of Chih.[11] Here, too, then, Chün must be the same individual as K'u. These considerations lead Wang to suggest that it is more satisfactory to identify Chün 夋 (= Chün 俊 , Ch'ün 逡 , Chi 岌) with K'u, following Huang-fu Mi, than to identify him with Shun, as Kuo P'u does.[12] As a matter of fact, he says, the character *chün* 夋 (= *chün* 俊 , *ch'ün* 逡 , *chi* 岌) that appears in *Ti-wang shih-chi* and *Shan-hai ching* as another name for K'u is an error for *k'uei* 夒 .[13]

On the basis of the foregoing considerations, Wang concludes that K'uei 夒 (= Chün 夋 , Chün 俊 , Ch'ün 逡 , Chi 岌) may be identified with K'u 嚳 (= Kao 告 , Kao 誥 , Kao 俈 ; also = Kao

Hsin Shih 高辛氏), who according to literary documents was the
First Ancestor of the Shang royal lineage. It must be, he suggests,
because K'uei (= K'u) was the father of the founder of the House of
Tzu that the Shang kings performed the *ti* sacrifice to him (*Li chi*,
"Chi fa") and bone inscriptions refer to him as "illustrious ancestor
K'uei."[14]

The genealogy of the Shang royal house as recorded by Ssu-ma
Ch'ien consists of two parts: predynastic ancestors and dynastic kings.
In the former category, according to the Historian's list (*Shih chi*, "Yin
pen-chi"), are fourteen lords in fourteen successive generations:

Hsieh	Wei
Chao Ming	Pao Ting
Hsiang T'u	Pao I
Ch'ang Jo	Pao Ping
Ts'ao Yü	Chu Jen
Ming	Chu Kuei
Chen	T'ien I/Ch'eng T'ang/T'ang/Wu Wang.[15]

Although he has virtually nothing to say about the ancestors whom
Ssu-ma Ch'ien calls Hsieh, Chao Ming, Ch'ang Jo, and Ts'ao Yü, Wang
Kuo-wei claims to have deciphered in bone inscriptions graphs de-
noting the names of four other Shang forebears mentioned by the
Historian and even that of one not mentioned by him.

The name T'u (following Wang's transcription of 且 as *t'u* 土)
that appears in divinatory inscriptions, Wang Kuo-wei suggests, may
probably be identified with the name Hsiang T'u 相土 that appears
in *Shih chi* ("Yin pen-chi") as well as in *Shih ching* ("Ch'ang fa"), *Tso
chuan* ("Hsiang 9"), *Shih pen* ("Tso") as quoted in Yang Liang's commentary on *Hsun Tzu* ("Chieh pi"), and *Ta-Tai li-chi* ("Ti hsi"). Although some literary sources record this progenitor's name as Ch'eng
Ya, Ch'eng Tu, or Hsiang Shih, Wang believes them to be in error.
His argument is roughly as follows.

Lü-shih ch'un-ch'iu ("Wu kung") relates that "Ch'eng Ya 乘雅 began the taming of horses." *Hsun Tzu* ("Chieh pi") states that "Ch'eng
Tu 乘杜 began the domestication of horses." And *Shih pen* ("Tso") as
quoted in the commentary on *Chou li* ("Ssu-ma cheng-kuan chih chih,"
'Chiao jen') relates that "Hsiang Shih 相土 began the domestication
of horses." Because the commentary on *Lü-shih ch'un-ch'iu* ("Wu kung")
says that *ya* 雅 is written alternatively as *ch'ih* 持, and because *ch'ih*
持 and *tu* 杜 anciently were phonetically similar, *T'u* 土, Wang Kuo-
wei argues, must be the correct, *Shih* 土 the incorrect, form of this
Shang ancestor's name.

As for *Lü-shih ch'un-ch'iu's* and *Hsun Tzu's* evident conviction that the character *ch'eng* formed a part of T'u's (= Ya, Tu, Shih) name, Wang notes that Yang Liang in his commentary on the latter work ("Chieh pi") says, "Since he began the domestication of horses (*tso ch'eng-ma* 作乘馬), he was called Ch'eng Tu 乘杜." According to Wang, this shows that the word *ch'eng* was not originally part of this lord's name. Perhaps, he speculates, this particular Shang forebear was simply called T'u 土, this name being sometimes written in literary texts as Tu 杜. If this supposition is correct, the name T'u that appears in oracle-bone inscriptions ought, Wang Kuo-wei argues, to be identical with Hsiang T'u 相土 (= Ch'eng Ya 乘雅, Ch'eng Tu 乘杜, Hsiang Shih 相士). Concerning the possible meaning of the character *hsiang* in the ancestor's name as it appears in *Shih chi* and elsewhere, Wang ventures no opinion.[16]

Wang Kuo-wei's theory concerning the identity of Wang Hai, a Shang progenitor whose name Lo Chen-yü had discovered in divinatory inscriptions in the winter of 1914–15, is one for which he is particularly famous. His study of Wang Hai provides an excellent example of the way in which, by mobilizing his vast knowledge of textual sources, Wang was able to elucidate records on shell and bone and, coincidentally, to demonstrate how certain characters in certain literary sources came to be in the forms in which we there find them.

Wang Kuo-wei's suspicions regarding the identity of Wang Hai seem to have been aroused, in the first instance, by the glaring absence in *Shih chi* of any predynastic lord with this name.

> From the fact that Wang Hai 王亥 is called "illustrious ancestor" in divinatory inscriptions, as well as from the fact that the rituals performed to him were extremely lavish, involving the use of five, thirty, forty, or even three hundred cattle, it appears certain beyond a shadow of a doubt that he was a former lord or former king of the Yin. There is no mention of any Yin ancestor named Wang Hai, however, in either the "Yin pen-chi" or the "San-tai shih-piao" section of *Shih chi*. [The former] says only, "When Ming died, he was succeeded by his son Chen 振; when Chen died, he was succeeded by his son Wei 微."[17]

Since (1) *Shih pen* as quoted in the So-yin commentary on *Shih chi* ("Yin pen-chi") writes Ho 核 instead of Chen 振, and (2) *Han shu* ("Ku-chin jen-piao") writes Kai 垓 instead of Chen 振, Wang Kuo-wei argues that the character *chen* 振 must be an error for either *ho* 核 or *kai* 垓, both of which it resembles in form.

As for *ho* 核 and *kai* 垓, Wang says that they are interchangeable with *hai* 亥, the character that appears in oracle-bone inscriptions and also, as he points out, in *Shan-hai ching* and both versions of *Chu-shu chi-nien*. "In the country called K'un-ming . . . there was a man by the name of Wang Hai 王亥," *Shan-hai ching* ("Ta-huang tung-ching") relates. "He held birds in both hands and devoured their heads. When Wang Hai was residing in Yu-i 有易 . . . the Yu-i killed Wang Hai and took his domesticated cattle (*p'u-niu* 僕牛)."[18]

In a similar vein, the ancient text of *Chu-shu chi-nien*, as quoted by Kuo P'u in his commentary on the above passage in *Shan-hai ching*, states: "While Wang Tzu Hai 王子亥 of Yin was a guest of the Yu-i, he behaved licentiously, as a result of which Mien-ch'en, lord of Yu-i, killed him and dispersed [his followers]. Chu Chia Wei 主甲微 of Yin therefore attacked the Yu-i with forces borrowed from Ho-po; he vanquished them and killed their lord, Mien-ch'en." The account recorded in the modern text of *Chu-shu chi-nien* is almost identical: "In the twelfth year of Ti Hsieh, while Hou Tzu Hai 侯子亥 of Yin was a guest of the Yu-i, the Yu-i killed him and dispersed [his followers]. In the sixteenth year the marquis of Yin, Wei 微, attacked the Yu-i with Ho-po's forces; he killed their lord, Mien-ch'en."[19]

Because *Shan-hai ching* and both versions of *Chu-shu chi-nien* refer to him as royalty and because, moreover, he is said to have belonged to the generation immediately preceding that of Shang Chia 上甲 (= Chu Chia Wei 主甲微, Wei 微),[20] Wang Kuo-wei suggests that the Hai of these texts may be identified with *Shih chi*'s Chen. Furthermore, he declares, since (1) the name Wang Hai that appears in *Shan-hai ching* is identical to the name of this ancestor as given in bone inscriptions, and (2) rituals were performed to Wang Hai on *hai* days,[21] it is clear that *Hai* 亥, not *Ho* 核 or *Kai* 垓, is the correct form of this Shang forebear's name.

While conceding that neither *Shan-hai ching* nor *Chu-shu chi-nien*, in either of its versions, is completely reliable, Wang Kuo-wei believes that we may nevertheless regard the ancient legends about Wang Hai recorded in them to be "not entirely without foundation" since the man's name does, after all, occur in divinatory inscriptions. Wang Hai's activities are, moreover, described in other literary works besides *Shan-hai ching* and *Chu-shu chi-nien*.[22]

Lü-shih ch'un-ch'iu ("Wu kung"), for instance, relates that "Wang Ping 王冰 began the domestication of cattle (*tso fu-niu* 作服牛)." Because in the seal style *ping* 冰 is written as 仌, which is similar in form to *hai* 亥, it is obvious, Wang asserts, that the former is an error for the latter. Indeed, *Shih pen*'s statement ("Tso" as quoted in *Ch'u-hsueh chi*, 29) that "Hai 胲 began the domestication of cattle (*tso fu-niu* 作服牛)" corroborates this point, he argues. (In this passage as quoted in *T'ai-p'ing yü-lan*, 899, Hai 胲 has been mistakenly written as Kun 鮌, Wang notes.) As for the term *fu-niu*, used in both

Lü-shih ch'un-ch'iu and *Shih pen,* it is equivalent, Wang says, to the term *p'u-niu,* used in *Shan-hai ching,* since *fu* and *p'u* anciently had the same sound.

Ch'u tz'u ("T'ien wen") is another text, Wang Kuo-wei observes, that has something to say on the matter at hand. "Kai 該 inherited Chi's prowess. His father was a goodly man. Why did he end by losing his herdsmen and his cattle and sheep in Yu-i 有扈 ?" *Ch'u tz'u* ("T'ien wen") also says: "Heng inherited Chi's prowess. How did he get back the domesticated cattle (*p'u-niu* 朴牛)?"[23] According to Wang, *kai* 該 is equivalent to *hai* 胲 , *yu-i* 有扈 is equivalent to *yu-i* 有易 , and *p'u-niu* 朴牛 is equivalent to *p'u-niu* 僕牛 and *fu-niu* 服牛.[24]

On the basis of the foregoing considerations, Wang Kuo-wei concludes that the names Wang Hai 王亥 (oracle-bone inscriptions and *Shan-hai ching*), Wang Tzu Hai 王子亥 (ancient text of *Chu-shu chi-nien*), Hou Tzu Hai 侯子亥 (modern text of *Chu-shu chi-nien*), Chen 振 (*Shih chi*), Kai 垓 (*Han shu*), Ho 核 (*Shih pen* as quoted in the So-yin commentary on *Shih chi*), Hai 胲 (*Shih pen* as quoted in *Ch'u-hsueh chi*), Kun 鮌 (*Shih pen* as quoted in *T'ai-p'ing yü-lan*), Wang Ping 王氷 (*Lü-shih ch'un-ch'iu*), and Kai 該 (*Ch'u tz'u*) all refer to the same Shang forebear, whom literary sources depict as the First Herdsman. It must be, Wang declares, because Wang Hai was not only a predynastic lord but also a cultural hero that the rituals offered to him by the late Shang kings were exceedingly lavish.[25]

As a result of his penetrating study of Wang Hai, Wang Kuo-wei thought that he could identify in bone inscriptions not only the name of the First Herdsman himself, but also the names of his father and brother. *Shih chi* ("Yin pen-chi"), Wang reminds us, says that "when Ts'ao Yü died, he was succeeded by his son Ming 冥 ; when Ming died, he was succeeded by his son Chen 振." Since, as *Ch'u tz'u* ("T'ien wen") makes clear, Kai 該 was Chi's 季 son ("Kai inherited Chi's prowess"), and since, as Wang has already established, Kai is the same person as Chen (= Wang Hai), the Shang progenitor who is called Chi in bone inscriptions as well as in *Ch'u tz'u* must be identical with the Ming of *Shih chi.* As for Wang Heng (following Wang Kuo-wei's transcription of 𡴂 and 𢍑 as *heng* 恆), he is surely identical with the Heng 恆 of *Ch'u tz'u* ("T'ien wen"), which describes him as the brother of Kai (= Wang Hai).[26]

The Royal Genealogy Recorded in Bone Inscriptions

Probing further into the matter of Wang Hai's relatives, Wang Kuo-wei eventually concluded that in the graphs 田 and 齒 he had discovered archaic forms of the name of the First Herdsman's son, who is called Shang Chia Wei 上甲微 in *Kuo yü* ("Lu yü"), Chu Chia Wei 主甲微 in the ancient text of *Chu-shu chi-nien* as quoted by Kuo P'u in his commentary on *Shan-hai ching* ("Ta-huang tung-ching"), Hun Wei 昏微 in *Ch'u tz'u* ("T'ien wen"), and simply Wei 微 in the modern text of *Chu-shu chi-nien* as well as in *Shih chi* ("Yin pen-chi"). His theory that the two very similar graphs that appear in oracle-bone inscriptions and the four names that are recorded in the transmitted literature all refer to one and the same Shang forebear, like his theory concerning the identity of Wang Hai, is one for which Wang Kuo-wei is especially noted.

The graph 田, Wang observes, when correctly written consists of a cross ＋, the ancient form of *chia* 甲, placed within a square enclosure ☐. By not extending the horizontal and vertical strokes of the cross to the boundary lines of the square enclosure, the Shang were able to make a distinction between this graph and a closely similar one, *t'ien* 田, which means "fields" or, in the phrase *t'ien-shou*, "to hunt."[27]

The modern character *chia* always appears in bone inscriptions as a simple cross, Wang notes, except when it is used especially to designate the Shang forebear whom *Kuo yü* calls Shang Chia Wei. In those instances alone, the cross is placed within a square enclosure, giving the form 田. Consisting as it does of a denary cyclical sign (*t'ien-kan*—literally, heavenly stem) placed within a square enclosure, this graph has obvious affinities, he remarks, with the archaic forms of the names Pao I 報乙, Pao Ping 報丙, and Pao Ting 報丁, all of which consist of a denary cyclical sign placed within a square bracket ⌐ , ⌐ . Why a square enclosure or square bracket should constitute part of the name of each of these four Shang ancestors, Wang Kuo-wei confesses, is a mystery.[28]

As regards the form 审 having an additional line above it, Wang observes that — is an abbreviation of 二, the archaic way of writing *shang* 上. Therefore, he declares, "田 and 审 are Shang Chia 上甲," as is 畓 (this last, Wang notes, is the full form of 审, as Lo Chen-yü was the first to point out).[29]

An important bone inscription, reconstructed by Wang Kuo-wei from fragments belonging to two different collections, reads in part: "to 田 (Shang Chia 上甲), ten; to 乙 (Pao I 報乙), three; to 丙 (Pao Ping 報丙), three; to 丁 (Pao Ting 報丁), three; to 示 壬 (Shih Jen 示壬), three; to 示 癸 (Shih Kuei 示癸), three; to 大 丁 (Ta Ting 大丁), ten; to 大 甲 (Ta Chia 大甲), ten."[30] This inscription, Wang observes, provides "an iron proof" that 田 stands for the first of the late Shang ancestors, an ancestor whose personal name (according to traditional literary sources) was Wei and whose posthumous appellation (as bone records reveal) was Shang Chia. This inscription, he adds, also fully confirms Lo Chen-yü's hypothesis that the graphs 𠬝, 𢎨, and 𢎥 may be identified with the late Shang ancestors whom Ssu-ma Ch'ien calls Pao I 報乙, Pao Ping 報丙, and Pao Ting 報丁. Wang notes, however, that the author of *Shih chi* has erred in placing Pao Ting before, instead of after, Pao I and Pao Ping. Lo's identifications of Shih Jen 示壬 and Shih Kuei 示癸 with the Historian's Chu Jen 主壬 and Chu Kuei 主癸 are also corroborated, Wang avers, by the bone document that he has reconstructed.[31]

As for Wang Kuo-wei's views concerning the name of the Shang figure who appears in the "Yin pen-chi" chapter of *Shih chi* as both the last of the predynastic ancestors and the first of the dynastic kings, they in the main follow those of Lo Chen-yü. Following Lo, Wang states that Ssu-ma Ch'ien has erred in writing the dynastic founder's name as T'ien I 天乙 rather than Ta I 大乙. In archaic script, Wang reminds us, the graphs for *t'ien* and *ta* are very similar. It is not to be wondered, therefore, that writers often confused the one with the other.

That the correct form of the dynastic founder's name is in fact Ta I can be verified, Wang says (following Lo), by repeated reference in bone inscriptions to other Shang kings who have *ta*, not *t'ien*, in their names: Ta Ting, Ta Chia, Ta Keng, Ta Wu. That the Ta I whose name is recorded in the inscriptions is in fact the same person as Ssu-ma Ch'ien's T'ien I can be confirmed by the occasional occurrence in bone documents of I Yin's name alongside that of Ta I (according to traditional literary sources, I Yin was the principal adviser of the founder of the Shang dynasty). As for the Historian's claim that the dynastic founder was also called Ch'eng T'ang 成湯, or simply T'ang 湯, Wang observes that the original form of *t'ang* 湯 is *t'ang* 唐 and that, indeed, the latter does appear in divinatory inscriptions as a name for Ta I.[32]

The propositions that the names Wang Hai and Wang Heng that occur in bone documents may be identified with *Shih chi*'s Chen and *Ch'u tz'u*'s Heng, respectively, over the years have won general acceptance by Shang scholars. Wang's theory that "囝 and 甶 are Shang Chia" has been widely accepted as well. His view that the oracle-bone name K'uei may be identified with the Historian's K'u and his argument that the names Chi (inscriptions) and Ming (*Shih chi*) refer to one and the same Shang forebear have been embraced by some specialists but rejected by others. As for his hypothesis that the T'u of the divinatory inscriptions may probably be identified with the

Hsiang T'u who is mentioned in some Chou texts and also in *Shih chi,* most scholars now subscribe to the view that T'u ("Earth"), like Ho and Yueh, was a nature spirit rather than a predynastic lord. Lo Chen-yü's and Wang Kuo-wei's clarifications concerning the dynastic founder's name, as well as the names and order of succession of his five immediate predecessors, have been universally accepted.

Having concluded his investigations into the Shang royal lineage in its predynastic phase, Wang Kuo-wei turns his attention to the Shang kings themselves. According to the "Yin pen-chi" chapter of *Shih chi,* he reminds us, the Shang dynasty had, in all, thirty kings belonging to seventeen successive generations (see the chart on pages 188-189).

The names of most of these sovereigns, Wang observes, have been discovered in identical or similar form by Lo Chen-yü in sacrifice inscriptions. He himself accepts all of Lo's transcriptions as well as all of his identifications of royal names recorded in oracle inscriptions with those given by Ssu-ma Ch'ien in the "Yin pen-chi" chapter of *Shih chi.*[33]

One of Wang Kuo-wei's great contributions to the study of oracle bones was his discovery that specific inscriptions can be periodized on the basis of the kin titles that occur in them. The way in which such titles can be used to date inscriptions, as explained by David N. Keightley, is this: "If an inscription refers to an ancestor as 'father' (*fu*) and we can place that 'father' in the Shang royal genealogy, we can then establish beyond doubt that the inscription refers to a divination performed during the generation of his 'sons.' Similarly, reference to an 'older brother' (*hsiung*) establishes that the divination was performed by a 'younger brother' of the same generation." These considerations also apply, Keightley notes, to the title "grandfather" (*tsu*), although this title is ambiguous because it refers to any deceased male ancestor two or more generations distant from the ruling sovereign.[34]

It is not always easy to ascertain the period of inscriptions by locating on the royal family tree the fathers, older brothers, and grandfathers mentioned in them. One difficulty, Wang observes, lies in the ambiguity of the ancestral titles themselves. An inscription that refers to Fu I, for instance, might date from the reign of Wu Ting (K22), who would have used this appellation to refer to Hsiao I (K21), but it could just as easily date from the time of Wen Wu Ting (K28), who would have used the title Fu I to refer to Wu I (K27).[35]

A second difficulty in dating inscriptions by equating the names of the Shang royal ancestors recorded in them to those given by Ssu-ma Ch'ien in his genealogy stems from the circumstance that not all the royalty whose names appear in oracle-bone inscriptions are mentioned in the "Yin pen-chi" chapter of *Shih chi*. Consider, for example, an inscription that refers to Fu Ting ("Father Ting"), Hsiung Chi ("Older Brother Chi"), and Hsiung Keng ("Older Brother Keng"). Wang Kuo-wei dates this inscription to the reign of Tsu Chia (K24) by identifying Fu Ting with *Shih chi*'s Wu Ting (K22) and Hsiung Keng with its Ti Tsu Keng (K23). Hsiung Chi, whose name does not appear in Ssu-ma Ch'ien's genealogy, Wang takes to be Hsiao Chi, an ancient worthy mentioned in a number of textual sources. From *Shih-shuo hsin-yü* ("Yen yü"), *Ti-wang shih-chi* as quoted by Liu Chün in his commentary on *Shih-shuo hsin-yü* ("Yen yü"), and *Chia-yü* ("Ti-tzu chieh"), he states, we may infer that Hsiao Chi was a son of Wu Ting who never took power.[36]

In Wang Kuo-wei's estimation, the royal genealogy recorded in the "Yin pen-chi" chapter of *Shih chi* more closely approximates the Shang's own view of their family tree, as we understand it from contemporary inscriptional evidence, than either of the rival genealogies that have been preserved in literary sources. One of the latter is the genealogy contained in the "San-tai shih-piao" chapter of *Shih chi*, which takes Hsiao Chia, Yung Chi, and T'ai Wu to be T'ai Keng's younger brothers rather than his sons. The other is the genealogy given in the "Ku-chin jen-piao" chapter of *Han shu*, which takes Chung Ting, Wai Jen, and Ho Tan Chia to be T'ai Wu's younger brothers rather than his sons and Hsiao Hsin to be P'an Keng's son rather than his younger brother. According to Wang, sacrifice inscriptions prove that both "San-tai shih-piao" and "Ku-chin jen-piao" are mistaken on these points. The "Yin pen-chi" account, by contrast, is very nearly correct, he states, its only error being that it lists Tsu I as the son of Ho Tan Chia ("San-tai shih-piao" makes the same mistake, while "Ku-chin jen-piao" makes a similar one); from the inscriptions we may infer that he was actually the son of Chung Ting.[37]

From the fact that he and Lo Chen-yü had been able in the main to confirm, with inscriptional evidence, Ssu-ma Ch'ien's record of the Shang kings' names and sequence, Wang Kuo-wei concluded that *Shih pen*, a text used by the Historian in writing the "Yin pen-chi" chapter of *Shih chi*, is completely trustworthy. His research on the royal genealogy of the Shang in both its predynastic and dynastic phases led Wang to conclude as well that even works which contain erroneous information and fanciful details, such as *Shan-hai ching*, and works which appeared at a late date, such as *Chu-shu chi-nien*, are partly reliable in their accounts of high antiquity. It is much to be regretted, we find Wang writing in the mid-1920s, that scholars with an overly skeptical view of antiquity (*i-ku chih kuo*) have not made full use of

The Shang Dynastic Kings (G = generation, K = king, + + = died before ascending the throne, * = elder/eldest brother), according to *Shih chi* ("Yin pen-chi")

G1 K1 T'ien I
        T'ang
        Ch'eng T'ang
        Wu Wang

G2 + + T'ai Ting*   K2 Wai Ping   K3 Chung Jen
                                 Ti Wai Ping   Ti Chung Jen

G3 K4 T'ai Chia
        Ti T'ai Chia
        T'ai Tsung

G4 K6 T'ai Keng   K5 Wu Ting*
        Ti T'ai Keng   Ti Wu Ting

G5 K9 T'ai Wu   K8 Yung Chi   K7 Ti Hsiao Chia*
        Ti T'ai Wu   Ti Yung Chi
        Chung Tsung

G6 K12 Ho Tan Chia   K11 Wai Jen   K10 Chung Ting*
         Ti Ho Tan Chia   Ti Wai Jen   Ti Chung Ting

G7 K13 Tsu I
         Ti Tsu I

G8 K14 Tsu Hsin*   K15 Wu Chia
         Ti Tsu Hsin   Ti Wu Chia

K18 Yang Chia*
Ti Yang Chia

K19 P'an Keng
Ti P'an Keng

K17 Nan Keng
Ti Nan Keng

K20 Hsiao Hsin
Ti Hsiao Hsin

K23 Ti Tsu Keng*

K25 Ti Lin Hsin*

G9

K16 Tsu Ting
Ti Tsu Ting

G10 K21 Hsiao I
Ti Hsiao I

G11 K22 Wu Ting
Ti Wu Ting
Kao Tsung

G12 K24 Tsu Chia
Ti Chia

G13 K26 Keng Ting
Ti Keng Ting

G14 K27 Wu I
Ti Wu I

G15 K28 Ti T'ai Ting

G16 K29 Ti I

G17 K30 Hsin
Ti Hsin
Chou
Ti Chou

the sources available to them for the study of ancient China. Because their instinctive distrust of traditional literary materials has not been tempered with a knowledge of the evidence contained in oracle-bone inscriptions, he implies, Ku Chieh-kang and his circle of "antiquity doubters" have failed to grasp that, with the aid of Shang documents on shell and bone, "we definitely are able to supplement and emend (*pu cheng*) the textual sources and also to confirm (*cheng-ming*) the complete factuality of certain portions of ancient books."[38]

15

The Later Years

It must have been with mixed feelings that Wang Kuo-wei set sail in early 1916 for Shanghai, where he had been offered a job by the wealthy British businessman Silas A. Hardoon (1847–1931). Through Lo Chen-yü's generosity, he had for four full years been freed of the necessity of supporting himself and his ever-growing family and had luxuriated in pursuing his scholarly interests in whatever direction they had happened to take him. There can be no doubt that Wang felt deeply obliged to his mentor for having put a roof over his head and food on his table, instructed him in the mysteries of bronze and bone inscriptions, and given him unrestricted access to a library so magnificent that Kyoto University had considered itself lucky to have been able briefly to house it. Nor can there be any doubt that, when by 1915 Lo's extensive publishing activities had begun to make a sizable dent in his monthly budget (during the years he lived in Japan, Lo edited and published several hundred works), Wang had thought-fully volunteered to remove his family from his mentor's payroll.

After 1911 Wang was drawn to Lo, as the latter subsequently observed, by his deepening conviction that the older man not only benefited him materially but also shared with him a commitment to traditional moral and political principles as well as a determination to preserve China's cultural heritage—in particular, its historical leg-acy. It was, indeed, precisely because he believed that Lo was per-forming an incalculable public service by doggedly persevering in his self-appointed chore of reproducing rare or hitherto unpublished historical materials that Wang Kuo-wei had decided to ease his men-tor's considerable financial burden by getting himself a job.[1] The two men parted, therefore, at Kobe on the best of terms: Lo presented one-tenth of his books to his protégé as a farewell gift and declared, as he took leave of Wang, "With your diligence and courage to pursue virtue, you will one day become another Ku Yen-wu."[2]

In Wang's own view, the years that he spent at Lo Chen-yü's side in Kyoto, years that wrought a profound change in his scholarship, appeared in retrospect to have been at once the simplest and the most productive of his life.[3] From our vantage point today, it is difficult not to attribute the simplicity and productivity of Wang's life in Japan, at least in part, to the sense of distance from contemporary Chinese political and social realities that he was undoubtedly able to attain by virtue of his lengthy residence abroad. Once, however, he had again set foot on native soil, Wang was thrown into the thick of a growing cultural storm. The exigencies of earning a living, together with the pain he must surely have felt as he watched his apostate compatriots deride the principles that he would continue to uphold in his person and his scholarship until the day he died, were enough to ensure that Wang's life would never again be simple or free from worry.

It is quite possible, therefore, that the "extraordinary sorrow and grief" that Ch'en Yin-k'o has said became integral features of his friend's emotional existence in his later years had their roots precisely here, in the kind of society that greeted Wang Kuo-wei on his return from his self-imposed exile.[4] "To live in troublous times . . . and yet to consider the preservation of scholarship one's own responsibility" are words Wang used in 1918 to describe his mentor's unenviable situation in the second decade of the twentieth century, but they are words that could just as easily be said to describe his own.[5] That Wang was able to carve out a niche for himself in cosmopolitan Shanghai, where he lived from early 1916 until mid-1923, was due in part to his intense concentration on scholarly research and in part to the sorts of circles in which he moved.

A Literary Talent of Shanghai

After he returned to China, Wang Kuo-wei initiated what in time would become a voluminous correspondence with Lo Chen-yü, to whom he continued to report his every cold and mood (when in a bad mood, he confides in one missive, he "passes the time" studying Tun-huang manuscripts and the historical geography of China's Northwest).[6] No number of letters either to or from Lo seems, however, to have been able to obscure from Wang the circumstance that he was now, for the first time in a decade, separated from his mentor. It was, perhaps, because Lo was now an entire ocean away that Wang's friendships with Chang Erh-t'ien, Sun Te-ch'ien (1869–1935), K'o Shao-min, and, particularly, Shen Tseng-chih and Chiang Ju-tsao (1877–?) blossomed at this time.

In light of his own conservative commitments in the sociopolitical and cultural spheres, it is undoubtedly significant that most of Wang's closest friends in later life were well-known Ch'ing loyalists and eminent scholars of the traditional type.[7] Chang Erh-t'ien, for example, had resigned his office (prefect of a district in Kiangsu) after the 1911 Revolution, in accordance with the neo-Confucian principle of loyalty, to devote himself to scholarly research. A devout Confucian, Chang was a member of the Confucian Society (K'ung-chiao hui) founded in Shanghai in 1912 by Shen Tseng-chih, Liang Ting-fen, and others, and he was as well a regular contributor to that society's journal. The author of many works upholding the values of the Old Learning and of at least one refuting those of the New, Chang was an authority on the Classics and Buddhism whose stature as a historian brought him in time to the attention of Chao Erh-hsun, a former governor-general of Szechwan and of Manchuria who in 1914 had accepted Yuan Shih-k'ai's offer to become director of the newly established Bureau of Ch'ing History (Ch'ing-shih kuan). Invited by Chao to serve as a compiler (tsuan-hsiu) of what would become the *Provisional History of the Ch'ing Dynasty* (Ch'ing-shih kao, 1927–28), Chang passed the latter part of the teens piously writing the "Biographies of the Empresses and Imperial Concubines" ("Hou fei chuan") and several other portions of the officially commissioned Ch'ing history.[8]

Much respected for his loyal devotion to his friends, Chang Erh-t'ien was on very good terms with several local scholars who shared his cultural concerns as well as his intellectual interests. Among them were Sun Te-ch'ien and Wang Kuo-wei, with the latter of whom Chang coauthored in the late teens a number of sections of the enlarged and revised edition of the *Gazetteer of Chekiang Province* (Che-chiang t'ung-chih) then being compiled under the supervision of Shen Tseng-chih. Chang's friendship with Sun, a noted Confucian and prominent scholar of the Old Learning, and with Wang was indeed so celebrated that the trio were known as "the three literary talents of Shanghai" (Hai-shang san-tzu).[9]

To K'o Shao-min, it will be recalled, Wang Kuo-wei had been introduced by Lo Chen-yü in 1909, when all three men had been employed at the Ministry of Education.[10] Having enjoyed a prosperous career as both an official and a scholar during the last decades of Ch'ing rule, K'o had refused on principle to accept the posts offered him by the Republican authorities. Instead, he redoubled his efforts to produce a new history of the Yuan dynasty (after fifty years' labor, the monumental *New History of the Yuan Dynasty* [Hsin Yuan-shih] would be published in 1922), wrote various treatises for the *Provisional History of the Ch'ing Dynasty*, and composed the poems that in 1924 would appear under the title *Poems from the Smartweed Garden* (Liao-yuan shih-ch'ao). While his close friend Wang Kuo-wei never became overly enthusiastic about his historical endeavors (Wang did not think that it was necessary for K'o to write an entirely new opus on the Yuan), he was decidedly partial to K'o's verses, which he preferred to those of any other poet during his later years. As for K'o, he so deeply admired Wang for his scholarly attainments that he sent his sons to study with him.[11]

One of the gentlemen whom Wang Kuo-wei is said to have respected most highly during his life was the stout monarchist and prominent scholar Shen Tseng-chih, who for three decades had served the Ch'ing government in a variety of official capacities. Fiercely loyal to the dynasty, Shen reportedly cried, on hearing of the Hsuan-t'ung Emperor's abdication, "For generations we have received benefits from the imperial house; dead or alive I shall remain faithful to it." A cofounder of the Confucian Society of Shanghai, Shen was as well a leading member of the Imperial Clan party (Tsung-she tang), which supported the Manchu royal house in particular and, more important, the monarchic principle in general. In 1917 he had the pleasure of serving as minister of education in the administration that Chang Hsun, the "Pigtailed General," inaugurated after restoring the Ch'ing scion to his throne. After the failure of the short-lived Restoration, the embittered Shen lived quietly in retirement in Shanghai, where he spent his time reading and writing poetry and discussing scholarly matters with such good friends as Chang Erh-t'ien, Cheng Hsiao-hsu (1859–1938), and Wang Kuo-wei.[12]

Although he had corresponded with him from the very beginning of his stay abroad, Wang Kuo-wei had been formally introduced to Shen Tseng-chih by his mentor only in 1915, when the two exiles had paid a short visit to China.[13] After a stimulating conversation on the advantages to be gained by studying alliterative initials (*shuang-sheng*) rather than rhyming finals (*tieh-yun*), Shen and Wang had found themselves much taken with one another.[14] During the latter part of the teens, the two phonologists developed an intimate friendship that would be severed only by Shen's death late in 1922.

That Wang thought highly of his learned, upright friend can be seen from the circumstance that he consulted him on every scholarly work he wrote during this period as well as from the fact that he mentioned him constantly in his letters to Lo Chen-yü. Wang and Shen, who lived in close proximity to one another, met frequently, it is said, to chant poetry together or to examine rubbings of bronze and stone inscriptions. After Shen Tseng-chih's demise, which profoundly grieved him, Wang would characterize his friend as a "great poet" (he ranked Shen's poems second only to K'o's), a "great scholar" (Wang's studies in the areas of phonology, the historical geography of the Northwest, and Yuan history were influenced by Shen), and an "even greater sage" who "was at home a filial son (*hsiao tzu*) and abroad a pure subject (*ch'un ch'en*)."[15]

Another of Wang's intimates was the recluse Chiang Ju-tsao, a wealthy bibliophile who, like Lo Chen-yü and his protégé and K'o Shao-min as well, had worked at the Ministry of Education in the waning years of the Ch'ing dynasty. Wang, who had not known Chiang prior to the 1911 Revolution, first made his acquaintance in Shanghai when, on the recommendation of Lo, he was hired to compile a descriptive catalogue of Chiang's Secret Rhyme Library (Mi-yun lou). In time Wang Kuo-wei and Chiang Ju-tsao, the latter of whose library is said to have compared favorably with those of the well-known bibliophiles Liu Ch'eng-kan and Chang Chün-heng, became fast friends. During the years he lived in Shanghai, Wang subsequently recollected, Chiang used to lend him books and, whenever new treasures had been acquired for the Secret Rhyme Library, invite him over to examine them. Chiang also undertook the costly task of publishing the massive collection of Wang's writings known as *Works by Kuan-t'ang* (*Kuan-t'ang chi-lin*, 1923).[16]

It was, then, in the company of such kindred spirits as Chang Erh-t'ien, Sun Te-ch'ien, K'o Shao-min, Shen Tseng-chih, and Chiang Ju-tsao that Wang Kuo-wei passed his years in Shanghai. Through Shen, he also met at this time the literary critic and former Hanlin compiler and prefect Yang Chung-hsi (1865–1940), who, like many other Ch'ing loyalists, had settled in Shanghai after the 1911 Revolution. Wang seems also to have seen a fair amount of his former Peking acquaintance Miao Ch'üan-sun, who had retired to Shanghai after the collapse of the dynasty to devote himself to bibliographical pursuits, as well as of the aforementioned bibliophile Liu Ch'eng-kan.[17] With access to the private collections of Chiang Ju-tsao and Liu Ch'eng-kan as well as to that of his principal Shanghai employers, Silas Hardoon and Lo Chia-ling (Mrs. Hardoon), Wang found that he could profitably engage in scholarly research even though he was now constrained to do without the resources of the fabulous Great Cloud Library.

The couple for whom Wang Kuo-wei went to work in 1916 had by the mid-teens acquired a reputation of being fanatic admirers of traditional Chinese learning, customs, conventions, and moral values. In the pre-1911 period, to be sure, the Hardoons had patronized the revolutionary artist-monk Huang Tsung-yang (1865–1921; also known by his sobriquet, Monk of Mount Wu-mu) as well as the revolutionary organizations with which he was connected: the Chinese Educational Association (Chung-kuo chiao-yü hui) and the Patriotic School (Ai-kuo hsueh-she). They had also permitted revolutionaries to rendezvous on the grounds of their large estate, Ai-li Garden (popularly called *Ha-t'ung hua-yuan,* or "The Hardoons' Garden"), and had even supported the 1911 Revolution.[18]

While old revolutionary friends such as Huang Tsung-yang and Chang Ping-lin (the latter of whom would one day write Hardoon's epitaph) continued after the collapse of the Ch'ing dynasty to be welcome in the Hardoons' home, the couple themselves seem by the early teens to have begun to drift in a distinctly conservative direction. For one thing, they had no reservations, once the Wuchang Uprising had actually occurred, about throwing open the gates of their estate to such high ex-officials as Ch'en K'uei-lung, Jui-ch'eng, and Ts'en Ch'un-hsuan, all of whom had been governors-general under the empire. For another thing, not long after the revolution the Hardoons began to spend considerable sums on preserving China's "national essence" through the publication of two antiquarian magazines, the *Journal of Art (I-shu ts'ung-pien)* and the *Journal of Scholarship (Hsueh-shu ts'ung-pien)*, as well as on preserving old-style educational arrangements through the establishment on their property of private primary and middle schools and even a college.[19]

Wang Kuo-wei had initially been hired by the Hardoons in early 1916 to serve as editor of their newly established *Journal of Scholarship.* As it happened, the most illustrious, and also the most frequent, contributor to the magazine proved to be Wang himself. The *Journal of Scholarship* and the monumental collectanea that he edited for the Hardoons a year or two later contain, between them, draft versions of every important work that Wang authored during this period: his critical study of the ceremonies associated with the publication of the dying charge of King Ch'eng and the enthronement of King K'ang as they are described in the latter part of the "Ku-ming" chapter of the *Book of Documents;* his article on the famous Mao Kung Ting; his essay on the probable date of composition of the poems that make up the "Shang sung" section of the *Book of Poetry;* his partial reconstruction of the text of what he considered the original *Bamboo Books (Chu-shu chi-nien*—literally, bamboo book annals); his analysis of the spurious modern text of the *Bamboo Books;* his critical study of the Hardoons' collection of inscribed bones; his essay on the origins of ancient China's basic political and social institutions; and his articles on Shang genealogy, among others.[20]

In addition to his editorial responsibilities, Wang Kuo-wei reportedly assumed from 1918 onward the task of teaching at the Hardoons' College to Propagate the Sage Ts'ang Chieh's Wisdom (Ts'ang-sheng ming-chih ta-hsueh). The mission of this college, as its president, Lo Chia-ling, is said to have envisioned it, was to give promising but penurious youths (tuition was free, as were meals and lodging) a good, old-fashioned education. Employed at the College to Propagate the Sage Ts'ang Chieh's Wisdom, accordingly, were a handful of classically trained scholars with conservative outlooks. Especially memorable was Professor Wang Kuo-wei, whose skull cap and queue made him appear to his charges as the most curiously costumed member of the entire college faculty.[21]

Like Ts'ao Chan's famous Grand View Garden (Ta-kuan yuan), on which it was partially modeled, Ai-li Garden constituted a small, secluded world all of its own. The lives of its numerous young denizens seem to have been indeed so cloistered (those attending the Hardoons' schools were permitted neither to read newspapers nor to leave the estate grounds) and the efforts of Lo Chia-ling to manage her educational enterprises along traditional lines indeed so intense that, we are told, students could easily imagine themselves to be dwelling in the nineteenth century rather than the twentieth. Reflecting Lo Chia-ling's policy of "preserving the old," the College to Propagate the Sage Ts'ang Chieh's Wisdom was run not on a seven-day but on a ten-day week, and the school year commenced not in July but in the first moon of the lunar year. The opening-school-day ritual, presided over by the Hardoons' business manager, Chi Chueh-mi (also known by his Buddhist sobriquet, Fo-t'o), consisted in part of requesting students to perform the kowtow ceremony in honor of Ts'ang Chieh, the legendary inventor of Chinese writing and the college's patron saint. At Lo Chia-ling's behest, Chi Chueh-mi also sometimes staged performances of ancient rites. Wang Kuo-wei, who served as Chi's consultant for one of them, regarded these performances in principle as the "most exquisite" aspect of life in Ai-li Garden.[22]

It should not be thought that Wang considered all aspects of life in Ai-li Garden pleasurable. As a matter of fact, Wang did not care in the least for Chi Chueh-mi, a man whom he considered ill-bred, mean-spirited, self-important, ostentatious, and unlearned. His bête noire is a "low-class person," we find Wang confiding to Lo Chen-yü in a letter written shortly after the former had landed in Shanghai. Chi also, he says, "spends money like water" and "understands neither scholarly nor administrative matters." Although his is a fundamentally vulgar mind, incapable of any true finesse or delicacy, Chi is unfortunately a powerful figure in Ai-li Garden, Wang tells Lo. His mentor need not, however, fear that he will compromise his integrity. "If we had been inclined to toady, we could have gone far before 1911, and what could we not have attained after 1912?"[23]

Like other members of his circle, Wang continued during the teens tenaciously to cling to traditional notions of duty and honor, in particular to the orthodox Confucian dictum that virtue resides in the loyalty a subject shows his lord, the respect a son shows his father, and the obedience a wife shows her husband. One reads with interest, in the last connection, the epitaph Wang wrote in 1922 for his mentor's daughter-in-law, a young woman who from his description appears fully to have embodied the particular virtue exemplified in the third of China's Three Major Relationships (*san-kang*). During the illness that eventually claimed the life of Lo Fu-ch'ang, a gifted linguist of whom both Wang Kuo-wei and Shen Tseng-chih thought very highly, his spouse courageously but vainly (husband and wife died within one hundred days of one another) tried to cure her husband by the traditional procedure of self-mutilation. "When residents of the capital heard that she had cut a piece of flesh from her arm," Wang writes with evident admiration, "they were deeply moved." Even the emperor (*ti*), he notes, was so overcome by the virtuous act of Lo Chen-yü's daughter-in-law that he conferred on the family a piece of imperial calligraphy (*yü-shu*) bearing the motto, "Extraordinary conduct expressing the utmost devotion."[24]

Wholly traditional in its moral orientation, the life that Wang Kuo-wei carved out for himself in Shanghai may be described as a bastion of decorum and decency in a world that, from the conservative point of view, was growing ever more lawless. The years that he passed in Shanghai seem, for this reason, to have been on the whole not unpleasant. That they were intellectually stimulating and productive as well is evident both from the number of important scholarly works Wang authored during this period and from the substance of much of his correspondence with Lo Chen-yü. The impression one derives of Wang from his letters—which are filled with accounts of his most recent intellectual discoveries, requests for Lo's opinion on baffling Shang graphs, plans for future research—is, indeed, one of a scholar so completely engrossed in his historical and antiquarian pursuits that he is even able, for short intervals at least, to ignore the new storm brewing on China's cultural horizon.

Dark clouds had, however, begun to gather on the horizon. Already in 1918 Ch'en Tu-hsiu and Hu Shih were boldly declaring war on what they derisively referred to as the "old ethics" and the "old literature" (ridding China of simply the "old politics," they now believed, would not be enough to cure the country of its multifarious ills). Already in 1918 these and other cultural iconoclasts were beginning to demand a "new literature," written in a "new language," whose aim it would be to discredit traditional ("cannibalistic" was the word Lu Hsun used) notions of morality, in particular the hoary doctrine of the Three Major Relationships, and to popularize in their stead the alien ideals of political, generational, and sexual equality. Even before the New Culture Movement had gotten fully under way, in short, the battle lines were beginning to be drawn between the radical May Fourth activists and those members of the older, more conservative 1890s generation who, in both their scholarship and their lives, were committed to upholding traditional values. It is no coincidence that, long after the Literary Revolution had become a fait accompli, members of the transitional generation of intellectuals would still be trying to conserve, not destroy, China's literary legacy and would themselves still be writing in classical, not colloquial, Chinese.

Companion of the Southern Study

Although he had, at Lo Chen-yü's invitation, ushered in the New Year of 1917 in Kyoto, and although Lo had paid him a visit in Shanghai in mid-1917, Wang Kuo-wei got back into regular personal contact with his mentor only in 1919, after the older man had finally decided to return permanently to his native land. Having sailed first to Shanghai to see his protégé and to arrange the marriage of his youngest daughter to Wang's eldest son, Lo proceeded to Tientsin, an asylum (like Shanghai and Tsingtao) in which many Ch'ing loyalists had taken refuge after the collapse of the dynasty. Here, in the foreign sector of Tientsin, Lo would live for the next ten years, and here, during the late teens and early twenties, Wang often visited him.[25]

It seems likely that, as one consequence of his renewed intimacy with his sociable and gregarious mentor, Wang's contacts with other Ch'ing loyalists increased in number at this time. Among his friends and acquaintances Lo Chen-yü counted the former grand secretary Sheng-yun, a stalwart monarchist who is said to have been especially active in plots to restore the dynasty; the imperial tutor Liang Ting-fen, who was much admired in conservative circles for the courage and loyalty he showed during the Restoration; the Manchu scholar-writer Chin-liang, who, like Sheng-yun, was deeply involved in efforts to bring the deposed Hsuan-t'ung Emperor back to power; Lao Nai-hsuan, president of Tsingtao's Confucian society; and Chang Tseng-yang, a former governor of Chekiang who in 1907 had ordered the execution of the flamboyant poet-revolutionary Ch'iu Chin. While staying with his mentor in the latter part of 1919 to nurse a painful illness (beriberi), for example, Wang was introduced by Lo to Sheng-yun, who reportedly took an instantaneous liking to him.[26]

In 1923–24 a number of distinguished Chinese intellectuals were selected by the sometime emperor to serve as either Companions of the Southern Study (Nan shu-fang hsing-tsou) or Companions of the

Great Diligence Hall (Mao-ch'in tien hsing-tsou) in that part of the Forbidden City which was still occupied by the imperial family and the Imperial Household Department. According to the Ch'ing scion's tutor Reginald F. Johnston, these appointments were intended, on the one hand, to honor gentlemen of exceptional loyalty to the dynasty and, on the other, "[to add] lustre to the court in its time of twilight." Among those who were thus inducted into the imperial service were Yang Chung-hsi, K'o Shao-min, Cheng Hsiao-hsu, Lo Chen-yü, and Wang Kuo-wei.[27]

Wang Kuo-wei learned of his appointment as a Companion of the Southern Study, which was made on the personal recommendation of Sheng-yun, in early 1923. Since his intimate friend Shen Tseng-chih had recently passed away, and since, moreover, he had just completed his catalogue of the Secret Rhyme Library, it is possible that Wang at this time felt less uneasy about the prospect of leaving Shanghai than he would have in earlier years. To one close friend, Chiang Ju-tsao, who expressed doubts about the post, Wang stated simply, "As a matter of principle, I cannot decline the appointment."[28]

"In the summer of 1923," Lo Chen-yü subsequently recalled, "Mr. Wang went to the capital to assume his new position. His remuneration was equivalent to that of a fifth-grade official, and he was granted permission to ride a horse in the Forbidden City." Wang was, according to his mentor, grateful for his sudden promotion from commoner to courtier, and in his memorials he reportedly gave repeated thanks to the young man whom he acknowledged as the heir and representative of the Ch'ing dynasty.[29]

One imagines that Wang Kuo-wei had little difficulty adjusting to the new environment in which, from mid-1923 onward, he found himself. He must surely have taken comfort in the thought that here in the Forbidden City, as in Ai-li Garden, time had in a number of respects stood still. Here, within the quiet halls and palaces of the Great Within, a titular monarch still occupied his throne, holding audiences in the customary fashion and ruling over all who dwelled or worked inside the Gate of Spiritual Valor. Here the reign title "Hsuan-t'ung," the lunar calendar, traditional court functions, and innumerable other manners of a former age were still routinely observed. Here queues, although few, were still in evidence.[30] Here a gentleman's biggest problem, as Wang discovered shortly after his arrival in Peking, was where to obtain the dragon-embroidered gown required on ceremonial occasions.[31] For many of those who, like Wang himself, were in the former emperor's service, the Chinese Republic might just as well have been a thousand miles away in space, instead of a few hundred yards, a thousand years away in time, instead of contemporaneous.

From the single document he submitted to "His Majesty" (*huang-shang*) that has been published, however, we know that Wang did occasionally concern himself with developments in the bustling world that existed on the far side of the Gate of Spiritual Valor. Of particular interest in this document is his explicit repudiation of the West. In a dramatic reversal of his view of foreigners in the pre-1911 period, during which he had repeatedly extolled the great minds of Europe for their preoccupation with the human spirit and the meaning of life, Wang now (1923–24) maintains that the principal traits of Westerners are greed, aggressiveness, selfishness, and competitiveness. In fact, he counsels the emperor, China's present debilities may be attributed in no small measure to the pernicious influence of Western ideas, ideas that unfortunately since 1911 have gained the upper hand over the Old Learning. His Majesty, Wang suggests, need not envy the Europeans their prosperity and power (*fu ch'iang*), for the recent world war has revealed that foreign peoples lack the wherewithal to govern themselves either peaceably or long. They ought, he says, to study the thought of the Duke of Chou and Confucius, sages who grasped the secrets of good government.[32]

Wang Kuo-wei's major assignment as a Companion of the Southern Study, as it developed, was to assist in the inventory of palace treasures for which the Ch'ing scion and certain of his advisers had called in order both to end peculation in the Forbidden City and to ascertain the net assets of the imperial family. A portion of the imperial collection of books, bronzes, porcelains, jades, paintings, and other kinds of valuables—that is, the portion housed in the Wen-hua and Wu-ying palaces—had, it is true, been appraised fully a decade earlier as part of an agreement worked out by representatives of the royal house and representatives of the Republic. The rarities comprising the bulk of the collection, however, had never even been catalogued. To catalogue them was the task set Lo Chen-yü, Yang Chung-hsi, and Wang Kuo-wei, among others.[33]

While affording him the opportunity to pursue his historical and antiquarian interests with the aid of materials to which scholars normally had no access, the chore of inventorying the vast and enormously valuable imperial collection plunged Wang into the mounting controversy between the royal family and Republican authorities over that collection's status. For several years articles had been appearing in the press protesting the sale of various palace treasures on the grounds that those treasures were owned by the state rather than by the imperial family and were, therefore, not at the latter's absolute disposal. Since the period 1923–24 in particular was one of intense "popular" animosity toward the royal house, it is not altogether surprising that even the inventory of the palace collection that Lo, Yang, Wang, and other courtiers were then engaged in making should have come under attack from certain quarters.[34] Neither is it altogether surprising that Wang, who seems from the first to have realized that at stake in the disputes over palace treasures was nothing less than the imperial family's honor, bitterly terminated his affiliation with National Peking University because of the stance taken on the imperial collection's status by Ma Heng (1880–1955), Shen Chien-shih (1885–1947), and others belonging to the university's Archaeological Society.

Acting on the instructions of Peking University administrators, Ma Heng had initially offered his friend Wang Kuo-wei a position on the university's faculty in mid-1919. Although he had declined the offer, Wang was approached by Ma again in the following year. Again he turned down the opportunity to join the faculty of Peking University. Ma Heng and his associates, however, were both insistent and persistent. In 1922, accordingly, Ma sent Wang a sum of money, asking him to accept both it and a position at the university's newly established Institute for Sinological Research (Yen-chiu so kuo-hsueh men). Wang returned the money and refused the offer. When, however, a month later Ma forwarded the money to Wang for a second time, begging him to reconsider, the latter finally agreed to accept both the money and a nominal post, adviser-by-correspondence (t'ung-hsin tao-shih), at the Institute for Sinological Research.[35] Wang's reservations about Peking University appear to have stemmed in the first instance from a fear that he might, if formally affiliated with it, become embroiled in politics. As it happened, this fear proved toward the end of 1924 or thereabouts to have been well justified.[36]

While reading the paper one day, Wang was startled, as he later informed Ma Heng and Shen Chien-shih, to see that the Archaeological Society of Peking University had published a manifesto deploring Prince Tsai-hsun's destruction of "state property" and accusing the Ch'ing scion of having "taken ancient artifacts handed down through the ages to be his own personal property." The society's charges, in Wang's view, were objectionable on many grounds, and he lost no time writing his Peking University colleagues to enumerate them.[37]

In the first place, he suggests to Ma and Shen, the status of the antiquities that Prince Tsai-hsun destroyed is not nearly as clear as the Archaeological Society's manifesto would lead one to believe. "Whether they should be considered state property or whether they should be considered the private property of the imperial family, and whether, moreover, the imperial family presented them to Prince Tsai-hsun or whether Prince Tsai-hsun himself purchased them from some other source or whether, as the manifesto says, he forcibly seized them are all questions that bear looking into."[38]

In the second place, Wang writes, the manifesto's claim that the Ch'ing scion has "taken ancient artifacts handed down through the ages to be his own personal property" is indefensible. All those treasures still in the hands of the imperial family, as well as all the objects on display in the Wen-hua and Wu-ying palaces ("the items in these two palaces have been purchased, but not yet paid for, by the Republic," he reminds Ma and Shen), can be shown on historical and legal grounds, Wang contends, "to be every one of them the private property of the imperial family." As regards the history of the palace collection, the thrust of Wang Kuo-wei's argument is that the priceless valuables, with four exceptions, were all amassed during "the present dynasty" by the forebears of the tenth Ch'ing sovereign. That they therefore belong to the imperial family, not to the state, is a proposition that would, Wang claims, be accepted under the legal system of any country at any time. As a matter of fact, he observes, the Republic itself has, in its Articles Providing for the Favorable Treatment of the Great Ch'ing Emperor after His Abdication, declared the palace collection to be the private property of the imperial family, and the latter's right to their property has been acknowledged by successive administrations in public documents.[39]

He cannot understand his colleagues' motives in publishing their manifesto, Wang confesses. "Not to study either the history of the palace collection or the Articles of Favorable Treatment is unwise (pu-chih). To be familiar with both and yet deliberately to say [what you have said in your manifesto] is unkind (pu-jen)." And to slander the imperial family while voicing not a single criticism of the Republican authorities' mishandling of antiquities, being as it is a case of "devouring the weak and spitting out the strong," is uncourageous (wu-yung).[40]

Mention of the Archaeological Society's wanton affronts to the dignity of the imperial family brings Wang Kuo-wei, in the long letter he sent Ma Heng and Shen Chien-shih, to two final complaints about the stance taken by his Peking University colleagues in their manifesto. His first complaint is that the society's members, by adopting the position set forth in their manifesto, have ignored their legal duty as citizens of the Republic of China.

According to the Articles of Favorable Treatment, the citizens of the Republic are to treat the Great Ch'ing emperor [after his abdication] "with the courtesies it is customary to accord to foreign monarchs." While in the manifesto you repeatedly impugn the imperial name, I know of no country in the world that treats foreign monarchs in this fashion. If you have abolished the Republic and established a new state, that is one thing. If, however, you are still a national university [founded] by the Republic of China, it is most certainly your duty to comply with the Articles by which the Republic was created as well as with its laws regarding the protection of [private] property.[41]

As for the latter of Wang's two final complaints about the Archaeological Society's manifesto, it is that its authors have ignored their sacred duty as scholars. "Universities are the highest institutions of learning in the entire country, and you gentlemen [who are professors at one of them] have the responsibility of [upholding] scholarship. When you make statements, therefore, you ought not to speak carelessly, as you have done here." Preserving antiquities, moreover, is only one of scholarship's functions, Wang reminds Ma and Shen. "If, for the sake of [preserving antiquities], you violate fundamental rights recognized in both law and morality, both state and society will disintegrate and where will scholarship be then?"[42]

It is obvious from the contents of his angry missive that Wang Kuo-wei believed his colleagues to have transformed the Archaeological Society from a nonpartisan to a partisan body. It is obvious too that he believed the authors of the society's manifesto to have forsaken their legal obligations as citizens, their moral obligations as human beings, and their professional obligations as scholars. That he felt personally betrayed by Ma Heng, who had prevailed on him to become an affiliate of the Institute for Sinological Research, is clear as well. We are not surprised, therefore, to learn that Wang wished to have no further dealings with Peking University.

> The graduate students whom you two earlier assigned me came to my house to consult me about something; please ask them to stop. Please also annul my status as an adviser in the Institute for Sinological Research. I would be most grateful if you would please also stop the publication of those articles [of mine] that are scheduled to appear in *The Journal of Sinological Studies*—namely, my article titled "My Views on Tai Chen's Edition of the *Commentary on the 'Classic of Waterways'* " ("Shu Tai chiao 'Shui-ching' chu̱ hou"), solicited by Mr. Hu Shih, and the notes on epigraphy that Mr. Jung Keng is in the process of fair-copying—since I am planning to make further revisions in them.[43]

In late 1924 Wang's tenure as a Companion of the Southern Study was brought to an abrupt and brutal close by Feng Yü-hsiang's coup d'état. Having betrayed the warlord Wu P'ei-fu, under whom he held an important command, the "Christian General" (as Feng was called) seized Peking and, on 2 November, established a regency government. Since he had long cherished the ambition of eliminating the royal house, it is not surprising that, once in control of the capital, Feng Yü-hsiang moved quickly to gain control of the Forbidden City itself. On 5 November, a day that Chinese loyalists would later recall with intense anguish and bitterness, a detachment of Feng's troops marched up to the Gate of Spiritual Valor, disbanded the imperial bodyguard, and ordered the Ch'ing scion both to accept a "revision" of the Articles of Favorable Treatment and to quit the palace immediately. Under the "protection" of an armed escort, the former emperor was driven to the northern section of Peking and deposited unceremoniously on the doorstep of the Northern Mansion, his father's residence. Here he would remain under guard for several weeks, until with the assistance of his tutor Reginald Johnston he would escape to the Japanese Legation.[44]

The molestation of the Ch'ing scion possessed, from the conservative point of view, a number of repugnant features. In the first place, the Christian General staged his dramatic second coup during a time of mourning (the dowager-consort Tuan-k'ang had recently passed away), a serious breach of propriety within the Confucian context. In the second place, Feng's staff officers demanded an interview with "Mr. P'u-i," which form of address was considered revoltingly gross by all those who still regarded what had been the imperial throne with respect or even reverence. In the third place, the Articles of Favorable Treatment, a formal document representing the Republicans' contribution to the compromise by which Empress Dowager Lung-yü (on behalf of the baby Hsuan-t'ung Emperor) in 1912 had acceded to the establishment of the Republic, was unilaterally abrogated. And in the fourth place, the Ch'ing scion was coerced into accepting, on 5 November 1924, a drastic modification of the original Articles.

It would be difficult to overstate the extent to which Wang Kuo-wei was troubled by the 5 November incident, during which he felt obliged, as he would later write Kano Naoki, "to accompany His Majesty out of the palace" and through town "amidst bayonets and bombs" to the Northern Mansion.[45] The immediate effect of his fearful trip through the streets of Peking on that ignominious fall day was, as one might imagine, to fill Wang with dread about the Ch'ing scion's personal safety. During the entire frightful and humiliating episode, Wang stood loyally by the former emperor's side, refusing to leave him unattended for even a second.[46]

The ultimate effect that Feng Yü-hsiang's violation of the Forbidden City had on Wang appears to have been so to offend his
sensibilities that he began darkly to contemplate suicide. Together
with Lo Chen-yü and K'o Shao-min (both, like himself, Companions
of the Southern Study), Wang Kuo-wei reportedly vowed to cast himself into the moat in front of the Gate of Spiritual Valor on the same
principle that, twenty-five years earlier, had inspired the scholar-
official Wang I-jung to jump down a well, namely, that "the subject
must die when his lord has been humiliated."[47] In an elegy written
shortly after Wang's demise, Ch'en Yin-k'o poignantly recaptures the
emotional intensity of what seems to have been a bleak, desperate
moment for some members of the Ch'ing scion's entourage:

> By the moat in front of the Gate of Spiritual Valor,
> They contemplated requiting their lord for his great
>   benevolence.
> The Companions of the Southern Study wished to drown
>   themselves;
> The Scholars of the Northern Gate desired to perish with them.[48]

Although neither he nor his friends did in the end commit suicide
during those unhappy last weeks of 1924 (Wang's family is said to
have kept a close eye on him at this time),[49] the winter of 1924–25
was without a doubt one of the cruelest that Wang Kuo-wei was ever
constrained to endure.[50] He was, indeed, so distraught in the weeks
following the Christian General's coup that, looking back on this period several months later, he confided to Chiang Ju-tsao that "no
words can adequately express how I then felt."[51]

Once the Ch'ing scion had arrived safely at the Japanese Legation,
however, Wang's mood brightened considerably. Neither the machinations of Feng Yü-hsiang, whose troops continued to occupy the
Forbidden City, nor Tuan Ch'i-jui's and Chang Tso-lin's entry into
the fray, nor the threatening movements of the Nationalist "revolutionaries," nor the imminence of the Communist "disaster" overly
perturbs him anymore, we find Wang writing to Kano Naoki, now
that "His Majesty" has reached the protective enclosure of the Japanese Legation. A frequent visitor at the legation, Wang seems to have
derived a certain measure of grim satisfaction from the elaborateness
of the security arrangements made by the Japanese to ensure the
deposed emperor's personal safety. He appears as well to have felt
pleased by the "especially kind" treatment that he noticed the Ch'ing
scion to be receiving at the hands of Minister Yoshizawa. As a result
of these felicitous developments, Wang was finally able, as he said,
"to relax somewhat."[52]

No sooner had the sometime emperor quit the Japanese Legation, after a three months' stay there (29 November 1924–23 February 1925), to settle on a long-term basis in the Japanese Concession in Tientsin than Wang Kuo-wei's worries about him began to revive. Of greatest concern to Wang in early 1925 were the intramural conflicts of various factions of loyalists, conflicts that he seems to have feared would undermine the Ch'ing scion's future safety. "Although [the imperial master] is in dire straits," he complains to Chiang Ju-tsao, "the cliques surrounding him continue to maneuver for position, precisely as they used to do when times were peaceful." The situation has proved so distressing, Wang confides to his friend, that he has decided to accept a professorship offered him by Ch'ing-hua University. "It is a good idea [for me] to leave the crowd. I have not been doing much reading lately, and I have been feeling that my thoughts are disorganized. I must now pull myself together so I can get back to my old career."[53]

Last Years

Although he had earlier been approached, on Chancellor Ts'ao Yun-hsiang's behalf, by Hu Shih concerning an appointment at Ch'ing-hua, Wang had initially declined Hu's offer, reportedly because he could not bring himself to leave the former emperor's side during the latter's hour of need.[54] After the Ch'ing scion's escape to the Japanese Legation, however, Wang clearly believed him to be in good hands, and, goaded by financial necessity, may have begun to reconsider Hu Shih's offer. Precisely at this juncture, as it happened, Chancellor Ts'ao wrote Reginald Johnston, requesting him to speak to the Ch'ing scion on the university's behalf; Hu Shih as well evidently contacted the former emperor on the subject.[55] As a result of the combined efforts of Johnston and Hu, Wang is said to have been summoned to the Japanese Legation one day in early 1925 and commanded by the sometime emperor to accept the position of professor of history at Ch'ing-hua's newly established Sinological Research Institute (Kuo-hsueh yen-chiu yuan).[56] While Wang seems to have obeyed the Ch'ing scion's order with alacrity, it is obvious from his subsequent letter to Chiang that by early 1925 the former emperor's thoughts on Wang Kuo-wei's future coincided with that gentleman's own.

Wang's life at Ch'ing-hua, in its initial phase, appears to have been quite agreeable to him. In the first place, at the institute he was surrounded by colleagues (among them Ch'en Yin-k'o, Wu Mi, and Liang Ch'i-ch'ao) and students (including Chao Wan-li, Hsu Chung-shu, and Yao Ming-ta) who admired him as both a scholar and a man of principle. Not once during his two years at Ch'ing-hua, we are told, despite the fact that he retained his queue and dressed in an old-fashioned cloth gown and jacket, was Wang ever ridiculed by anyone at the university for his loyalist sympathies.[57]

In the second place, Wang had ample time while employed at Ch'ing-hua to pursue his own intellectual interests, which of late had come to focus on the history and geography of the early Mongol period. Since he and his family had moved to the Ch'ing-hua campus months before classes were scheduled to begin, Wang was able to spend the summer of 1925 completing in draft a chronological biography (nien-p'u) of Yeh-lü Ch'u-ts'ai, secretary-astrologer to Ching-gis Khan, and a series of annotations to Li Chih-ch'ang's Record of a Journey to the West (Hsi-yu chi). Even after school had opened in the fall, Wang found that his teaching duties were light enough (he lectured only three or four hours per week on subjects very familiar to him—his own work on the Shang, the Book of Documents, and the ancient dictionary Shuo-wen chieh-tzu) to afford him sufficient leisure in which to conduct his own research.[58]

After his terrifying, humiliating encounter with Feng Yü-hsiang's troops during the coup of late 1924, Wang seems to have developed something of an aversion to Peking proper. His old friend Aoki Masaru, who visited him in the spring of 1925 in his new home on the Ch'ing-hua campus, was in fact startled to note that Wang was beginning to resemble one of those reclusive worthies of former times who, for years at a stretch, refused to sully themselves by going into a city. "Since I moved here," Wang told Aoki, "I have not set foot in the city."[59] Even when, later on, he was compelled occasionally to go into town on business of one sort or another, Wang always declined to spend the night there.[60] It is easy to imagine that, after his harrowing experience of November 1924, Wang Kuo-wei found the bucolic suburbs of Peking far more to his liking than the city itself, where during most of 1925 the antagonistic warlords Feng Yü-hsiang and Chang Tso-lin jockeyed for political supremacy.

Although he appears to have enjoyed his quiet surroundings at Ch'ing-hua, from time to time Wang would travel to Tientsin either to pay his respects to the Ch'ing scion or to visit with his mentor. While Lo Chen-yü had been included in the small group of scholars invited by Hu Shih, on Ts'ao Yun-hsiang's behalf, to assume professorships at Ch'ing-hua, he seems by early 1925 to have become too deeply involved in politics to have had much time for purely academic pursuits. Instead of accepting Hu's offer, therefore, as his protégé had done, Lo had chosen to move back to Tientsin (he and one of his sons had personally escorted the former emperor from the Japanese Legation in Peking to the Japanese Concession in Tientsin) and to establish himself there as one of the Ch'ing scion's principal advisers. During the latter part of the twenties, accordingly, Lo's energies were devoted mostly to collaborating with the Japanese for the purpose of placing the Ch'ing scion again on the throne (in March 1932, in part through Lo's efforts, the puppet state of Manchoukuo would be proclaimed with the Ch'ing scion as its nominal head) and to squabbling with Cheng Hsiao-hsu, another of the former emperor's closest advisers and one with whom Lo never saw eye to eye.[61]

Although no one will ever know how heavy his emotional burden really was during the last years of his life, we may hazard the opinion that the 5 November incident so profoundly disturbed Wang Kuo-wei that he never completely recovered from it. Indeed, in the eyes of his childhood friend Ch'en Shou-ch'ien, Wang was, so to speak, a suicide waiting to happen.[62] Whether in fact Wang would have felt constrained a second time to contemplate taking his own life had other distressing developments, after 1924, not subsequently occurred, we can, of course, never know. Other distressing developments did, however, subsequently occur, and in the aggregate they would serve to drive Wang to his grave.

During late 1926 and early 1927, Wang Kuo-wei's outlook on life became, for a variety of reasons, gloomier than it had ever been before. Already during the winter of 1925–26 his close friend Chiang Ju-tsao, with every one of whose books Wang was intimately acquainted by virtue of having compiled a descriptive catalogue of them, had lost the Secret Rhyme Library. On hearing of Chiang's misfortune, Wang had been "unhappy for days," unable to think of any way to ease the grief of a man "who loves books as if they were his life" and "who has sedulously collected them for twenty years."[63]

Another, and far more severe, blow was dealt Wang Kuo-wei in the latter part of 1926 when his eldest son, Ch'ien-ming (the one married to Lo Chen-yü's youngest daughter, Hsiao-ch'un), fell seriously ill in Shanghai. By the time Wang senior arrived on the scene, he found that his son's disease had already reached the incurable stage. We can only imagine how crushed Wang must have felt as he watched helplessly the life of his firstborn, aged twenty-seven, flow away before his eyes. During the months that remained to him, his student Chao Wan-li has reported, Wang's mood darkened appreciably.[64]

While due in part to his son's premature demise, Wang's darkening mood was in all probability due as well to the unhappy severance, at the time of Ch'ien-ming's funeral, of relations between Lo

Chen-yü and himself. According to Lo Chen-yü's grandson Lo Chi-
tsu, the abrupt rupture of the two men's thirty-year friendship was
occasioned by a conflict that arose between Mrs. Wang Kuo-wei and
her daughter-in-law over the funeral arrangements being made by
the former for the latter's husband. Since the women had not been
on good terms even before Wang Ch'ien-ming's death, this particular
clash, so Lo Chi-tsu informs us, caused a fatal breach between
them. When Lo Chen-yü heard of the incident from his distraught
daughter, Lo Chi-tsu further informs us, it caused a fatal breach
between him and Wang as well. Holding his protégé personally
responsible for Hsiao-ch'un's unhappiness, Lo Chen-yü took a measure that, from the Confucian perspective, can only be described as
extreme: he asked his daughter permanently to return to her natal
family (ta-kuei).[65]

Despite the loss of face that he suffered as one result of his
daughter-in-law's removal to Tientsin, Wang Kuo-wei apparently hoped
to heal the rift between Lo and himself through conciliatory gestures.
No sooner had the aggrieved young woman settled in her father's
home, therefore, than Wang sent Lo a letter profoundly earnest, even
apologetic, in tone. "Because I am lacking in virtue, Heaven sends
calamities down on me; that is why [Ch'ien-ming] perished last month.
He was my son and your son-in-law, so we grieve equally much for
him. Unexpectedly a misunderstanding has arisen between us, but
this misunderstanding will eventually resolve itself." In the meantime,
Wang says, he would like to entrust Lo with two sums of money to
manage on behalf of Ch'ien-ming's widow. One sum, he notes, had
been given to him on an earlier occasion by his daughter-in-law herself, while the other had just recently been paid out by Ch'ien-ming's
former employer, the Maritime Customs Service. "Please assume full
responsibility for managing [this money], as I am unfamiliar with this
sort of thing . . . In the Underworld my late son will be most grateful."[66]

When Lo Chen-yü returned the money that he had expected him
to accept, Wang Kuo-wei's hopes for a reconciliation in the near future
seem to have begun to evaporate. "It is really unreasonable for your
daughter to say that she will never touch a penny [of this money],"
we find him complaining in a subsequent letter to Lo. "May I inquire
to whom my late son's money should go if it is not to go to your
daughter? Please talk some sense into her." Lo appears, however, to
have been either unwilling or unable to reason with his daughter.
Mentor and protégé, as a result, reportedly never saw one another
again, and the money remained in Wang Kuo-wei's reluctant hands
until the day he died.[67]

During his last months, Wang Kuo-wei was both oppressed by personal woes and anxious about the Ch'ing scion's future among men grown implacably hostile to him. In view of his abiding concern for the sometime emperor, Wang in all likelihood regarded the Northern Expedition, launched by the Nationalists in mid-1926 to reunify China by military force, with grave foreboding. Since most of North China, including Shantung and Chihli, was in 1926 under the sway of Chang Tso-lin, a "conservative" warlord favorably disposed to the Ch'ing scion, he could hardly have been expected to refrain from worrying about what might happen to the former emperor in the event that the revolutionary forces of Chiang Kai-shek should succeed in vanquishing Chang's Feng-t'ien army during their sweep northward. It seems, indeed, to have been with fears of precisely this sort in mind that Wang began in the fall of 1926 to pay more frequent visits to Chang Garden than he had hitherto.[68]

Whatever reassurance he may have hoped to obtain from the Ch'ing scion's retainers in Tientsin, however, completely eluded Wang. To his dismay, these men proved to be blissfully ignorant of the increasing precariousness of the military status quo in North China. After one particularly consternating visit to Chang Garden, which he made in February 1927 on the occasion of the lunar New Year, Wang Kuo-wei returned to Ch'ing-hua University so distraught, Chao Wan-li tells us, that he actually fell ill with tuberculosis.[69]

Under these unhappy circumstances, Wang could not have been in any mood to hear, early in the New Year, that his old nemesis, the Christian General, was back in business in central and northern China. Having in late 1926 declared his allegiance to the Nationalists, Feng Yü-hsiang zestfully joined its Northern Expedition by invading Honan in the spring of 1927 in cooperation with the revolutionary armies of T'ang Sheng-chih and Chang Fa-k'uei. The pressure that these troops brought to bear against those of Chang Tso-lin did in the end, as Wang Kuo-wei appears to have feared, deal a serious blow to the Feng-t'ien army's position in North China. On 28 May General Chang was constrained to order all Feng-t'ien forces fighting on the southern front to withdraw to Chihli and Shantung. With Honan now firmly in his grip, Feng Yü-hsiang poised his troops for the march northward to Peking, eastward to Tientsin.

Those who spoke with Wang Kuo-wei during the last days of May and on the first day of June noticed that he had become unusually despondent about the outlook for his country and for the Ch'ing scion. Jung Keng, whom he visited several days before his death in order to return all the books he had borrowed, found Wang profoundly pessimistic about the current political situation. Liang Ch'i-ch'ao did as well. Chin-liang, who called on him at the end of May, found Wang so upset about the deteriorating military situation in North China and so worried about its implications for the former emperor's safety that he seemed on the point of weeping.[70]

To two students who visited him at his home the night before his suicide, Wang remarked gloomily: "I hear that Feng Yü-hsiang is about to enter the capital and that Chang Tso-lin is going to order a general withdrawal in order to hold the territory east of Shanhaikuan. There will be a major upheaval in Peking within days."[71] Although Wang was not the only resident of the Peking area to worry, at the beginning of June, about his immediate future, he had, in view of his former service to the Ch'ing scion and mortifying prior encounter with the Christian General's troops, more cause for anxiety than most. Indeed, according to Chao Wan-li, Wang Kuo-wei feared that Feng's second seizure of the capital might prove even more catastrophic than the first. "Having already experienced one upheaval, as a matter of principle I see no reason to allow myself to be humiliated again," Wang wrote in his suicide note the evening before his demise.[72]

With rumors that Feng's takeover of the capital was imminent flying about the Ch'ing-hua campus, some of Wang's colleagues, such as Liang Ch'i-ch'ao, publicly announced their intention to flee Peking temporarily. Wang, however, quietly kept his own counsel. To those who inquired privately about his plans, he simply implied vaguely that he, too, would seek refuge from the approaching turmoil in some distant place.[73]

In view of the numerous disappointments of his later years, one is tempted to speculate that Wang Kuo-wei must have ridden out to the well-ordered and tranquil grounds of I-ho Park on the morning of 2 June 1927 with a certain sense of relief. This park was, as we know, inextricably associated in his mind with the imperial family in particular and the Ch'ing dynasty in general and, by extension, with the manners and mores that had been China's under the empire. In his moroseness and desolation, Wang's thoughts had in fact recently turned toward the unearthly little world that Empress Dowager Tz'u-hsi had created, four decades earlier, on the quiet outskirts of Peking; just three days before his death he had agitatedly confided to Chin-liang that K'un-ming Lake was "the only clean (kan-ching) spot left today" in an otherwise hopelessly muddy world.[74]

As he tarried in the Fishes-among-Pondweed Pavilion, was Wang, one wonders, recounting to himself the lines of the ancient poem to which the pavilion's name is an allusion?

> The fishes are there, there among the pondweed,
> Sheltered by the rushes.
> The king is here, here in Hao,
> Dwelling in tranquillity.[75]

Everything, with the exception of himself, Wang may have been thinking as he stood alone on the margin of K'un-ming Lake, was in its proper place: the fishes in their pond, the king in his capital, the spirit of Old China in I-ho Park. Perhaps Wang may have been reflecting that it was high time that he, too, assume his rightful place in the natural order of things by following the Ch'ing dynasty, and the cultural order of which it had been an integral part, into oblivion. Like his former English teacher Taoka Sayoji, who had sacrificed his life after the death of the Meiji Emperor to protest the demise of traditional Japanese culture, Wang Kuo-wei seems by mid-1927 to have regarded suicide as the only constructive action a gentleman could take in nihilistic times.

We are able, of course, only to guess at the sorts of thoughts that may have crossed Wang's mind as he stood poised on the brink of eternity. It is not, however, too farfetched to suggest, as many of his contemporaries have done, that Wang Kuo-wei's last desperate act was made in the lofty spirit of Confucian idealism.

> The detached palace still belongs to the former dynasty;
> When the lord has been humiliated, in it his subject may grieve.
> Into the Mi-lo River, in a different age, disappeared Ch'ü Yuan.
>
> The calamity has now overtaken us;
> The man has perished and the country is diseased.
> All under Heaven, in a single voice, weep for Cheng Ssu-hsiao,

writes Wang's friend Wu Mi.[76]

According to Wu Mi and others of his friends and colleagues, it was by no means a coincidence that Wang chose as the site of his suicide the Ch'ing dynasty's park and selected as the date of his suicide the anniversary of Ch'ü Yuan's death.[77] Over and over again in the elegies they composed after his demise, Wang's intimates describe his death as a sacrifice made for the sake of high principle, similar for that reason to the suicides of Po-i and Shu-ch'i, Ch'ü Yuan, Wang Ping (his own ancestor), Wu K'o-tu, and Liang Chi. " 'He sought to act virtuously and [he] did so,' " declares Wang's old friend and former teacher Fujita Toyohachi.[78]

In the estimation of those closest to him, Wang Kuo-wei was one of those "determined scholars and men of virtue" whom Confucius extolled for "not seeking to live at the expense of injuring their virtue."

From the poems and essays they have left posterity, we can see that his friends and colleagues regarded Wang in the same incandescent light in which, indeed, that gentleman for a lifetime had regarded himself. He was, they say, a man of scrupulous integrity, as pure in spirit as the driven snow. Wang was, they say, precisely the sort of person who "will even sacrifice his life to preserve his virtue complete."[79]

In their descriptions of what they believe to have been his probable motivation in committing suicide, some of Wang's circle appear implicitly to have drawn a distinction between, on the one hand, certain symbolic acts that their righteous friend had performed during his later years and, on the other, the symbolic significance that these acts seem likely to have possessed for him. As intimates such as Ch'en Yin-k'o appear to have discerned, the paradoxical fact of the matter seems to be this: in throwing himself to the fishes in K'un-ming Lake, Wang Kuo-wei was performing what of necessity would be the last, and most dramatic, of a number of ostensibly political acts whose symbolic significance to him was not exclusively, or even primarily, political.

There can, of course, be no doubt that Wang in later life was intensely loyal to the Ch'ing. His loyalty stemmed, however, neither from a conviction that the monarchical form of government was superior to the republican (although he believed this to be the case), nor from any expectation that the dynasty might return to power (although for some time he seems to have entertained the hope that it might), but rather from an emotional devotion to the principle of loyalty itself. Wang Kuo-wei's determination to resign his post at the Ministry of Education after the Wuchang Uprising, to retain his queue even after the collapse of the dynasty of whose authority it was a token, to do his duty by the Ch'ing scion while a Companion of the Southern Study, and to end his life spectacularly in a park associated in the public mind—as well as his own—with the imperial family, that is to say, was fraught with deep emotional significance and arose in the first instance out of his fierce commitment to Confucian moral tenets, salient among which is the hoary notion of the oneness of the virtues of loyalty to one sovereign, filial piety, and wifely subservience to one husband.[80]

Because of his extreme devotion to the twin causes of conserving traditional moral ideals and preserving the literary record wherein these ideals are enshrined, those who knew Wang Kuo-wei best considered him the apologist par excellence for traditional Chinese culture. This was, in their view, both the source of his heroic virtue and the cause of his extraordinary grief. "Whenever a culture is in decline," Ch'en Yin-k'o writes in a thoughtful essay published shortly after Wang's death, "anyone who has received benefits from this culture will necessarily suffer. The more a person embodies [the underlying principles of] this culture, the deeper will be his suffering. Once his suffering has become extreme, such a person may resort to suicide in order to attain peace of mind and discharge his moral obligations." Since the political and social upheavals of recent decades have fatally undermined traditional Chinese culture, "how," Ch'en inquires, "can a man who personifies the very spirit of this culture not meet the same fate and come to an end along with it?"[81]

16

Epilogue: Across the Barriers of Culture and Time

The project to make China "wealthy and strong" was initiated over one hundred years ago by Confucian scholar-officials who felt supremely confident of the superiority of their own political, ethical, and cultural values but who were deeply troubled by the Chinese people's material backwardness and military weakness. When late Ch'ing bureaucrats began energetically to move the empire in the direction of industrialization and away from the traditional ideal of a subsistence-level agrarian economy, they therefore did so on the happy assumption that new technology, modern industry, and Western commercial practices could be incorporated into a Confucian society. The lesson that these patriotic and innovative administrators eventually derived from the dynasty's extended experiment in "self-strengthening" was, however, a sobering one, namely, that the practical knowledge that China sought in the West was in fact deeply implicated in a cultural mesh subversive of the very social order the central government had expected it to defend.

Thus it was that sensitive members of the 1890s generation came in the end to realize, and to regret, that by championing Western ideas at variance with Confucian wisdom they had unwittingly contributed to the subversion of traditional Chinese culture. This was the irony, indeed the tragedy, of the watershed generation of Chinese intellectuals: having themselves set the empire on a radical course that would lead eventually to the demise of Confucian China, they lived to decry many of the features of the new society whose emergence was due in no small measure to their own youthful examination and enamoration of foreign strands of thought. No one better exemplifies this type of transitional intellectual, the type who helped to subvert a culture that he would later cherish above all else, than Wang Kuo-wei.

Many of the concepts that Wang acquired from the German men-

tors of his youth are, of course, by no means incompatible with traditional Chinese values. Some, such as Kant's view of the nature of
duty and Schopenhauer's doctrine of redemption through a Bud-
dhistic negation of the will, are even in close harmony with, respectively, the Confucian emphasis on moral obligation and the Buddhist
stress on self-abnegation. Schopenhauer's dynamic vision of the universe and human society as a seething tumult of mutually antagonistic
elements, however, while having affinities with the social Darwinian
image of "nature red in tooth and claw" that captivated Yen Fu as
well as an entire generation of young, iconoclastic intellectuals, bears
no resemblance whatsoever to traditional Chinese world views, which
characteristically exalt quietude and passivity. Nietzsche's doctrines of
the will to power, the overman, and the revaluation of values, all of
which Wang introduced to his contemporaries in the opening years
of the twentieth century via Lo Chen-yü's *Journal of the Educational
World,* are also the very antipodes of central Confucian ideals.

It was doubtless because he belatedly perceived Schopenhauer's
and Nietzsche's great heresies that, shortly after the Wuchang Uprising, Lo Chen-yü urgently entreated his protégé to repudiate his
earlier love affair with German philosophy. Lo evidently took particular exception to the thought of Nietzsche, whose violent excoriation
of the "uncourageous" virtues of benevolence, humility, and self-re-
straint he found especially pernicious in the volatile atmosphere of
the times. It was doubtless because, after listening carefully to his
mentor's hortatory speech, Wang fully comprehended the extent to
which his former excursions in foreign thought had helped to undermine the traditional fabric of Chinese society that he refused after
1911 to discuss, or even to allude to, his former philosophical investigations.[1]

Wang Kuo-wei apparently lived to regret not only his pioneering
study of German philosophy, but also his ground-breaking research
on Chinese vernacular literature and literature that contains vernacular elements. Wang's interest in this kind of literature, as we have
seen, had first been aroused by his German sages, whose "unusual"
ideas in the literary sphere enabled him to free himself from the
Chinese scholar's traditionally contemptuous view of vernacular literature and to see it in a brand-new light.

The seriousness with which Wang Kuo-wei himself took up the
study of *Dream of the Red Chamber* (which is written in a vernacular
style), Sung lyrics (which incorporate a limited number of colloquial
language elements), and Yuan drama (which makes extensive use of
colloquial language elements) had consequences, however, that in his
earlier years he evidently did not foresee. By commending traditional

literary works written in a vernacular style or containing vernacular elements, Wang inadvertently helped pave the way toward a general acceptance of Hu Shih's revolutionary proposition that it is actually works written in the colloquial, rather than the classical, language that best represent the peculiar excellence of traditional Chinese literature. By proclaiming the worth and importance of the vernacular as a literary medium, he inadvertently helped pave the way as well toward a general acceptance of Hu Shih's revolutionary proposal that all Chinese literature in future be written in the vernacular.[2]

One has little difficulty imagining Wang Kuo-wei's repugnance, during his later years, toward Hu Shih's contention that Chinese literary works written in the classical language are both aesthetically ungratifying and socially irrelevant. Odious to him as well, no doubt, was Hu Shih's ambition to make the written word accessible to peasants as well as to intellectuals, at the heart of which lies a radical rejection of a fundamental traditional value, namely, the sharp distinction between ruler and ruled, between those who labor with their minds and those who labor with their hands. It is not coincidental that the intellectual elitist Wang Kuo-wei declined ever to write in the vernacular himself or that he paid no attention when in the early 1920s Ch'en Nai-ch'ien republished *Catalogue of Plays*. Nor is it accidental that Wang retitled the new edition of *Lyrics in the World of Men* that reportedly appeared in 1917 *Bignonia Lyrics* (*T'iao-hua tz'u*), which connotes despair in the midst and in consequence of China's cultural decline.[3]

A humanist whose extended quest for meaning led him, after the 1911 Revolution, existentially to commit himself to the Confucian ethicoreligious tradition, Wang Kuo-wei seems in his later years both to have considered China's actual cultural situation wretched in the extreme and to have possessed an abiding faith in the value and importance of the Confucian ideals from which the present, as this latter-day Jeremiah believed, was a grievous departure. While he has thus been regarded as an anachronism by some "progressive" and "revolutionary" writers, it is very far from certain that the ideas for which Wang bled and finally died have, in fact, passed into history. Antitraditionalist dogma notwithstanding, it is not self-evidently true, for example, that the impulse to overthrow a civilization's cultural ideals and social forms is more estimable than the impulse to preserve them, or that in their management of public affairs progressives and revolutionaries are juster, more humane, and more efficient than conservatives are. Neither is it at all obvious that, as May Fourth and post–May Fourth iconoclasts have long insisted, Confucian humanism has no constructive role to play in the modern world.[4]

It should not be taken for granted that we who live in the late twentieth century have managed to solve, once and for all, the "problems of the universe and human life" that, in one form or another, wholly engaged Wang's attention over the course of a lifetime. Precisely because the questions to which he addressed himself—the questions of higher belief, artistic form, and moral value—are both fundamental and elusive, Wang's writings on philosophy, literature, and history will always possess a universal interest distinct from their many technical merits. Across the barriers of culture and time, Wang Kuo-wei will forever be talking to his fellow man about truth and beauty and virtue, about the world of substantial things.

Abbreviations

Notes

Selected Bibliography

Glossary

Index

Abbreviations

AWL	Wang Kao-ming et al., eds. and comps., *Wang Chung-ch'ueh kung ai-wan lu*
CASTK	Wang Kuo-wei, *Ching-an shih-tz'u kao*
CLP	Lo Chen-yü, *Chi-liao pien*
JCTH	Wang Kuo-wei, *Jen-chien tz'u-hua*
LHTCC	Lo Chen-yü, *Lo Hsueh-t'ang hsien-sheng ch'üan-chi*
"NP"	Chao Wan-li, "Wang Ching-an hsien-sheng nien-p'u"
NP	Wang Te-i, *Wang Kuo-wei nien-p'u*
SYHCK	Wang Kuo-wei, *Sung Yuan hsi-ch'ü k'ao*
TWWR	Arthur Schopenhauer, *The World as Will and Representation*
WKTCC	Wang Kuo-wei, *Wang Kuan-t'ang hsien-sheng ch'üan-chi*

Full references for the works listed above as well as for all other incompletely cited works appearing in the Notes are given in the Selected Bibliography.

Notes

Preface

1. My account of Wang's activities on the morning of 2 June 1927 is based on Tai Chia-hsiang [Po Sheng], "Chi Wang Ching-an hsien-sheng tzu-ch'en-shih shih-mo," in *WKTCC*, 16:7148. According to another source, however, Wang did not dive headfirst into K'un-ming Lake and choke to death, as Tai has inferred; rather, he jumped feet-first into the lake and, finding the water only waist-deep, immediately submerged his head (Chin-liang, "Wang Chung-ch'üeh kung hsun-chieh chi," in *AWL*, p. 1). (I have arbitrarily chosen to follow Tai's account.) However he cast himself into K'un-ming Lake, both writers agree that Wang was under water for only a minute or two (indeed, Chin-liang maintains that his back never even got wet)—long enough to take the life of a frail, despairing "old" man, but not long enough to render his suicide note, secreted about his person, illegible.

1. Prologue

1. *CLP*, p. 710. In the decades immediately following its establishment in Shanghai in 1865, the Kiangnan Arsenal translated many Western scientific treatises and manuals.

2. Lo Chen-yü, "Hai-ning Wang Chung-ch'üeh kung chuan," in *WKTCC*, 16:7019.

3. For Yen Fu's criticism of Chang Chih-tung's slogan, see Teng Ssu-yu and John K. Fairbank, eds., *China's Response to the West*, p. 151. The account that follows of Yen Fu's intellectual orientation is based on Benjamin I. Schwartz, *In Search of Wealth and Power*.

4. As translated in Schwartz, *In Search of Wealth and Power*, p. 49.

5. As translated in ibid., p. 48.

6. As translated in Teng and Fairbank, *China's Response to the West*, p. 76 (with a minor revision).

2. The Early Years

1. Liu Chun-jen, *Chung-kuo ti-ming ta tz'u-tien* [The Geographical Dictionary of China] (Peking: Kuo-li Pei-p'ing yen-chiu yuan, 1930), pp. 578, 1084. *Hsien* and *chou* were the smallest administrative units within a province in imperial times. They consisted of a *hsien* or *chou* seat, which was a walled city, surrounded by several towns and dozens or even hundreds of villages. The

population of a *hsien* or *chou* varied from several tens of thousands of households to several hundred thousand.

2. As early as the seventh century A.D., flooding had become a serious problem along the northern coastline of the bay (Liu Chun-jen, *Ti-ming ta tz'u-tien*, p. 578), and in no place was the problem more serious than in Yen-kuan. Of the entire system of dikes (*hai-t'ang*) eventually constructed from Chiang-yin on the south shore of the Yangtze River around the Yangtze Cape and thence past Cha-p'u and Yen-kuan to Hangchou, the dikes of Yen-kuan are the oldest (H. von Heidenstam, "The Growth of the Yangtze Delta," *Journal of the North-China Branch of the Royal Asiatic Society* 53 [1922]:31).

3. Hsu San-li et al., comps., *Hai-ning hsien chih* [Gazetteer of Hai-ning District] (1683), 1:11b.

4. This discussion of Wang Kuei is based on Wang Kuo-wei, "Pu chia-p'u Chung-chuang kung chuan" (original title: "*Sung shih* 'Chung-i chuan' Wang Ping pu-chuan"), 1917; revised version rpt. in *WKTCC*, 3:1097–1099.

5. This account of Wang Kuang-tsu's career is based on ibid., pp. 1099–1102.

6. The foregoing account of Wang Ping's heroic deeds is based on ibid., pp. 1116–1117.

7. Ibid., pp. 1120–1121; *NP*, p. 1.

8. Sun Feng-tsao, ed., Chu Hsi-en, comp., *Hai-ning chou chih kao* [Provisional Gazetteer of Hai-ning Department] (n.p., 1922), 25:7b, 10, 9b; *NP*, p. 1.

9. On the Ch'en family, see Arthur W. Hummel, ed., *Eminent Chinese of the Ch'ing Period (1644–1912)*, 2 vols. with successive pagination, pp. 96–97, and Ho Ping-ti, *The Ladder of Success in Imperial China: Aspects of Social Mobility, 1368–1911* (1962; rpt. New York: Da Capo Press, 1976), pp. 137–141.

10. "NP," p. 7051. Although the academic title of *chien-sheng* was a purchased one, it admitted its holder to gentry status and entitled him to participate in the examinations for the *chu-jen* and *chin-shih* degrees. If Wang Kuo-wei's immediate forebears did, as seems' probable, take advantage of their student status to sit for the *chu-jen* examination, they evidently did not succeed in passing it. "Mr. Wang's great-grandfather and grandfather were virtuous men but unknown," says Lo Chen-yü ("Hai-ning Wang Chung-ch'üeh kung chuan," in *WKTCC*, 16:7019).

11. "NP," pp. 7051–7052. On the system of privately hired advisers, see Kenneth E. Folsom, *Friends, Guests, and Colleagues: The Mu-fu System in the Late Ch'ing Period* (Berkeley: University of California Press, 1968), pp. 33–57. By the late nineteenth century there were about six hundred thousand regular first-degree holders (*sheng-yuan*) and another six hundred thousand lower-degree holders who had purchased their rank (Ho, *The Ladder of Success*, pp. 181–182).

12. Lo Chen-yü, "Chung-ch'üeh kung chuan," p. 7019.

13. *NP*, p. 5.

14. Wang Kuo-wei, "Tzu-hsu," 1907; rpt. in *WKTCC*, 5:1823.

15. Ibid. See also "NP," p. 7051.

16. "NP," p. 7052.

17. Ibid. It seems that Wang Nai-yü had been "adopted out" to the family of his paternal uncle, Wang Ssu-tuo, and was thus obliged to observe the mourning rites for him on the occasion of his death.

18. Ch'en Shou-ch'ien, "Chi Wang Chung-ch'üeh kung wen," in *WKTCC,* 16:7117.

19. "NP," p. 7052.

20. Wang, "Tzu-hsu," p. 1823.

21. *NP,* pp. 7–8. Serious preparation for the higher examinations took place not in the community schools but in academies, of which each provincial capital usually had several. One or more offered special courses to help students prepare for the triennial *chü-jen* examinations.

22. Ch'en Shou-ch'ien, "Chung-ch'üeh kung wen," p. 7117; ibid.

23. Ibid. The provincial examination of 1893 was one given by imperial grace; the next regularly scheduled examination was to be held in 1894. Unaware that there was in 1893 a "provincial examination by imperial grace" (*en-k'o*), Wang Te-i (*NP,* p. 8) thinks that Wang Kuo-wei must have sat for the special preliminary examination in 1894.

24. Wang, "Tzu-hsu," p. 1823; ibid. The text says simply "learning" (*hsueh*), but, like his Chinese biographers, I take Wang to mean "New Learning" (*hsin-hsueh*).

25. This biographical account is based on data contained in "NP," p. 7053.

26. Ibid., p. 7054; *NP,* pp. 10–11.

27. Lo Chen-yü, "Chung-ch'üeh kung chuan," p. 7019.

28. Ibid., p. 7022. See also Wang's letter to Hsu T'ung-lin of 13 April 1898, in Wang Kuo-wei, *Wang Kuo-wei ch'üan-chi: shu-hsin,* ed. Wu Tse, p. 5.

29. In his autobiography Lo Chen-yü recalls how he became interested in agriculture: "I thought to myself that if the world would not make use of me, I would establish myself in one of the professions to earn my living. Reflecting that agriculture is the foundation of the country and that the ancients farmed when not in office, I conceived the ambition of studying agriculture" (*CLP,* p. 710). He read what materials he could obtain, including "such foreign works on agriculture as had been translated into Chinese" (ibid.). His curiosity, Lo says, was aroused by these foreign works. "According to them, crop yields could be increased with new methods. Regretting that these works were not very specific, I thereupon discussed with my late friend Mr. Chiang Fu the idea of founding an Agricultural Society in Shanghai" (ibid.).

30. *CLP,* p. 714. An ardent Japanophile from at least the mid-1890s, Lo Chen-yü was on excellent terms at the turn of the century with many Japanese intellectuals, including Naitō Torajirō and Kano Naoki.

31. "NP," p. 7054; Wang, "Tzu-hsu," pp. 1823–1824. Lo and Fujita apparently first met in 1897 (Lo Chen-yü, "Jih-pen T'ai-pei ta-hsueh chiao-shou wen-hsueh po-shih T'eng-t'ien [Fujita] chün mu-piao," in *LHTCC,* 1st series, 4:1539). Lo seems immediately to have invited Fujita to join his translating enterprise, and in time the two men became fast friends. After the establishment of the Eastern Language Institute, Fujita continued to translate agricultural materials for Lo while simultaneously teaching science at the institute (*CLP,* p. 714). For a synopsis of Fujita's career, see *The Japan Biographical*

Encyclopedia and Who's Who, compiled and edited by the staff of the Japan Biographical Research Department of the Rengo Press, 3rd ed. (Tokyo: Rengo Press, 1964–65), p. 159. On him, see also *Ajia rekishi jiten* [The Historical Encyclopedia of Asia], 10 vols. (Tokyo: Heibonsha, 1959–1962), 8:113.

32. Lo Chen-yü, "Chung-ch'ueh kung chuan," p. 7019. Lo also befriended Fan Ping-ch'ing and Shen Hung, two other students at the institute (*CLP,* p. 715).

33. "NP," p. 7054. For the full text of this quatrain, see *WKTCC,* 4:1458.

34. Wang, "Tzu-hsu," p. 1824.

35. Lo Chen-yü, "Chung-ch'ueh kung chuan," p. 7022. The preceding account is based also on *CLP,* p. 714, and "NP," p. 7054.

36. Wang, "Tzu-hsu," p. 1824.

37. *The Japan Biographical Encyclopedia and Who's Who,* pp. 1663–1664; Lo Chen-yü, "T'eng-t'ien chün mu-piao," p. 1539.

38. Quoted in *NP,* p. 14.

39. Kano Naoki, "Ō Seian [Wang Ching-an] kun o omou," *Geibun* 18, no. 8 (August 1927):38–39. The foregoing account of the institute's curriculum is drawn from Wang, "Tzu-hsu," p. 1824, and *CLP,* p. 715.

40. Chou Shu-jen [Lu Hsun], preface to *Call to Arms* (*Na han*); trans. according to Yang Hsien-yi and Gladys Yang, *Selected Stories of Lu Hsun,* 3rd ed. (Peking: Foreign Languages Press, 1972), pp. 1–2.

41. As translated in William A. Lyell, Jr., *Lu Hsün's Vision of Reality* (Berkeley: University of California Press, 1976), pp. 50–51.

3. Wang as Educational Critic

1. As translated in Teng Ssu-yu and John K. Fairbank, eds., *China's Response to the West,* p. 196 (with a minor revision).

2. David S. Nivison, "Protest against Conventions and Conventions of Protest," in *The Confucian Persuasion,* ed. Arthur F. Wright (Stanford, Calif.: Stanford University Press, 1960), p. 200. On the serious reservations that some Chinese have had about the examination system, see also the great mid-Ch'ing novel *Ju-lin wai-shih* [The Scholars], by Wu Ching-tzu.

3. Chang Chih-tung, *Ch'üan-hsueh p'ien,* p. 58.

4. As translated in William Ayers, *Chang Chih-tung and Educational Reform in China* (Cambridge, Mass.: Harvard University Press, 1971), p. 160 (with minor revisions).

5. On educational reform, see Meribeth E. Cameron, *The Reform Movement in China, 1898–1912,* pp. 65–87, and David D. Buck, "Educational Modernization in Tsinan, 1899–1937," in *The Chinese City between Two Worlds,* ed. Mark Elvin and G. William Skinner (Stanford, Calif.: Stanford University Press, 1974), pp. 171–212.

6. Liang Ch'i-ch'ao, "Chiao-yü cheng-ts'e ssu i" [My Views on Educational Policy], *Hsin-min ts'ung-pao* [New Citizen Journal], no. 8 (1902):60.

7. Quoted in Ch'en Ch'i-t'ien, *Tsui-chin san-shih nien Chung-kuo chiao-yü shih* [The History of Chinese Education in the Last Thirty Years], ed. Wu Hsiang-hsiang (1930; rpt. as vol. 5 in Chung-kuo hsien-tai shih-liao ts'ung-shu [Taipei: Wen-hsing shu-tien, 1962]), p. 68.

8. For the Ministry of Education's regulations concerning county-level educational matters, see Shu Hsin-ch'eng, ed., *Chin-tai Chung-kuo chiao-yü shih-liao* [Historical Materials on Modern Chinese Education], 4 vols. (Shanghai: Chung-hua shu-chü, 1928), 2:131–135.

9. Wang Kuo-wei, "Tzu-hsu," 1907; rpt. in *WKTCC*, 5:1824–1825.

10. "NP," p. 7055.

11. Mo Jung-tsung, "Lo Hsueh-t'ang hsien-sheng nien-p'u," in *LHTCC*, 1st series, 20:8704. The School of Agriculture had been established by Chang Chih-tung in 1898 in order, so he said, to enrich the country, alleviate suffering, and reduce reliance on others. Chinese agriculture lagged behind that of other countries, in Chang's opinion, because of China's neglect of scientific studies. He challenged officials to take the lead in improving agricultural knowledge, methods, and yields and himself set a good example by founding and maintaining the School of Agriculture. On the school, see Ayers, *Chang Chih-tung and Educational Reform*, pp. 132, 223.

12. *NP*, p. 17. Founded by Lo Chen-yü in the spring of 1901, the *Chiao-yü shih-chieh tsa-chih* was edited by Wang Kuo-wei.

13. *North-China Herald*, 18 September 1901, p. 557; Mo Jung-tsung, "Nien-p'u," p. 8705; Ayers, *Chang Chih-tung and Educational Reform*, p. 219; "NP," p. 7055.

14. John K. Fairbank, Edwin O. Reischauer, and Albert M. Craig, *A History of East Asian Civilization*, vol. 2, *East Asia, The Modern Transformation* (Boston: Houghton Mifflin, 1965), p. 618.

15. Wang, "Tzu-hsu," p. 1825; "NP," p. 7055.

16. Wang Kuo-wei, preface to *Ching-an wen-chi*, 1905; preface rpt. in *WKTCC*, 5:1547. In his autobiographical sketch ("Tzu-hsu," p. 1825) Wang Kuo-wei asserts that he did not undertake his background reading in Western philosophy until 1903 and that he began his examination of the critical philosophy only in 1904. Since his first published piece on Kant ("Han-te hsiang-tsan") appeared in the fall of 1903, Wang's recollection as given there is obviously faulty.

17. Marian von Galik, "Nietzsche in China (1918–1925)," *Zeitschrift fur Kultur und Geschichte Ost-und Sudostasiens* 110 (1971):5–6; William A. Lyell, Jr., *Lu Hsün's Vision of Reality* (Berkeley: University of California Press, 1976), p. 60.

18. "NP," p. 7055.

19. Ibid.; Albert Feuerwerker, *China's Early Industrialization: Sheng Hsuan-huai (1844–1916) and Mandarin Enterprise* (Cambridge, Mass.: Harvard University Press, 1958), p. 70; Wang Ch'ü-ch'ang, "Chia-hsing Shen Mei-sou hsien-sheng nien-p'u ch'u-kao [part one]," *Tung-fang tsa-chih* 26, no. 15 (10 August 1929):69.

20. *NP*, p. 18. Fujita Toyohachi also became an educational adviser to Ts'en in 1902 (*Ajia rekishi jiten* [The Historical Encyclopedia of Asia], 10 vols. [Tokyo: Heibonsha, 1959–1962], 8:113). On the T'ung-chou Normal School, also called the Nan-t'ung Normal School, see Samuel C. Chu, *Reformer in Modern China: Chang Chien, 1853–1926* (New York: Columbia University Press, 1965), pp. 94, 100.

21. During 1902 Wang was absorbed in the study of the works of Arthur Fairbanks, William Stanley Jevons, Harald Høffding, Friedrich Paulsen, and Wilhelm Windelband. See "Wang's Discovery of Kant's Works" in chapter 5.

22. "NP," pp. 7056–7057.

23. *CLP*, p. 728; Huang Hsiao-k'o, "T'eng-t'ien [Fujita] po-shih hsiao-chuan," *Yen-ching hsueh-pao*, no. 8 (December 1930): 1653–1654. The Kiangsu Normal School was also called the Su-chou Normal School.

24. "NP," p. 7057; Chin Shunhsin, "Taoka Reiun to Kanō Jigorō," in *Kindai Nihon to Chūgoku*, ed. Takeuchi Yoshimi and Hashikawa Bunzō, 2 vols., 1:192. Taoka taught Japanese at the school.

25. Wang, "Tzu-hsu," p. 1826.

26. *NP*, pp. 34, 36, 40.

27. "NP," p. 7059.

28. Wang Kuo-wei, "Shu-pen-hua chih che-hsueh chi ch'i chiao-yü hsueh-shuo," 1904; rpt. in *WKTCC*, 5:1598. Wang's educational essays, as well as his philosophical essays, youthful literary essays, and early poetry, were published originally in the *Chiao-yü shih-chieh tsa-chih*, no issues of which I have been able to consult. Some of these essays Wang himself republished in 1905 in an anthology titled *Ching-an wen-chi* [Essays by Ching-an]. Others were republished some years after Wang's death by Chao Wan-li (*NP*, p. 417) in *Hai-ning Wang Ching-an hsien-sheng i-shu* as part of an anthology titled *Ching-an wen-chi hsu-pien* [Further Essays by Ching-an]. The two works are reprinted as the fifth vol. of *WKTCC*; original dates of publication of the essays contained therein are according to "NP."

29. Wang Kuo-wei, "Chiao-yü ou-kan ssu tse," 1904; rpt. in *WKTCC*, 5:1759.

30. Wang, "Shu-pen-hua chih che-hsueh," p. 1598.

31. Ibid., pp. 1596–1597; ibid., p. 1597.

32. Wang Kuo-wei, "Lun chiao-yü chih tsung-chih," n.d.; rpt. in *WKTCC*, 5:1767.

33. Ibid.

34. Wang, "Shu-pen-hua chih che-hsueh," pp. 1620–1621. The passage just quoted is a paraphrase of *TWWR*, 2:71. There follows on pp. 1621–1623 a plagiarism of selected passages from *TWWR*, 2:71–80. Throughout his educational and philosophical essays, Wang quotes, paraphrases, and plagiarizes Schopenhauer's magnum opus. Since in his day plagiarism was an acceptable practice, one may view Wang's "borrowings" from Schopenhauer as merely another indication of the extent of his admiration of, and indebtedness to, the philosopher. For bibliographical information on Schopenhauer's major work, see chapter 5, n. 4.

35. Wang, "Shu-pen-hua chih che-hsueh," p. 1622; ibid.; ibid., pp. 1622–1623; ibid., p. 1622. These ideas are taken directly from *TWWR*, 2:74, 78. On Wang's understanding of Schopenhauer's theory of perception, see also "Wang's View of Schopenhauer's Epistemology" in chapter 6.

36. Wang, "Lun chiao-yü chih tsung-chih," p. 1769.

37. Wang, "Shu-pen-hua chih che-hsueh," p. 1623; Wang, "Lun chiao-yü chih tsung-chih," p. 1769.

38. In chapters 6 and 7.

39. On Schopenhauer's view of philosophical determinism, which he endeavored to interpret in such a way as to reconcile it with a belief in ultimate human liberty and responsibility, see Patrick Gardiner, *Schopenhauer*, pp. 247–274.

40. Wang, "Shu-pen-hua chih che-hsueh," pp. 1627–1628.

41. By "philosophy" (*che-hsueh*), or "pure philosophy" (*ch'un-ts'ui che-hsueh*), a pleonasm to which he occasionally resorts, Wang has in mind primarily those areas of philosophical inquiry that in the West are called metaphysics, aesthetics, logic, and epistemology; see "China's Lack of a Pure Philosophical Tradition" in chapter 4.

42. Wang, "Chiao-yü ou-kan," p. 1760.

43. Wang Kuo-wei, " 'Tsou-ting ching-hsueh-k'o ta-hsueh wen-hsueh-k'o ta-hsueh chang-ch'eng' shu hou," n.d.; rpt. in *WKTCC*, 5:1858.

44. Wang, "Chiao-yü ou-kan," p. 1758. For a list of the subjects Chang Chih-tung planned to include in the curriculum of the university's Literature Department, see *Tsou-ting hsueh-t'ang chang-ch'eng*, vol. 3, pp. 17–32b.

45. Wang, " 'Tsou-ting chang-ch'eng,' " pp. 1858–1859. For a list of the subjects Chang envisioned including in the curriculum of the university's Classics Department, see *Tsou-ting hsueh-t'ang chang-ch'eng*, vol. 3, pp. 4–11. For his promotion of "real results" and denigration of "empty talk," see *Tsou-ting hsueh-t'ang chang-ch'eng*, vol. 1, p. 23.

46. Wang, "Chiao-yü ou-kan," p. 1758; Wang, " 'Tsou-ting chang-ch'eng,' " pp. 1869–1870.

47. Wang, "Chiao-yü ou-kan," p. 1758. Wang maintains that although Japanese universities have literature departments rather than philosophy departments, the principal subject matter of these departments is philosophy (Wang, " 'Tsou-ting chang-ch'eng,' " p. 1858).

48. Wang, "Chiao-yü ou-kan," p. 1758; ibid.

49. Wang Kuo-wei, "Lun chin-nien chih hsueh-shu chieh," 1905; rpt. in *WKTCC*, 5:1740. Ibid.

50. Ibid.

51. Wang, " 'Tsou-ting chang-ch'eng,' " p. 1860; ibid.

52. Ibid., p. 1861.

53. Wang, "Chiao-yü ou-kan," pp. 1758–1759.

54. Wang Kuo-wei, "Chi-yen," 1906; rpt. in *WKTCC*, 5:1879, 1877.

55. Wang Kuo-wei, "Chiao-yü hsiao-yen shih-erh tse," n.d.; rpt. in *WKTCC*, 5:1881.

56. Ibid., p. 1882; ibid., pp. 1882–1883.

57. Wang, "Chin-nien chih hsueh-shu chieh," p. 1738; ibid.

58. Ibid.

59. Ibid., pp. 1738–1739; ibid., p. 1739; ibid.

60. Wang Kuo-wei, "Chiao-yü hsiao-yen shih tse," 1906 or 1907; rpt. in *WKTCC*, 5:1899. Ibid. Ibid.

61. Ibid., p. 1900.

62. Ibid.

63. Wang Kuo-wei, "Chiao-yü hsiao-yen shih-san tse," 1907; rpt. in *WKTCC*, 5:1896.

64. Wang Kuo-wei, "Wen-hsueh hsiao-yen," 1906; rpt. in *WKTCC*, 5:1839–1840. Wang, "Chiao-yü hsiao-yen shih-san tse," p. 1897.

65. Wang, "Chiao-yü hsiao-yen shih-san tse," p. 1897; ibid., p. 1898.

66. Ibid., p. 1898. It may be remarked that Ku T'ang-sheng (Hung-ming) also deplored the late Ch'ing government's emphasis on universal education, criticized the official policy of sending students abroad to be educated and of making them officials when they returned, and believed that education should be for its own sake. See R. David Arkush, "Ku Hung-ming (1857–1928)," *Papers on China* 19 (December 1965):213.

4. Declaration of Principles

1. Wang Kuo-wei, "Lun chin-nien chih hsueh-shu chieh," 1905; rpt. in *WKTCC*, 5:1735–1736.

2. Wang Kuo-wei, "Tzu-hsu," 1907; rpt. in *WKTCC*, 5:1825. Wang, "Chin-nien chih hsueh-shu chieh," p. 1741.

3. Wang Kuo-wei, "Lun che-hsueh chia yü mei-shu chia chih t'ien-chih," 1905; rpt. in *WKTCC*, 5:1749.

4. Ibid., p. 1748; ibid., p. 1749.

5. Ibid., pp. 1748–1749.

6. Ibid., p. 1749; ibid.; ibid., p. 1752.

7. Benjamin I. Schwartz, "Some Polarities in Confucian Thought," in *Confucianism and Chinese Civilization*, ed. Arthur F. Wright (Stanford, Calif.: Stanford University Press, 1964), p. 5; Wang, "Che-hsueh chia yü mei-shu chia," p. 1750.

8. Wang, "Che-hsueh chia yü mei-shu chia," p. 1751; ibid.

9. Ibid. Wang Kuo-wei, "Shu Ku shih T'ang-sheng ying-i *Chung-yung* hou," 1907; rpt. in *WKTCC*, 5:1803.

10. Wang, "Ku shih T'ang-sheng," p. 1803; ibid., pp. 1803–1804.

11. Ibid., p. 1804; ibid., p. 1805.

12. Ibid., p. 1805.

13. Ibid., p. 1804.

14. Ibid., p. 1806. "Ego," "Absolute," "Idea," and "Unconscious" are written in English.

15. Wang, "Che-hsueh chia yü mei-shu chia," p. 1751.

16. Wang, "Chin-nien chih hsueh-shu chieh," p. 1734.

17. Ibid., p. 1735; ibid. It is unclear why Wang regards Christianity as being "material."

18. Wang, "Chin-nien chih hsueh-shu chieh," p. 1735. Yen Fu gave Huxley's work the incomplete Chinese title of *T'ien-yen lun* [Theory of Evolution], as Wang mentions parenthetically in the passage just quoted.

19. Wang, "Chin-nien chih hsueh-shu chieh," p. 1736.

20. Ibid., p. 1737; ibid.; ibid. For "Chin-shih ti-i ta-che K'ang-te chih hsueh-shuo" [The Philosophy of the Great Modern Philosopher Kant], Liang's article on Kant, see *Hsin-min ts'ung-pao* [New Citizen Journal], no. 25 (1903):11–24, and no. 26 (1903):9–18.

21. Wang, "Chin-nien chih hsueh-shu chieh," pp. 1736–1737.

22. Ibid., p. 1737. Henry Wood's *Ideal Suggestion through Mental Photography*

(1893) was translated by John Fryer in 1896 under the title *Chih-hsin mien-ping fa* [The Prevention of Disease through Mental Healing]. For a brief consideration of the influence of Wood's book on T'an, who was reportedly "ecstatic" after reading it, see Richard H. Shek, "Some Western Influences on T'an Ssu-t'ung's Thought," in *Reform in Nineteenth-Century China*, ed. Paul A. Cohen and John E. Schrecker (Cambridge, Mass.: East Asian Research Center, Harvard University, 1976), pp. 200–203.

23. Wang, "Chin-nien chih hsueh-shu chieh," p. 1738; ibid., p. 1741. As late as 1911, Wang would still be stressing this theme of the universality of learning and elaborating on it in terms very similar to those used in this essay of 1905. See the opening remarks he made on the occasion of the publication of the first issue of Lo Chen-yü's *Kuo-hsueh ts'ung-k'an* [Sinological Publications] (1911); remarks rpt. in *WKTCC*, 4:1408.

5. The Critical Philosophy

1. See, for example, Ts'ai Yuan-p'ei, "Wu-shih nien lai Chung-kuo chih che-hsueh" [Chinese Philosophy in the Last Fifty Years], 1923; rpt. in idem, *Ts'ai Yuan-p'ei ch'üan-chi* [The Complete Works of Ts'ai Yuan-p'ei] (Tainan: Wang-chia ch'u-pan she, 1975), p. 307; Kuo Chan-po, *Chin wu-shih nien Chung-kuo ssu-hsiang shih* [Chinese Intellectual History of the Past Fifty Years], 2nd ed. enlarged (Hong Kong: Lung-men shu-tien, 1965), p. 71; Chiang Wei-ch'iao, *Chung-kuo chin san-pai nien che-hsueh shih* [The History of Chinese Philosophy in the Last Three Hundred Years] (Taipei: Chung-hua shu-chü, 1971), p. 153; and Fung Yu-lan, *A Short History of Chinese Philosophy*, ed. Derk Bodde (1948; rpt. New York: Free Press, 1966), pp. 326–327.

2. See "Wang's View of Schopenhauer's Epistemology" and "Wang's View of Schopenhauer's Metaphysics" in chapter 6 as well as Wang's article on *Dream of the Red Chamber* ("Hung-lou meng p'ing-lun," 1904; rpt. with punctuation in I Su, comp., *"Hung-lou meng" chüan*, 2 vols. in 1, 1:244–265), which contains a number of references to Buddhist and Taoist ideas.

3. Wang Kuo-wei, "Tzu-hsu," 1907; rpt. in *WKTCC*, 5:1825–1826. Since it is unclear whether in 1902 Wang read *Logic* or *Elementary Lessons in Logic*, I have arbitrarily identified the work he calls *Ming-hsueh* as the former; on these two works, see chapter 11, n. 1. Harald Høffding's *Psykologi i Omrids på Grundlag af Erfaring* (1881) was translated from the German edition by Mary E. Loundes as *Outlines of Psychology* (1892); Friedrich Paulsen's *Einleitung in die Philosophie* (1892) was translated from the 3rd edition by Frank Thilly as *Introduction to Philosophy* (1895); and Wilhelm Windelband's *Lehrbuch der Geschichte der Philosophie* (1892) was translated by James H. Tufts as *A History of Philosophy* (1893; 2nd ed. 1901).

4. Wang Kuo-wei, preface to *Ching-an wen-chi*, 1905; preface rpt. in *WKTCC*, 5:1547. Wang, "Tzu-hsu," p. 1825. By the close of the nineteenth century, Immanuel Kant's *Kritik der reinen Vernunft* (1781; 2nd ed. 1787) had been translated into English by Francis Heywood (1838), J. M. D. Meiklejohn (1854), and F. Max Müller (1881, 2 vols.). Arthur Schopenhauer's *Die Welt als Wille und Vorstellung* (1818 [dated 1819]; 2nd ed. enlarged by fifty chapters, 1844) had been translated into English by R. B. Haldane and J. Kemp (1883, 3

vols.). Although they were of course not available to Wang, in this study we shall rely on Norman Kemp Smith's masterful translation of the first *Critique* (1929; rpt. 1965) and E. F. J. Payne's brilliant translation of Schopenhauer's magnum opus (1958, 2 vols.), which is cited in these notes as *TWWR*.

5. Wang, preface to *Ching-an wen-chi*, p. 1547; ibid.; Wang, "Tzu-hsu," p. 1826; ibid.

6. Wang Kuo-wei, "Han-te hsiang-tsan," 1903; rpt. in *WKTCC*, 5:1830.

7. Kant, *Critique of Pure Reason*, trans. Smith, p. 22.

8. Wang, "Han-te hsiang-tsan," p. 1830.

9. Wang, "Tzu-hsu," pp. 1825–1826.

10. Wang Kuo-wei, "Shu-pen-hua chih che-hsueh chi ch'i chiao-yü hsueh-shuo," 1904; rpt. in *WKTCC*, 5:1599.

11. *TWWR*, 1:425; ibid.

12. Wang, "Shu-pen-hua chih che-hsueh," p. 1600.

13. Ibid., p. 1601.

14. Wang Kuo-wei, "Shih li," 1904; rpt. in *WKTCC*, 5:1576. Ibid., p. 1578.

15. Ibid., p. 1578; ibid., pp. 1578–1579. The source of these quotations from the first *Critique* is not actually that work itself but *TWWR*, 1:432. See ibid. for his quotation from Schopenhauer's "Criticism of the Kantian Philosophy." Regarding Wang's remark that Kant gives many definitions for the term 'understanding', compare *TWWR*, 1:433. Regarding the last part of the passage, compare *TWWR*, 1:444.

16. Norman Kemp Smith, *A Commentary to Kant's "Critique of Pure Reason,"* p. 2.

6. The Philosophy of Metaphysical Pessimism

1. Wang Kuo-wei, preface to *Ching-an wen-chi*, 1905; preface rpt. in *WKTCC*, 5:1547. By the end of the nineteenth century Schopenhauer's main works had all been translated into English: *Die Welt als Wille und Vorstellung*, as previously noted, by Haldane and Kemp as *The World as Will and Idea*; *Über die vierfache Wurzel des Satzes vom zureichenden Grunde* (1813) and *Über den Willen in der Natur* (1836) by Mme. Karl Hillebrand as *"On the Fourfold Root of the Principle of Sufficient Reason" and "On the Will in Nature"* (rev. ed. [London: George Bell & Sons, 1891]); and part of *Parerga und Paralipomena* (1851, 2 vols.) by T. Bailey Saunders as *Studies in Pessimism: A Series of Essays by Arthur Schopenhauer* (London: Swan Sonnenschien & Co., 1891). As mentioned earlier, all references in this book to Schopenhauer's magnum opus are to Payne's translation (*TWWR*).

2. Wang, preface to *Ching-an wen-chi*, p. 1547. Wang Kuo-wei, "Tzu-hsu," 1907; rpt. in *WKTCC*, 5:1825. Idem, "Shu-pen-hua chih che-hsueh chi ch'i chiao-yü hsueh-shuo," 1904; rpt. in *WKTCC*, 5:1598.

3. Wang, "Shu-pen-hua chih che-hsueh," pp. 1614–1615.

4. Ibid., p. 1597; ibid., p. 1614; ibid., p. 1597. See *TWWR*, 2:391.

5. *TWWR*, 1:3; ibid., p. 15; ibid., p. 419.

6. Wang, preface to *Ching-an wen-chi*, p. 1547. Wang Kuo-wei, *"Hung-lou meng p'ing-lun,"* 1904; rpt. with punctuation in I Su, comp., *"Hung-lou meng" chüan*, 2 vols. in 1, 1:259. Wang, preface to *Ching-an wen-chi*, p. 1547.

7. Wang, "Shu-pen-hua chih che-hsueh," p. 1612.

8. Ibid., pp. 1612–1613; ibid., p. 1611.

9. See "Wang's Educational Philosophy" ("The Aims of Education") in chapter 3.

10. Wang, "Shu-pen-hua chih che-hsueh," pp. 1615–1616. The passage just quoted is a paraphrase of *TWWR*, 1:69.

11. See Patrick Gardiner, *Schopenhauer*, pp. 106–109.

12. Wang, "P'ing-lun," p. 245. Wang's discussion of the essentiality of suffering to life is based on *TWWR*, 1:312; the remark about the pendulum is a plagiarism of ibid.

13. Wang, "P'ing-lun," p. 249. For "The Metaphysics of Love," see *TWWR*, 2:531–560.

14. Wang, "P'ing-lun," pp. 250–251.

15. Wang Kuo-wei, "Shu Shu-pen-hua 'I-ch'uan shuo' hou," 1905; rpt. in *WKTCC*, 5:1709–1710.

16. Ibid., pp. 1710, 1713, 1716. The fathers of Ssu-ma Ch'ien and Pan Ku were both noted scholars. For "The Hereditary Nature of Qualities," see *TWWR*, 2:517–530. For Wang's translation, which is appended to his essay "Shu Shu-pen-hua 'I-ch'uan shuo' hou," see *WKTCC*, 5:1717–1733.

17. Wang, "Shu-pen-hua chih che-hsueh," pp. 1601–1603.

18. In "The Possibility of Knowing the Thing-in-Itself" (*TWWR*, 2:191–200), a supplementary chapter of his major work, Schopenhauer did in fact greatly qualify his earlier claims about the knowability of the will.

19. Wang Kuo-wei, "Shu-pen-hua yü Ni-ts'ai," 1904; rpt. in *WKTCC*, 5:1671. See also ibid., p. 1672.

20. There is, of course, the problem of how an irrational impulse to live that is not at the same time the striving of some subject can objectify itself at all.

21. The will has spontaneity but no moral freedom, the precondition of guilt.

22. Wang, "P'ing-lun," p. 254.

23. Ibid., p. 258; ibid.

24. While inspired by Plato, this conception of eternal Ideas serves distinctive ends in Schopenhauer's theory of art.

25. Although Schopenhauer usually seems to say that genius involves both the ability to intuit the Ideas and the ability to express them in art, he sometimes seems to imply that genius refers only to the faculty of apprehending the Ideas, the ability to express them being simply a matter of technique.

26. E. Joan Smythe, "The Early Thought of Wang Kuo-wei: An Analysis of His Essays on German Voluntaristic Philosophy (1903–1907)," *Papers on China* 18 (December 1964):10–11. Writers such as Tolstoy and Turgenev, and subsequently Hardy and Mann, were influenced in different ways by Schopenhauer's vision of the world.

27. Wang, "P'ing-lun," pp. 245–246; Wang, "Shu-pen-hua chih che-hsueh," pp. 1605-1606.

28. For Wang's Schopenhauerian account of the origin and nature of human consciousness, see "Shu-pen-hua chih che-hsueh," pp. 1602–1604.

29. Wang, "Shu yü Ni," pp. 1690–1691; *TWWR*, 1:314. See also *TWWR*, 2:203.

30. Wang, "Shu yü Ni," p. 1685; ibid., p. 1682. In another article ("Shu-pen-hua chih che-hsueh," pp. 1607–1608), however, which was probably written earlier than the one from which I have just quoted, Wang accepts without reservation the philosopher's views on universal love.

31. Wang, "P'ing-lun," pp. 257, 251–252.

32. Ibid., pp. 250–252. On this point see also "*Dream* and Schopenhauerian Ethics" in chapter 7.

33. Wang Kuo-wei, "Lun hsing," n.d.; rpt. in *WKTCC*, 5:1550.

34. Wang, "P'ing-lun," pp. 259–260.

35. Ibid., pp. 260–261. For Schopenhauer's words, see *TWWR*, 1:381.

36. Wang, "P'ing-lun," p. 260; Wang, "Shu yü Ni," p. 1672.

7. Analysis of "Dream of the Red Chamber"

1. For his criticisms of his contemporaries' understanding of *Hung-lou meng*, see Wang Kuo-wei, "*Hung-lou meng* p'ing-lun," 1904; rpt. with punctuation in I Su, comp., "*Hung-lou meng*" *chüan*, 2 vols. in 1, 1:262–265. Unlike the rest of his early essays, Wang's "Critique" has received considerable scholarly attention. See, for instance, Wang Ching-hsien, "Recognition and Anticipation in Wang Kuo-wei's 'Criticism of *Hung-lou meng*,' " *Tsing Hua Journal of Chinese Studies*, n.s. 10, no. 2 (July 1974):91–112; Yeh Chia-ying, "Ts'ung Wang Kuo-wei '*Hung-lou meng* p'ing-lun' chih te-shih t'an tao *Hung-lou meng* chih wen-hsueh ch'eng-chiu chi Chia Pao-yü chih kan-ch'ing hsin-t'ai" [A Discussion, in the Light of the Merits and Demerits of Wang Kuo-wei's "Critique of *Dream of the Red Chamber*," of *Dream of the Red Chamber*'s Literary Achievement and Chia Pao-yü's Marked Sensibility], *Tou-sou* 27 (May 1978):27–43; and Anthony C. Yu, "Self and Family in the *Hung-lou Meng*: A New Look at Lin Tai-yü as Tragic Heroine," *Chinese Literature: Essays, Articles, Reviews* 2, no. 2 (July 1980):199–202.

2. C. T. Hsia, "Yen Fu and Liang Ch'i-ch'ao as Advocates of New Fiction," in *Chinese Approaches to Literature from Confucius to Liang Ch'i-ch'ao*, ed. Adele Austin Rickett, p. 251. For Hsia's own brilliant study of *Hung-lou meng*, which is superior to Wang's in its appreciation of the psychological complexity of the novel, see his book *The Classic Chinese Novel: A Critical Introduction* (New York: Columbia University Press, 1968), pp. 245–297.

3. See "Wang's View of Schopenhauer's Metaphysics" in chapter 6.

4. Wang, "P'ing-lun," p. 250.

5. Ibid.

6. Ibid., p. 254.

7. Ibid., p. 251.

8. *TWWR*, 1:254; ibid.

9. Wang, "P'ing-lun," p. 254; ibid., p. 251; ibid., p. 252.

10. Ibid., p. 255.

11. *TWWR*, 1:398.

12. Wang, "P'ing-lun," p. 251; ibid.; ibid.; ibid.

13. Ibid.

14. See "Wang's View of Schopenhauer's Ethics" in chapter 6.

15. Wang, "P'ing-lun," p. 250.

16. Ibid., pp. 251–252.

17. Ibid., p. 257.

18. As noted in "Wang's View of Schopenhauer's Metaphysics" in chapter 6, Wang usually speaks as if he holds man himself responsible for his existence, even though it is difficult to see how this could possibly be the case in a universe dominated by the will.

19. Wang, "P'ing-lun," p. 251.

20. Quoted in John C. Y. Wang, "The Chih-yen-chai Commentary and the *Dream of the Red Chamber:* A Literary Study," in *Chinese Approaches to Literature from Confucius to Liang Ch'i-ch'ao,* ed. Adele Austin Rickett, p. 199. Following Wang, I take this poem to be the work of the commentators.

21. "Without this turn of events, not only would there be no end to the whole thing, but also it would be too illogical" (quoted in ibid., p. 219).

22. The publication in 1792 of Kao E and Ch'eng Wei-yuan's 120-chapter printed version of *Hung-lou meng* gradually put an end to the circulation of the various 80-chapter manuscript versions of the novel, which contain the comments of Red Inkstone and others. The commentators were rescued from literary oblivion only in 1928, when Hu Shih published "K'ao-cheng *Hung-lou meng* ti hsin ts'ai-liao" [New Material for the Study of *Dream of the Red Chamber*], an examination of the *chia-hsu* (1754) version of the novel accompanied by Red Inkstone's comments. See Wang, "The Chih-yen-chai Commentary and the *Dream of the Red Chamber*," p. 189.

8. Disillusionment with Philosophy

1. Wang Kuo-wei, preface to *Ching-an wen-chi,* 1905; preface rpt. in *WKTCC,* 5:1547. Although he made this statement in the fall of 1905, Wang says he had "fully developed" this view of Schopenhauer's thought by the time he wrote his article on Nietzsche, which was probably toward the end of 1904 (ibid.).

2. Wang Kuo-wei, "Shu-pen-hua yü Ni-ts'ai," 1904; rpt. in *WKTCC,* 5:1691.

3. Ibid., p. 1694.

4. Ibid., p. 1693; ibid.

5. Ibid., pp. 1692–1693.

6. Maurice Meisner, *Li Ta-chao and the Origins of Chinese Marxism* (1967; rpt. New York: Atheneum, 1973), pp. 52, 274n2.

7. On Chinese interest in Nietzsche in the early part of the twentieth century, see Marian von Galik, "Nietzsche in China (1918–1925)," *Zeitschrift fur Kultur und Geschichte Ost-und Sudostasiens* 110 (1971):5–47.

8. Wang, "Shu yü Ni," p. 1671.

9. See "Wang's View of Schopenhauer's Metaphysics" and "Wang's View of Schopenhauer's Ethics" in chapter 6.

10. Wang, "Shu yü Ni," p. 1675.

11. Ibid., p. 1693; ibid.; ibid.; ibid., p. 1672.

12. *TWWR,* 2:146; quoted in Wang, "Shu yü Ni," p. 1679. Wang, "Shu yü Ni," p. 1671.

13. Wang, "Shu yü Ni," p. 1695; ibid., p. 1685; ibid., p. 1681; ibid., p. 1671.

14. Ibid., p. 1677. See *TWWR*, 2:393.

15. Wang, "Shu yü Ni, " p. 1694; ibid., p. 1686.

16. Ibid., p. 1686; ibid., pp. 1691–1692; ibid., p. 1686.

17. Ibid., p. 1695; ibid.

18. Wang Kuo-wei, "Tzu-hsu erh," 1907; rpt. in *WKTCC*, 5:1827.

19. For his characterization of Schopenhauer's metaphysics as "great," see Wang Kuo-wei, *"Hung-lou meng* p'ing-lun," 1904; rpt. with punctuation in I Su, comp., *"Hung-lou meng" chüan*, 2 vols. in 1, 1:259.

20. Wang, "Shu yü Ni," p. 1693.

21. Harald Høffding, *Psykologi i Omrids pà Grundlag af Erfaring* (1881); translated from the German edition by Mary E. Loundes as *Outlines of Psychology* (1892); translated from the English edition by Wang Kuo-wei as *Hsin-li hsueh kai-lun* (1907).

22. Høffding, *Outlines of Psychology*, trans. Loundes, p. 14.

23. Wang, "Tzu-hsu erh," p. 1828.

24. Ibid., pp. 1828, 1827. In his autobiographical sketch of 1907, Wang observes that "my temperament is such that my emotions are too powerful and my intellect too weak for me to become a philosopher, and yet my emotions are too weak and my intellect too powerful for me to become a poet" (ibid., pp. 1827–1828). This description of himself as a cross between a philosopher and a poet, as well as the ambivalent stance that Wang adopts in the 1907 sketch toward his hybrid condition (elsewhere in this same piece of writing he declares that he is one of the greatest poets in the *tz'u*, or lyric, genre that the world has ever seen), remind one powerfully of Schiller. Schiller, too, considered himself, as he said, a "hermaphrodite." Schiller, too, vacillated between moments of deep despair, when he thought that his creative powers would preclude his ever becoming a serious philosopher while his intellectual powers would preclude his ever becoming a serious poet, and moments of high confidence, when he felt his interest in philosophy and poetry to be an asset to his endeavors in both. See Elizabeth M. Wilkinson and L. A. Willoughby, trans. and eds., *On the Aesthetic Education of Man in a Series of Letters*, by Friedrich Schiller, editors' introduction, p. xxix.

It is entirely possible that Wang had Schiller very much in mind when he wrote his autobiographical account of 1907. On Wang's knowledge of Schiller's ideas, see "The Origin and Nature of the Aesthetic Impulse" in chapter 9.

9. The Aesthetic Education of Man

1. Wang Kuo-wei, "Jen-chien shih-hao chih yen-chiu," 1907; rpt. in *WKTCC*, 5:1801. Idem, "Wen-hsueh hsiao-yen," 1906; rpt. in *WKTCC*, 5:1840–1841.

2. I am indebted to Donald Fleming for this view of Schiller.

3. Wang, "Shih-hao," pp. 1795–1796. The yawning boredom dreaded by Schopenhauer and Wang resembles Leopardi's *noia* and Heidegger's *angst*.

4. Wang, "Shih-hao," p. 1796; ibid., p. 1797. "To kill time" is written in English.

5. Wang, "Shih-hao," pp. 1799–1800; ibid., p. 1799; ibid., p. 1800; ibid.

6. Ibid., p. 1801; ibid.

7. Ibid., p. 1800; ibid., pp. 1800–1801.

8. Ibid., p. 1802; ibid. In his literary essays of 1906–07 Wang sometimes argues, with Nietzsche, that both the creation and the appreciation of literary works involve considerations of power, but he sometimes argues, with Schiller, that literature—good literature, at any rate—is produced for the sake of beauty alone and, with Kant, that aesthetic contemplation is entirely disinterested (see "The Role of Art in Society" and "Types of Beauty Found in Art" in this chapter). Sensing, perhaps, that "a foolish consistency is the hobgoblin of little minds," Wang seems to have had no difficulty embracing the conflicting claims that are here under consideration.

9. Wang Kuo-wei, "Ch'ü-tu p'ien," 1906; rpt. in *WKTCC*, 5:1875.

10. Ibid., p. 1873; ibid., p. 1874; ibid.

11. Ibid., p. 1875; ibid.

12. Ibid.; ibid.; ibid.; ibid., p. 1876.

13. Wang, "Wen-hsueh hsiao-yen," pp. 1847–1848.

14. Ibid., p. 1848. On the literary views of Yen Fu and Liang Ch'i-ch'ao, see C. T. Hsia, "Yen Fu and Liang Ch'i-ch'ao as Advocates of New Fiction," in *Chinese Approaches to Literature from Confucius to Liang Ch'i-ch'ao*, ed. Adele Austin Rickett, pp. 221–257.

15. Wang Kuo-wei, "Lun che-hsueh chia yü mei-shu chia chih t'ien-chih," 1905; rpt. in *WKTCC*, 5:1750. Ibid., p. 1751.

16. Wang Kuo-wei, "Ch'ü-tzu wen-hsueh chih ching-shen," 1906; rpt. in *WKTCC*, 5:1850. Wang, "Shih-hao," pp. 1801–1802.

17. *TWWR*, 1:249.

18. Immanuel Kant, *Kritik der Urteilskraft* (1790), translated by J. H. Bernard in 1892 as *Kritik of Judgement* and reprinted in 1951 as *Critique of Judgment*, p. 44.

19. Ibid., p. 54.

20. Ibid., p. 73.

21. Ibid., p. 77; ibid., p. 74.

22. Wang Kuo-wei, "Ku-ya chih tsai mei-hsueh shang chih wei-chih," 1907; rpt. in *WKTCC*, 5:1831.

23. Ibid., p. 1832; ibid., p. 1836. Kant actually says not that what one person regards as beautiful all other persons *necessarily* also regard as beautiful, but merely that when we assert that something is beautiful, we claim that everyone else *ought* to consider it beautiful as well.

24. Wang Kuo-wei, "*Hung-lou meng* p'ing-lun," 1904; rpt. with punctuation in I Su, comp., "*Hung-lou meng*" *chüan*, 2 vols. in 1, 1:247–248. Idem, "Shupen-hua chih che-hsueh chi ch'i chiao-yü hsueh-shuo," 1904; rpt. in *WKTCC*, 5:1606. Wang, "P'ing-lun," p. 248.

25. Wang, "Ku-ya," pp. 1831–1832.

26. Ibid., pp. 1830–1831.

27. Ibid., p. 1833; ibid.; ibid.; ibid.

28. Translation of the lines from Tu Fu's "Ch'iang ts'un shih" [Ch'iang Village] is according to William Hung, *Tu Fu, China's Greatest Poet* (Cambridge,

Mass.: Harvard University Press, 1952), p. 115. Translation of those from Yen Chi-tao's lyric to the tune "Che-ku t'ien" [Partridge Sky] is according to James J. Y. Liu in *Sunflower Splendor: Three Thousand Years of Chinese Poetry,* ed. Liu Wu-chi and Irving Yucheng Lo (Garden City, N.Y.: Anchor Press/ Doubleday, 1975), p. 340. Translation of the line from "Po hsi" is according to James Legge, trans., *The Chinese Classics,* 5 vols. in 4, 4:105. (I have changed Legge's romanizations wherever necessary to accord with the system used in this study.) Translation of the lines from Ou-yang Hsiu's lyric to the tune "Tieh lien hua" [Butterflies Lingering over Flowers] is according to James J. Y. Liu, *Major Lyricists of the Northern Sung,* p. 41. All these lines are quoted by Wang in "Ku-ya," pp. 1833–1834.

29. Wang, "Ku-ya," p. 1834; ibid.

30. Ibid., p. 1839; ibid., p. 1838; ibid., pp. 1838–1839.

31. Ibid., p. 1836; ibid.; ibid.

32. Ibid., pp. 1836–1837.

33. Wang, "Wen-hsueh hsiao-yen," pp. 1842–1843. Translation of the lines from Yen Shu's lyric is according to Liu, *Major Lyricists of the Northern Sung,* p. 22; translation of those from Ou-yang Hsiu's lyric is according to ibid., p. 41; and translation of those from Hsin Ch'i-chi's lyric is according to Irving Yucheng Lo in *Sunflower Splendor,* ed. Liu and Lo, p. 395.

34. Wang, "Wen-hsueh hsiao-yen," p. 1843.

35. In a free translation of Schopenhauer's statement that "I have still to add here a special remark on the *childlike* character of genius, on a certain resemblance between genius and the age of childhood" (*TWWR,* 2:393), Wang had written in 1904 that "the genius is one who has not lost his childlike character" ("Shu-pen-hua yü Ni-ts'ai," rpt. in *WKTCC,* 5:1677).

36. Wang, "Wen-hsueh hsiao-yen," p. 1842. Later on (in 1908–09) we will find him insisting that "the lyricist is one who has not lost his childlike character" (*JCTH,* p. 197 [original remark 16]).

37. Wang, "Wen-hsueh hsiao-yen," p. 1844; ibid., p. 1845. Tung Shih was an ugly woman of yore who tried to make herself appear beautiful by imitating the mannerisms of the stunning Hsi Shih.

10. Lyrics, Criticism, Aesthetics

1. See *WKTCC,* 5:1771–1786. In Lo Chen-yü's edition of his protégé's works, these poems are reprinted separately under the title *Kuan-t'ang ping-wu i-ch'ien shih* [Regular Poems Written by Kuan-t'ang Prior to 1906].

2. "NP," pp. 7059–7061. Both volumes of Wang's lyrics apparently were first published in Lo's *Chiao-yü shih-chieh tsa-chih* (ibid., pp. 7059–7060). They are said to have been republished in incomplete form as a single volume in 1917, evidently under the title by which they are now known, *T'iao-hua tz'u.* (On this point, see Ch'u Wan-feng, "Wang Ching-an hsien-sheng chu-shu piao," in *WKTCC,* 16:7200; and *NP,* p. 416.) The version of *T'iao-hua tz'u* contained in Lo Chen-yü's edition of Wang's works is reportedly based on the 1917 volume, although it includes four lyrics dating from 1918–1920 (*NP,* p. 416). Other lyrics written by Wang during the years 1905–1909 were published, or possibly republished, in his *Kuan-t'ang chi-lin* [Works by Kuan-

t'ang, 1923] under the title "Ch'ang-tuan chü." All the lyrics contained in *T'iao-hua tz'u* and "Ch'ang-tuan chü" are reprinted with punctuation in *CASTK*.

James Robert Hightower has described the *tz'u* as "a song-form character-ized by lines of unequal length, prescribed rhyme and tonal sequences, oc-curring in a large number of variant patterns, each of which bears the name of a musical air" (*Topics in Chinese Literature: Outlines and Bibliographies*, rev. ed. [Cambridge, Mass.: Harvard University Press, 1966], p. 90). The *tz'u* is further distinguished by its vocabulary, which "admits colloquial language elements not common in the *shih*" (ibid.). Although all *tz'u* lyrics were originally set to music, over time the musical tunes were lost because of an inadequate notation system; as a result, the names of the musical airs, or tune titles, became in effect the names of meters.

3. *CASTK*, p. 59. The term that I have translated as "enlightened," *t'ien-yen* (literally, heavenly eyes), is itself a translation of *divyacaksus*, which in Buddhist terminology means "divine sight" or "unlimited vision." On Wang Kuo-wei's lyrics, see also Tu Ching-i, "A Group of Wang Kuo-wei's Tz'u Poems with an Introduction," in *Transition and Permanence*, ed. David C. Buxbaum and Frederick W. Mote, pp. 379–393.

4. *CASTK*, p. 54.

5. Ibid., pp. 60–61. *Ko-tao* (literally, suspended walkway, but translated freely here as "high road around the palace") and *wu-chang ch'i* ("banners fifty [Chinese] feet long") are allusions to Ssu-ma Ch'ien's description of the E-p'ang Palace (*Shih chi*, "Ch'in Shih-huang pen-chi"). I am indebted to Chow Tse-tsung for the suggestion that *lien-ch'ien* (literally, linked coins, but here translated as "weeds by the water"), which sometimes refers to a kind of horse, in this lyric is more likely to be "an allusion to the weeds growing by an imperial pond described in *Tung-ming chi* by Kuo Hsien of the Later Han dynasty" (letter dated 15 August 1983). "These weeds," Chow writes, "are said to have existed along with a certain aquatic grass [called] *tao-chih tsao* [and], forming like a 'nest,' were able to trap wild geese." The character *tao*, he notes, also appears in the lyric.

6. I am indebted to Chow Tse-tsung for this interpretation of the first stanza. According to official reports, Emperor Te-tsung's concubine threw herself down a well on the morning of 15 August 1900 in an act of patriotic martyrdom (the Allied Relief Expedition had entered Peking the day before), but in certain circles it was thought that she actually had been shoved into the well. The Pearl Concubine's mysterious demise, Chow says (ibid.), became the subject of a number of poems by late Ch'ing literati, who frequently used falling leaves or blossoms as a metaphor. On this concubine's earlier misdeeds, see Luke S. K. Kwong, *A Mosaic of the Hundred Days*, pp. 59–60.

7. *CASTK*, p. 60. On this and the preceding lyric, see also Chow Tse-tsung, *Lun Wang Kuo-wei "Jen-chien tz'u,"* pp. 9, 47–51.

8. *CASTK*, p. 47.

9. Ibid., p. 49.

10. Ibid., p. 48.

11. Ibid., p. 58.

12. Ibid., p. 59. On this lyric as well as on the first lyric translated and

discussed in this chapter, see also Lao Kan, *Chung-kuo ti she-hui yü wen-hsueh*, pp. 59–67.

13. I am indebted to James J. Y. Liu for this view of Wang's lyrics (letter dated 27 April 1979).

14. Fan Ping-ch'ing [Fan Chih-hou], foreword to *Jen-chien tz'u i-kao*, by Wang Kuo-wei, with punctuation in *CASTK*, p. xix. Wang himself also thought that the ideas embedded in his lyrics are their most excellent feature; see Wang Kuo-wei, *"Jen-chien tz'u-hua" hsin-chu*, edited and annotated by T'eng Hsien-hui, p. 29.

It was long ago suggested by Chao Wan-li ("NP," p. 7058), and subsequently by others as well, that Wang Kuo-wei himself wrote the forewords to both *Jen-chien tz'u i-kao* and *Jen-chien tz'u chia-kao* (by Wang Kuo-wei, with punctuation in *CASTK*, pp. xvii–xviii) using the nom de plume Fan Chih-hou. Chao appears to have reached this conclusion solely on the basis of the fact that the author of the forewords praises Wang's lyrics as extravagantly as Wang himself does in an essay we *know* he wrote ("Tzu-hsu erh," 1907). The similarity in tone between the forewords and "Tzu-hsu erh" does not, in my view, constitute conclusive proof that Wang wrote the former as well as the latter.

It is true that the opinions on Wang's lyrics and other literary matters that are expressed in the forewords are perfectly compatible with Wang's opinions as we are familiar with them from "Tzu-hsu erh," *Jen-chien tz'u-hua*, and a long passage in the 1906 foreword devoted to "Mr. Wang's" views on various lyricists; however, it does not necessarily follow that the forewords had to have been written by Wang Kuo-wei himself rather than by his intimate friend Fan Ping-ch'ing. Fan and Wang had met, we recall, at the Eastern Language Institute, where they had both been favorites of Lo Chen-yü. Subsequently Fan and Wang had worked for Lo in Wuchang, where, presumably, they began their custom of reading poetry together, as described in the 1906 foreword (p. xvii). Under these circumstances, it is surely possible that Fan's ideas on poetry might have developed along lines very similar to those of Wang. Indeed, Fan may have been invited to write the forewords precisely because he shared Wang's views on many literary matters and entertained as high an opinion of Wang's lyrics as Wang himself ("no one understands my lyrics better than you," Wang is quoted as saying of Fan in the 1906 foreword [p. xvii]). In a passage appearing in the hand-written draft of *Jen-chien tz'u-hua* but deleted from the published text of 1908–09, Wang Kuo-wei refers to the forewords as being by Fan (Wang, *"Jen-chien tz'u-hua" hsin-chu*, p. 29).

In the absence of testimony from handwriting experts or other kinds of evidence to the contrary, we will therefore assume in the present work that the forewords were in fact written by Fan Ping-ch'ing but reflect the views of both Fan and Wang. For reasons similar to my own, Liu Yü also believes that Fan wrote the forewords (*"Jen-chien tz'u* hsu tso-che k'ao," *Wen-hsueh p'ing-lun*, 1982, no. 2:141).

15. For a list of the thirty-eight occurrences of the characters *jen-chien* in Wang's lyrics, see Chow Tse-tsung, *Lun Wang Kuo-wei "Jen-chien tz'u,"* pp. 37–40. The phrase "in the world of men" was made famous by Li Yü in a lyric

the pertinent lines of which are quoted in "Wang's View of Other Lyricists" in this chapter.

16. Fan Ping-ch'ing, 1906 foreword, p. xvii; ibid.; ibid.; ibid.

17. Wang Kuo-wei, "Tzu-hsu erh," 1907; rpt. in *WKTCC*, 5:1828. Fan Ping-ch'ing, 1907 foreword, p. xix.

18. *JCTH*, p. 197 (original remark 15). See also ibid. (original remark 14). In preparing my translations of specific passages from *JCTH*, I have profitably consulted Tu Ching-i's *Poetic Remarks in the Human World: Jen Chien Tz'u Hua*, a translation of the sixty-four items that constitute the 1908–09 text of this work. Concerning the addition of "expunged remarks" and "supplementary remarks" to these "original remarks" in modern editions of *Jen-chien tz'u-hua*, see the introductory comments in "Wang's Mature Aesthetic Theory" in this chapter.

19. *JCTH*, pp. 197–198 (original remark 16); ibid., p. 197 (original remark 16); ibid., p. 198 (original remark 18), quoting from Zarathustra's speech "On Reading and Writing" in Nietzsche's *Thus Spoke Zarathustra; JCTH*, p. 198 (original remark 18).

20. The first lines quoted are from Li Yü's lyric to the tune "Wu yeh t'i" [Crows Crying at Night]; my translation of them is adapted from that of James J. Y. Liu, *Essentials of Chinese Literary Art*, p. 5. The other lines quoted are from Li Yü's lyric to the tune "Lang t'ao sha" [Ripples Sifting Sand]; my translation of them is adapted from that of David Hawkes, trans., *The Story of the Stone*, vol. 2, *The Golden Days*, by Cao Xueqin (Bloomington: Indiana University Press, 1979), p. 467. These lines from Li Yü's lyrics are quoted by Wang in *JCTH*, p. 197 (original remark 15).

21. Fan Ping-ch'ing, 1907 foreword, p. xix; *JCTH*, p. 213 (original remarks 44–46).

22. *JCTH*, p. 206 (original remark 33); ibid. For an excellent introduction to Wang's favorite Northern Sung lyricists, see James J. Y. Liu, *Major Lyricists of the Northern Sung*.

23. Fan Ping-ch'ing, 1906 foreword, p. xvii; *JCTH*, p. 215 (original remark 50). My translations of the line from Wu's lyric and the line from Chang's lyric are according to Tu, *Poetic Remarks*, p. 34 (with a minor change).

24. On Chou Mi, see *JCTH*, pp. 235–236 (expunged remarks 28, 29, 31); Chu Hsi is quoted in expunged remark 28. On Chiang K'uei, see ibid., pp. 212–213 (original remarks 42–43), and Fan Ping-ch'ing, 1907 foreword, pp. xviii–xix.

25. Liu, *Major Lyricists*, p. 200. On Hsin Ch'i-chi, see *JCTH*, p. 213 (original remarks 43–46).

26. Fan Ping-ch'ing, 1907 foreword, p. xix; ibid. See also *JCTH*, p. 217 (original remark 52) and p. 230 (expunged remark 18).

27. I am indebted to James J. Y. Liu for this view of the degree of Wang's originality as a critic of lyrics (letter dated 27 April 1979). On the Ch'ang-chou school, see Chao Yeh Chia-ying, "The Ch'ang-chou School of *Tz'u* Criticism," in *Chinese Approaches to Literature from Confucius to Liang Ch'i-ch'ao*, ed. Adele Austin Rickett, pp. 151–188.

28. As regards the original edition of *Jen-chien tz'u-hua*—that is, the edition

published in 1908–09 in the *Kuo-ts'ui hsueh-pao*—remarks 1–21 were published in no. 47 (tenth moon of Kuang-hsu 34), remarks 22–39 in no. 49 (twelfth moon of Kuang-hsu 34), and remarks 40–64 in no. 50 (first moon of Hsuan-t'ung 1). On the basis of an interpolation that appears in subsequent editions of *Jen-chien tz'u-hua*, many scholars over the years have erroneously believed that Wang did not complete the work until 1910.

Following Wang Yu-an, editor of the edition of *Jen-chien tz'u-hua* used in the present study (*JCTH*, 1961), I indicate whether a particular item was included in the 1908–09 text, expunged from it, or unrelated to it by writing "original remark," "expunged remark," or "supplementary remark" in parentheses after the relevant page number.

29. Much has been written concerning Wang Kuo-wei's conception of poetry. See, for instance, James J. Y. Liu, *The Art of Chinese Poetry*, pp. 84–87, 94; Tu Ching-i, "Some Aspects of the *Jen-chien tz'u-hua*," *Journal of the American Oriental Society* 93, no. 3 (July–September 1973):306–316; Jao Tsung-i, *"Jen-chien tz'u-hua" p'ing-i* [A Critical Discussion of *Remarks on Lyrics in the World of Men;* n.p., n.d.]; Yeh Chia-ying, *"Jen-chien tz'u-hua* ching-chieh shuo yü Chung-kuo ch'uan-t'ung shih-shuo chih kuan-hsi," *Tou-sou* 14 (March 1976):1–18; idem, *"Jen-chien tz'u-hua* chung p'i-p'ing chih li-lun yü shih-chien," *Wen-hsueh p'ing-lun* 1 (May 1975):199–291.

30. *JCTH*, p. 193 (original remark 6); ibid., p. 225 (expunged remark 10).

31. Translation of Wang Fu-chih's comment is adapted from that of Liu, *The Art of Chinese Poetry*, p. 83. Wang Kuo-wei, "Wen-hsueh hsiao-yen," 1906; rpt. in *WKTCC*, 5:1842.

32. Translation of Yen Yü's words, which are quoted by Wang in *JCTH*, p. 194 (original remark 9), is according to James J. Y. Liu, *Chinese Theories of Literature* (with a minor change), p. 39. *JCTH*, p. 191 (original remark 1).

33. *JCTH*, p. 219 (original remark 56); ibid., p. 211 (original remark 40); ibid., p. 207 (original remark 36). See also ibid., pp. 206–207 (original remarks 34–35) and p. 219 (original remark 57).

34. Ibid., p. 192 (original remark 4); ibid., p. 191 (original remark 3). Translation of the lines from the fifth of T'ao Ch'ien's "Yin chiu" [Drinking Wine] poems is according to Tu, *Poetic Remarks*, p. 2 (with a minor change), as is that of the lines from Yuan Hao-wen's poem "Ying-t'ing liu-pieh" [Taking Leave at Ying Pavilion]. The aforementioned lines are quoted by Wang in *JCTH*, p. 191 (original remark 3).

35. *JCTH*, p. 192 (original remark 4); ibid., p. 191 (original remark 3). Translation of the lines from Ou-yang Hsiu's lyric to the tune "Tieh lien hua" is according to Liu, *Major Lyricists*, p. 43. Translation of the lines from Ch'in Kuan's lyric to the tune "T'a so hsing" [Treading on Grass] is according to Lai Ming, *A History of Chinese Literature* (New York: John Day, 1964), p. 224 (with a minor change). The aforementioned lines are quoted by Wang in *JCTH*, p. 191 (original remark 3).

36. *JCTH*, p. 252 (supplementary remark 16); *TWWR*, 2:391.

37. *JCTH*, p. 252 (supplementary remark 16).

38. Ibid., p. 194 (original remark 9).

39. "NP," pp. 7054–7055, 7058, 7060–7061. For information on Mrs. Mo (d. 1935), P'an Tsu-i, and Wang Kuo-wei's second wife (d. 1965, according to *NP*, p. 387), see Wang Tung-ming, "Wei mu-ch'in shuo chi-chü hua," *Chung-kuo shih-pao*, 23 October 1984.

40. "NP," p. 7061. In ibid., p. 7062, Chao Wan-li gives the impression that he believes "Hsi-ch'ü k'ao-yuan" to have been completed only in mid-1909, but compare his "Wang Ching-an hsien-sheng chu-shu mu-lu," in *WKTCC*, 16:7175.

11. Critique of Yuan Drama

1. Lo Chen-yü, "Hai-ning Wang Chung-ch'üeh kung chuan," in *WKTCC*, 16:7019–7020. Wang published *Elementary Lessons in Logic*, a widely used textbook introductory to Mill, under the title *Pien-hsueh* (Chao Wan-li, "Wang Ching-an hsien-sheng chu-shu mu-lu," in *WKTCC*, 16:7177; Ch'u Wan-feng, "Wang Ching-an hsien-sheng chu-shu piao," in *WKTCC*, 16:7201). Around the time that Wang was translating this work, Yen Fu was engaged in preparing a translation of another of Jevons's books, one titled *Logic* (1880); having already translated the first part of Mill's *Logic* in 1905 under the Chinese title *Ming-hsueh*, Yen Fu called his translation of Jevons's *Logic* (a primer) *Ming-hsueh ch'ien-shuo*.

2. "NP," p. 7063; *NP*, p. 62.

3. "NP," p. 7063; Sun Hsiung, "Wan shih," in *AWL*, pp. 15b–16.

4. According to Hsu Chung-shu ("Wang Ching-an hsien-sheng chuan," in *WKTCC*, 16:7046), Wang wrote a draft of *Sung Yuan hsi-ch'ü k'ao* during this period as well, but since the manuscript assumed its final form only in 1912–13, it is not counted here. "Sung ta-ch'ü k'ao" is also known as "T'ang Sung ta-ch'ü k'ao" [On the Great Melodies of the T'ang and Sung].

5. Kano Naoki, "Ō Seian [Wang Ching-an] kun o omou," *Geibun* 18, no. 8 (August 1927):39.

6. "Hsi-ch'ü k'ao-yuan," as mentioned earlier, was published in the *Kuo-ts'ui hsueh-pao*, nos. 48 and 50 (1908–09), and, in revised form, in *Ch'en-feng ko ts'ung-shu* [Collectanea from the Ch'en-feng Pavilion], comp. Shen Tsung-ch'i and ed. Lo Chen-yü, 16 vols. (n.p., 1909), 13. "Yu yü-lu" was published in the *Kuo-ts'ui hsueh-pao*, nos. 63–66 (1910), "Sung ta-ch'ü k'ao" in the *Kuo-ts'ui hsueh-pao*, nos. 67–68 (1910), and "Lu-ch'ü yü-t'an" in the *Kuo-ts'ui hsueh-pao*, no. 69 (1910). *Ch'ü lu*, however, was published in *Ch'en-feng ko ts'ung-shu*, comp. Shen Tsung-ch'i and ed. Lo Chen-yü, vols. 10–12, while "Ku-chü chiao-se k'ao" was published in Lo Chen-yü's *Kuo-hsueh ts'ung-k'an* [Sinological Publications], no. 1 (1911). "Ch'ü-tiao yuan-liu piao" was never published and the draft is said no longer to be extant (*NP*, p. 60).

On the establishment of the Society for the Protection of National Studies, the founding of the *National Essence Journal*, and the political affiliations of the men most intimately connected with the society, see Laurence A. Schneider, *Ku Chieh-kang and China's New History*, pp. 34–40.

7. *TWWR*, 1:252. Wang Kuo-wei, "Wen-hsueh hsiao-yen," 1906; rpt. in *WKTCC*, 5:1846–1847.

8. Wang, "Wen-hsueh hsiao-yen," p. 1846.

9. Wang Kuo-wei, "Tzu-hsu erh," 1907; rpt. in *WKTCC*, 5:1828–1829. Ibid., p. 1829.

10. Wu Ch'i-ch'ang, "Wang Kuan-t'ang hsien-sheng hsueh-shu," in *WKTCC*, 16:7277.

11. Wang Kuo-wei, draft preface to *Ch'ü lu*, 1908; rpt. in *WKTCC*, 4:1426–1428.

12. Wang Kuo-wei, preface to *Ch'ü lu*, 1909; rpt. in *WKTCC*, 14:6198. Ibid., p. 6197.

13. Wang Kuo-wei, preface to *SYHCK*, p. 3.

14. Ibid. Originally titled *Sung Yuan hsi-ch'ü shih* [The History of Sung and Yuan Drama], this work was published serially in the *Tung-fang tsa-chih* ([The Eastern Miscellany], vol. 9, nos. 10–11, and vol. 10, nos. 3–6, 8–9) in 1913–14. In the present study we will refer to *Sung Yuan hsi-ch'ü k'ao* as a work of 1912–13 rather than of 1913–14 because, for our purposes, its date of composition is more important than its date of publication.

15. *SYHCK*, p. 105; ibid.; ibid., p. 111; Wang, preface to *SYHCK*, p. 3.

16. Aoki Masaru, preface to *Shina kinsei gikyoku shi*, p. 1.

17. Wang, "Wen-hsueh hsiao-yen," p. 1846; Wang, "Tzu-hsu erh," p. 1829.

18. *SYHCK*, p. 106; ibid.

19. For Wang's view of the elegant, see "Types of Beauty Found in Art" in chapter 9.

20. *SYHCK*, p. 105; ibid., pp. 105–106. It is said that in antiquity scholars who feared that their works might perish encased them in stone containers and deposited them on famous mountains.

21. *SYHCK*, p. 106; ibid., p. 127; ibid.

22. Ibid., p. 109. *Ch'en-tzu* is sometimes translated as "extrametric," "additional," "foil," or "padding" words. On these words, see Shih Chung-wen, *The Golden Age of Chinese Drama: Yüan "Tsa-chü,"* pp. 121–124. For Wang's examples of the apt use of nonmetric words, onomatopoeia, and other devices of the Yuan dramatists, see *SYHCK*, pp. 109–110.

23. *SYHCK*, p. 110.

24. As translated by Shih Chung-wen in *Injustice to Tou O*("*Tou O Yüan*") (Cambridge: At the University Press, 1972), pp. 149–153; quoted by Wang Kuo-wei in *SYHCK*, p. 107.

25. *SYHCK*, p. 107; ibid.

26. As translated by Liu Jung-en in *Six Yüan Plays* (Harmondsworth, Middlesex, England: Penguin Books, 1972), pp. 102–103; quoted by Wang Kuo-wei in *SYHCK*, pp. 107–108.

27. *SYHCK*, p. 108.

28. Ibid., p. 127; ibid., p. 132.

29. Ibid., p. 134.

30. As translated by Donald Keene in *Anthology of Chinese Literature from Early Times to the Fourteenth Century*, comp. and ed. Cyril Birch (New York: Grove Press, 1965), pp. 442–443; quoted by Wang Kuo-wei in *SYHCK*, p. 108.

31. *JCTH*, p. 225 (expunged remark 10).

32. *SYHCK*, p. 112; ibid.; ibid.; ibid. On the use of the term *pen-se* by drama critics, see James I. Crump, "Giants in the Earth: Yuan Drama as Seen by Ming Critics," *Tamkang Review* 5, no. 2 (October 1974):54–56.

33. Wang Kuo-wei, "*Hung-lou meng* p'ing-lun," 1904; rpt. with punctuation in I Su, comp., "*Hung-lou meng*" *chüan*, 2 vols. in 1, 1:253.

34. Ibid. Concerning the authorship of the last part of *The Romance of the Western Chamber*, see C. T. Hsia's critical introduction to S. I. Hsiung's translation of the work (New York: Columbia University Press, 1968), pp. xxii–xxiii.

35. Wang, "P'ing-lun," p. 253; ibid.

36. *JCTH*, p. 221 (original remark 64). Wang Kuo-wei, "Lu-ch'ü yü-t'an," 1910; rpt. with punctuation in idem, *Wang Kuo-wei hsi-ch'ü lun-wen chi*, p. 276. *SYHCK*, p. 106.

37. Ch'ien Chung-shu, "Tragedy in Old Chinese Drama," *T'ien Hsia Monthly* 1 (August 1935):37–46.

38. Wang, preface to *SYHCK*, p. 3; ibid. As part of his effort to promote the serious study of drama, Wang suggested that "investigators of antiquity can find useful materials in plays, historians can discuss human motivation as it is portrayed in plays, men of letters can study the language of plays, and musicians can examine the music of plays" (preface to *Ch'ü lu*, p. 6198). He also said that drama "is able to depict contemporary political and social conditions" (*SYHCK*, p. 112). Although Communist critics such as Chao Hang have made much of these comments, Wang Kuo-wei personally (as we have seen) had not the slightest interest in the "political and social conditions" depicted in Chinese drama. In *Sung Yuan hsi-ch'ü k'ao* Wang reveals himself to be, on the contrary, well within the tradition of what Perng Ching-Hsi has called the "poetic" school of dramatic criticism, whose adherents are distinguished by their preoccupation with the poetic subtleties of the arias of Chinese plays. See Chao Hang, "Tu *Sung Yuan hsi-ch'ü shih*" [On Reading *The History of Sung and Yuan Drama*], 1956; rpt. in *Yuan Ming Ch'ing hsi-ch'ü yen-chiu lun-wen chi* [An Anthology of Critical Writings on Yuan, Ming, and Ch'ing Drama], edited by the staff of the editorial department of the Jen-min wen-hsüeh ch'u-pan she (Peking: Jen-min wen-hsüeh ch'u-pan she, 1959), pp. 410–419. See also Perng Ching-Hsi, *Double Jeopardy: A Critique of Seven Yüan Courtroom Dramas* (Ann Arbor: Center for Chinese Studies, University of Michigan, 1978), pp. 4–10.

12. Conservative Commitments

1. Benjamin I. Schwartz, "Notes on Conservatism in General and in China in Particular," in *The Limits of Change: Essays on Conservative Alternatives in Republican China*, ed. Charlotte Furth, pp. 3–21.

2. It is precisely because they recognized that traditional literature is a repository of traditional values that May Fourth iconoclasts such as Hu Shih, Ch'en Tu-hsiu, and Ch'ien Hsuan-t'ung thought the creation of a new literature an essential feature of their larger project to destroy Confucianism and create, in its stead, a new culture based on alien ideas. Ch'ien went so far as to suggest that, were it only feasible (Mao Tse-tung would later dem-

onstrate that it was), the cultural revolutionaries ought to round up all traditional books and lock them away in libraries in order to prevent them from contaminating Chinese minds with their old-fashioned notions of duty and honor. For Ch'ien's remark, see C. T. Hsia, *A History of Modern Chinese Fiction*, 2nd ed. (New Haven: Yale University Press, 1971), p. 10.

3. *CLP*, p. 754; ibid. Lo considered Yuan Shih-k'ai an avatar of the notorious General Tung Cho of the Later Han (ibid., p. 763).

4. If he had, it seems unlikely that he would have rushed into print with scathing criticisms of Yuan immediately after the fall of the Ch'ing. See Wang's poem "I-ho yuan tz'u" ([I-ho Park], 1912; punctuated rpt. of the revised version in *CASTK*, pp. 16–18), translated in this chapter in "A Threnody for the Ch'ing." See, too, his poem "Lung-yü huang-t'ai-hou wan-ko-tz'u" [Dirge to Empress Dowager Lung-yü], 1913; rpt. with punctuation in *CASTK*, pp. 24–27.

5. *CLP*, pp. 754–755. Ōtani Kōzui, who in 1902–03 had led an expedition to Central Asia, India, and China, presumably had heard of Lo in connection with the latter's well-known interest in, and researches on, the historical materials (documents on wood, records on shell and bone, paper manuscripts, and so on) brought to light during the earliest years of the twentieth century by foreign explorers, Chinese antiquaries, and others.

6. *CLP*, p. 755. At this time Wang already had, from his two marriages, a handful of children. Before he died he would father, in all, eleven children (six male, five female): Ch'ien-ming (1899), Kao-ming (1902), Chen-ming (1905), Ming-chu (1909), Chi-ming (1911), Tung-ming (1913), Tz'u-ming (1915), Sung-ming (1917), Teng-ming (1919), T'ung-ming (1921), and Tuan-ming (1922). Names and dates of birth of Wang's offspring are according to "NP," pp. 7054–7093, and Yao Ming-ta, "Wang Ching-an hsien-sheng nien-piao," in *WKTCC*, 16:7111.

7. Mo Jung-tsung, "Lo Hsueh-t'ang hsien-sheng chu-shu nien-piao," in *LHTCC*, 2nd series, 20:8263.

8. Lo was only one of a number of educated Chinese who, during the difficult last years of the dynasty, apparently wished for little more than a restoration of social order by the legitimately constituted government and who, after the Ch'ing collapse, withdrew from office in accordance with the neo-Confucian concept of loyalty. For the names of other scholar-officials who resigned their posts after the 1911 Revolution out of a sense of loyalty to the defunct dynasty, see "A Literary Talent of Shanghai" in chapter 15.

9. See "Wang's Educational Philosophy" in chapter 3.

10. See Wang's poem "I-ho yuan tz'u," translated and discussed in this chapter in "A Threnody for the Ch'ing."

11. Wang Kuo-wei, "Shu tao nan," 1912; rpt. with punctuation in *CASTK*, pp. 19–21.

12. It was precisely Po-i's extreme insistence on personal purity that Liang Ch'i-ch'ao would have in mind when, after his colleague's death, he compared Wang's character to that of this ancient worthy ("Wang Ching-an hsien-sheng mu-ch'ien tao-tz'u," in *WKTCC*, 16:7122). "Po-i would not serve a prince whom he did not approve, nor associate with a friend whom he did not

esteem," declares Mencius (*Meng Tzu*, bk. 2, pt. 1, chap. 9, sect. 1; trans. according to James Legge, trans., *The Chinese Classics*, 5 vols. in 4, 2:206).

13. Wang Kuo-wei, "Sung Jih-pen Shou-yeh [Kano] po-shih yu Ou-chou," 1912; rpt. with punctuation in *CASTK*, p. 18.

14. Aoki Masaru, "Ō Seian [Wang Ching-an] sensei no bempatsu," *Geibun* 18, no. 8 (August 1927):62.

15. Chang Erh-t'ien thought very highly of *Ch'ing lieh-ch'ao hou-fei chuan kao* [Biographies of Empresses and Concubines of the Successive Reigns of the Ch'ing Dynasty, 1929], a revision of the monograph he had written on the subject for the *Ch'ing shih kao* [Provisional History of the Ch'ing Dynasty]; indeed, he regarded it as perhaps his most important work (Teng Chih-ch'eng, "Chang chün Meng-ch'ü pieh-chuan," *Yen-ching hsueh-pao*, no. 30 [June 1946]:323). Chang's opinion of Tz'u-hsi's reign as well as of her person is very similar to that of Wang, six lines of whose poem "I-ho yuan tz'u" he even quotes approvingly in *Ch'ing lieh-ch'ao hou-fei chuan kao* (p. 442).

On the lack of credibility of K'ang's and Liang's writings in the post-1898 period, see Luke S. K. Kwong, *A Mosaic of the Hundred Days*, especially pp. 5–13. See also Sue Fawn Chung, "The Much Maligned Empress Dowager: A Revisionist Study of the Empress Dowager Tz'u-hsi (1835–1908)," *Modern Asian Studies* 13, pt. 2 (1979):177–196; and Hao Yen-p'ing and Liu Kwang-Ching, "The Importance of the Archival Palace Memorials of the Ch'ing Dynasty: *The Secret Palace Memorials of the Kuang-hsü Period, 1875–1908*," *Ch'ing-shih wen-t'i* 3, no. 1 (November 1974):78.

16. In *Shih chi* ("Po-i Shu-ch'i chuan") we read that when Wu Wang was about to revolt against the last Shang emperor, Po-i and his brother, Shu-ch'i, detained Wu Wang's horse and vainly expostulated against his disloyal plans. Considering it unrighteous to "eat the grain of Chou"—that is, to depend for a living on the new dynasty—the outraged siblings fled after the conquest to Mount Shou-yang, where they died of starvation.

17. In 1917 he would be interested enough in his "roots" to write a biography of Wang Ping, a twelfth-century ancestor who, along with his son Wang Hsun, had nobly cast himself into the Fen River after the Jurched took T'ai-yuan in 1126. On Wang's ancestors, see "The Wang Family" in chapter 2.

18. During the Hsien-feng period (1851–1861), when the seventh Ch'ing monarch, Emperor Wen-tsung (I-chu, 1831–1861), occupied the Dragon Throne.

19. *Feng-ai* ("wind-blown dust") is a stock metaphor for warfare.

20. The Taiping Rebellion, which began in Kwangsi.

21. In 12 B.C. the keys to the gates in Ch'ang-an and at Han-ku Pass mysteriously disappeared. The significance of their disappearance was construed by a contemporary official, Ku Yung, in light of a "children's song" that went, "To say that the gates shake and the keys fly away is tantamount to saying that the realm has lost the Way and the ministers are doing evil, that affairs are in chaos and the ministers plotting to seize power" (*Han shu*, "Wu-hsing chih"); hence, an allusion to the panic of 1860 caused by the Anglo-French expedition.

22. Emperor Wen-tsung.

23. A term belonging to the nomenclature of the T'ang and signifying a locality in Mongolia; hence, an allusion to Wen-tsung's flight to Jehol in 1860 in response to the British and French allies' entry into Peking.

24. Emperor Wen-tsung died in Jehol on 22 August 1861.

25. The future Emperor Mu-tsung (Tsai-ch'un, 1856–1875, whose reign title was T'ung-chih), the only son of Emperor Wen-tsung, who on his death-bed proclaimed the boy heir apparent.

26. Wen-tsung's demise precipitated a bitter power struggle between Empress Dowager Tz'u-an (née Niuhuru, 1837–1881, the late emperor's senior consort), Empress Dowager Tz'u-hsi (née Yehe Nara [Yehonala], Tsai-ch'un's mother), Prince Kung (see n. 30 below), and other highly placed Manchus and Chinese officials, on the one hand, and eight powerful "officials designated by the late emperor on his deathbed" (*ku-ming chih ch'en*), on the other. After the party of Tsai-yuan, Tuan-hua, Su-shun, Ching-shou, Mu-yin, K'uang Yuan, Tu Han, and Chiao Yu-ying had been routed, the empresses dowager formed a joint regency, a practice known as "attending to governmental affairs from behind the screen" (*ch'ui-lien t'ing-cheng*). On the coup d'état of 1861, see Luke S. K. Kwong, "Imperial Authority in Crisis: An Interpretation of the Coup D'état of 1861," *Modern Asian Studies* 17, pt. 2 (April 1983):221–238.

27. Tz'u-an was also known as the Eastern Empress Dowager, Tz'u-hsi as the Western Empress Dowager, after their residences, which were located in the eastern and western sectors, respectively, of the Forbidden City.

28. Paraphrase: The empresses dowager did not indulge in nepotism.

29. Paraphrase: They managed affairs so privately that they actually directed the government from their own living quarters.

30. After the suppression of the Tsai-yuan conspiracy, Prince Kung (I-chu's half-brother I-hsin, 1833–1898) was appointed prince counselor (*i-cheng wang*) to advise the regents on all affairs of state.

31. Paraphrase: Entrusted by the court with great military power, statesmen-generals such as Tseng Kuo-fan (1811–1872), Tso Tsung-t'ang (1812–1885), and Li Hung-chang carried their campaigns against the Taiping, Nien, and Moslem rebels to a victorious conclusion.

32. The rebels.

33. The sovereign imperial authority of the Ch'ing.

34. The T'ung-chih Restoration (1862–1874).

35. Loyal officers of King Hsuan (r. 827–782 B.C.) of the Western Chou dynasty, Fang-shu and Earl Hu of Shao suppressed revolts of the Man of Ching-chou and of the Huai I, respectively. They here stand for Tseng Kuo-fan and Tso Tsung-t'ang, both of whom were appointed full grand secretaries (Tseng in 1867, Tso in 1874) after winning stunning victories in the field.

36. Paraphrase: The throne committed the defense of the capital area to Li Hung-chang.

Pei-men ("north gate") originally referred to the gate in the north wall of the capital of the ancient state of Cheng by virtue of this passage in *Tso chuan* ("Hsi 32," as translated by Legge, *The Chinese Classics*, 5:221): "*Now* Ch'i

Tzu had sent information from Cheng to Ch'in, saying, 'The people of Cheng have entrusted to my charge the key of their north gate. If an army come secretly upon it, the city may be got.' "

Hsi-p'ing wang ("prince of Hsi-p'ing") was the title of the distinguished T'ang general Li Sheng, who in the early 780s crushed the revolts of Chu Tz'u and of Li Huai-kuang, thereby enabling Emperor Te-tsung (r. 780–805) to return to Ch'ang-an from his self-imposed exile in Feng-t'ien. He here stands for one of the military heroes of the Taiping Rebellion, Li Hung-chang, who for his part in quashing the rebels was made a first-class earl with the designation Su-i. From 1870 to 1895 Li's principal post was that of governor-general of Chihli.

37. An allusion to her reconstruction, during the years 1886–1891, of I-ho Park ("park of smiling harmony," with the additional connotation, "to give rest and peace to Heaven-sent old age") from one of the imperial gardens, Ch'ing-i Park, which had been partially destroyed by the British and French in 1860. *Lou-ch'uan* ("storied boat") originally had associations with Emperor Wu of the Former Han dynasty, who in his capital at Ch'ang-an dug a lake, which he called K'un-ming, and built a fleet of storied ships to practice naval warfare (*Han shu*, "P'ing-chun shu").

38. Yuan-ming Park, which (along with other imperial parks in the vicinity) was looted and burned by the British and French in 1860, causing Wen-feng, the official in charge of it, to drown himself in the park lake. On Ch'ing pleasure resorts in the Peking area, see Carroll Brown Malone, *History of the Peking Summer Palaces under the Ch'ing Dynasty* (1934; rpt. New York: Paragon Book Reprint Corp., 1966), and L. C. Arlington and William Lewisohn, *In Search of Old Peking* (1935; rpt. New York: Paragon Book Reprint Corp., 1967).

39. Because I-ho Park lies to the northwest of Peking, Tz'u-hsi in traveling there always passed through Hsi-chih Gate, the northerly of the two west gates of the so-called Tartar City.

40. Approximately three miles northwest of I-ho Park lies Yü-ch'üan Hill, a beautiful park that Tz'u-hsi at one time hoped to restore to its former glory, when it had been a pleasure resort of Emperors Sheng-tsu (Hsuan-yeh, 1654–1722, whose reign title was K'ang-hsi) and Kao-tsung (Hung-li, 1711–1799, who ruled under the reign title Ch'ien-lung).

41. A false antithesis since, in fact, Emperor Kao-tsung (r. 1736–1795) not only gave to the hill that until his time had been called Weng the new name Wan-shou, but also dredged the lake, bestowing on it the new name K'un-ming.

42. The phrase *p'ai-yun ch'i* ("rise up to the clouds") plays on the name of the main hall on Wan-shou Hill, P'ai-yun tien, which is situated just below the Fo-hsiang ko ("Buddha's fragrant incense pavilion").

43. The painted gallery.

44. The Fo-hsiang ko.

45. A second reference to the Fo-hsiang ko.

46. The Ch'i-nien tien ("hall for praying for a bountiful year"), in which

the emperor prayed each year at the Festival of the Commencement of Spring for a propitious year, in particular a bountiful harvest, is a blue-tiled, triple-roofed circular building (part of the Temple of Heaven) in Peking.

47. Paraphrase: She directed that countless lanterns be suspended on scaffolds.

48. A metaphor for gleaming lanterns.

49. Ch'ang-lo, a Han dynasty palace located in the capital, and Kan-ch'üan, Emperor Wu's summer retreat, here stand for the Ning-shou Palace, Tz'u-hsi's official residence in the Forbidden City (after 1889), and I-ho Park, her summer palace.

50. The Feast of Ch'ung-yang, which fell on the ninth day of the ninth moon.

51. A Han palace located in Ch'ang-an; hence, an allusion to her return each year to Peking at the approach of winter (when yang gives way to yin).

52. The emperor's palace.

53. Toast of long life. *Yü-chih* ("jade goblet") originally had associations with Emperor Kao-tsu (r. 206–194 B.C.), the founder of the Former Han dynasty, who once held up a jade wine-cup in the Wei-yang Palace and, before the assembled guests, drank a toast to the health of the grand emperor (*Han shu*, "Kao-ti chi").

54. According to one such house rule, an empress dowager, by virtue of her place in the genealogical record of the imperial family, took precedence of the emperor himself. One of the many indications of Tz'u-hsi's exalted status, cited by Wang Kuo-wei in the foregoing line, was Emperor Te-tsung's use of the term *ch'en-tzu* ("your servant-son")—which signified his willingness to defer to the empress dowager in familial and even political matters—when addressing her. Another indication of Tz'u-hsi's exalted status, noted by Wang in the following line, was the emperor's obligation, when visiting her, to remain standing until invited to sit down. Concerning Tz'u-hsi's authority over Emperor Te-tsung even after her "retirement" in 1889, see Reginald F. Johnston, *Twilight in the Forbidden City*, pp. 27–30.

55. When in January 1875 Tz'u-hsi chose her nephew, the future Emperor Te-tsung (Tsai-t'ien, 1871–1908, whose reign title was Kuang-hsu), as successor to the throne, she adopted him as her son.

56. Paraphrase: She never proposed that they be "just family" together.

57. *Tung-p'ing wang* ("king of Tung-p'ing") was the title of Liu Ts'ang, the eighth son of Emperor Kuang-wu (r. A.D. 25–56) and a powerful figure at court after the "restoration" of the Han dynasty; he here stands for Prince Kung, one of the principal architects of the T'ung-chih Restoration. "The young daughter of Tung-p'ing" refers to Prince Kung's eldest daughter (1854–1911), who as a child was adopted by the empresses dowager, ennobled as Princess Jung-shou, and raised in the palace. On her, see Kao Pai-shih's article "T'an-t'an Ch'ing-mo liang-ko kung-chu" [Remarks concerning Two Princesses of the Late Ch'ing Period] in his *Ku ch'un-feng lou suo-chi* [Anecdotes from the Ku ch'un-feng Library], 20 vols. (1960; rpt. Taipei: Tai-wan hsin-sheng pao-she, 1979), 5:1–16. See also Arthur W. Hummel, ed., *Eminent*

Chinese of the Ch'ing Period (1644–1912), 2 vols. with successive pagination, p. 383.

58. In 1866 Princess Jung-shou was married to Chih-tuan, a descendant of Ming-jui. After her husband's death in 1871, the young widow lived in the palace as Tz'u-hsi's constant companion. ("Purple Chambers" refers to the empresses dowager.)

59. Miao Chia-hui, a widow. On her, see Chang Erh-t'ien, *Hou-fei chuan kao*, pp. 442–443. See, too, Isaac Taylor Headland, *Court Life in China: The Capital, Its Officials and People* (New York: Fleming H. Revell, 1909), pp. 87–88.

60. On her seventieth birthday, Tz'u-hsi's honorific titles numbered sixteen characters: *Tz'u-hsi tuan-yu k'ang-i chao-yü chuang-ch'eng shou-kung ch'in-hsien ch'ung-hsi (huang-t'ai-hou)*.

61. The name of a T'ang treasury constructed by Emperor Te-tsung to serve as a repository for tribute.

62. The name of a Chou depository for gold, jade, and other valuables given as tribute to the emperor.

63. Tz'u-hsi was, after her own fashion, a devout Buddhist.

64. Paraphrase: Thinking only of the welfare of the empire, she never asked anything for herself.

65. Since the dynasty toppled three years after Tz'u-hsi's body was laid to rest, Wang surely intends this line to make us feel a stab of pathos.

66. Another allusion to Emperor Wen-tsung's protracted stay in Jehol.

67. Ch'ing-shu shan-kuan was one of a number of scenic spots at Pi-shu Country Villa, the imperial summer palace in Jehol, on which Emperor Sheng-tsu (r. 1661–1722) bestowed a four-character name but which were not among the "thirty-six prospects" he chose to honor with a poem and painting. On the summer palace in Jehol, see Yuan Sen-po, "Ch'ing-tai k'ou-wai hsing-kung ti yu-lai yü Ch'eng-te Pi-shu shan-chuang ti fa-chan kuo-ch'eng" [The Origins of the Ch'ing Summer Palaces beyond the Great Wall and the History of Pi-shu Country Villa in Ch'eng-te], *Ch'ing-shih lun-ts'ung* [Articles on Ch'ing History] 2 (1980):286–319.

68. Designated an imperial concubine of the fourth rank on entering the palace in 1851, Tz'u-hsi was raised in status by Emperor Wen-tsung in 1854 and again in 1856, when she gave birth to Tsai-ch'un. As her child was Wen-tsung's only heir, and hence destined to inherit the throne, Tz'u-hsi's position was greatly strengthened after 1856. The emperor reportedly tutored her in state affairs and allowed her to classify memorials. According to Fang Chao-ying (in the biographical sketch he wrote of Tz'u-hsi for Hummel, ed., *Eminent Chinese*, p. 295; but compare Kwong, "Imperial Authority in Crisis," pp. 228–229), Wen-tsung before expiring gave to Tz'u-an a seal inscribed with the characters *yü-shang*, to be impressed at the beginning of each edict issued by the new administration; to Tz'u-hsi he allegedly entrusted, on behalf of the young emperor-designate (who could not be expected for some years to make vermilion endorsements in his own hand), a seal bearing the characters *t'ung-tao t'ang*, to be impressed at the end of every edict.

69. After casting a tripod at the base of Mount Ching, the Yellow Emperor encountered a dragon, which he thereupon mounted, as did many of his ministers and women. Those who had no opportunity properly to mount the dragon before it soared heavenward all clung to its whiskers, which, however, broke off, leaving them behind (*Shih chi*, "Feng shan shu"). Here the story is used as a metaphor for Emperor Wen-tsung's death and his women's, especially Tz'u-hsi's, bereavement.

70. *Ti-tzu* ("child of God") and *pei-chu* ("the northern bank") are allusions to the first line of "Hsiang fu-jen" [The Lady of the Hsiang] in *Ch'u tz'u*. (My translation of these terms follows that of David Hawkes, trans., *Ch'u Tz'u: The Songs of the South*, p. 38.) The Lady of the Hsiang, or Child of God, is Nü-ying, Yao's second daughter and Shun's concubine; she here stands for Tz'u-hsi.

71. In an edict dictated just before he died, Wen-tsung authorized the four adjutant-generals Tsai-yuan, Tuan-hua, Su-shun, and Ching-shou, together with four grand councillors then in Jehol, "to advise and assist (*tsan-hsiang*) in all affairs of government." The authority bestowed on these eight officials, as Liu Kwang-Ching has pointed out, was by no means absolute since it did not involve entrusting them with vicarious government, "either *she-cheng* (in charge of government) as in the case of Dorgon during the Shun-chih Emperor's minority or *fu-cheng* (associates in government) as in the case of Oboi and three other officials during the K'ang-hsi Emperor's minority" ("The Ch'ing Restoration," in *The Cambridge History of China*, ed. Denis Twitchett and John K. Fairbank [Cambridge: Cambridge University Press, 1978–], vol. 10, *Late Ch'ing, 1800–1911*, pt. 1, ed. John K. Fairbank, [1978], p. 419). In order to transact business, the eight men were thus obliged to appeal to the inherent authority of the empresses dowager, who by virtue of their maternal status could legitimately use the imperial seals. (On the natural connection between the rights of mothers and the institution of female rulers in China, see Yang Lien-sheng, "Female Rulers in Imperial China," *Harvard Journal of Asiatic Studies* 23 [1960–61]:47–61.) From the start Su-shun and his colleagues were at odds with the empresses dowager, whose role in the new administration they endeavored in every conceivable way to minimize.

72. As soon as the empresses dowager and the child monarch had arrived back in Peking (1 November), an edict was issued charging the eight advisers, in particular Tsai-yuan, Su-shun, and Tuan-hua, with having committed heinous political crimes, including arrogation of imperial authority. Soon thereafter, Su-shun and Tuan-hua were decapitated and Tsai-yuan "invited" to commit suicide.

73. Mu-tsung.

74. An allusion to Tz'u-an and Tz'u-hsi's first regency, which lasted twelve years (1862–1873). After Su-shun and his associates had been eliminated, the empresses dowager began to rule "from behind the screen."

75. Paraphrase: Mu-tsung died without issue.

Chia-kuan ("the first lodge") and *shih-ti* [*huang*]-*sun* ("[imperial] grandson who is the heir by the principal wife") allude to the following passage in *Han shu* ("Ch'eng-ti chi," as translated by Homer H. Dubs, trans., *The History of the Former Han Dynasty,* 2:373): "While Emperor Yüan [was living] in the Heir-apparent's Palace, [the future Emperor Ch'eng] was born in the Painted Hall of the First Lodge. He was [called] the Imperial Grandson Who is the Heir by the First Wife."

Hou-kung ("the imperial harem") and *ts'ai-jen tzu* ("son of a gifted concubine") also allude to a passage in *Han shu* ("Kao-hou chi," as translated by Dubs, *History of the Former Han,* 1:191): "The Empress . . . had no issue. [So the Empress Dowager] took the son of a Beauty from the [imperial] harem, pronounced him [the son of the Empress] and made him Heir-apparent."

76. The future Emperor Te-tsung, whose father was a younger brother of Wen-tsung and whose mother was a younger sister of Tz'u-hsi. On the controversial selection in early 1875 of Emperor Mu-tsung's cousin as successor to the throne, see Kwong, *A Mosaic of the Hundred Days,* pp. 41–44.

77. Paraphrase: She again became regent for a child emperor.

78. By virtue of the words *chu-ju* ("pearl jacket") and *wu-chang* ("martial canopy") this line refers to the first and most famous case of dethronement by an empress dowager in Chinese history, namely, the dethronement in 74 B.C. of the king of Ch'ang-i (Liu Ho) by his aunt (née Shang-kuan), the widow of Emperor Chao (*Han shu,* "Huo Kuang Chin Mi-ti chuan"); hence, an allusion to the so-called coup d'état of 21 September 1898. On the coup, see Kwong, *A Mosaic of the Hundred Days,* pp. 201–224.

Empress Dowager Tz'u-hsi possessed a fabulous cape reportedly made of 3,500 pearls of perfect shape and color. Whether she had donned it on that particular fall day in 1898 I do not know.

79. The Oirats captured the Ming emperor Ying-tsung (r. 1436–1449, 1457–1464) at the battle of T'u-mu (near Huai-lai) and besieged Peking in 1449; hence, an allusion to Tz'u-hsi's flight, via Huai-lai, to Sian in 1900 as well as to the Allied Relief Expedition, which entered Peking on 14 August 1900.

80. *Tuan-ku ch'e* ("a cart with shortened hubs") has the connotation of "a fleeing cart" because of the story of Ch'ih-chang Man-chih: foreseeing the invasion of his small state, this ancient official cut off the wheel-knaves of his chariot (in order to negotiate the narrow road then existing) and fled (*Lü-shih ch'un-ch'iu,* "Shen-ta lan"). Tz'u-hsi began her flight from Peking on 15 August 1900 in a common cart, being provided with a litter only after she had reached Kuan-shih.

81. During one of the arduous military campaigns that eventually won him the throne as the first emperor of the Later Han dynasty, Liu Hsiu arrived cold, exhausted, and famished at Wu-lou Station. Offered bean gruel to eat by General Feng I, the future Emperor Kuang-wu consumed his simple fare gratefully and gustily, and felt much better (*Hou Han shu,* "Feng I chuan"). Having fled through the Hsi-chih Gate before dawn on 15 August, Tz'u-hsi arrived at nightfall chilled, weary, and hungry (she had eaten nothing all day) at Kuan-shih. Here the locals offered her their own coarse fare—millet porridge—for dinner (Chin-liang, *Ch'ing-ti wai-chi; Ch'ing-hou wai-chuan* [Unofficial Annals of Ch'ing Emperors and Unofficial Biographies of Ch'ing Empresses; Peking, 1934], p. 233).

82. Li Hung-chang, governor-general of Chihli and minister plenipotentiary, represented the throne in the negotiations that resulted in the Boxer Protocol of 1901.

83. The governors-general and governors of the central and southern provinces, by treating the Boxer Uprising as a rebellion against the legitimate authority of Tz'u-hsi, were able both to maintain peace in the Yangtze region and to consider themselves loyal to the imperial house.

84. Paraphrase: She preserved the vitality of the regime.

85. The empress dowager's return to Peking in January 1902 was celebrated by a two-hour imperial procession through the city streets, during which yellow (the imperial color) banners were carried aloft.

86. Paraphrase: Tz'u-hsi and Te-tsung were restored to power.

87. Paraphrase: That sacrifices to the sacred forebears were again being performed at the imperial ancestral temples was one indication that imperial authority had been restored.

88. Paraphrase: That I-ho Park continued to be well maintained was another proof of the regime's vitality in the years immediately following the Boxer troubles.

89. *Ching-she* ("take care of one's health," which I freely translate in this line as "indisposed") is a term that had been used both by Emperor Wen-tsung to justify his lengthy stay in Jehol (his illness, he said, required him to remain put and "take care of his health") and by Tz'u-hsi in her valedictory edict (although she had not been feeling well for several months, the empress dowager confided, affairs of state had allowed her no leisure in which to "take care of her health"). For Wen-tsung's remark, see Chin-liang, *Ch'ing-ti wai-chi; Ch'ing-hou wai-chuan*, p. 141. For Tz'u-hsi's, see *Ta-Ch'ing Te-tsung Ching (Kuang-hsu) huang-ti shih-lu* [The Veritable Records of the Great Ch'ing Emperor Te-tsung (Kuang-hsu)], 8 vols. (Taiwan: Hua-lien ch'u-pan she, 1964), 8:5460. On Te-tsung's health, see Chung, "The Much Maligned Empress Dowager," pp. 192–194.

90. Paraphrase: Owing to Te-tsung's fragile health, she expected that she would be constrained to work for the public weal right up to the day she died.

Han-i nung-sun ("eating sweets and fondling grandchildren") are words associated with the Later Han Empress Dowager Ma, who, like Tz'u-hsi, had begun her career as a concubine. After the death of Emperor Ming (r. A.D. 57–75) and assumption to power of Emperor Chang (r. A.D. 76–88), whose foster mother she was, the empress dowager actively involved herself in governmental affairs. Later she announced her intention to retire from the public arena to enjoy her old age by saying that henceforth she wished merely "to eat sweets and fondle grandchildren" (*Hou Han shu*, "Huang-hou chi").

91. Tz'u-hsi's excellent health and vitality are legendary.

92. This line may simply mean that she realized the dynasty's days were numbered, or it may contain an oblique criticism of Emperor Te-tsung for his unfilial conduct during the Hundred Days' Reform.

93. Ch'ing officials referred to Tz'u-hsi and Te-tsung as the Two Palaces (*liang-kung*).

94. Paraphrase: Who would have thought that Emperor Te-tsung would predecease Empress Dowager Tz'u-hsi?

Being the Son of Heaven, the emperor is the Heavenly Pillar; being female, the empress dowager is the Earthly Support.

95. Paraphrase: How many descendants of the dynasty's capable and energetic early rulers could there be?

The Ch'ing analogues of the Former Han emperors Kao-tsu and Wu are Sheng-tsu and Kao-tsung.

96. Since Emperor Ch'eng (r. 32–7 B.C.) died without leaving an heir to the throne, he was succeeded by Emperor Ai (r. 6–1 B.C.), a grandson of Emperor Ch'eng's father, Emperor Yuan. Because Emperor Ai died without issue, he was succeeded by his cousin Emperor P'ing (r. A.D. 1–5), also a grandson of Emperor Yuan. And because Emperor P'ing left no heir, he was succeeded by Young Prince Ying (r. A.D. 6–9), a great-great-grandson of Emperor Yuan's father, Emperor Hsuan. While the line of succession was thus disrupted three times during the last years of the Former Han, it was broken only twice during the last years of the Ch'ing—after the deaths of Emperors Mu-tsung and Te-tsung, both of whom died without issue.

97. In November 1908 Tz'u-hsi fell ill while celebrating her seventy-third birthday at I-ho Park. From her sickbed she designated as heir to the throne the future Hsuan-t'ung Emperor (P'u-i, 1906–1967, eldest son of the second Prince Ch'un [Tsai-feng, 1883–1951]) and appointed as prince regent (*she-cheng wang*) the baby's father. Po Ch'in, the first Duke of Lu, was the eldest son of the celebrated Duke of Chou of the Western Chou dynasty.

98. Paraphrase: On her deathbed Tz'u-hsi consulted with her closest advisers.

99. An-shih refers to Chang An-shih (d. 62 B.C.), an eminent Former Han official who at one time held the central government's highest posts. Pen-ch'u was the courtesy name of Yuan Shao (d. A.D. 202), a warlord who flourished at the tumultuous end of the Later Han dynasty. Here An-shih stands for Chang Chih-tung and Pen-ch'u for Yuan Shih-k'ai. Chang and Yuan were in the latter half of 1907 simultaneously made grand councillors, Chang concurrently in charge of the Ministry of Education and Yuan concurrently in charge of the Ministry of Foreign Affairs under Prince Ch'ing (I-k'uang, 1836–1916).

100. According to Yuan Shih-k'ai's son, Tz'u-hsi entreated the senior ministers Chang Chih-tung, Yuan Shih-k'ai, Shih-hsu, and Lu Chuan-lin as well as the regent and Prince Ch'ing to work together in the new administration (Yuan K'o-wen, *Yuan-shang ssu-ch'eng* [A Personal Account of Yuan-shang, n.d.; rpt. as vol. 9 in Yuan Shih-k'ai shih-liao hui-k'an, Taipei: Wen-hai ch'u-pan she, 1966], pp. 6–7).

101. Liu Tse, King of Lang-ya, was a venerable cousin of Emperor Kao-tsu of the Former Han dynasty; he here stands for Prince Ch'ing, who served as chief grand councillor and, finally, premier during the dynasty's last days.

102. *Ju-tzu* ("young prince"), a designation that here ostensibly refers to the Hsuan-t'ung Emperor, simultaneously alludes to Young Prince Ying (Ju-

tzu Ying), the last ruler of the Former Han, whose fate was identical to that of the last Ch'ing sovereign.

103. Her late husband, Emperor Wen-tsung (*tsung* has been changed to *tsu* to fit the rhyme scheme).

104. This line is derived from "Tiao Wei Wu-ti wen" [Mourning Emperor Wu of Wei], in which the third-century poet Lu Chi laments that Ts'ao Ts'ao (Emperor Wu), whose stature in life had been so great that it filled the heavens, blocking out the clouds (*mi-t'ien*), should be reduced in death to a corpse that could be contained in a single coffin (*i-kuan*).

105. This is the first of several bitter denunciations of Yuan Shih-k'ai, who as a grand councillor and one of the empress dowager's most trusted advisers, had been with her at the end. *Hsin-ch'ao* ("new dynasty"), which here ostensibly refers to the Republic over which Yuan presided after arranging the Hsuan-t'ung Emperor's abdication in early 1912, simultaneously alludes to the Hsin dynasty established in A.D. 9 by the usurper Wang Mang after he had deposed the child emperor of *his* day, Young Prince Ying.

106. *Chia-chang* ("elegant draperies") originally had associations with Emperor Wu of the Former Han, who, like Tz'u-hsi, loved fine things (Morohashi Tetsuji, *Dai Kan-Wa jiten* [The Great Chinese-Japanese Dictionary], 13 vols. [Tokyo: Taishūkan shoten, 1955–1960], 7:7979).

107. Probably the Chang-hua Tower, built by King Ling of Ch'u (see Legge, *The Chinese Classics*, 5:611, 615). That splendid tower, which was a symbol of the ancient state of Ch'u, stands here for Tz'u-hsi's summer palace, I-ho Park, which was a symbol of the late Ch'ing dynasty.

108. According to several early sources, Shun besieged Yao at Yao-ch'eng. Yao's unhappy situation at that time was thus identical to that of the Hsuan-t'ung Emperor, who was to all intents and purposes placed under house arrest by *his* disloyal successor, Yuan Shih-k'ai, in 1912.

109. Like Wang Mang, who had bullied a widow and baby into giving up the empire in A.D. 9, Yuan Shih-k'ai (who with the analogy of the Former Han clearly in mind had in late 1911 sworn never to betray "the widow" and "the infant") inveigled Empress Dowager Lung-yü (née Yehe Nara [Yeho-nala], 1868–1913, known up until 1908 as Empress Hsiao-ting) and the baby emperor into surrendering the throne in 1912. Lung-yü played a conspicuous role in the so-called abdication because memorials of surrender (*hsiang-piao*) were always sent in the name of both mother and son. (Since the Hsuan-t'ung Emperor was the adopted son of Emperor Mu-tsung and simultaneously the "spiritual" son of Emperor Te-tsung, he was obliged to regard as "mothers" not only his natural mother but also the three surviving consorts of Mu-tsung, the surviving consort of Te-tsung, and Te-tsung's empress.)

110. Paraphrase: Although he may now be enjoying his moment of power, Yuan Shih-k'ai will become a byword with future generations, a synonym for immorality and unscrupulousness.

111. Lung-yü and the young Hsuan-t'ung Emperor.

112. Paraphrase: The difficulties that the recently widowed Lung-yü and her adopted son experienced in trying to keep the throne in 1911–12 remind one of Tz'u-hsi and Mu-tsung's ordeal in 1861, when the grieving widow of

Emperor Wen-tsung was confronted with the machinations of Tsai-yuan's cabal.

Luan-yang is another name for Ch'eng-te, so called because of its location north of the Luan River; hence, an allusion to Tz'u-hsi and Mu-tsung's flight to Jehol in 1860.

113. Paraphrase: There was, however, one difference between Lung-yü and the baby emperor's situation in 1911–12 and Tz'u-hsi and Mu-tsung's in 1861, namely, that whereas the populace in the mid-nineteenth century had supported the empress dowager's valiant efforts to preserve the throne for her son and had sympathized with the young monarch's plight, in 1911–12 not even the Hsuan-t'ung Emperor's most compassionate subjects pitied him.

According to *Chuang Tzu* ("T'ien ti"), when a leper woman (*li-jen*) delivers in the night, she immediately lights a torch and examines her baby, fearing that it may look like herself.

114. Paraphrase: Some men change their colors so frequently that it becomes impossible to determine whether they are noble characters (tigers and dragons) or mean, unprincipled creatures (rats and fish).

115. Paraphrase: Yuan Shih-k'ai, who having occupied a series of high posts under Tz'u-hsi has now seen fit to transfer his allegiances to the Republic (which has rewarded him with the privileged position of president), is the unprincipled individual par excellence.

116. These lines are derived from Ts'ao Chih's (A.D. 192–232) sequence of poems presented to his half-brother Ts'ao Piao, Prince of Po-ma ("Tseng Po-ma wang Piao"), one of which contains the lines, "Take loving care, dear prince, of your jade-like body, / May we both get to enjoy the age of yellowing hair!" Because Ts'ao Chih is attempting to cheer up Ts'ao Piao by saying that they should both expect to live to a ripe old age, even though he is in fact worried that they might both be killed by the emperor (Ts'ao P'i), it seems probable that Wang is here expressing the fear that P'u-i and other members of the imperial clan might be put to death by Republican authorities. (This interpretation was suggested to me by James J. Y. Liu in a letter dated 14 January 1982.) Translation of the lines from Ts'ao Chih's poem quoted above is according to Hans H. Frankel, "Fifteen Poems by Ts'ao Chih: An Attempt at a New Approach," *Journal of the American Oriental Society* 84, no. 1 (January–March 1964):5.

117. Located eighty miles northeast of Peking, Ting-ling, where Emperor Wen-tsung and his empress are buried, and Ting-tung-ling, where Emperor Wen-tsung's consorts—Tz'u-an and Tz'u-hsi—are buried, constitute part of the Eastern Imperial Mausolea.

118. Paraphrase: It is lamentable that the Ch'ing dynasty, like the Ming before it, has at last come to an end; all that one can hope is that China's new rulers will protect the descendants of the Ch'ing royal house, permitting them to perpetuate the sacrifices to their ancestors, in the same magnanimous way that the early Ch'ing monarchs protected the scions of the Ming ruling house, allowing them to perform their sacrificial duties at their forebears' tombs.

By Manchu imperial magnanimity, the hereditary dignity of marquis (*hou*) and the title "extended grace" (*yen-en*) had been bestowed during the

Yung-cheng period (1723–1735) on a descendant of the Ming monarchs, whose surname was Chu. In return for the imperial favor, each Ming marquis was thereafter expected to pay ceremonial visits twice a year to the Thirteen Imperial Tombs (*shih-san ling*), which contain the remains of as many Ming emperors. After the 1911 Revolution, the "loyalist" Marquis of Extended Grace, Chu Yü-hsun, went on fulfilling his mission to the Ming tombs under the auspices of the deposed Ch'ing emperor.

119. Aoki Masaru, "Ō Seian sensei no bempatsu," p. 62. As further tokens of Wang's "convictions, integrity, and resentment," we may cite his use in the post-1911 period of traditional calendrical systems—usually the "stems and branches" system, but on occasion the "reign title" system (Hsuan-t'ung such-and-such a year)—as well as his use of the phrase "the present dynasty" (*pen-ch'ao*) to refer to the Ch'ing. On these and other standard loyalist writing practices, see Chou Chün-shih, *Wei-Man kung-t'ing tsa-i*, pp. 4–5.

It is exceedingly improbable that Wang, as Ku Chieh-kang has curiously alleged, cut off his queue during his first sojourn in Japan (1901–02). For his unsubstantiated claim, see Ku Chieh-kang, "Tao Wang Ching-an hsien-sheng," in *WKTCC*, 16:7135.

120. Joseph R. Levenson, *Confucian China and Its Modern Fate*, vol. 2, *The Problem of Monarchical Decay* (Berkeley: University of California Press, 1964), p. 10.

121. *NP*, pp. 88, 86; "NP," p. 7066.

122. Kano Naoki, "Ō Seian [Wang Ching-an] kun o omou," *Geibun* 18, no. 8 (August 1927):41; *CLP*, p. 756.

123. Concerning Lo's outlook in the months following the 1911 Revolution, see Hsu Chung-shu, "Wang Ching-an hsien-sheng chuan," in *WKTCC*, 16:7047; and Lo Chen-yü, "Hai-ning Wang Chung-ch'üeh kung chuan," in *WKTCC*, 16:7020.

124. Lo Chen-yü, "Chung-ch'üeh kung chuan," p. 7020. For a brief biographical account of Ts'ui Shu (1740–1816), see Hummel, ed., *Eminent Chinese*, pp. 770–777.

125. Lo Chen-yü, "Chung-ch'üeh kung chuan," p. 7020. I have followed Immanuel C. Y. Hsü in translating *hsiao-hsueh* as "traditional linguistics" and *hsun-ku* as "philology" (Immanuel C. Y. Hsü, trans., *Intellectual Trends in the Ch'ing Period*, by Liang Ch'i-ch'ao [Cambridge, Mass.: Harvard University Press, 1959], p. 132n2).

126. Lo Chen-yü, "Chung-ch'üeh kung chuan," p. 7020.

127. "NP," pp. 7062–7063, 7065; Ch'en Shou-ch'ien, "Chi Wang Chung-ch'üeh kung wen," in *WKTCC*, 16:7117. In late 1909 Wang had helped Lo compile *Tun-huang shih-shih i-shu* [Lost Manuscripts from the Stone Chamber in Tun-huang] and had translated, evidently at his mentor's request, part of a talk that Stein had delivered earlier in the year to the Royal Geographical Society; see "Wang's First Historical Works" in chapter 13. " 'Sui T'ang ping-fu t'u-lu' fu-shuo," the first of Wang's articles on ancient artifacts (*ku-ch'i-wu hsueh*), was published in Lo's *Kuo-hsueh ts'ung-k'an* [Sinological Publications] (no. 3) early in 1911. Inspired to write this short work by his mentor's "T'ang che-ch'ung fu k'ao pu" [Supplement to *A Study of the T'ang's Intrepid Militia*

Units], which was published in the first issue of *Kuo-hsueh ts'ung-k'an* together with an appendix titled "Sui T'ang ping-fu t'u-lu" [Reproductions of Military Tallies of the Sui and T'ang Periods], Wang subsequently revised and republished his study as "Sui t'ung-hu-fu pa" [A Note on Metal Tiger Tallies of the Sui Period] and "Wei-Chou erh kuei-fu pa" [A Note on Two Tortoise Tallies of the Wei-Chou Period]. The former provides an overview of the principal features of the system of military tallies as it evolved during the early imperial period, while the latter demonstrates that two tortoise tallies formerly thought by Wu Ta-ch'eng (to whom they at one time belonged) to date from the late seventh century are in fact forgeries of a later date.

128. Kano Naoki, "Ō Seian kun o omou," pp. 40–41.

129. Aoki Masaru, preface to *Shina kinsei gikyoku shi*, p. 1.

130. *NP*, p. 87. See also Lo Chen-yü, foreword to *Kuan-t'ang chi-lin*, by Wang Kuo-wei; foreword rpt. in *WKTCC*, 1:2.

131. Lo Chen-yü, "Chung-ch'ueh kung chuan," pp. 7020–7021.

132. Ibid., p. 7020; ibid.

133. Ibid., pp. 7020–7021.

134. For biographical information on Lo Chen-ch'ang, see Hashikawa Tokio, ed., *Chūgoku bunkakai jimbutsu sōkan*, p. 786, and Richard L. Rudolph, "Lo Chen-yü Visits the Waste of Yin," in *"Nothing Concealed": Essays in Honor of Liu Yü-yün*, ed. Frederic Wakeman, Jr., pp. 5–10. For information on Lo Chen-yü's sons, see Hashikawa Tokio, ed., *Chūgoku bunkakai jimbutsu sōkan*, p. 790. See, too, the following three sources. Paul Pelliot, Review of *A Brief Manual of the Si-hia Characters with Tibetan Inscriptions*, by Nicolas Nevsky, *T'oung Pao* 24, nos. 2–3 (1926):399–403. Wang Kuo-wei, "Lo Chün-ch'u chuan," 1922; rpt. in *WKTCC*, 3:1121–1125. Shen Tseng-chih, "Lo Chün-ch'u mu-chieh," *Ya-chou hsueh-shu tsa-chih* 1, no. 3 (April 1922): various pagination. Lo Chen-yü's brother and sons are also mentioned frequently in Wang Kuo-wei's correspondence with his mentor; see Wang Kuo-wei, *Wang Kuo-wei ch'üan-chi: shu-hsin*, ed. Wu Tse.

135. Lo Chen-yü, "Chung-ch'ueh kung chuan," p. 7022.

136. Quoted in Lo Chen-yü, foreword to *Kuan-t'ang chi-lin*, by Wang Kuo-wei, p. 2; ibid., p. 3.

13. Archaeological Enthusiasms

1. When in 1909 he heard that documents belonging to the Grand Secretariat were slated for destruction, Lo Chen-yü convinced Chang Chih-tung to move the endangered materials (vermilion edicts, routine memorials, interoffice memos, examination essays, and the like) to the Ministry of Education for safekeeping. After the 1911 Revolution the Grand Secretariat's official files were moved to the National History Museum, whose managers in the winter of 1921–22 felt constrained for financial reasons to sell three-quarters of their collection to a paper merchant for recycling. Lo Chen-yü learned of the sale in March 1922, when he happened to notice in the Peking bookstalls a memorial written by Hung Ch'eng-ch'ou (1593–1665) and a list of tributary articles presented by the king of Korea. Tracking down the paper merchant to whom the nine thousand burlap bags of Ch'ing documents had been sold,

Lo purchased the entire collection from him and built a library to house it. (Subsequently Lo sold the archives to Li Sheng-to, who in turn sold the archives to Fu Ssu-nien, head of the Academia Sinica's Institute of History and Philology.) On Lo and the Ch'ing archives, see Wang Kuo-wei, "K'u-shu lou chi," 1922; rpt. in *WKTCC*, 3:1164–1168. See also Tung Tso-pin, "Lo Hsueh-t'ang hsien-sheng chuan-lueh," in *LHTCC*, 1st series, 1:iv; and *NP*, p. 243.

2. This seems to have been the opinion of many of Lo's friends and admirers, and in particular of Wang Kuo-wei, who considered his mentor's publishing efforts positively heroic: "Publishing, in one work after another, the oracle bones from the Ruins of Yin and the ancient wooden documents and lost manuscripts from Tun-huang was a task that an entire country with its collective resources was unable to accomplish; in the end it was accomplished through the efforts of a single man living abroad" (foreword to *Hsueh-t'ang chiao-k'an ch'ün-shu hsu-lu*, by Lo Chen-yü, foreword dated 1918; rpt. in *WKTCC*, 3:1137). For similar views, see also K'o Ch'ang-ssu, "Tiao Shang-yü Lo hsien-sheng," in *LHTCC*, 5th series, 20:8599–8604; and Tung Tso-pin, *Chia-ku-hsueh liu-shih nien*, pp. 46–47.

3. *CLP*, p. 750; Weng Tu-chien, "Po-hsi-ho [Pelliot] chiao-shou," *Yen-ching hsueh-pao*, no. 30 (June 1946):329–330; Mo Jung-tsung, "Lo Hsueh-t'ang hsien-sheng nien-p'u," in *LHTCC*, 1st series, 20:8707. Lo also corresponded with Stein (*CLP*, p. 760).

4. *NP*, p. 58. The Taoist priest apparently did not surrender all of the remaining documents to the government's emissaries, however, for Stein succeeded in obtaining four more cases of manuscripts from him during his third Central Asian expedition of 1913–1916. See Jeannette Mirsky, *Sir Aurel Stein, Archaeological Explorer* (Chicago: University of Chicago Press, 1977), pp. 369–370.

5. "NP," p. 7062. *Tun-huang shih-shih i-shu* is reprinted in *LHTCC*, 3rd series, 6:1977–2324, without the appendix. The appendix, which is titled "Liu-sha fang-ku chi" [Explorations in Drift-Sand], is a collection of reports on different foreign expeditions to remote parts of China, translated from English, French, and Japanese sources into classical Chinese by Wang Kuo-wei and his old friends from the Eastern Language Institute, Shen Hung and Fan Ping-ch'ing; it is reprinted in *LHTCC*, 2nd series, 7:3015–3100. The paper that Stein read at the Royal Geographical Society on 8 March 1909 was subsequently published under the title "Explorations in Central Asia, 1906–8" in two installments in *The Geographical Journal* (vol. 34, no. 1 [July 1909]:5–36; and vol. 34, no. 3 [September 1909]:241–264); Wang Kuo-wei was sent a copy of the September issue by Fujita Toyohachi ("NP," p. 7063).

6. Wang Kuo-wei, "Chien-tu chien-shu k'ao," 1912; rpt. of the revised version in *WKTCC*, 6:2344–2346. When he wrote this article, Wang was apparently unaware that in 1905 Chavannes had published "Les livres Chinois avant l'invention du papier" (*Journal Asiatique*, series 10, vol. 5, no. 1 [January–February]:5–75), which covers much of the same ground as his own work.

7. Wang, "Chien-tu chien-shu k'ao," pp. 2321–2325. The Han foot was equal to approximately 10.5 inches, or 23 centimeters.

8. Although *Shuo-wen chieh-tzu* defines *hsi* as "a document measuring two feet in length" (*erh-ch'ih shu*), Tuan Yü-ts'ai subsequently emended the text to read "a document measuring one foot two inches in length" (*ch'ih-erh shu*); his reading has been accepted by such modern scholars as Chavannes and Morohashi, but was rejected by Wang.

9. The emperor wrote on wooden stationery one foot one inch in length to demonstrate his superiority.

10. The foregoing synopsis of Wang's views on the lengths of different kinds of wooden documents is based on "Chien-tu chien-shu k'ao," pp. 2335–2338.

11. Ibid., pp. 2340–2342. According to M. Aurel Stein (*Ruins of Desert Cathay*, 2 vols., 2:55), most of the wooden slips he discovered measure from a quarter- to a half-inch in width.

12. Wang, "Chien-tu chien-shu k'ao," pp. 2329–2330, 2343–2344.

13. Ibid., pp. 2331–2332, 2342–2343.

14. Ibid., p. 2333.

15. Ibid., pp. 2346–2352, 2357–2359.

16. Ibid., pp. 2353–2355. For a discussion in English of many of the points made by Wang in his article on the technical features of ancient Chinese stationery, see chapter 5 of Tsien Tsuen-hsuin's masterful study, *Written on Bamboo and Silk*. In his work Tsien provides translations of numerous passages from textual sources adduced by Wang in his article but omitted in the foregoing résumé of it. For criticisms of some of the ideas advanced by Wang in "Chien-tu chien-shu k'ao," see Ma Hsien-hsing, "Chien-tu hsing-chih" [Forms of Bamboo and Wooden Documents], *Chien-tu hsueh-pao* [Journal of Bamboo and Wooden Documents], no. 7 (1980):87–118.

17. Shen Tseng-chih as quoted in *NP*, p. 91.

18. It is unclear when Wang Kuo-wei learned enough French to enable him to get the gist of Chavannes's critical remarks.

19. For details, see "NP," pp. 7067–7068.

20. Concerning Lo Chen-yü's influence on Wang's researches on bronze inscriptions, see the following. Kano Naoki, "Ō Seian [Wang Ching-an] kun o omou," *Geibun* 18, no. 8 (August 1927):41. Wang Kuo-wei, preface to *Kuo-ch'ao chin-wen chu-lu piao* [A Table of Books and Catalogues Written during the Present Dynasty That Concern Bronze Inscriptions], 1914; preface rpt. in *WKTCC*, 10:3890. Lo Fu-i's comments as quoted in *NP*, pp. 119–120. Lo Chen-yü, preface to *San-tai chi-chin wen-ts'un* [Bronze Inscriptions of the Three Dynasties Period], 1936; preface rpt. in *LHTCC*, 2nd series, 2:405–406. Regarding the circumstances under which Wang began his investigations into the identity of Wang Hai, see Wang Kuo-wei, preface to "Yin pu-tz'u chung so-chien hsien-kung hsien-wang k'ao," 1917; preface rpt. in *WKTCC*, 2:391. See also the introductory remarks to chapter 14. On the authorship of *Yin-hsu shu-ch'i k'ao-shih*, see "Lo Chen-yü and Bone Inscriptions" in this chapter.

Hsu in the connection that here concerns us means not "waste" but "ruins"; on this point, see Herrlee Glessner Creel, *Studies in Early Chinese Culture*, pp. 6–8. Since, as David N. Keightley has noted (*Sources of Shang History*, p. xiv), oracle inscriptions make no reference to a great settlement (*ta-i*) called Yin but do mention repeatedly the "great settlement Shang," and since, as Noel Barnard has observed (review of Chou Hung-hsiang's *Shang-Yin ti-wang pen-chi, Monumenta Serica* 19 [1960]:500), "Yin" is never used to refer to the dynasty in scientifically excavated bronzes, I will, except when translating titles of, or passages from, documents containing the term "Yin," refer to the polity as the Shang. For an introduction to the problem, see Creel, *Studies in Early Chinese Culture*, pp. 64–66, and Keightley, *Sources of Shang History*, pp. xiii–xiv.

21. Both of these articles were first published in 1915 in Lo's *Hsueh-t'ang ts'ung-k'o* [Lo Chen-yü's Miscellany (original title: *Kuo-hsueh ts'ung-k'an*)], edited by Wang Kuo-wei. The latter article was subsequently republished by Wang as six separate essays: "Shuo tzu Hsieh chih-yü Ch'eng T'ang pa ch'ien" [On the (Shang's) Eight Moves from Hsieh to Ch'eng T'ang], "Shuo Shang" [On Shang], "Shuo Po" [On Po], "Shuo Keng" [On Keng], "Shuo Yin" [On Yin], and "Ch'in tu-i k'ao" [On Ch'in's Capital Cities]. All of the above are reprinted in vol. 2 of *WKTCC*.

22. "NP," p. 7056. Although not all the inscriptions are oracular, the name "oracle bones" is widely used to refer generally to inscribed turtle plastrons and carapaces, which are, technically speaking, composed of bone, and cattle scapulas.

23. Lo Chen-yü, preface to "Yin-Shang chen-pu wen-tzu k'ao," in *LHTCC*, 3rd series, 1:325–326. Tung Tso-pin, "Lo Hsueh-t'ang hsien-sheng chuan-lueh," p. iii. Wang Kuo-wei, "Tsui-chin erh-san-shih nien chung Chung-kuo hsin fa-chien chih hsueh-wen," 1925; rpt. in *WKTCC*, 5:1917. Lo also wrote a foreword to Liu E's work, the first collection of ink squeezes of bone inscriptions (1903), as did Wu Ch'ang-shou.

24. See Tung Tso-pin, *Chia-ku-hsueh liu-shih nien*, pp. 48–49, for the names of Japanese, American, British, and German scholars interested in oracle bones. Wang I-jung had died much earlier—in 1900.

25. In 1913 Lo published his great *Yin-hsu shu-ch'i ch'ien-pien* [Inscriptions from the Ruins of Yin, Part One], which Creel, writing in 1937, could still call "the most important single work of its sort" (*Studies in Early Chinese Culture*, p. 5). In 1914 Lo published his *Yin-hsu shu-ch'i ching-hua* [*La Crème de la Crème* of Inscriptions from the Ruins of Yin], in 1915 *T'ieh-yun ts'ang-kuei chih yü* [Additional Items from Liu E's Collection of Turtle Shells], and in 1916 *Yin-hsu shu-ch'i hou-pien* [Inscriptions from the Ruins of Yin, Part Two]. In 1916 Lo published as well his *Yin-hsu shu-ch'i tai-wen pien* [Inscriptions from the Ruins of Yin Awaiting Further Investigation], on graphs not yet deciphered, and his *Yin-hsu ku-ch'i-wu t'u-lu* [A Catalogue of Ancient Artifacts from the Ruins of Yin], containing illustrations of various objects unearthed at Anyang and presumably of Shang date.

26. Herrlee Glessner Creel, "Dragon Bones," *Asia* (published by Asia Magazine) 35, no. 1 (January 1935):182. On Hayashi's initial reaction to *T'ieh-yun ts'ang-kuei,* see Tung Tso-pin, *Chia-ku nien-piao*, pp. 5b–6. On the conditions that encouraged forgery in the early years of oracle-bone studies, see Li Chi, *Anyang*, pp. 19–20, and Creel, *Studies in Early Chinese Culture*, pp. 2–3. The

problem, as defined by Noel Barnard, is this: "Spurious inscriptions in genuine bone can be comparatively easily incised and made to appear quite authentic; when rubbings are taken from them the deception may be hidden altogether" (review of Jao Tsung-i's *Yin-tai chen-pu jen-wu t'ung-k'ao, Monumenta Serica* 19 [1960]:481). Since, according to Creel, writing in 1935, "only about ten per cent of the bones excavated are inscribed," the forgers had plenty of genuine bones to incise ("Dragon Bones," p. 182).

27. Keightley, *Sources of Shang History*, p. 141n30. For Ku Chieh-kang's remark, see his *Autobiography of a Chinese Historian*, trans. Arthur W. Hummel, p. 46. For Chang Ping-lin's denunciation, see his *Kuo-ku lun-heng* (1919; rpt. Shanghai: Ti-i shu-chü, 1924), p. 63; the well-known allegation is also quoted by Wang Sen-jan in his short biography of Chang Ping-lin (*Chin-tai erh-shih chia p'ing-chuan*, p. 187) as well as by Tung Tso-pin in his *Chia-ku-hsueh liu-shih nien*, pp. 56–57. For Granet's comment, see his *Chinese Civilization* (New York: Alfred A. Knopf, 1930), p. 59. For additional information on Chang Ping-lin's attitude toward oracle bones in general and Lo Chen-yü in particular, see Tung Tso-pin, *Chia-ku-hsueh liu-shih nien*, pp. 57–60.

28. Fu Ssu-nien, foreword to *Yin-li-p'u*, by Tung Tso-pin, 4 vols., 1:ib; Kuo Mo-jo, "Lu Hsun yü Wang Kuo-wei," in idem, *Li-shih jen-wu*, p. 297; Ai-hsin-chueh-lo P'u-i, *P'u-i tzu-chuan*, p. 261.

Fu Ssu-nien's allegation that Lo paid his protégé five hundred (Chinese) dollars to write *Yin-hsu shu-ch'i k'ao-shih* is open to suspicion on the following grounds. First, prior to 1945 no Shang scholars, or even his fiercest political enemies, seem to have entertained doubts that Lo Chen-yü was the author of this monograph. Neither Lionel C. Hopkins, writing in 1917 ("The Sovereigns of the Shang Dynasty, B.C. 1766–1154," *Journal of the Royal Asiatic Society*, p. 70), nor Jung Keng, writing in 1927 ("Wang Kuo-wei hsien-sheng k'ao-ku-hsueh shang chih kung-hsien," in *WKTCC*, 16:7347), nor Creel, writing in 1935 (*Studies in Early Chinese Culture*, pp. 5, 9), for example, finds any reason to question Lo's authorship of *Yin-hsu shu-ch'i k'ao-shih*. Shih Ta (a pseudonymous author), writing in 1927 ("Wang Ching-an hsien-sheng chih-ssu ti chen-yin," *Wen-hsueh chou-pao* 5, nos. 1–4 combined [August 1927]:73), does not even mention the work, although he has much to say—all of it negative—about Lo Chen-yü.

Second, Fu Ssu-nien declines to tell us where, in 1945, he has obtained his new "information" pertaining to events that had occurred three decades earlier and that involved men who by this time were both dead (Wang, whom Fu himself says he never met [see *NP*, p. 9], had died in 1927, Lo in 1940). Third, Wang Kuo-wei and his large family were already fully supported by Lo Chen-yü while they lived in Kyoto. And fourth, as already noted, Fu Ssu-nien, like the anti-Japanese polemicist Kuo Mo-jo, abominated the Japanese collaborator Lo Chen-yü.

As for P'u-i, he wrote his memoirs under Communist pressure and, indeed, with party "assistance." See Jerome Ch'en, "The Last Emperor of China," *Bulletin of the School of Oriental and African Studies* 28 (1965):352–354, 338–339; *The Cambridge Encyclopedia of China* (Cambridge: Cambridge University Press, 1982), p. 251; and Howard L. Boorman, ed., *Biographical Dictionary of Republican China*, 4 vols. (New York: Columbia University Press, 1967–1971), 3:85–86.

29. Benjamin A. Elman, "Wang Kuo-wei and Lu Hsün: The Early Years," *Monumenta Serica* 34 (1979–80):390n4; Elman's source is Kuo Mo-jo. Li Chi, *Anyang*, p. 268n14; Li Chi's source is probably Fu Ssu-nien, director for many years of the Academia Sinica's Institute of History and Philology, with whom he worked closely from 1928 (the year Fu hired him to head the institute's Archaeological Section) until Fu's death in 1950.

In a work published in 1980, Chou Chün-shih also claims that *Yin-hsu shu-ch'i k'ao-shih* was written by Wang (*Wei-Man kung-t'ing tsa-i*, p. 50).

30. According to Li Chi (*Anyang*, p. 26), Lo Chen-yü "benefited from" Sun I-jang's *Ming yuan* [Origin of Names], published in 1906, and "took advantage of" Sun I-jang's *Ch'i-wen chü-li* [Examples of Incised Writings], written in 1904 but published only in 1917, when he wrote "Yin-Shang chen-pu wen-tzu k'ao," published in 1910. The "benefits" that Li Chi claims Lo derived from *Ming yuan*—(1) the idea of comparing bronze inscriptions with bone inscriptions, (2) the notion of selecting a handful of pictographs for special scrutiny, and (3) the choice of the pictographs for sheep, horse, deer, pig, dog, and dragon among those meriting special study—seem to me to be of too general a nature to justify the charge of plagiarism.

Since Li Chi does not specify in what ways he believes Lo Chen-yü "took advantage of" *Ch'i-wen chü-li*, it is difficult to know what to make, substantively, of this allegation. The allegation itself is apparently based on Lo's own admission that his friend Sun I-jang once sent him *shou-kao* on the subject of bone inscriptions (preface to "Yin-Shang chen-pu wen-tzu k'ao," p. 325). Lo may mean by this that Sun sent him an actual handwritten manuscript or manuscripts. Since, however, Lo has also said that the only work by Sun on bone inscriptions that he ever saw consisted of *cha-chi* ("notes"), he may mean merely that Sun sent him research notes, not a draft of a monograph or drafts of monographs. (For the statement that he saw *cha-chi*, see the preface Lo wrote to his *Yin-hsu shu-ch'i ch'ien-pien* in 1913; preface rpt. in *LHTCC*, 7th series, 4:1289.) It is not at all clear from Lo's vague prefatory remarks precisely what materials he was sent by Sun—a draft of *Ch'i-wen chü-li*, a draft of *Ming yuan*, drafts of both, or research notes. Despite these difficulties, Li Chi seems to take Lo Chen-yü's comments as definite proof that he received, and was therefore in a position to "take advantage of," *Ch'i-wen chü-li*.

From sources available to Li Chi at the time he made his allegation (for example, "NP," p. 7076, and *NP*, p. 162), as well as from sources that have come to light since then (specifically, Wang Kuo-wei, "Kuan-t'ang shu-cha: yü Lo Chen-yü hsien-sheng lun-hsueh shou-cha," *Chung-kuo li-shih wen-hsien yen-chiu chi-k'an* 1 [1980]: letters 27, 28), we know that *Ch'i-wen chü-li* disappeared from view sometime after Sun completed it and remained lost from view for a number of years. In late 1916 Wang Kuo-wei discovered it by chance in Shanghai and purchased it for five (Chinese) dollars from a local book dealer. "I think you will be happy to learn that this manuscript is still extant," we then find Wang writing to Lo in a letter dated 14 December (Wang, "Kuan-t'ang shu-cha: yü Lo," letter 27). From the description of *Ch'i-wen chü-li* that Wang gives his mentor in his letters (number of characters per line, number of lines per page, total number of pages, expression of his general disappointment with it, an example of the kinds of errors it contains), it would appear that Lo was unfamiliar with the contents of the work, although both he and Wang evidently had known for years that Sun had written a monograph titled *Ch'i-wen chü-li*.

Even if, as Li Chi supposes, Lo *had* had an opportunity to read *Ch'i-wen chü-li* before he wrote "Yin-Shang chen-pu wen-tzu k'ao," and—as I have tried to make clear—it is very far from certain that he did, there is still a distinction to be made between consulting another scholar's work and "taking advantage of" it. In this connection, we may note that *Ch'i-wen chü-li*, while a pioneering monograph, is by no means an infallible guide to the study of bone inscriptions. In a letter to his mentor dated 28 December (ibid., letter 28), Wang Kuo-wei reports that, on reading *Ch'i-wen chü-li*, he has found numerous errors in both Sun I-jang's transcriptions and his critical remarks, but he recommends that Lo publish the manuscript anyway because of its historical interest. (Lo Chen-yü did in fact publish *Ch'i-wen chü-li* in 1917. Why, if he really had "taken advantage of" this work in 1910, he should care to publish it seven years later is a question Li Chi does not discuss.)

Wang Kuo-wei was not the only scholar to find fault with *Ch'i-wen chü-li*. Creel has called the work "primitive" (*Studies in Early Chinese Culture*, p. 4), while Tung Tso-pin has stated baldly that Sun really could not read oracle-bone inscriptions (*Chia-ku-hsueh liu-shih nien*, p. 54). (In a retrospective account of the early years of oracle-bone studies made near the end of his life, Wang Kuo-wei attributes Sun's mistakes in *Ch'i-wen chü-li* and *Ming yuan* to the circumstance that he had only a small sample of rubbings, *T'ieh-yun ts'ang-kuei*, with which to work ["Chung-kuo hsin fa-chien chih hsueh-wen," p. 1918].)

As for Lo Chen-yü, he appears from the first to have entertained a low opinion of Sun I-jang's research on bone inscriptions. Based on the materials that Sun had sent him, he concluded that his friend "was unable to penetrate their mysteries" (preface to "Yin-Shang chen-pu wen-tzu k'ao," p. 325). According to Lo, the dominant influence on him at the time he wrote his 1910 article was the Japanese collector and student of bone inscriptions Hayashi Taisuke. "My Japanese friend Mr. Hayashi in 1910 sent me his [1909 article titled 'Turtle Shells and Animal Bones Discovered in T'ang-yin District, Honan Province, Ch'ing China' ('Shinkoku Kanansho Tōinken hakken no kikkō gyūkotsu ni tsukite')], a work more systematic and orderly than Mr. Sun's notes. [Mr. Hayashi] also sent me a letter containing questions that he himself had been unable to answer. On the basis of what I had already learned [about oracle bones], I thereupon wrote 'On Divinatory Inscriptions of the Yin-Shang Period' to answer them" (preface to *Yin-hsu shu-ch'i ch'ien-pien*, p. 1290).

For a review of Lo's "brief but important essay"—the characterization is Creel's (*Studies in Early Chinese Culture*, p. 4)—see Edouard Chavannes, "La divination par l'écaille de tortue dans le haute antiquité Chinoise (d'après un livre de M. Lo Tchen-yu)," *Journal Asiatique*, series 10, vol. 17, no. 1 (January–February 1911):127–137.

On the source "Kuan-t'ang shu-cha: yü Lo," see chapter 15, n. 6.

31. Lo had developed an interest in epigraphy as early as 1882 (Mo Jung-tsung, "Nien-p'u," pp. 8696, 8707).

32. Wang Kuo-wei, postface to *Yin-hsu shu-ch'i k'ao-shih*, by Lo Chen-yü; postface dated winter of 1914–15 and rpt. in *WKTCC*, 3:1134. I have not been able to consult the original—that is, the 1915—edition of *Yin-hsu shu-ch'i k'ao-shih*, but according to Tung Tso-pin (*Chia-ku nien-piao*, p. 10), it contains a preface by Lo and a postface by Wang. I have seen both the 1923 edition, published as vol. 7 of Shang Ch'eng-tso's *Yin-hsu wen-tzu lei-pien* (with critical remarks by Lo Chen-yü, foreword by Wang Kuo-wei, and preface by Shang Ch'eng-tso), and the revised and enlarged edition of early 1927 (*Tseng-ting "Yin-hsu shu-ch'i k'ao-shih"* [Tung-fang hsueh-hui]). Although the former has neither preface nor postface, Wang and Shang both state, in the prefatory matter to *Yin-hsu wen-tzu lei-pien*, that *Yin-hsu shu-ch'i k'ao-shih* was authored by Lo. The latter contains not only Lo's preface and Wang's postface, but also a foreword by Wang; all three are dated winter of 1914–15. References in this work to *Yin-hsu shu-ch'i k'ao-shih* are to the 1923 edition.

33. For examples, see "NP," pp. 7067–7069, and *NP*, p. 114.

34. Lo Chen-yü, *K'ao-shih*, pp. 1–2b. There are no paragraphs in the original. The claim that Wu I's is the last name recorded in divinatory inscriptions is refuted in a later section of *K'ao-shih* (p. 6b), which identifies the Wen Wu Ting of the bone inscriptions with *Shih chi's* T'ai Ting/Ti T'ai Ting, the king who succeeded Wu I.

35. I have omitted from my translation that part of the text which demonstrates that the Yin-hsu near Anyang was not, as some earlier scholars had imagined, the site of Ho Tan Chia's capital. In preparing the foregoing translation, I have profitably consulted that of W. Perceval Yetts ("The Shang-Yin Dynasty and the An-yang Finds," *Journal of the Royal Asiatic Society*, July 1933, pp. 665–668).

36. The statements made in *Shih chi* ("Yin pen-chi" and "San-tai shih-piao"), the modern text of *Chu-shu chi-nien*, and *Ti-wang shih-chi* are compatible insofar as they all agree that P'an Keng moved the Shang capital "south of the River" and, further, that a later king (Wu I, Keng Ting, or Ti I) moved it back "north of the River." According to Wang Kuo-wei, however, the testimony of *Shih chi* on this point is worthless because it is based on an error contained in the preface to the modern text of *Shang shu.* (Following the fourth-century scholar Shu Hsi, Wang thinks that the characters *chih po* in the sentence, *P'an Keng . . . chiang chih Po Yin* ["P'an Keng . . . proposed to establish the capital at Po (in the land of) Yin"], ought to read *shih chai;* this gives the sentence the meaning, "P'an Keng . . . proposed first to dwell at Yin.") Wang notes also that the testimony of the modern text of *Chu-shu chi-nien* is open to suspicion because the passage in question does not occur in the genuine (that is, the ancient) text of that work. For Wang's views on the sources, see his "Shuo Yin," pp. 505–507.

37. Wang's inscriptional evidence consists of pieces of bone that can be dated by the writing on them to a time not earlier than Ti I ("Shuo Yin," p. 507).

38. Compare "Yin-Shang chen-pu wen-tzu k'ao," pp. 329–331, with *K'ao-shih*, pp. 2b–9, with respect to both the substance and the wording of the critical remarks. For Lo's views on the oracular names of the Shang ancestors, see also "The Royal Genealogy Recorded in Bone Inscriptions" in chapter 14. For his views on the Shang kings' oracular names, see chapter 14, n. 33.

39. Bernhard Karlgren, "Yin and Chou in Chinese Bronzes," *Bulletin of the Museum of Far Eastern Antiquities*, no. 8 (1936):17; Kano Naoki, "Ō Seian kun o omou," p. 41. Among other contemporaries who held Lo's work in very high regard, we may mention K'o Shao-min, Shen Tseng-chih, Shang Ch'eng-tso, Pelliot, Chavannes, Hopkins, Yetts, Creel, Hummel, Hayashi Taisuke, Naitō Torajirō, Tomioka Kenzo, and Fujita Toyohachi.

That Lo and Wang had a mutually stimulating intellectual association during the teens is strongly suggested not only by the reminiscences of Japanese colleagues who knew them at this time, but also by the correspondence of the men themselves. See those of Wang's letters to Lo which date from this period (relevant excerpts constitute Wang, "Kuan-t'ang shu-cha: yü Lo") as well as the two letters from Lo to Wang whose subject matter is noted in chapter 14, n. 3 (letters rpt. in *WKTCC*, 2:417–419). It does not seem likely that Wang Kuo-wei would have looked back on his years in Kyoto as especially pleasant and productive ("NP," p. 7072) if, as Fu Ssu-nien, Kuo Mo-jo, P'u-i, and Shih Ta have alleged, he was during this period nothing more than Lo's scholarly tool.

Tung Tso-pin, who, like myself, has dismissed Chang Ping-lin's and Fu Ssu-nien's allegations as libelous, also believes that Lo Chen-yü was the author of *Yin-hsü shu-ch'i k'ao-shih* (*Chia-ku-hsüeh liu-shih nien*, p. 47).

14. Wang as Shang Genealogist

1. Wang Kuo-wei, "Yin pu-tz'u chung so-chien hsien-kung hsien-wang k'ao," 1917; revised version of 1923 rpt. in *WKTCC*, 2:391. In general I have cited Wang's "Yin pu-tz'u chung so-chien hsien-kung hsien-wang k'ao" (revised version) and his "Yin pu-tz'u chung so-chien hsien-kung hsien-wang hsu-k'ao" (1917; rpt. in *WKTCC*, 2:419–432). Whenever additional information has been inserted or the logic of the argument improved, however, I have used Wang Kuo-wei's *Ku-shih hsin-cheng* (1927; rpt. in *WKTCC*, 6:2077–2111), which incorporates these articles with slight modifications.

2. Wang, "Hsien-kung hsien-wang k'ao," p. 391; Naitō Torajirō, "Ōi," in idem, *Naitō Konan zenshū*, 10 vols., 7:469; idem, "Zoku Ōi," in ibid., p. 481.

3. "NP," pp. 7076–7077. One copy of the draft of "Yin pu-tz'u chung so-chien hsien-kung hsien-wang k'ao" Wang sent to Lo, who after reading it mailed his protégé two letters confirming his interpretation of the graph 田; these letters Wang published as an appendix to his article (Wang Kuo-wei, postscript to "Hsien-kung hsien-wang k'ao," p. 419). Another copy of his draft manuscript Wang sent to Naitō, who published the gist of it, in Japanese translation, under the title "Zoku Ōi" (Naitō Torajirō, "Zoku Ōi," p. 481).

4. As the last of the predynastic lords and the first of the Shang kings, the dynastic founder traditionally, and here as well, has been counted twice. Lo also discovered in oracle inscriptions the name of Ta Ting (*Shih chi*'s T'ai Ting), whom textual sources claim died before ascending the throne. For Lo Chen-yü's views on the names of the dead Shang sovereigns recorded in bone inscriptions, see n. 33 below. As for the predynastic ancestors whose names Lo thought he could decipher in the inscriptions, they are those whom *Shih chi* ("Yin pen-chi") calls Pao I, Pao Ping, Pao Ting, Chu Jen, Chu Kuei, and T'ien I; see Lo Chen-yü, *Yin-hsu shu-ch'i k'ao-shih*, pp. 8b–9b, 3, and "The Royal Genealogy Recorded in Bone Inscriptions" in this chapter.

5. Wang, *Ku-shih hsin-cheng*, pp. 2080–2081. In the draft version of "Hsien-kung hsien-wang k'ao," published in 1917 in *Hsueh-shu ts'ung-pien* (vol. 14, p. 2), Wang transcribes these graphs as *chün* 夋, rather than as *k'uei* 夒.

6. Only three Shang ancestors—K'uei, Wang Hai, and Ta I (according to Wang Kuo-wei, Tung Tso-pin, and Kuo Mo-jo)—are called *kao-tsu* in the bone inscriptions.

7. Wang, "Hsien-kung hsien-wang k'ao," pp. 393–394. For Kao 告, see the preface to *Shang shu*. *Shih chi* ("Yin pen-chi") writes Kao 誥 instead of Kao 告. According to the So-yin commentary on *Shih chi* ("Yin pen-chi"), the character *kao* 誥 is also written as *kao* 俈. *Shih chi* ("San-tai shih-piao" and "Feng-shan shu") and *Kuan Tzu* ("Ch'ih mi") take Kao 俈 to be K'u. Although Chien-ti is said miraculously to have conceived Hsieh through the agency of a bird (*Shih ching*, "Hsuan niao"; *Ch'u tz'u*, "Li sao" and "T'ien wen"; *Shih chi*, "Yin pen-chi"), her husband, K'u, was nevertheless regarded as Hsieh's formal and lawful father.

8. Wang, "Hsien-kung hsien-wang k'ao," p. 394.

9. *Shan-hai ching* ("Ta-huang nan-ching") says that Chün had a consort named Wo-huang. This passage, perhaps along with two others ("Hai-nei ching" and "Ta-huang pei-ching"), the latter of which associates Chün with bamboo (in many legends Shun's two wives, Wo-huang and Nü-ying, are mentioned in connection with bamboo), leads Kuo P'u in his commentary on the work ("Ta-huang tung-ching") to suggest that the character *chün* 俊 is a loan for *shun* 舜.

10. Wang, "Hsien-kung hsien-wang k'ao," pp. 394–395. This argument is weakened, however, by the fact that *Tso-chuan* ("Wen 18") says not only that Kao Hsin Shih had a son named Chung-hsiung, but also that Kao Yang Shih had a son named Chung-jung. If we take the Chung-jung mentioned in *Shan-hai ching* to be the same person as the man in *Tso chuan* who has an identical, rather than merely similar, name, then Chün in the "Ta-huang tung-ching" passage must be the same individual as Kao Yang Shih (= Chuan-hsu), not Kao Hsin Shih (= K'u).

11. For details, see Wang, "Hsien-kung hsien-wang k'ao," p. 395.

12. Ibid. To bolster his argument that Chün is identical with K'u, Wang might also have cited a passage in *Shan-hai ching* ("Ta-huang tung-ching") that associates Chün with birds. Since a bird, usually a swallow, plays a conspicuous role in stories concerning the miraculous birth of K'u's son, Hsieh, Chün seems here as well to be identical with K'u.

13. Wang, "Hsien-kung hsien-wang k'ao," p. 394.

14. Ibid., p. 395. *Kuo-yü* ("Lu yü") says that the Shang performed the *ti* sacrifice to Shun, rather than to K'u, but Wang thinks that the text ought to read "Chün" 夋 (= K'u), not "Shun" 舜. K'u, he notes, was a direct forebear of the Shang (Shun was not).

15. Regarding Ssu-ma Ch'ien's list of fourteen predynastic lords in fourteen generations, compare (1) *Kuo yü* ("Chou yü"): "The Dark King [Hsieh] labored for the cause of Shang, which rose to power after fourteen generations"; and (2) *Hsun Tzu* ("Ch'eng hsiang"): "Hsieh, the Dark King, begat Chao Ming . . . After fourteen generations there was T'ien I, who was Ch'eng T'ang." Concerning the ambiguity of these formulations, Bernhard Karlgren has remarked: "We must conclude that in both cases [the figure '14 generations'] refers, not to the number of princes after Sie [Hsieh] and Chao Ming respectively, but to the complete number of princes after the Royal ancestor K'u, Sie counted as the first, and T'ang, who rose to Royal power, as the 14th" ("Legends and Cults in Ancient China," *Bulletin of the Museum of Far Eastern Antiquities*, no. 18 [1946]:335).

16. The foregoing discussion of T'u (= Hsiang T'u) is based on Wang, "Hsien-kung hsien-wang k'ao," pp. 395–396.

17. Wang, *Ku-shih hsin-cheng*, p. 2084.

18. In this passage as quoted in ibid., Wang has mistakenly written *fu-niu* instead of *p'u-niu*.

19. On Ho-po, who appears in many literary accounts as a spirit of the waters but here seems to be a feudal lord, see Karlgren, "Legends and Cults," p. 320.

20. On Shang Chia, see "The Royal Genealogy Recorded in Bone Inscriptions" in this chapter.

21. As a matter of fact, rituals were performed to Wang Hai mostly on *hsin* days; see Chang Kwang-chih, "T'ien kan: A Key to the History of the Shang," in *Ancient China: Studies in Early Civilization*, ed. David T. Roy and Tsien Tsuen-hsuin, pp. 33–35. Wang Kuo-wei mistakenly thought that they were performed on *hai* days because, at the time he wrote "Hsien-kung hsien-wang k'ao," he had seen only two oracle-bone inscriptions that record the days on which sacrifices were to be offered to Wang Hai, and by chance both days were *hsin-hai*.

22. Wang, "Hsien-kung hsien-wang k'ao," pp. 398–399.

23. Translation adapted from that of David Hawkes, trans., *Ch'u Tz'u: The Songs of the South*, p. 52.

24. Wang, "Hsien-kung hsien-wang k'ao," p. 399.

25. Ibid., p. 400.

26. Ibid., pp. 396–397, 400–401, 403. Based on Wang's discoveries concerning Wang Hai's identity, Lo had suggested in *K'ao-shih* (p. 17b) that Chi must be Ming. As for Wang Heng, very little is known about him even today; see Chang, "T'ien kan," p. 36.

27. Wang, "Hsien-kung hsien-wang k'ao," p. 404.

28. Ibid., pp. 404–405; Wang Kuo-wei, *Chien-shou t'ang so-ts'ang Yin-hsu wen-tzu k'ao-shih*, published together with *Chien-shou t'ang so-ts'ang Yin-hsu wen-*

tzu, comp. Chi Chueh-mi [Chi Fo-t'o] (actually compiled by Wang Kuo-wei), foreword dated 1917, vol. 2, p. 3.

29. Wang, *Chien-shou t'ang so-ts'ang,* p. 3. Already in 1915 (*K'ao-shih,* p. 18b) Lo had transcribed 田 and 冊 as *shang chia.* For his comments on the form 宮, see the two letters he wrote Wang that are appended to the latter's "Hsien-kung hsien-wang k'ao" (letters rpt. in *WKTCC,* 2:417–419).

30. On the reconstituted document, see Wang, "Hsien-kung hsien-wang hsu-k'ao," p. 421. Wang seems to read 田, 又, 网, and 可 as *shang chia, pao i, pao ping,* and *pao ting,* respectively; he ventures no opinion on the possible phonetic significance of either the square enclosure or the square bracket.

31. Wang, *Ku-shih hsin-cheng,* p. 2093.

32. For Lo's comments on Ta I, see his "Yin-Shang chen-pu wen-tzu k'ao," rpt. in *LHTCC,* 3rd series, 1:330; and *K'ao-shih,* p. 3. For Wang's comments on him, see "Hsien-kung hsien-wang k'ao," pp. 409–411.

33. Lo Chen-yü's views on the names and identities of the kings mentioned in oracle-bone inscriptions (*K'ao-shih,* pp. 3–6b, 15b) may be summarized as follows:

A name in *Shih chi*	Name(s) in bone inscriptions, according to Lo
T'ien I (K1)	Ta I
Wai Ping (K2)	Pu Ping
T'ai Chia (K4)	Ta Chia
T'ai Keng (K6)	Ta Keng
Ti Hsiao Chia (K7)	same
T'ai Wu (K9)	Ta Wu
Chung Ting (K10)	same
Wai Jen (K11)	Pu Jen
Tsu I (K13)	same
Tsu Hsin (K14)	same
Tsu Ting (K16)	same
Nan Keng (K17)	same
Yang Chia (K18) 陽甲	Yang Chia 羊甲 /Fu Chia
P'an Keng (K19)	Pan Keng/Fu Keng
Hsiao Hsin (K20)	same/Fu Hsin
Hsiao I (K21)	same
Wu Ting (K22)	same
Ti Tsu Keng (K23)	Tsu Keng
Tsu Chia (K24)	same
Keng Ting (K26)	K'ang Ting/K'ang Tsu Ting
Wu I (K27)	same/Wu Tsu I
Ti T'ai Ting (K28)	Wen Wu Ting

According to Tung Tso-pin and Ch'en Meng-chia, the graphs that Lo transcribes as *yang chia* 羊甲 ought to be transcribed as *ch'iang chia* 羌甲 and this ancestor identified not with the king *Shih chi* calls Yang Chia but with the one it calls Wu Chia (*Chia-ku-hsueh liu-shih nien,* p. 53; *Yin-hsu pu-tz'u tsung-*

shu, p. 334). David N. Keightley takes the graph Lo transcribes as *k'ang* 康 in the name K'ang Tsu Ting to be *keng* 庚 (*Sources of Shang History,* p. 207).

34. Keightley, *Sources of Shang History,* p. 95. He has placed the kinship terms in quotation marks, Keightley says, "to indicate that they were classificatory, not just biological" (ibid.).

35. Wang, "Hsien-kung hsien-wang k'ao," p. 416.

36. Ibid., p. 413.

37. Wang, "Hsien-kung hsien-wang hsu-k'ao," pp. 428–429. Recent scholarship has revealed that the "Yin pen-chi" genealogy does not tally with the genealogy recorded in sacrifice inscriptions as neatly as Wang Kuo-wei imagined; for an introduction to the problems involved, see Keightley, *Sources of Shang History,* pp. 185–187, 204–209.

38. Wang, *Ku-shih hsin-cheng,* p. 2078. See also ibid., pp. 2108, 2077. On antiquity doubting, see Ku Chieh-kang, *The Autobiography of a Chinese Historian,* trans. Arthur W. Hummel, and Laurence A. Schneider, *Ku Chieh-kang and China's New History.*

15. The Later Years

1. Wang Kuo-wei, foreword to *Hsueh-t'ang chiao-k'an ch'ün-shu hsu-lu,* by Lo Chen-yü, foreword dated 1918; rpt. in *WKTCC,* 3:1137. "NP," p. 7071.

2. Lo Chen-yü, "Hai-ning Wang Chung-ch'ueh kung chuan," in *WKTCC,* 16:7021.

3. "NP," p. 7072.

4. For Ch'en Yin-k'o's view of Wang's character in later life, see the foreword he wrote in 1934 to *Hai-ning Wang Ching-an hsien-sheng i-shu,* by Wang Kuo-wei, in *WKTCC,* 1:i–iii. See also Ch'en's prose preface to his elegy "Wang Kuan-t'ang hsien-sheng wan-tz'u," in *WKTCC,* 16:7120.

5. Wang, foreword to *Hsueh-t'ang chiao-k'an ch'ün-shu hsu-lu,* by Lo Chen-yü, p. 1135.

6. Wang Kuo-wei, "Kuan-t'ang shu-cha: yü Lo Chen-yü hsien-sheng lun-hsueh shou-cha," *Chung-kuo li-shih wen-hsien yen-chiu chi-k'an* 1 (1980): letter 95. According to his daughter Tung-ming (as quoted in *NP,* p. 381), shortly before his death Wang Kuo-wei burned all of the letters he had received from Lo Chen-yü over the years. Many, although by no means all, of the letters that Wang wrote to Lo during the 1916–1926 period, however, are said by the latter's grandson Lo Chi-tsu (the son of Lo Fu-ch'eng) to have been preserved by the Lo family for several decades. According to Lo Chi-tsu, the majority of these letters were destroyed during the Cultural Revolution, although handwritten copies of them, prepared by himself in 1962, were not ("Pa 'Kuan-t'ang shu-cha,' " *Tu-shu,* 1982, no. 8:100–101). Excerpts from Wang's hitherto unpublished correspondence with his mentor constitute "Kuan-t'ang shu-cha: yü Lo" and appear in Lo Chi-tsu, "Pa 'Kuan-t'ang shu-cha,' " pp. 102–103; in idem, "Wang Kuo-wei hsien-sheng pi-hsia ti Ha-t'ung Ts'ang-sheng ming-chih ta-hsueh," *She-hui k'o-hsueh chan-hsien* 5, no. 2 (1982):168–170; in idem, "*Wang Kuo-wei chi ch'i wen-hsueh p'i-p'ing* tu hou," *Tou-sou* 54 (November 1983):46–50; and here and there in idem [Kan Ju], *Yung-feng hsiang jen hsing-nien lu (Lo Chen-yü nien-p'u).* The full texts of the

letters excerpted in the aforementioned works may be found in the collection of Wang's correspondence edited by Wu Tse, to whom Lo Chi-tsu made all his materials available, and published in 1984 under the title *Wang Kuo-wei ch'üan-chi: shu-hsin.* There are, however, numerous small discrepancies between the wording of the excerpts published by Lo Chi-tsu himself and the wording of these same passages as they appear in *Shu-hsin.* There are also numerous small discrepancies between the wording of letters written by Wang to other friends and colleagues and excerpted in various pre-1984 sources, including *NP,* and the wording of these same missives as they appear in *Shu-hsin.*

7. Tai Chia-hsiang [Po Sheng] has also noted that Wang Kuo-wei's most intimate friends—specifically, Lo Chen-yü, Shen Tseng-chih, and K'o Shao-min—were Ch'ing loyalists ("Chi Wang Ching-an hsien-sheng tzu-ch'en-shih shih-mo," in *WKTCC,* 16:7150).

8. Yuan Shih-k'ai established the Bureau of Ch'ing History for several reasons: to seal formally the termination of Ch'ing rule, thereby forestalling a Manchu restoration (expecting that the Ch'ing scion would one day be restored to power, some loyalists declined invitations to work on the history project); to provide elder statesmen of the fallen dynasty (*i-ch'en*) with a means of support; and to perpetuate Confucian ideals and a Confucian outlook, which, having dynastic ambitions himself, he evidently hoped to turn to his own advantage in the future. It is therefore no coincidence that the project's personnel were traditional-style scholars of monarchist bent. Among friends and acquaintances of Wang Kuo-wei who served under Director Chao were K'o Shao-min, substitute director; Yuan Chin-k'ai, supervisor of publication; Chin-liang, proofreader and collator; Miao Ch'üan-sun, a member of the Chief Editing Commission; the above-mentioned Chang Erh-t'ien, a compiler; and Wu Ch'ang-shou, an assistant compiler. For detailed information on the history of the project, see Thurston Griggs, "The *Ch'ing Shih Kao:* A Bibliographical Summary," *Harvard Journal of Asiatic Studies* 18, nos. 1–2 (June 1955):105–123. See also Charles S. Gardner, *Chinese Traditional Historiography* (Cambridge, Mass.: Harvard University Press, 1938; 3rd printing, 1970), pp. 97–99.

9. The above account of Chang Erh-t'ien is based on Teng Chih-ch'eng, "Chang chün Meng-ch'ü pieh-chuan," *Yen-ching hsueh-pao,* no. 30 (June 1946):323–325; "NP," p. 7086; Wang Yi-t'ung, "Biographic Sketches of Twenty-nine Classical Scholars of the Late Manchu and Early Republican Era," pp. 1–3; and Howard L. Boorman, ed., *Biographical Dictionary of Republican China,* 4 vols. (New York: Columbia University Press, 1967–1971), 1:54–56.

On Sun Te-ch'ien, see Wu P'i-chi's incomplete chronological biography (it covers the years 1869–1911), "Sun Ai-k'an nien-p'u ch'u-kao," *Hsueh-hai* 1, no. 1 (July 1944):86–94; *Hsueh-hai* 1, no. 6 (December 1944):92–96; and *Hsueh-hai* 2, no. 2 (February 1945):54–56. According to Wu, Sun Te-ch'ien and Chang Erh-t'ien had met and become good friends as early as 1894.

10. See the introductory remarks to chapter 11.

11. While he lived in Kyoto and Shanghai, Wang is said to have been in correspondence with K'o (Lo Chen-yü, "Chung-ch'ueh kung chuan," p. 7021;

"NP," p. 7080). Although K'o was apparently living in Peking during the teens, there is every indication that his friendship with Wang was becoming close at this time. For biographical information on K'o Shao-min, see Wang Sen-jan, *Chin-tai erh-shih chia p'ing-chuan*, pp. 53–68; Wang, "Biographic Sketches," pp. 35–37; and Boorman, ed., *Biographical Dictionary*, 2:241–242. For Wang's view of the *Hsin Yuan-shih*, see Hsu Chung-shu, "Wang Ching-an hsien-sheng chuan," in *WKTCC*, 16:7048. For his opinion of K'o's poetry, see "NP," p. 7066. Regarding K'o Ch'ang-ssu and K'o Ch'ang-chi, see *NP*, p. 224, as well as Wang, "Kuan-t'ang shu-cha: yü Lo," letter 94.

12. For Wang's high opinion of Shen, see *NP*, p. 292. Concerning Shen's last supper under the monarchy, during the course of which he reportedly uttered his loyalist vow, see Reginald F. Johnston, *Twilight in the Forbidden City*, pp. 88–89. For biographical information on Shen, see Wang Sen-jan, *Erh-shih chia p'ing-chuan*, pp. 31–52; and Wang Ch'ü-ch'ang, "Chia-hsing Shen Mei-sou hsien-sheng nien-p'u ch'u-kao," *Tung-fang tsa-chih* 26, no. 15 (10 August 1929):59–71, and no. 16 (25 August 1929):63–74. On Shen's deep involvement in Chang Hsun's effort to restore the monarchy, see also the excerpts from Wang Kuo-wei's correspondence with Lo Chen-yü that are cited in Lo Chi-tsu, "*Wang Kuo-wei chi ch'i wen-hsueh p'i-p'ing tu hou*," pp. 47–48.

A prominent official under the empire, Cheng Hsiao-hsu had resigned from office after the 1911 Revolution, and, repeatedly refusing positions offered him by Yuan Shih-k'ai and Li Yuan-hung, he had moved to Shanghai to study Chinese history, improve his calligraphy, and write poetry. See Johnston, *Twilight in the Forbidden City*, pp. 342–343.

13. Lo Chen-yü, "Chung-ch'ueh kung chuan," p. 7021; "NP," pp. 7069–7070. Lo and Wang had originally planned to travel together to Anyang and Loyang, but the latter developed eye trouble and had to remain put in Shang-hai while his mentor pressed on alone to those archaeologically important cities.

14. Wang thought his conversation with Shen so interesting that he re-corded the gist of it for posterity. See Wang Kuo-wei, preface to "*Erh ya* ts'ao mu ch'ung yü niao shou shih-li" [Examples of the *Erh ya*'s Elucidations of the Terms for Grass, Tree, Worm, Fish, Bird, and Animal], 1916; preface rpt. in *WKTCC*, 4:1414–1418. Lo Chen-yü reports that Wang had studied both etymology and phonology in Kyoto under his tutelage, although he had done so "only on the side" (foreword to *Kuan-t'ang chi-lin*, by Wang Kuo-wei; fore-word rpt. in *WKTCC*, 1:2).

15. "NP," pp. 7093, 7066. According to the editor of those of Wang's letters to Lo that were published in 1980, no one is mentioned more frequently therein than Shen Tseng-chih (Wang, "Kuan-t'ang shu-cha: yü Lo," p. 11n4).

16. Wang Kuo-wei, "Shou hsu," 1926; quoted in *NP*, p. 319. "NP," p. 7086. *NP*, p. 233. Whether Chiang was a Confucian who had withdrawn from public life or a Buddhist lay-associate is unclear, as the term *chü-shih* ("recluse") refers to both.

17. Yang Chung-hsi, epitaph for Wang Kuo-wei (private manuscript copy); Wang, "Kuan-t'ang shu-cha: yü Lo"; *NP*, pp. 163–164.

18. Born in Iraq, Silas Hardoon had begun his career in Shanghai as a janitor at David Sassoon's business firm, which (among other things) was an importer of opium. In time he became one of the wealthiest men in all of China, largely through his speculation in real estate. Lo Chia-ling's mother was a Chinese woman surnamed Shen, her father a Frenchman (known to the Chinese as Lo-shih) who was at one time chief of French police in Shanghai. Orphaned at a tender age, Lo Chia-ling lived in reduced circumstances with her maternal grandmother until old friends of her father came to her aid. Chia-ling, the name by which she was known throughout her adult life, is derived from the Chinese transliteration of the Sanskrit word *kalavinka*, *chia-ling p'in-chieh* (a kind of bird, known for its beautiful voice, indigenous to the valleys of the Himalayas). On the Hardoons' respective backgrounds, see "Tang-nien Shang-hai hao-fu Ha-t'ung fu-fu ch'uan-ch'i (shang)," *Ch'un-ch'iu*, no. 151 (n.d.):5–6; and "Lo Chia-ling nü-shih chuan," *Hsin-min ts'ung-pao*, no. 25 (1903):165.

Regarding the couple's revolutionary connections, see Chiang Chün-chang, "Ts'ang-sheng ming-chih ta-hsueh ti hui-i," *Chuan-chi wen-hsueh* 9, no. 6 (December 1966):13; and Mary Backus Rankin, *Early Chinese Revolutionaries: Radical Intellectuals in Shanghai and Chekiang, 1902–1911* (Cambridge, Mass.: Harvard University Press, 1971), pp. 59–60, 64–65, 208, 296n26. Although Huang Tsung-yang himself apparently never joined a political party, he was widely regarded as one of Shanghai's leading radicals at the dawn of the twentieth century, primarily because of his ability to obtain funds for revolutionary causes from his patrons, in particular Lo Chia-ling, who was a devout Buddhist.

19. "Ha-t'ung fu-fu ch'uan-ch'i (shang)," p. 7; Chiang Chün-chang, "Ming-chih ta-hsueh," p. 13; Liao K'o-yü, with the collaboration of Wang K'eng, "Ha-t'ung fu-fu i-shih tien-ti," *She-hui k'o-hsueh chan-hsien* 2, no. 3 (1979):161; "NP," pp. 7071–7072. Jui-ch'eng and Ts'en Ch'un-hsuan are said both to have died in the Hardoons' garden.

20. Wang's " 'Chou shu' 'Ku ming' li-cheng" (subsequently retitled " 'Chou shu' 'Ku ming' k'ao") appeared in *Hsueh-shu ts'ung-pien*, vol. 1, and in Wang Kuo-wei, ed., *Kuang-Ts'ang hsueh-ch'ün ts'ung-shu chia-lei* ([Collectanea of the School to Propagate Ts'ang-chieh's Wisdom, Series A]; Shanghai: Ts'ang-sheng ming-chih ta-hsueh, n.d.), vol. 1. His " 'Chou shu' 'Ku ming' hou-k'ao" was published in *Hsueh-shu ts'ung-pien*, vol. 7, and in *Ts'ung-shu chia-lei*, vol. 1; his "Mao kung ting ming k'ao-shih" in *Hsueh-shu ts'ung-pien*, vol. 4, and in *Ts'ung-shu chia-lei*, vol. 4; his "Yueh-shih k'ao-lueh" (the relevant section of which was subsequently republished separately as "Shuo 'Shang sung' hsia") in *Hsueh-shu ts'ung-pien*, vol. 3, and in *Ts'ung-shu chia-lei*, vol. 1; his *Ku-pen "Chu-shu chi-nien" chi-chiao* in *Hsueh-shu ts'ung-pien*, vol. 15, and in *Ts'ung-shu chia-lei*, vol. 23; his *Chin-pen "Chu-shu chi-nien" shu-cheng* in *Hsueh-shu ts'ung-pien*, vols. 17–18 (according to *NP*, pp. 423–424—I have been unable to consult the volumes in question), and in *Ts'ung-shu chia-lei*, vols. 23–24. His *Chien-shou t'ang so-ts'ang Yin-hsu wen-tzu k'ao-shih* was published in Wang Kuo-wei, ed., *Kuang-Ts'ang hsueh-ch'ün ts'ung-shu i-lei* ([Collectanea of the School to Propagate Ts'ang-chieh's Wisdom, Series B]; Shanghai: Ts'ang-sheng ming-

chih ta-hsueh, n.d.), vol. 24; this work was also published together with *Chien-shou t'ang so-ts'ang Yin-hsu wen-tzu*, comp. Chi Chueh-mi [Chi Fo-t'o] (actually compiled by Wang Kuo-wei), as a separate two-volume work. "Yin Chou chih-tu lun" was published in *Ts'ung-shu chia-lei*, vol. 22 (since I have not seen any volumes of *Hsueh-shu ts'ung-pien* past vol. 16, I cannot say whether this article was also published in that journal). As for those of Wang's articles on the Shang that we discussed earlier in some detail, "Yin pu-tz'u chung so-chien hsien-kung hsien-wang k'ao" was published in *Hsueh-shu ts'ung-pien*, vol. 14, and in *Ts'ung-shu chia-lei*, vol. 22; and "Yin pu-tz'u chung so-chien hsien-kung hsien-wang hsu-k'ao" was published in *Hsueh-shu ts'ung-pien*, vol. 16, and in *Ts'ung-shu chia-lei*, vol. 22.

21. "NP," p. 7084; Chiang Chün-chang, "Ming-chih ta-hsueh," pp. 12–13. According to Chiang, the conservative elder statesman and eminent scholar Wang Hsien-ch'ien also taught at the Hardoons' college. How Chiang, who says he became a student at the college only in 1921, can recall seeing Wang Hsien-ch'ien there (he died in Changsha in 1918) is unclear. On the perils of being seen with a queue on the streets of Shanghai at this time, as well as on Wang's determination not to be parted from *his*, see the lines he wrote Lo Chen-yü about the matter; lines quoted in Lo Chi-tsu, "*Wang Kuo-wei chi ch'i wen-hsueh p'i-p'ing* tu-hou," p. 49.

22. Chiang Chün-chang, "Ming-chih ta-hsueh," p. 12; "Tang-nien Shang-hai hao-fu Ha-t'ung fu-fu ch'uan-ch'i (hsia)," *Ch'un-ch'iu*, no. 152 (n.d.):14; Wang Kuo-wei, letter to Lo Chen-yü, quoted in part in Lo Chi-tsu, "Wang Kuo-wei hsien-sheng pi-hsia ti Ming-ta," p. 170.

23. Wang Kuo-wei, letter to Lo Chen-yü, quoted in part in Lo Chi-tsu, "Wang Kuo-wei hsien-sheng pi-hsia ti Ming-ta," p. 169; ibid.; ibid.; ibid.

24. Wang Kuo-wei, "Lo Chün-ch'u ch'i Wang ju-jen mu-chieh-ming," 1922; rpt. in *WKTCC*, 3:1126. See also idem, "Lo Chün-ch'u chuan," 1922; rpt. in *WKTCC*, 3:1121–1125. Well into the twentieth century, as Wang's remarks attest, many Chinese continued to believe that an ill person might regain his health by taking "medicine" consisting of a piece of human flesh voluntarily sacrificed by a close relative or friend; the divine powers, it was thought, might be moved by the selflessness thus shown by the loyal relative or friend to cure the patient.

At the time of the Hsuan-t'ung Emperor's abdication, the Republican government guaranteed, in Article One of the Articles Providing for the Favorable Treatment of the Great Ch'ing Emperor after His Abdication, that "his title of dignity is to be retained and will not be abolished" (translation is according to Johnston, *Twilight in the Forbidden City*, p. 96). Chinese loyalists, and others as well, thus continued in the post-1911 period to refer to the Ch'ing scion by his title of dignity, without adding the prefix "ex."

25. Wang Kuo-wei, "Yin pu-tz'u chung so-chien hsien-kung hsien-wang hsu-k'ao," 1917; rpt. in *WKTCC*, 2:420. "NP," p. 7076. *CLP*, p. 765. According to Chao Wan-li ("NP," p. 7082), Lo returned to China in 1918. Hsiao-ch'un, who married Wang Ch'ien-ming, was Lo Chen-yü's only daughter by his second wife; he had two daughters by his first (Mo Jung-tsung, "Nien-p'u," p. 8755).

26. *CLP,* pp. 766–767; "NP," p. 7085. Liang Ting-fen's act of courage consisted of proceeding, as duty required, through a shower of bullets (the rival armies of Chang Hsun and Tuan Ch'i-jui were fighting in the vicinity of the Forbidden City) to the Ch'ing scion's palace in order to keep an appointment with his imperial pupil. The incident is described by Johnston in *Twilight in the Forbidden City,* p. 189.

27. Johnston, *Twilight in the Forbidden City,* p. 342. See also Ai-hsin-chueh-lo P'u-i, *P'u-i tzu-chuan,* p. 204. Chin-liang, in whose house Wang lived during the summer of 1923, also entered the service of the Ch'ing scion at this time ("NP," p. 7094; Ai-hsin-chueh-lo P'u-i, *P'u-i tzu-chuan,* p. 204).

28. Wang, "Shou-hsu," p. 319; "NP," p. 7094. On Wang's reaction to the news of his appointment, see also the lines he wrote to Lo Chen-yü on the subject; lines quoted in Lo Chi-tsu, "*Wang Kuo-wei chi ch'i wen-hsueh p'i-p'ing tu-hou,*" p. 49.

29. Lo Chen-yü, "Chung-ch'ueh kung chuan," p. 7021.

30. After the disappearance of the imperial queue in 1921 or thereabouts, many of the Ch'ing scion's retainers, following suit, sheared their own plaits away. Thereafter, only the deposed emperor's tutors, a few senior members of the Imperial Household Department, and a handful of die-hard conservatives continued to wear their hair according to the traditional Manchu fashion; among them were K'o Shao-min, Lo Chen-yü, and Wang Kuo-wei (Ai-hsin-chueh-lo P'u-i, *P'u-i tzu-chuan,* p. 204).

31. Chester Chen-I Wang, "Wang Kuo-wei (1877–1927): His Life and Scholarship" (Ph.D. diss., University of Chicago, 1962), p. 19.

32. Wang's (draft) document is quoted by Lo Chen-yü in his essay "Wang Chung-ch'ueh kung pieh-chuan," in *Hai-ning Wang Chung-ch'ueh kung i-shu,* by Wang Kuo-wei, 1:iiib–vb. While I have here assumed that Wang Kuo-wei really wrote the document in question, I have not been able independently to confirm its authenticity. However, with one possible exception—namely, his claim that just before Wang died he wrote a last memorial to the Ch'ing scion (for the view that *that* document was forged by Lo himself, see Lo Chi-tsu, "Pa 'Kuan-t'ang shu-cha,' " p. 103)—I have found Lo Chen-yü to be a highly reliable source of information on Wang's life; the document that concerns us here, in my view, is thus probably genuine.

33. Lo Chen-yü, "Chung-ch'ueh kung chuan," p. 7021; Yang Chung-hsi, epitaph for Wang Kuo-wei. The agreement reached by the imperial family and the Republican authorities in 1916 concerned treasures that in 1914 had been brought from the Ch'ing palaces in Mukden and Jehol to Peking and deposited in three throne halls taken over by the Republic as well as in the Wen-hua and Wu-ying palaces. According to Johnston, the agreement that the two sides reached in 1916 was reflected in a legal document which explains that the treasures in question had been brought to Peking by a joint deputation; that they were acknowledged to be the private property of the imperial family; that they were to be purchased by the Republican government, at a price determined by independent experts, whenever finances permitted; and that in the meantime they were to be considered on loan from the imperial family to the Republic (*Twilight in the Forbidden City,* p. 301).

34. Ai-hsin-chueh-lo P'u-i, *P'u-i tzu-chuan*, p. 212.

35. "NP," p. 7093; *NP*, p. 251; Wang Kuo-wei, "Kuan-t'ang shu-cha: yü Ma Heng hsien-sheng lun-hsueh shou-cha," *Chung-kuo li-shih wen-hsien yen-chiu chi-k'an* 2 (1981): letter 2; ibid., letter 3. Ma Heng also asked Wang if he would contribute articles to the university's *Kuo-hsueh chi-k'an* [The Journal of Sinological Studies], and the latter said that he would (Wang, "Kuan-t'ang shu-cha: yü Ma," letter 3).

36. In early 1924 Wang declined an offer to become director of the Institute for Sinological Research precisely because he feared that those who had offered him the directorship had done so in the hope that he would help them with their cultural work (*wen-hua shih-yeh*). "I am by no means a political creature (*tang-p'ai chih jen*—literally, a party person)," Wang writes to his friend Chiang Ju-tsao in a letter dated 6 April, "and I have no desire to become involved in this business" (letter to Chiang Ju-tsao, quoted in part in *NP*, p. 283).

37. Wang Kuo-wei, "Chih Pei-ching ta-hsueh mou chiao-shou shu" [A Letter to Certain Professors at Peking University], in *Wang Kuan-t'ang wen-hsuan*, by Wang Kuo-wei, ed. Tanaka Keitarō, p. 5. Tanaka's text of Wang's letter to Ma and Shen, which was published in 1941, differs somewhat from the text published as letter 39 in Wang, "Kuan-t'ang shu-cha: yü Ma." Also compare Wang, *Shu-hsin*, pp. 405–407.

38. Wang, "Chih Pei-ching ta-hsueh," p. 5.

39. Ibid., p. 7; ibid. Wang is evidently thinking of Article Seven of the Articles of Favorable Treatment, which does not mention the palace collection specifically but does state that "after the abdication of the Great Ch'ing emperor, his private property will be safeguarded and protected by the Republic of China" (translation is according to Johnston, *Twilight in the Forbidden City*, p. 97, with one small change).

40. Wang, "Chih Pei-ching ta-hsueh," p. 8. The *locus classicus* of the words that I have translated as "devouring the weak and spitting out the strong" is the poem "Cheng-min" in *Shih ching*, which reads in part (following the translation of James Legge, trans., *The Chinese Classics*, 5 vols. in 4, 4:543–544):

> The people have a saying.—
> "The soft is devoured,
> And the hard is ejected from the mouth."
> But Chung Shan-fu
> Does not devour the soft,
> Nor eject the powerful.
> He does not insult the poor or the widow [*sic*];
> He does not fear the strong or the oppressive.

41. Wang, "Chih Pei-ching ta-hsueh," pp. 8–9.

42. Ibid., p. 9; ibid.

43. Wang, "Kuan-t'ang shu-cha: yü Ma," letter 39 (postscript). Neither his opening salutation nor his closing postscript appears in the 1941 text of Wang's letter.

My view that the letter in question dates from the latter part of 1924 or thereabouts is based on the following considerations. First, Ku Chieh-kang says, in an article published in the latter part of 1927, that both the Archaeological Society's manifesto and Wang's letter criticizing it were written "three years ago" ("Tao Wang Ching-an hsien-sheng," *Wen-hsueh chou-pao* 5, nos. 1–4 combined [August 1927]; rpt. in *WKTCC*, 16:7129). Second, Wang's article on Tai Chen's text of the *"Shui ching" chu* was completed, according to Chao Wan-li, in early 1925 ("NP," p. 7100). In the postscript to his letter to Ma and Shen, Wang asks his colleagues to return his manuscript to him since he would like to revise it; presumably Wang had submitted a draft article to the editors of the *Kuo-hsueh chi-k'an* (many of Wang's works, we recall, were originally published in draft form) at some earlier date, perhaps summer or fall of 1924. It is this draft version of the article on Tai Chen's edition of the *"Shui ching" chu*, not the revised version of early 1925, one supposes, that Wang asks to have returned to him in the postscript to his letter. The revised article, retitled "*'Shui ching' chu* pa-wei" [Notes on the *Commentary on the "Classic of Waterways"*], was published in June 1925 in the *Ch'ing-hua hsueh-pao* [The Tsing Hua Journal, vol. 2, no. 1]. The issue of the *Kuo-hsueh chi-k'an* in which Wang's article had been scheduled to appear, a special one devoted entirely to Tai Chen, was published in December 1925 (vol. 2, no. 1).

Third, from the letter's subject matter and tone it would appear that Feng Yü-hsiang's coup of 5 November 1924 had not yet occurred. After Feng's seizure of the Forbidden City, after all, the treasures housed in its palaces passed into *his* hands. It is even possible that both Ma Heng and Shen Chien-shih were appointed members of the Commission for the Readjustment of the Affairs of the Ch'ing House (Ch'ing-shih shan-hou wei-yuan hui), whose mission was to divide into public and private portions the property remaining in the Forbidden City after the Ch'ing scion had been expelled from it, precisely because the new Peking administration found their position on the palace collection's status (as set forth in the Archaeological Society's manifesto) most agreeable. (Although Ma's name does not appear in the list of commission members given in Ai-hsin-chueh-lo P'u-i, *P'u-i tzu-chuan* [p. 246], Ma himself has said that he was a member; see his "Sui shu 'Lü-li chih' shih-wu teng ch'ih" [Fifteen Different Classes of Measures as Given in the "Lü-li chih" Section of the *History of the Sui Dynasty;* Peking, 1932], p. 8.) The fact that Wang tells his colleagues that he is sending them this letter in his capacity not as courtier but as archaeologist presumably indicates that it dates from the period of his closest association with the Ch'ing scion (that is, the years he served as a Companion of the Southern Study), but this does not help us very much. The fact that in his letter Wang repeatedly invokes the Articles of Favorable Treatment helps us not at all because neither the imperial family nor any Ch'ing loyalist ever recognized the legal validity of the "revised" Articles imposed on the Ch'ing scion on 5 November 1924.

On Wang's letter to Ma and Shen, see also Wang Ching-hsien [Yang Mu], "Tsai lun Wang Kuo-wei chih ssu," *Lien-ho pao*, 21–22 November 1982.

44. See Johnston, *Twilight in the Forbidden City*, pp. 376–396, for a detailed description of the day on which, as he puts it (p. 396), "the twilight that had lingered in the Forbidden City for thirteen years at last deepened into night."

Since at least 1917, when he denounced the Restoration and led his troops to Peking to fight those of Chang Hsun, Feng Yü-hsiang had wanted to eliminate the royal house. The measures against the Ch'ing scion and his family that Feng actually took in 1924 he had been on record since 1917 as wishing to take. See James Sheridan, *Chinese Warlord: The Career of Feng Yü-hsiang* (Stanford, Calif.: Stanford University Press, 1966), p. 66.

45. Wang's letter to Kano Naoki of 1 December 1924 is quoted in Kano Naoki, "Ō Seian [Wang Ching-an] kun o omou," *Geibun* 18, no. 8 (August 1927):43.

46. "NP," p. 7096.

47. Lo Chen-yü, "Chi Wang Chung-ch'üeh kung wen," in *WKTCC*, 16:7115; Lo Chen-yü, "Chung-ch'üeh kung chuan," p. 7021. Yeh Chia-ying has questioned the truth of Lo's claim that Wang entertained suicidal thoughts in 1924 ("I-ko hsin-chiu wen-hua chi-pien chung ti pei-chü jen-wu: Wang Kuo-wei ssu-yin chih t'an-t'ao," *Hsiang-kang Chung-wen ta-hsueh hsueh-pao* 3, no. 1 [1975]:37). However, I believe it unlikely that Lo would have falsified the record on this point since K'o Shao-min was still alive at the time (1927) that Lo made this assertion. Indeed, K'o himself has indirectly corroborated Lo's statement by publishing a short biography of Wang Kuo-wei in the *Ch'ing-shih kao* (*lieh-chuan* 282), of which he became editor-in-chief after Chao Erh-hsun's death in September 1927; according to this biographical account, after the coup Wang vowed that he would die. K'o presumably would not have published this biography had he not believed its contents to be true.

(I have not been able to ascertain who wrote the biography in question. Since, on the one hand, its wording is virtually identical at points to that in Lo Chen-yü's "Chung-ch'üeh kung chuan," one might suppose that Wang's mentor authored it. But since, on the other hand, many of Wang's colleagues wrote essays about him that incorporate lines or even whole passages from Lo's writings, it is possible that someone else, perhaps K'o Shao-min himself, authored it.)

In addition to Lo Chen-yü and K'o Shao-min, other close friends of Wang Kuo-wei were convinced that he wished to take his own life after Feng's coup. Among them were Yang Chung-hsi, who during the period in question was also serving as an adviser to the Ch'ing scion (epitaph for Wang Kuo-wei), and Ch'en Yin-k'o, who knew Wang intimately during the years immediately following the coup ("Wang Kuan-t'ang hsien-sheng wan-tz'u," p. 7121). Ch'en Shou-ch'ien depicts Wang's death as emerging naturally out of the 5 November incident ("Chi Wang Chung-ch'üeh kung wen," in *WKTCC*, 16:7117–7118). Hsu Chung-shu ("Wang Ching-an hsien-sheng chuan," p. 7048) and Lo Chi-tsu (letter dated 24 March 1984) also believe that Wang Kuo-wei wished to commit suicide after the distressing developments of 5 November. Wang Te-i as well believes this to have been the case (*NP*, p. 291).

48. Ch'en Yin-k'o, "Wang Kuan-t'ang hsien-sheng wan-tz'u," p. 7121. In January 1979 the late William Hung told me that he could recall hearing that after the 5 November 1924 incident some persons had talked about committing suicide, but he could not recollect hearing that anyone had actually

done so. On the propriety of dying at this time, see Ch'en Shou-ch'ien, "Chung-ch'ueh kung wen," pp. 7117–7118.

49. Hsu Chung-shu, "Wang Ching-an hsien-sheng chuan," p. 7048.

50. He barely lived through the winter of 1924–25, Wang subsequently confessed ("Shou hsu," p. 319).

51. Wang's letter to Chiang Ju-tsao of 25 March 1925 is quoted in part in *NP*, p. 297.

52. The foregoing is based on Wang, letter to Kano, quoted in Kano Naoki, "Ō Seian kun o omou," p. 43; "NP," p. 7096; Ai-hsin-chueh-lo P'u-i, *P'u-i tzu-chuan*, p. 247; and Wang, letter to Chiang, quoted in *NP*, p. 297.

53. Wang, letter to Chiang, quoted in *NP*, p. 297; ibid.

54. "NP," p. 7096; Johnston, *Twilight in the Forbidden City*, p. 473n5.

55. Johnston, *Twilight in the Forbidden City*, p. 473n5; Lan Wen-cheng as quoted in *NP*, p. 295.

56. "NP," p. 7098; Fan Ping-ch'ing, "Wang Chung-ch'ueh kung shih-lueh," in *AWL*, p. 3.

57. Yao Ming-ta as quoted in *NP*, p. 304; Johnston, *Twilight in the Forbidden City*, p. 473n5.

58. "NP," p. 7099; Wang, "Kuan-t'ang shu-cha: yü Ma," letter 6.

59. Aoki Masaru, "Ō Seian [Wang Ching-an] sensei no bempatsu," *Geibun* 18, no. 8 (August 1927):60.

60. Wang, "Kuan-t'ang shu-cha: yü Ma," letter 33.

61. On Hu Shih's recommendation that Lo Chen-yü be invited to teach at Ch'ing-hua, see Lan Wen-cheng's remarks as quoted in *NP*, p. 295. On Lo's involvement after 1924 in politics, see the section on Lo Chen-yü in the Ch'ing scion's biased but still useful autobiography (Ai-hsin-chueh-lo P'u-i, *P'u-i tzu-chuan*, pp. 257–270). The contest between Lo and Cheng was eventually won by the latter, who was appointed premier of Manchoukuo (the former was made a mere privy councillor).

62. Ch'en Shou-ch'ien, "Chung-ch'ueh kung wen," pp. 7117–7118.

63. Wang, "Shou hsu," p. 320; ibid., p. 319; ibid., p. 320.

64. "NP," p. 7101. Chao Wan-li, who lived in a Ch'ing-hua apartment adjacent to that of the Wang family, was Wang Kuo-wei's teaching assistant in the 1925–1927 period; he was also a relative of Mrs. Wang Kuo-wei (their mothers were cousins). (I am indebted to Wang Tung-ming [letter dated 18 March 1985] for this information.)

65. Lo Chi-tsu, "Pa 'Kuan-t'ang shu-cha,'" pp. 101–102; Lo Chi-tsu, *Yung-feng hsiang jen*, p. 95. After reading the latter account of the affair that occasioned the dissolution of Wang Kuo-wei and Lo Chen-yü's friendship, Tai Chia-hsiang sent Lo Chi-tsu a letter stating that his own understanding of that affair was identical to Lo's. Mrs. Wang Kuo-wei, it seems, confided in Chao Wan-li, who in turn confided in Tai (Tai Chia-hsiang as quoted in Lo Chi-tsu, " 'Kuan-t'ang shu-cha' tsai pa," *Shih-hsueh chi-k'an*, 1983, no. 4:40). While asserting that her mother and sister-in-law had not been on bad terms prior to her half-brother's death, Wang Tung-ming maintains a view of the incident that estranged her father and Lo Chen-yü which is otherwise very

similar to that of Lo Chi-tsu ("Wei mu-ch'in shuo chi-chü hua," *Chung-kuo shih-pao*, 23 October 1984).

66. Wang Kuo-wei, letter to Lo Chen-yü of 24 October 1926, quoted in part in Lo Chi-tsu, "Pa 'Kuan-t'ang shu-cha,'" p. 102; ibid.

67. Wang Kuo-wei, letter to Lo Chen-yü of 25 October 1926, quoted in part in Lo Chi-tsu, "Pa 'Kuan-t'ang shu-cha,'" p. 102; ibid. If we are justified in taking the aforementioned correspondence to be genuine, and if we are justified in accepting the account of the events of late 1926 given by Lo Chi-tsu, confirmed by Tai Chia-hsiang, and partially endorsed by Wang Tung-ming, then we may dismiss as libelous the claim of Shih Ta, a pseudonymous author, that Wang Kuo-wei was driven to suicide by financial pressure exerted on him by Lo Chen-yü. (According to Shih Ta, when Lo Chen-yü took his daughter back into his own household, he demanded that Wang Kuo-wei contribute two thousand [Chinese] dollars per year to her support. Again according to Shih Ta, Lo also at this time began to dun Wang for repayment of debts. The financial pressure thus exerted on Wang by Lo in late 1926–early 1927, he alleges, drove the former to take his life. See Shih Ta, "Wang Ching-an hsien-sheng chih-ssu ti chen-yin," *Wen-hsueh chou-pao* 5, nos. 1–4 combined [August 1927]:74.) The mystery of Shih Ta's identity has yet to be solved; as for the view of Wang's death that he advances in his essay, its most prominent identifiable spokesman in the latter part of 1927 was Lo Chen-yü's archenemy, Cheng Hsiao-hsu (Chou Chün-shih, *Wei-Man kung-t'ing tsa-i*, pp. 50–51).

68. "NP," p. 7102.

69. Ibid., pp. 7102–7103. That his poor health contributed to Wang's depression in the last months of his life seems highly likely. (On this point, see also Hsiao Ai, "Kuan-yü Wang Kuo-wei ti kung-kuo," *Tu-shu*, 1981, no. 8:134.) What role, if any, it played in Wang's decision to commit suicide we cannot, however, say at present; the sources currently available—namely, the writings of Wang himself as well as those of his closest friends and colleagues—are absolutely silent on the subject of how Wang felt about his health, which (as we know) had always been very fragile, during the spring of 1927.

70. Jung Keng, "Wang Kuo-wei hsien-sheng k'ao-ku-hsueh shang chih kung-hsien," in *WKTCC*, 16:7340; Liang Ch'i-ch'ao, letter to his daughter of 15 June 1927, quoted in Ting Wen-chiang, *Liang Jen-kung hsien-sheng nien-p'u ch'ang-pien ch'u-kao*, p. 739; Chin-liang, "Wang Chung-ch'üeh kung hsun-chieh chi," in *AWL*, p. 1. According to Liang, Wang had most recently been plunged into melancholy reflections on the contemporary scene by the news that Yeh Te-hui and Wang Pao-hsin had been shot to death for political reasons by Hunan government officials (letter to his daughter, quoted in Ting Wen-chiang, *Liang Jen-kung*, p. 739).

From Chin-liang's account it would appear that Wang was among those who in the spring of 1927 wished the Ch'ing scion, for his own safety, to go abroad ("Chung-ch'üeh kung hsun-chieh chi," p. 1). Lo Chen-yü also repeatedly urged the former emperor to leave Tientsin at this time, but his recommendations were not followed (Ai-hsin-chueh-lo P'u-i, *P'u-i tzu-chuan*,

p. 266). On the tense, fearful mood in Tientsin as well as in Peking in late May and early June, see Liang Ch'i-ch'ao, letter to his daughter, quoted in Ting Wen-chiang, *Liang Jen-kung*, pp. 739–740.

71. Tai Chia-hsiang, "Tzu-ch'en-shih shih-mo," p. 7150.

72. For the text of Wang's suicide note, which was addressed to his third son (Chen-ming), see "NP," p. 7103. The meaning of the note's opening lines—*"wu-shih chih nien, chih ch'ien i ssu; ching tz'u shih-pien, i wu tsai ju"*—has been much debated.

According to Wang Shih-chao, shortly before Wang's death the *Shih-chieh jih-pao* [Daily News of the World] published a list of persons whom it assumed would be arrested when the revolutionary army reached Peking, and (again according to Wang Shih-chao) Wang Kuo-wei's name was on the list (*Chung-kuo wen-jen hsin-lun* [From Confucius to Hu Shih; Hong Kong: Hsin shih-chi ch'u-pan she, 1953], p. 156). What role, if any, this news played in Wang's decision to commit suicide or whether, in fact, he even read the paper on the day in question or whether, indeed, there ever was published such a list (none of Wang's intimates mention it in their reminiscences) is unclear.

73. Tai Chia-hsiang, "Tzu-ch'en-shih shih-mo," p. 7147.

74. Chin-liang, "Chung-ch'ueh kung hsun-chieh chi," p. 1.

75. "Yü tsao" in *Shih ching;* trans. according to Legge, *The Chinese Classics,* 4:401.

76. Wu Mi, "Wan lien," in *AWL,* p. 26. One of the most famous Chinese literary figures ever to commit suicide by drowning, Ch'ü Yuan preferred in 278 B.C. to cast himself into the Mi-lo River than to allow the jewel of his integrity to be besmirched. Cheng Ssu-hsiao (1241–1318), a well-known Sung loyalist, was only a young man when Hangchou fell to the Mongols, and he had never held an official post in the Sung government. Cheng nevertheless spent the rest of his life expressing his intense devotion to the defunct dynasty as well as his loathing for China's new rulers. On Cheng's "extreme" loyalism, see Frederick W. Mote, "Confucian Eremitism in the Yüan Period," in *The Confucian Persuasion,* ed. Arthur F. Wright (Stanford, Calif.: Stanford University Press, 1960), pp. 234–235.

77. Although Wang took his life on 2 June (the third day of the fifth moon), his friends refer to his suicide in a loose way as having occurred on the anniversary of Ch'ü Yuan's death (the fifth day of the fifth moon).

78. Fujita Toyohachi (quoting *Lun yü,* bk. 7, chap. 14, sect. 2; trans. according to Legge, *The Chinese Classics,* 1:199) as quoted in Lo Chen-yü, "Jih-pen T'ai-pei ta-hsueh chiao-shou wen-hsueh po-shih T'eng-t'ien [Fujita] chün mu-piao," in *LHTCC,* 1st series, 4:1542. On Wu K'o-tu (1812–1879), see Arthur W. Hummel, ed., *Eminent Chinese of the Ch'ing Period (1644–1912),* 2 vols. with successive pagination, pp. 874–875. On Liang Chi (1859–1918), see Lin Yu-sheng, "The Suicide of Liang Chi: An Ambiguous Case of Moral Conservatism," in *The Limits of Change: Essays on Conservative Alternatives in Republican China,* ed. Charlotte Furth, pp. 151–168; and Guy S. Alitto, *The Last Confucian: Liang Shu-ming and the Chinese Dilemma of Modernity* (Berkeley: University of California Press, 1979), pp. 17–69.

79. *Lun yü,* bk. 15, chap. 8; trans. according to Legge, *The Chinese Classics,*

1:297. Ibid. Among those who considered Wang Kuo-wei one of those rare men of principle who, knowing that there is something a gentleman "loves more than life" (*Meng Tzu*, bk. 6, chap. 10), chose to preserve their integrity by "refusing to surrender their wills, or to submit to any taint in their persons" (*Lun yü*, bk. 18, chap. 8, sect. 2, as translated by Legge, *The Chinese Classics*, 1:336); we may mention Ch'en Yin-k'o, Yang Chung-hsi, Liang Ch'i-ch'ao, Fan Ping-ch'ing, and Sun Hsiung. See Ch'en Yin-k'o, foreword to *Wang Ching-an hsien-sheng i-shu*, by Wang Kuo-wei, p. ii, and preface to "Wang Kuan-t'ang hsien-sheng wan-tz'u," p. 7120; Yang Chung-hsi, epitaph for Wang Kuo-wei; Liang Ch'i-ch'ao, "Wang Ching-an hsien-sheng mu-ch'ien tao-tz'u," in *WKTCC*, 16:7122; Fan Ping-ch'ing, "Wan lien," in *AWL*, p. 26; and Sun Hsiung, "Wan shih," in ibid., p. 15.

80. It is also significant that in the Republican era Wang declined to date his writings in accordance with the Republican system (Min-kuo such-and-such a year). In deference to his late friend's cultural outlook, Ch'en Yin-k'o also declined to use that system in dating the foreword he wrote to the second edition of Wang Kuo-wei's collected works. See chapter 12, n. 119, and Ch'en Yin-k'o as quoted in Chiang T'ien-shu, *Ch'en Yin-k'o hsien-sheng pien-nien shih-chi*, p. 81.

81. Ch'en Yin-k'o, preface to "Wang Kuan-t'ang hsien-sheng wan-tz'u," p. 7120; ibid.

On 5 June the Ch'ing scion, who had learned of Wang's death from Lo Chen-yü, bestowed on his former courtier the posthumous title "loyal and upright," delegated Prince P'u-chin to attend the funeral, and contributed a sum of money toward the family's funeral expenses ("NP," p. 7103). Lo Chen-yü, who is said bitterly to have regretted ever having quarreled with his protégé, traveled to Peking to help the Wangs with the funeral arrangements; he also spent a year compiling, editing, and publishing Wang Kuo-wei's collected works (ibid.; Lo Chi-tsu, "Pa 'Kuan-t'ang shu-cha,' " p. 103). On 14 August Wang was laid to rest, as he had requested in his suicide note, in a grave near Ch'ing-hua.

16. Epilogue

1. See "Reformulation of Principles" in chapter 12. So repugnant did Lo Chen-yü, in retrospect, find his protégé's youthful researches in foreign thought that in 1923 he attempted in his foreword to *Kuan-t'ang chi-lin* to minimize the actual extent of Wang Kuo-wei's heretical thinking in the pre-1911 period. "In pursuing the study of philosophy, Mr. Wang was never so partial to new ideas that he disregarded traditional learning. In pursuing the study of literature written in a vernacular style, he never so venerated the colloquial language that he made light of classical expressions" (foreword rpt. in *WKTCC*, 1:2). When in 1927–28 he compiled his well-known edition of Wang's surviving works, Lo went so far as to omit all of the educational, philosophical, and literary essays that his protégé had originally published in Lo's own *Chiao-yü shih-chieh tsa-chih*.

2. On Hu Shih's literary proposals, see his article "Chien-she-ti wen-hsueh ko-ming lun" [On a Constructive Literary Revolution], 1918; rpt. in idem,

Hu Shih wen-hsuan [Selected Writings of Hu Shih] (Taipei: Yuan-tung t'u-shu kung-ssu, 1967), pp. 146–165.

3. *NP*, p. 55. Ch'en republished the two-*chüan* version of *Ch'ü lu* in 1921 and the six-*chüan* version of it in 1925. On the date of publication of *T'iao-hua tz'u*, see chapter 10, n. 2. On the metaphorical poem in *Shih ching* to which the work's title is an allusion, see James Legge, trans., *The Chinese Classics*, 5 vols. in 4, 4:lxxiii, 423.

4. For a brief but thoughtful critique of the Levensonian thesis concerning the fate of Confucianism in the modern world, see Tu Wei-ming, "Hsiung Shih-li's Quest for Authentic Existence," in *The Limits of Change: Essays on Conservative Alternatives in Republican China,* ed. Charlotte Furth, pp. 242–245. On the rise of the so-called new Confucianism (*hsin ju-chia*) in recent decades, see Hao Chang, "New Confucianism and the Intellectual Crisis of Contemporary China," in ibid., pp. 276–302.

Selected Bibliography

Works by Wang Kuo-wei

"Han-te hsiang-tsan" 汗德像贊 [An Appreciation of Kant]. 1903. Reprint. *WKTCC*, 5:1830.

"Chiao-yü ou-kan ssu tse" 教育偶感四則 [Occasional Reflections on Education: Four Items]. 1904. Reprint. *WKTCC*, 5:1753–1762.

"*Hung-lou meng* p'ing-lun" 紅樓夢評論 [A Critique of *Dream of the Red Chamber*]. 1904. Punctuated reprint. *"Hung-lou meng" chüan* 紅樓夢卷 [Sources on *Dream of the Red Chamber*], compiled by I Su 一粟. 2 vols. in 1, 1:244–265. Peking: Chunghua shu-chü 中華書局, 1963. Also in *WKTCC*, 5:1628–1671.

"Shih li" 釋理 [An Elucidation of the Term 'Reason']. 1904. Reprint. *WKTCC*, 5: 1570–1596.

"Shu-pen-hua chih che-hsueh chi ch'i chiao-yü hsueh-shuo" 叔本華之哲學及其教育學說 [Schopenhauer's Philosophy and His Pedagogical Theory]. 1904. Reprint. *WKTCC*, 5:1596–1628.

"Shu-pen-hua yü Ni-ts'ai" 叔本華與尼采 [Schopenhauer and Nietzsche]. 1904. Reprint. *WKTCC*, 5:1671–1695.

"Lun che-hsueh chia yü mei-shu chia chih t'ien-chih" 論哲學家與美術家之天職 [On the Callings of Philosopher and Artist]. 1905. Reprint. *WKTCC*, 5:1748–1753.

"Lun chiao-yü chih tsung-chih" 論教育之宗旨 [On the Purpose of Education]. N.d. Reprint. *WKTCC*, 5:1767–1770.

"Lun chin-nien chih hsueh-shu chieh" 論近年之學術界 [On the World of Scholarship in Recent Years]. 1905. Reprint. *WKTCC*, 5:1734–1741.

"Lun hsing" 論性 [On Human Nature]. N.d. Reprint. *WKTCC*, 5:1549–1570.

Preface to *Ching-an wen-chi* 靜安文集 [Essays by Ching-an]. 1905. Reprint. *WKTCC*, 5:1547–1548.

"Shu Shu-pen-hua 'I-ch'uan shuo' hou" 書叔本華遺傳說後 [My Views on Schopenhauer's "Hereditary Nature of Qualities"]. 1905. Reprint. *WKTCC*, 5: 1709–1733.

"Chi yen" 紀言 [A Record of What I Said (to Visitors on the Subject of Primary School Education)]. 1906. Reprint. *WKTCC*, 5:1877–1880.

"Ch'ü-tu p'ien" 去毒篇 [On Extirpating the Poison]. 1906. Reprint. *WKTCC*, 5: 1870–1877.

"Ch'ü-tzu wen-hsueh chih ching-shen" 屈子文學之精神 [The Spirit of Ch'ü Yuan's Poetry]. 1906. Reprint. *WKTCC*, 5:1848–1855.

"Wen-hsueh hsiao-yen" 文學小言 [Comments on Literature]. 1906. Reprint.

WKTCC, 5:1839–1848.

"Chiao-yü hsiao-yen shih tse" 教育小言十則 [Ten Comments on Education]. 1906 or 1907. Reprint. *WKTCC*, 5:1898–1902.

"Chiao-yü hsiao-yen shih-erh tse" 教育小言十二則 [Twelve Comments on Education]. N.d. Reprint. *WKTCC*, 5:1880–1887.

"Chiao-yü hsiao-yen shih-san tse" 教育小言十三則 [Thirteen Comments on Education]. 1907. Reprint. *WKTCC*, 5:1892–1898.

"Jen-chien shih-hao chih yen-chiu" 人間嗜好之研究 [A Study of Man's Pastimes]. 1907. Reprint. *WKTCC*, 5:1795–1803.

"Ku-ya chih tsai mei-hsueh shang chih wei-chih" 古雅之在美學上之位置 [The Place of the Elegant in Aesthetics]. 1907. Reprint. *WKTCC*, 5:1830–1839.

"Shu Ku shih T'ang-sheng ying-i *Chung-yung* hou" 書辜氏湯生英譯中庸後 [My Views on Ku T'ang-sheng's English Translation of the *Doctrine of the Mean*]. 1907. Reprint. *WKTCC*, 5:1803–1822.

T'iao-hua tz'u 苕華詞 [Bignonia Lyrics]. Originally published, along with other material, under the title *Jen-chien tz'u* 人間詞 [Lyrics in the World of Men]. Part One, 1906; Part Two, 1907. Punctuated reprint of the 1917 edition (?), enlarged. *CASTK*, pp. 53–77. Also in *WKTCC*, 4:1511–1537.

" 'Tsou-ting ching-hsueh-k'o ta-hsueh wen-hsueh-k'o ta-hsueh chang-ch'eng' shu hou" 奏定經學科大學文學科大學章程書後 [My Views on the "Regulations concerning the Establishment of Departments of Classical Studies and Literary Studies in the University, as Memorialized and Approved"]. N.d. Reprint. *WKTCC*, 5:1857–1870.

"Tzu-hsu" 自序 [Autobiography]. 1907. Reprint. *WKTCC*, 5:1822–1827.

"Tzu-hsu erh" 自序二 [A Second Autobiography]. 1907. Reprint. *WKTCC*, 5: 1827–1830.

Draft preface to *Ch'ü lu* 曲錄 [Catalogue of Plays]. 1908. Reprint. *WKTCC*, 4: 1426–1428.

"Ch'ang-tuan chü" 長短句 [Long-and-Short Lines]. Composed during the period 1905–1909. Published (some lyrics possibly republished) in 1923. Punctuated reprint. *CASTK*, pp. 47–52. Also in *WKTCC*, 3:1200–1206.

Jen-chien tz'u-hua 人間詞話 [Remarks on Lyrics in the World of Men]. *Kuo-ts'ui hsueh-pao* 國粹學報 [National Essence Journal], nos. 47, 49, 50 (1908–09), various pagination.

Preface to *Ch'ü lu*. 1909. Reprint. *WKTCC*, 14:6197–6199.

"Lu-ch'ü yü-t'an" 錄曲餘談 [Miscellaneous Observations on Drama]. 1910. Punctuated reprint. *Wang Kuo-wei hsi-ch'ü lun-wen chi* (see under "Wang Kuo-wei," 1957), pp. 267–282. Also in *WKTCC*, 15:6717–6736.

"Sui t'ung-hu-fu pa" 隋銅虎符跋 [A Note on Metal Tiger Tallies of the Sui Period]. Originally published, along with other material, under the title " 'Sui T'ang ping-fu t'u-lu' fu-shuo" 隋唐兵符圖錄附說 [A Note on "Reproductions of Military Tallies of the Sui and T'ang Periods"]. 1911. Reprint of the revised version of 1917. *WKTCC*, 3:892–894.

"Wei-Chou erh kuei-fu pa" 偽周二龜符跋 [A Note on Two Tortoise Tallies of the Wei-Chou Period]. Originally published, along with other material, under the title " 'Sui T'ang ping-fu t'u-lu' fu-shuo." 1911. Reprint of the revised version of 1917. *WKTCC*, 3:894–895.

"Chien-tu chien-shu k'ao" 簡牘檢署考 [On Bamboo and Wooden Documents and the Methods of Packaging and Addressing Them]. 1912. Reprint of the revised version of 1914. *WKTCC*, 6:2319–2361.

"I-ho yuan tz'u" 頤和園詞 [I-ho Park]. 1912. Reprint of the draft version. *Ch'ing-ch'ao yeh-shih ta-kuan* 清朝野史大觀 [A Comprehensive Unofficial History of the Ch'ing Dynasty], 3rd edition, 12 vols. Shanghai: Chung-hua shu-chü 中華書局, 1917. Vol. 2, pp. 85–87.

"I-ho yuan tz'u." 1912. Punctuated reprint of the revised version. *CASTK*, pp. 16–18. Also in *WKTCC*, 3:1169–1172.

"Sung Jih-pen Shou-yeh po-shih yu Ou-chou" 送日本狩野博士游歐洲 [Seeing the Japanese Dr. Kano Off on a Trip to Europe]. 1912. Punctuated reprint. *CASTK*, pp. 18–19. Also in *WKTCC*, 3:1173–1174.

Sung Yuan hsi-ch'ü k'ao (SYHCK) 宋元戲曲考 [On Sung and Yuan Drama]. Originally titled, and still sometimes called, *Sung Yuan hsi-ch'ü shih* 宋元戲曲史 [The History of Sung and Yuan Drama]. 1913–14. Punctuated reprint. *Wang Kuo-wei hsi-ch'ü lun-wen chi* (see under "Wang Kuo-wei," 1957), pp. 1–148. Also in *WKTCC*, 14:5975–6187.

Foreword to *Yin-hsu shu-ch'i k'ao-shih* (see under "Lo Chen-yü," 1915). Foreword dated winter of 1914–15. Reprint. *WKTCC*, 3:1130–1132.

Postface to *Yin-hsu shu-ch'i k'ao-shih* (see under "Lo Chen-yü," 1915). Postface dated winter of 1914–15. Reprint. *WKTCC*, 3:1132–1135.

"Shuo Yin" 說殷 [On Yin]. Originally published, along with other material, under the title "San-tai ti-li hsiao-chi" 三代地理小記 [A Brief Account of the Geography (of China) during the Three Dynasties Period]. 1915. Reprint. *WKTCC*, 2:505–507.

" 'Chou shu' 'Ku ming' k'ao" 周書顧命考 [On the "Ku ming" Chapter of the "Chou shu" Section (of the *Book of Documents*)]. Originally titled " 'Chou shu' 'Ku ming' li-cheng" 周書顧命禮徵 [A Critical Examination of the Rituals Described in the "Ku ming" Chapter of the "Chou shu" Section (of the *Book of Documents*)]. 1916. Reprint. *WKTCC*, 1:32–40.

" 'Chou shu' 'Ku ming' hou-k'ao" 周書顧命後考 [Further Information on the "Ku ming" Chapter of the "Chou shu" Section (of the *Book of Documents*)]. 1916. Reprint. *WKTCC*, 1:40–49.

"Mao Kung Ting ming k'ao-shih" 毛公鼎銘考釋 [A Critical Study of the Inscription on the Mao Kung Ting]. 1916. Reprint. *WKTCC*, 6:1989–2022.

"Shuo 'Shang sung' hsia" 說商頌下 [On the "Shang sung" Section (of the *Book of Poetry*), Part Two]. Originally published, along with other material, under the title "Yueh-shih k'ao-lueh" 樂詩考略 [A Brief Study of Musical Poetry]. 1916. Reprint of the revised version of 1923. *WKTCC*, 1:97–100.

Chien-shou t'ang so-ts'ang Yin-hsu wen-tzu k'ao-shih 戩壽堂所藏殷虛文字考釋 [A Critical Study of the Chien-shou Building's Inscriptions from the Ruins of Yin]. Published together with *Chien-shou t'ang so-ts'ang Yin-hsu wen-tzu*, allegedly compiled by Chi Chueh-mi 姬覺彌 [Chi Fo-t'o 姬佛陀] but actually compiled by Wang Kuo-wei (see the latter's letter to Lo Chen-yü dated 30 June and 2 July 1917; letter published in the source listed under "Wang Kuo-wei," 1984, pp. 194–195). 2 vols. Vol. 2. Shanghai: Ts'ang-sheng ming-chih ta-hsueh 倉聖明智大學, foreword dated 1917.

Chin-pen "Chu-shu chi-nien" shu-cheng 今本竹書紀年疏證 [A Commentary on, and Critical Examination of, the Modern Text of the *Bamboo Book Annals*]. 1917. Reprint. *WKTCC*, 13:5559–5678.

Ku-pen "Chu-shu chi-nien" chi-chiao 古本竹書紀年輯校 [Edited Quotations from the Ancient Text of the *Bamboo Book Annals*]. 1917. Reprint. *WKTCC*, 13:5513–5558.

"Pu chia-p'u Chung-chuang kung chuan" 補家譜忠壯公傳 [A Supplement to the Family Genealogy's Biography of Wang Ping]. Originally titled "*Sung shih* 'Chung-i chuan' Wang Ping pu-chuan" 宋史忠義傳王稟補傳 [A Supplement to the "Biographies of the Loyal" Section of the *History of the Sung Dynasty:* The Biography of Wang Ping]. 1917. Reprint of the revised version of 1923. *WKTCC*, 3: 1097–1121.

"Yin Chou chih-tu lun" 殷周制度論 [On Yin and Chou Institutions]. 1917. Reprint. *WKTCC*, 2:433–462.

"Yin pu-tz'u chung so-chien hsien-kung hsien-wang k'ao" 殷卜辭中所見先公先王考 [Former Lords and Former Kings of the Yin (Whose Names) Appear in Divinatory Inscriptions]. 1917. Reprint of the revised version of 1923. *WKTCC*, 2:391–419.

"Yin pu-tz'u chung so-chien hsien-kung hsien-wang hsu-k'ao" 殷卜辭中所見先公先王續考 [Further Information on Former Lords and Former Kings of the Yin (Whose Names) Appear in Divinatory Inscriptions]. 1917. Reprint. *WKTCC*, 2: 419–432.

Foreword to *Hsueh-t'ang chiao-k'an ch'ün-shu hsu-lu* 雪堂校刊羣書敍錄 [A Descriptive Catalogue of Works Edited and Printed by Lo Chen-yü], by Lo Chen-yü 羅振玉. Foreword dated 1918. Reprint. *WKTCC*, 3:1135–1137.

"K'u-shu lou chi" 庫書樓記 [An Account of K'u-shu Library]. 1922. Reprint. *WKTCC*, 3:1164–1168.

"Lo Chün-ch'u ch'i Wang ju-jen mu-chieh-ming" 羅君楚妻汪孺人墓碣銘 [Epitaph for Lo Fu-ch'ang's Late Wife, Née Wang]. 1922. Reprint. *WKTCC*, 3:1125–1126.

"Lo Chün-ch'u chuan" 羅君楚傳 [A Biography of Lo Fu-ch'ang]. 1922. Reprint. *WKTCC*, 3:1121–1125.

" 'Kao Tsung yung jih' shuo" 高宗肜日説 [On the "Kao Tsung yung jih" Chapter (of the *Book of Documents*)]. 1925. Reprint. *WKTCC*, 1:9–13.

"Tsui-chin erh-san-shih nien chung Chung-kuo hsin fa-chien chih hsueh-wen" 最近二三十年中中國新發見之學問 [Scholarship on the New Discoveries of the Last Twenty or Thirty Years]. 1925. Reprint. *WKTCC*, 5:1915–1924.

"Shou hsu" 壽序 [Felicitating (Mr. Chiang Ju-tsao on the Occasion of his Fiftieth *Sui* Birthday)]. 1926. Quoted in *NP*, pp. 319–320.

Ku-shih hsin-cheng 古史新證 [New Evidence concerning Ancient History]. 1927. Reprint. *WKTCC*, 6:2077–2111.

Hai-ning Wang Chung-ch'üeh kung i-shu 海寧王忠慤公遺書 [The Collected Works of Wang Chung-ch'üeh kung of Hai-ning]. Compiled and edited by Lo Chen-yü. 42 vols. N.p., 1927–28.

"*Jen-chien tz'u-hua* wei-k'an kao chi ch'i-t'a" 人間詞話未刊稿及其他 [(Remarks on Lyrics Excerpted from) the Unpublished Draft of *Remarks on Lyrics in the World of Men* and Other (Remarks on Literature)]. Edited by Chao Wan-li 趙萬里.

Hsiao-shuo yueh-pao 小説月報 [Fiction Monthly] 19, no. 3 (March 1928):375–381.

Hai-ning Wang Ching-an hsien-sheng i-shu 海寧王靜安先生遺書 [The Collected Works of Mr. Wang Ching-an of Hai-ning]. Edited by Wang Kuo-hua 王國華 and Chao Wan-li. 48 vols. Shanghai: Shang-wu yin-shu kuan 商務印書館, 1940.

Wang Kuan-t'ang wen-hsuan 王觀堂文選 [Selected Writings of Wang Kuan-t'ang]. Edited by Tanaka Keitarō 田中慶太郎. Tokyo: Bunkyūdo shoten 文求堂書店, 1941.

Wang Kuo-wei hsi-ch'ü lun-wen chi 王國維戲曲論文集 [An Anthology of Wang Kuo-wei's Writings on Drama]. Peking: Chung-kuo hsi-chü ch'u-pan she 中國戲劇出版社, 1957.

Jen-chien tz'u-hua (*JCTH*). Enlarged edition. In *Hui-feng tz'u-hua; Jen-chien tz'u-hua* 蕙風詞話, 人間詞話 [K'uang Chou-i's Remarks on Lyrics; Remarks on Lyrics in the World of Men]. Edited by Wang Yu-an 王幼安 and annotated by Hsu T'iao-fu 徐調孚. 1960. Reprint. Hong Kong: Shang-wu yin-shu kuan 商務印書館, 1961.

Wang Kuan-t'ang hsien-sheng ch'üan-chi (*WKTCC*) 王觀堂先生全集 [The Complete Works of Mr. Wang Kuan-t'ang]. 16 vols. Taipei: Wen-hua ch'u-pan kung-ssu 文華出版公司, 1968.

Poetic Remarks in the Human World: Jen Chien Tz'u Hua. Translated and annotated by Tu Ching-i. Taipei: Chung-hua shu-chü 中華書局, 1970.

Ching-an shih-tz'u kao (*CASTK*) 靜庵詩詞彙 [Ching-an's Poetry]. Taipei: I-wen yin-shu kuan 藝文印書館, 1974.

Wang Kuo-wei hsien-sheng ch'üan-chi 王國維先生全集 [The Complete Works of Mr. Wang Kuo-wei]. 25 vols. Taipei: Ta-t'ung shu-chü 大通書局, 1976.

"Kuan-t'ang shu-cha: yü Lo Chen-yü hsien-sheng lun-hsueh shou-cha" 觀堂書札 (與羅振玉先生論學手札) [Kuan-t'ang's Correspondence: Letters to Mr. Lo Chen-yü concerning Scholarly Matters]. *Chung-kuo li-shih wen-hsien yen-chiu chi-k'an* 中國歷史文獻研究集刊 [Research on Chinese Historical Documents] 1 (1980):10–45.

"Jen-chien tz'u-hua" hsin-chu 人間詞話新注 [Remarks on Lyrics in the World of Men, Newly Annotated]. Edited and annotated by T'eng Hsien-hui 滕咸惠. Ch'i-lu shu-she 齊魯書社, 1981.

"Kuan-t'ang shu-cha: yü Ma Heng hsien-sheng lun-hsueh shou-cha" 觀堂書札 (與馬衡先生論學手札) [Kuan-t'ang's Correspondence: Letters to Mr. Ma Heng concerning Scholarly Matters]. *Chung-kuo li-shih wen-hsien yen-chiu chi-k'an* 2 (1981): 1–10.

Wang Kuo-wei ch'üan-chi: shu-hsin 王國維全集(書信) [The Complete Works of Wang Kuo-wei: Correspondence]. Edited by Wu Tse 吳澤. Peking: Chung-hua shu-chü, 1984.

Works by Others

Ai-hsin-chueh-lo P'u-i 愛新覺羅溥儀. *P'u-i tzu-chuan* 溥儀自傳 [(Aisin Gioro) P'u-i's Autobiography]. Taipei: Ch'ang-ko ch'u-pan she 長哥出版社, 1975.

Aoki Masaru 青木正兒. "Ō Seian sensei no bempatsu" 王靜庵先生の辮髪 [Mr. Wang Ching-an's Queue]. *Geibun* 藝文 [Literature] 18, no. 8 (August 1927):59–62.

——— Preface to *Shina kinsei gikyoku shi* 支那近世戲曲史 [A History of Modern

Chinese Drama]. 1930. Reprint. Tokyo: Kōbundo 弘文堂, 1955.

Brunnert, H. S., and Hagelstrom, V. V. *Present Day Political Organization of China*. Translated by A. Beltchenko and E. E. Moran. Shanghai: Kelly & Walsh, 1912.

Cameron, Meribeth E. *The Reform Movement in China, 1898–1912*. 1931. Reprint. New York: Octagon Books, 1963.

Chang Chih-tung 張之洞. *Ch'üan-hsueh p'ien* 勸學篇 [Exhortation to Learn]. 1898. Reprint. Chin-tai Chung-kuo shih-liao ts'ung-k'an 近代中國史料叢刊 [Historical Materials on Modern China Series], edited by Shen Yun-lung 沈雲龍, 84. Taipei: Wen-hai ch'u-pan she 文海出版社, 1967.

Chang Erh-t'ien 張爾田. *Ch'ing lieh-ch'ao hou-fei chuan kao* 清列朝后妃傳稿 [Biographies of Empresses and Concubines of the Successive Reigns of the Ch'ing Dynasty]. 1929. Reprint. Chin-tai Chung-kuo shih-liao ts'ung-k'an, edited by Shen Yun-lung, 742. Taipei: Wen-hai ch'u-pan she, 1972.

Chang Kwang-chih. "*T'ien kan:* A Key to the History of the Shang." In *Ancient China: Studies in Early Civilization*, edited by David T. Roy and Tsien Tsuen-hsuin, pp. 13–42. Hong Kong: Chinese University Press, 1978.

——— *Shang Civilization*. New Haven: Yale University Press, 1980.

Chang Po-hsi 張百熙, Jung-ch'ing 榮慶, and Chang Chih-tung. *Tsou-ting hsueh-t'ang chang-ch'eng* 奏定學堂章程 [Regulations Governing Education, as Memorialized and Approved]. 5 vols. Hu-pei hsueh-wu ch'u 湖北學務處, 1904.

Chao Wan-li 趙萬里. "Wang Ching-an hsien-sheng chu-shu mu-lu" 王靜安先生著述目錄 [A Catalogue of Mr. Wang Ching-an's Works]. 1928. Reprint. *WKTCC*, 16:7169–7178.

——— "Wang Ching-an hsien-sheng nien-p'u" ("NP") 王靜安先生年譜 [A Chronological Biography of Mr. Wang Ching-an]. 1928. Reprint. *WKTCC*, 16: 7051–7104.

Chavannes, Edouard. "Les livres Chinois avant l'invention du papier." *Journal Asiatique*, series 10, vol. 5, no. 1 (January–February 1905):5–75.

——— "La divination par l'écaille de tortue dans la haute antiquité Chinoise (d'après un livre de M. Lo Tchen-yu)." *Journal Asiatique*, series 10, vol. 17, no. 1 (January–February 1911):127–137.

Ch'en Meng-chia 陳夢家. *Yin-hsu pu-tz'u tsung-shu* 殷墟卜辭綜述 [A Comprehensive Account of the Divinatory Inscriptions from the Ruins of Yin]. Peking: K'o-hsueh ch'u-pan she 科學出版社, 1956.

Ch'en Shou-ch'ien 陳守謙. "Chi Wang Chung-ch'ueh kung wen" 祭王忠慤公文 [Wang Chung-ch'ueh kung: A Memorial Essay]. 1927 (in *AWL*). Reprint. *WKTCC*, 16:7116–7119.

Ch'en Yin-k'o 陳寅恪. "Wang Kuan-t'ang hsien-sheng wan-tz'u (ping hsu)" 王觀堂先生挽詞(并序) [An Elegiac Poem, with a Prose Preface, on Mr. Wang Kuan-t'ang]. 1927. Reprint. *WKTCC*, 16:7120–7121.

——— Foreword to *Hai-ning Wang Ching-an hsien-sheng i-shu* (see under "Wang Kuo-wei," 1940). Foreword dated 1934. Reprint. *WKTCC*, 1:i–iii.

Chiang Chün-chang 蔣君章. "Ts'ang-sheng ming-chih ta-hsueh ti hui-i" 倉聖明智大學的回憶 [A Reminiscence of the College to Propagate the Sage Ts'ang Chieh's Wisdom]. *Chuan-chi wen-hsueh* 傳記文學 [Biographical Literature] 9, no. 6 (December 1966):12–16.

Chiang T'ien-shu 蔣天樞. *Ch'en Yin-k'o hsien-sheng pien-nien shih-chi* 陳寅恪先生編年

事輯 [Events in the Life of Mr. Ch'en Yin-k'o, Arranged Chronologically]. Shanghai: Shang-hai ku-chi ch'u-pan she 上海古籍出版社, 1981.

Ch'ien Chung-shu. "Tragedy in Old Chinese Drama." *T'ien Hsia Monthly* 1 (August 1935):37–46.

Chin-liang 金梁. "Wang Chung-ch'ueh kung hsun-chieh chi" 王忠慤公殉節記 [An Account of Wang Chung-ch'ueh kung's Martyrdom]. In *AWL*, pp. 1–2.

Chin Shunshin 陳舜臣. "Taoka Reiun to Kanō Jigorō" 田岡嶺雲と嘉納治五郎 [Taoka Reiun and Kanō Jigorō]. In *Kindai Nihon to Chūgoku* 近代日本と中国 [Japan and China in Recent Times], edited by Takeuchi Yoshimi 竹内好 and Hashikawa Bunzō 橋川文三, 2 vols. Vol. 1, pp. 187–200. Tokyo: Asahi shimbun-sha 朝日新聞社, 1974.

Chou Chün-shih 周君適. *Wei-Man kung-t'ing tsa-i* 偽滿宮廷雜憶 [Recollections regarding the Palace in Manchoukuo]. Ssu-chuan jen-min ch'u-pan she 四川人民出版社, 1980.

Chow Tse-tsung 周策縱. *Lun Wang Kuo-wei "Jen-chien tz'u"* 論王國維人間詞 [On Wang Kuo-wei's *Tz'u* Poetry]. Hong Kong: Wan-yu t'u-shu kung-ssu 萬有圖書公司, 1972.

Ch'u Wan-feng 儲皖峰. "Wang Ching-an hsien-sheng chu-shu piao" 王靜安先生著述表 [A Table of Mr. Wang Ching-an's Works]. 1927. Reprint. *WKTCC*, 16: 7179–7229.

Chung, Sue Fawn. "The Much Maligned Empress Dowager: A Revisionist Study of the Empress Dowager Tz'u-hsi in the Period 1898 to 1900." Ph.D. dissertation, University of California at Berkeley, 1975.

—— "The Much Maligned Empress Dowager: A Revisionist Study of the Empress Dowager Tz'u-hsi (1835–1908)." *Modern Asian Studies* 13, no. 2 (1979): 177–196.

Copleston, Frederick. *Arthur Schopenhauer, Philosopher of Pessimism*. The Bellarmine Series, 11. Andover, Hants: Chapel River Press, 1946.

Creel, Herrlee Glessner. *Studies in Early Chinese Culture, First Series*. 1937. Reprint. Philadelphia: Porcupine Press, 1978.

—— *The Origins of Statecraft in China*. Vol. 1, *The Western Chou Empire*. Chicago: University of Chicago Press, 1970.

Crump, James I. "Giants in the Earth: Yuan Drama as Seen by Ming Critics." *Tamkang Review* 5, no. 2 (October 1974):33–62.

Dubs, Homer H., trans. *The History of the Former Han Dynasty*. 3 vols. Baltimore: Waverly Press, 1938, 1944, 1955.

Elman, Benjamin A. "Wang Kuo-wei and Lu Hsun: The Early Years." *Monumenta Serica* 34 (1979–80):389–401.

Fan Ping-ch'ing 樊炳清 [Fan Chih-hou 樊志厚]. Foreword to *Jen-chien tz'u chia-kao* 人間詞甲稿 [Lyrics in the World of Men, Part One], by Wang Kuo-wei. 1906. Punctuated reprint. *CASTK*, pp. xvii–xviii. Also in *WKTCC*, 4:1505–1506, and in *JCTH*, pp. 255–256.

—— [Fan Chih-hou]. Foreword to *Jen-chien tz'u i-kao* 人間詞乙稿 [Lyrics in the World of Men, Part Two], by Wang Kuo-wei. 1907. Punctuated reprint. *CASTK*, pp. xviii–xix. Also in *WKTCC*, 4:1506–1509, and in *JCTH*, pp. 256–257.

—— "Wan lien" 挽聯 [An Elegiac Couplet]. In *AWL*, p. 26.

———— "Wang Chung-ch'ueh kung shih-lueh" 王忠愨公事略 [A Sketch of Wang Chung-ch'ueh kung]. In *AWL*, pp. 2–3.

Fu Ssu-nien 傅斯年. Foreword to *Yin-li p'u* 殷曆譜 [The Yin Calendar], by Tung Tso-pin 董作賓, 4 vols. Li-chuang, Szechwan: Kuo-li chung-yang yen-chiu yuan li-shih yü-yen yen-chiu so 國立中央研究院歷史語言研究所, 1945.

Furth, Charlotte, ed. *The Limits of Change: Essays on Conservative Alternatives in Republican China.* Cambridge, Mass.: Harvard University Press, 1976.

Galik, Marian von. "Nietzsche in China (1918–1925)." *Zeitschrift fur Kultur und Geschichte Ost-und Sudostasiens* 110 (1971):5–47.

Gardiner, Patrick. *Schopenhauer.* Harmondsworth, Middlesex, England: Penguin Books, 1963.

Han shu 漢書 [History of the Former Han Dynasty]. Chung-hua shu-chü edition. 12 vols. Peking, 1962.

Hashikawa Tokio 橋川時雄, ed. *Chūgoku bunkakai jimbutsu sōkan* 中國文化界人物總鑑 [Who's Who in the Chinese Cultural World]. Peking: Chung-hua fa-ling pien-yin kuan 中華法令編印舘, 1940.

Hawkes, David, trans. *Ch'u Tz'u: The Songs of the South, An Ancient Chinese Anthology.* Oxford: At the Clarendon Press, 1959.

Høffding, Harald. *Outlines of Psychology.* Translated from the German edition by Mary E. Loundes. London: Macmillan & Co., 1892.

———— *Hsin-li hsueh kai-lun* 心理學概論 [Outlines of Psychology]. Translated from the English edition by Wang Kuo-wei. 8th edition. Shanghai: Shang-wu yin-shu kuan, 1926.

Hopkins, Lionel C. "The Sovereigns of the Shang Dynasty, B.C. 1766–1154." *Journal of the Royal Asiatic Society*, January 1917, pp. 69–89.

———— "The Honan Relics: A New Investigator and Some Results." *Journal of the Royal Asiatic Society*, January 1921, pp. 29–45.

Hou Han shu 後漢書 [History of the Later Han Dynasty]. Chung-hua shu-chü edition. 12 vols. Peking, 1965.

Hsiao Ai 蕭艾. "Kuan-yü Wang Kuo-wei ti kung-kuo" 關於王國維的功過 [Wang Kuo-wei's Attainments and Deficiencies]. *Tu-shu* 讀書 [Study], 1981, no. 8:129–134.

Hsu Chung-shu 徐中舒. "Wang Ching-an hsien-sheng chuan" 王靜安先生傳 [A Biography of Mr. Wang Ching-an]. 1927. Reprint. *WKTCC*, 16:7042–7050.

Hu Shih 胡適. "Hu Shih chih Wang Kuo-wei shu-hsin shih-san feng" 胡適致王國維書信十三封 [Thirteen Letters from Hu Shih to Wang Kuo-wei]. *Wen-hsien* 文獻 [Documents], no. 15 (March 1983):3–10.

Huang Hsiao-k'o 黃孝可. "T'eng-t'ien po-shih hsiao-chuan" 藤田博士小傳 [A Short Biography of Dr. Fujita]. *Yen-ching hsueh-pao* 燕京學報 [Yenching Journal of Chinese Studies], no. 8 (December 1930):1653–1654.

Hummel, Arthur W., ed. *Eminent Chinese of the Ch'ing Period (1644–1912).* 2 vols. with successive pagination. Washington, D.C.: U.S. Government Printing Office, 1943–44.

Jevons, William Stanley. *Elementary Lessons in Logic: Deductive and Inductive.* London: Macmillan & Co., 1870.

———— *Logic.* New York: D. Appleton & Co., 1880.

Johnston, Reginald F. *Twilight in the Forbidden City.* 1934. Reprint. Wilmington,

Del.: Scholarly Resources, 1973.

Jung Keng 容庚. "Wang Kuo-wei hsien-sheng k'ao-ku-hsueh shang chih kung-hsien" 王國維先生考古學上之貢獻 [Mr. Wang Kuo-wei's Contributions to Archaeology]. 1927. Reprint. *WKTCC*, 16:7340–7356.

Kano Naoki 狩野直喜. "Ō Seian kun o omou" 王靜安君を憶ふ [Memorial Remarks concerning Mr. Wang Ching-an]. *Geibun* 18, no. 8 (August 1927):38–45.

Kant, Immanuel. *Critique of Judgment*. Translated by J. H. Bernard. 1892 (title then rendered as *Kritik of Judgement*). Reprint. New York: Macmillan, Hafner Press, 1951.

—— *Critique of Pure Reason*. Translated from the 2nd edition by Norman Kemp Smith. 1929. Reprint. New York: St. Martin's Press, 1965.

Karlgren, Bernhard. "Legends and Cults in Ancient China." *Bulletin of the Museum of Far Eastern Antiquities*, no. 18 (1946):199–365.

Keightley, David N. *Sources of Shang History: The Oracle-Bone Inscriptions of Bronze Age China*. Berkeley: University of California Press, 1978.

K'o Ch'ang-ssu 柯昌泗. "Tiao Shang-yü Lo hsien-sheng" 弔上虞羅先生 [Mourning Mr. Lo of Shang-yü]. Reprint. *LHTCC*, 5th series, 20:8599–8604.

Ku Chieh-kang 顧頡剛. "Tao Wang Ching-an hsien-sheng" 悼王靜安先生 [Memorial Remarks regarding Mr. Wang Ching-an]. 1927. Reprint. *WKTCC*, 16:7127–7135.

—— *The Autobiography of a Chinese Historian, Being the Preface to a Symposium on Ancient Chinese History (Ku shih pien)*. Translated and annotated by Arthur W. Hummel. Leyden: E. J. Brill, 1931.

—— "Ku Chieh-kang chih Wang Kuo-wei ti san-feng hsin" 顧頡剛致王國維的三封信 [Three Letters from Ku Chieh-kang to Wang Kuo-wei]. *Wen-hsien*, no. 15 (March 1983):11–13.

Kuo Mo-jo 郭沫若. "Lu Hsun yü Wang Kuo-wei" 魯迅與王國維 [Lu Hsun and Wang Kuo-wei]. 1946. Reprint. *Li-shih jen-wu* 歷史人物 [Historical Personalities], by Kuo Mo-jo, pp. 288–300. Shanghai: Hsin wen-i ch'u-pan she 新文藝出版社, 1956.

Kwong, Luke S. K. *A Mosaic of the Hundred Days: Personalities, Politics, and Ideas of 1898*. Cambridge, Mass.: Council on East Asian Studies, Harvard University, 1984.

Lao Kan 勞榦. *Chung-kuo ti she-hui yü wen-hsueh* 中國的社會與文學 [Chinese Society and Literature]. Taipei: Wen-hsing shu-tien 文星書店, 1964.

Legge, James, trans. *The Chinese Classics*. Hong Kong University Press edition. 5 vols. in 4. Hong Kong, 1960.

Li Chi. *Anyang*. Seattle: University of Washington Press, 1977.

Liang Ch'i-ch'ao 梁啓超. "Wang Ching-an hsien-sheng mu-ch'ien tao-tz'u" 王靜安先生墓前悼詞 [A Graveside Lament for Mr. Wang Ching-an]. 1927. Reprint. *WKTCC*, 16:7122–7124.

Liao K'o-yü 廖克玉, with the collaboration of Wang K'eng 王鏗. "Ha-t'ung fu-fu i-shih tien-ti" 哈同夫婦軼事點滴 [A Few Anecdotes concerning the Hardoons]. *She-hui k'o-hsueh chan-hsien* 社會科學戰綫 [Social Sciences Front] 2, no. 3 (1979): 161–162.

Liu, James J. Y. *The Art of Chinese Poetry*. Chicago: University of Chicago Press, 1962.

———*Major Lyricists of the Northern Sung,* A.D. *960–1126.* Princeton, N.J.: Princeton University Press, 1974.

——— *Chinese Theories of Literature.* Chicago: University of Chicago Press, 1975.

——— *Essentials of Chinese Literary Art.* The Duxbury Civilization in Asia Series. Belmont, Calif.: Wadsworth, Duxbury Press, 1979.

Liu Yü 劉雨. ''*Jen-chien tz'u* hsu tso-che k'ao'' 人間詞序作者考 [On the Authorship of the Forewords to *Lyrics in the World of Men*]. *Wen-hsueh p'ing-lun* (Peking) 文學評論 [Literary Criticism], 1982, no. 2:141.

Lo Chen-yü 羅振玉. ''Yin-Shang chen-pu wen-tzu k'ao'' 殷商貞卜文字考 [On Divinatory Inscriptions of the Yin-Shang Period]. 1910. Reprint. *LHTCC,* 3rd series, 1:323–388.

——— Preface to *Yin-hsu shu-ch'i ch'ien-pien* 殷虚書契前編 [Inscriptions from the Ruins of Yin, Part One]. 1913. Reprint. *LHTCC,* 7th series, 4:1289–1292.

——— *Yin-hsu shu-ch'i k'ao-shih* 殷虚書契考釋 [A Critical Study of Inscriptions from the Ruins of Yin]. 1915. Reprint. *Yin-hsu wen-tzu lei-pien* 殷虚文字類編 [A Classified List of Inscriptions from the Ruins of Yin], by Shang Ch'eng-tso 商承祚, with critical remarks by Lo Chen-yü and a foreword by Wang Kuo-wei, 8 vols. Vol. 7. N.p., 1923.

——— Foreword to *Kuan-t'ang chi-lin* 觀堂集林 [Works by Kuan-t'ang], by Wang Kuo-wei, 20 *chüan.* 1923. Reprint. *WKTCC,* 1:1–3.

——— ''Chi Wang Chung-ch'ueh kung wen'' 祭王忠愨公文 [Wang Chung-ch'ueh kung: A Memorial Essay]. 1927 (in *AWL*). Reprint. *WKTCC,* 16:7115–7116.

——— ''Hai-ning Wang Chung-ch'ueh kung chuan'' 海寧王忠愨公傳 [A Biography of Wang Chung-ch'ueh kung of Hai-ning]. 1927 (in *AWL*). Reprint. *WKTCC,* 16:7019–7022.

——— ''Wang Chung-ch'ueh kung pieh-chuan'' 王忠愨公別傳 [Another Biography of Wang Chung-ch'ueh kung]. In *Hai-ning Wang Chung-ch'ueh kung i-shu* (see under ''Wang Kuo-wei,'' 1927–28), 1:iiib–vb.

——— ''Jih-pen T'ai-pei ta-hsueh chiao-shou wen-hsueh po-shih T'eng-t'ien chün mu-piao'' 日本臺北大學教授文學博士藤田君墓表 [Tombstone for Mr. Fujita, Litt. D., Professor at Japan's Taihoku University]. 1929? Reprint. *LHTCC,* 1st series, 4:1539–1543.

——— *Chi-liao pien* (*CLP*) 集蓼編 [Amidst Bitter Experiences]. 1941. Reprint. *LHTCC,* 2nd series, 2:695–786.

——— *Lo Hsueh-t'ang hsien-sheng ch'üan-chi* (*LHTCC*) 羅雪堂先生全集 [The Complete Works of Mr. Lo Chen-yü]. 140 vols. in 7 series of 20 vols. each. Taipei: Wen-hua ch'u-pan kung-ssu, 1968–1970 (series 1–3). Taipei: Ta-t'ung shu-chü, 1972, 1973, 1976 (series 4–7).

Lo Chen-yü and Wang Kuo-wei. *Liu-sha chui-chien* 流沙墜簡 [Wooden Slips Buried in Drift-Sand]. 1914. Reprint. *LHTCC,* 2nd series, 7:2717–3012.

Lo Chi-tsu 羅繼祖 [Kan Ju 甘孺]. *Yung-feng hsiang jen hsing-nien lu* (*Lo Chen-yü nien-p'u*) 永豐鄉人行年錄(羅振玉年譜) [A Year-by-Year Account of the Life of the Man from Yung-feng hsiang (A Chronological Biography of Lo Chen-yü)]. Chiang-su jen-min ch'u-pan she 江蘇人民出版社, 1980.

——— ''Pa 'Kuan-t'ang shu-cha' '' 跋觀堂書札 [A Note concerning ''Kuan-t'ang's Correspondence'']. *Tu-shu,* 1982, no. 8:100–103.

——— ''Wang Kuo-wei hsien-sheng pi-hsia ti Ha-t'ung Ts'ang-sheng ming-chih ta-hsueh'' 王國維先生筆下的哈同倉聖明智大學 [Mr. Wang Kuo-wei's Written Descriptions of the Hardoons' College to Propagate the Sage Ts'ang Chieh's Wisdom]. *She-hui k'o-hsueh chan-hsien* 5, no. 2 (1982):168–170.

—— '' 'Kuan-t'ang shu-cha' tsai pa'' 觀堂書札再跋 [Another Note concerning ''Kuan-t'ang's Correspondence'']. *Shih-hsueh chi-k'an* 史學集刊 [Journal of History], 1983, no. 4:37–42.

—— ''*Wang Kuo-wei chi ch'i wen-hsueh p'i-p'ing* tu hou'' 王國維及其文學批評讀後 [My Views on (Yeh Chia-ying's Work Titled) *Wang Kuo-wei and His Literary Criticism*]. *Tou-sou* 抖擻 [Enlightenment] 54 (November 1983):45–50.

—— ''Wang Kuo-wei hsien-sheng ti cheng-chih ssu-hsiang'' 王國維先生的政治思想 [Mr. Wang Kuo-wei's Political Thought]. In *Wang Kuo-wei hsueh-shu yen-chiu lun-chi* 王國維學術研究論集 [Articles on Wang Kuo-wei's Scholarly Research], edited by Wu Tse, vol. 1, pp. 398–409. Shanghai: Hua-tung shih-fan ta-hsueh ch'u-pan she 華東師範大學出版社, 1983.

''Lo Chia-ling nü-shih chuan'' 羅迦陵女士傳 [A Biography of Lo Chia-ling]. *Hsin-min ts'ung-pao* 新民叢報 [New Citizen Journal], no. 25 (1903):165–167.

Loewe, Michael. ''Military Operations in the Han Period.'' *China Society Occasional Papers*, no. 12 (1961):1–26.

—— ''Some Notes on Han-time Documents from Tun-huang.'' *T'oung Pao* 50, nos. 1–3 (1963):150–189.

—— ''Some Military Despatches of the Han Period.'' *T'oung Pao* 51, nos. 4–5 (1964):335–354.

Ma Heng 馬衡 [Yin Nan 殷南]. ''Wo so-chih-tao ti Wang Ching-an hsien-sheng'' 我所知道的王靜安先生 [The Mr. Wang Ching-an Whom I Knew]. 1927. Reprint. *WKTCC*, 16:7165–7167.

''Ma Heng hsien-sheng chuan-lueh (1881–1955)'' 馬衡先生傳略 (1881–1955) [A Biographical Sketch of Mr. Ma Heng (1881–1955)]. *K'ao-ku hsueh-pao* 考古學報 [Journal of Archaeology] 10 (December 1955).

Miyazaki Ichisada. *China's Examination Hell: The Civil Service Examinations of Imperial China*. Translated by Conrad Schirokauer. New York: John Weatherhill, 1976.

Mo Jung-tsung 莫榮宗. ''Lo Hsueh-t'ang hsien-sheng chu-shu nien-piao'' 羅雪堂先生著述年表 [A Chronological List of Mr. Lo Chen-yü's Works]. 1962. Reprint. *LHTCC*, 2nd series, 20:8263–8284.

—— ''Lo Hsueh-t'ang hsien-sheng nien-p'u'' 羅雪堂先生年譜 [A Chronological Biography of Mr. Lo Chen-yü]. 1963. Reprint. *LHTCC*, 1st series, 20:8693–8757.

Naitō Torajirō 内藤虎次郎. ''Ōi'' 王亥 [Wang Hai]. 1916. Reprint. *Naitō Konan zenshū* 内藤湖南全集 [The Complete Works of Naitō Torajirō], by Naitō Torajirō, 14 vols. Vol. 7, pp. 469–480. Tokyo: Chikuma shobō 筑摩書房, 1970.

—— ''Zoku Ōi'' 續王亥 [Further Information on Wang Hai]. 1917, 1921. Reprint. *Naitō Konan zenshū*, by Naitō Torajirō, 14 vols. Vol. 7, pp. 481–499. Tokyo: Chikuma shobō, 1970.

Nietzsche, Friedrich. *Thus Spoke Zarathustra*. In *The Portable Nietzsche*, translated, edited, and annotated by Walter Kaufmann. 1954. Reprint. Harmondsworth, Middlesex, England: Penguin Books, 1976.

Paulsen, Friedrich. *Introduction to Philosophy*. Translated from the 3rd edition by Frank Thilly. New York: H. Holt & Co., 1895.

Pelliot, Paul. Review of *A Brief Manual of the Si-hia Characters with Tibetan Inscriptions*, by Nicolas Nevsky. *T'oung Pao* 24, nos. 2-3 (1926):399-403.

——— "Wang Kouo-wei." *T'oung Pao* 26, nos. 1-2 (1928):70-72.

——— "L'édition collective des oeuvres de Wang Kouo-wei." *T'oung Pao* 26, nos. 2-3 (1928):113-182.

Rickett, Adele Austin. "Wang Kuo-wei's *Jen-chien Tz'u-hua:* A Study in Chinese Literary Criticism." Ph.D. dissertation, University of Pennsylvania, 1967.

———, ed. *Chinese Approaches to Literature from Confucius to Liang Ch'i-ch'ao*. Princeton, N.J.: Princeton University Press, 1978.

Rudolph, Richard L. "Lo Chen-yü Visits the Waste of Yin." In *"Nothing Concealed": Essays in Honor of Liu Yü-yün*, edited by Frederic Wakeman, Jr., pp. 1-19. Taipei: Ch'eng-wen ch'u-pan she 成文出版社, 1970. Distributed by the Chinese Materials and Research Aids Service Center.

Schiller, Friedrich. *On the Aesthetic Education of Man in a Series of Letters*. Translated and edited by Elizabeth M. Wilkinson and L. A. Willoughby. Oxford: At the Clarendon Press, 1967.

Schneider, Laurence A. *Ku Chieh-kang and China's New History: Nationalism and the Quest for Alternative Traditions*. Berkeley: University of California Press, 1971.

Schopenhauer, Arthur. *The World as Will and Idea*. Translated from the 2nd edition, enlarged, by R. B. Haldane and J. Kemp. 3 vols. London: Routledge & Kegan Paul, 1883.

——— *The World as Will and Representation* (*TWWR*). Translated from the 2nd edition, enlarged, by E. F. J. Payne. 2 vols. Indian Hills, Colo.: Falcon's Wing Press, 1958.

Schwartz, Benjamin I. *In Search of Wealth and Power: Yen Fu and the West*. Cambridge, Mass.: Harvard University Press, Belknap Press, 1964.

"Shan-hai ching" chiao-chu 山海經校注 [The Annotated Classic of Mountains and Seas]. Edited and annotated by Yuan K'o 袁珂, with notes by Kuo P'u 郭璞 and others. Shanghai: Shang-hai ku-chi ch'u-pan she, 1980.

Shen Tseng-chih 沈曾植. "Lo Chün-ch'u mu-chieh" 羅君楚墓碣 [Epitaph for Lo Fu-ch'ang]. *Ya-chou hsueh-shu tsa-chih* 亞洲學術雜誌 [The Journal of the Asiatic Learning Society] 1, no. 3 (April 1922): various pagination.

Shih chi 史記 [Records of the Historian]. Chung-hua shu-chü edition. 10 vols. Peking, 1959.

Shih Chung-wen. *The Golden Age of Chinese Drama: Yuan "Tsa-chü."* Princeton, N.J.: Princeton University Press, 1976.

Shih Ta [pseud.] 史達. "Wang Ching-an hsien-sheng chih-ssu ti chen-yin" 王靜庵先生致死的真因 [The Real Cause of Mr. Wang Ching-an's Death]. *Wen-hsueh chou-pao* 文學週報 [Literature Weekly] 5, nos. 1-4 combined (August 1927):72-75.

Smith, Norman Kemp. *A Commentary to Kant's "Critique of Pure Reason."* 2nd edition, revised and enlarged. 1923. Reprint. Atlantic Highlands, N.J.: Humanities Press, 1962.

Smythe, E. Joan. "The Early Thought of Wang Kuo-wei: An Analysis of His Essays on German Voluntaristic Philosophy (1903-1907)." *Papers on China* 18 (December 1964):1-25.

Stein, M. Aurel. *Ancient Khotan: Detailed Report of Archaeological Explorations in Chinese*

Turkestan. 2 vols. Oxford: At the Clarendon Press, 1907.

—— *Ruins of Desert Cathay: Personal Narrative of Explorations in Central Asia and Westernmost China*. 2 vols. London: Macmillan & Co., 1912.

—— "Notes on Ancient Chinese Documents Discovered along the Han Frontier Wall in the Desert of Tun-huang." 1921–22. Reprint. N.p., 1940.

Sun Hsiung 孫雄. "Wan shih" 挽詩 [An Elegiac Poem]. In *AWL*, pp. 15–16b.

Tai Chia-hsiang 戴家祥 [Po Sheng 柏生]. "Chi Wang Ching-an hsien-sheng tzu-ch'en-shih shih-mo" 記王靜安先生自沈事始末 [A Complete Account of Mr. Wang Ching-an's Suicide]. 1927. Reprint. *WKTCC*, 16:7147–7151.

"Tang-nien Shang-hai hao-fu Ha-t'ung fu-fu ch'uan-ch'i" 當年上海豪富哈同夫婦傳奇 [The Legend of Old Shanghai's Wealthy Couple, the Hardoons]. *Ch'un-ch'iu* 春秋 [Spring and Autumn], no. 151 (n.d.):5–7; and *Ch'un-ch'iu*, no. 152 (n.d.):13–15.

Teng Chih-ch'eng 登之誠. "Chang chün Meng-ch'ü pieh-chuan" 張君孟劬別傳 [Another Biography of Mr. Chang Erh-t'ien]. *Yen-ching hsueh-pao*, no. 30 (June 1946):323–325.

Teng Ssu-yu and Fairbank, John K., eds. *China's Response to the West: A Documentary Survey, 1839–1923*. 1954. Reprint. New York: Atheneum, 1963.

Ting Wen-chiang 丁文江. *Liang Jen-kung hsien-sheng nien-p'u ch'ang-pien ch'u-kao* 梁任公先生年譜長編初稿 [A First Draft of a Chronological Biography of Mr. Liang Ch'i-ch'ao]. Taipei: Shih-chieh shu-chü 世界書局, 1959.

Tsien Tsuen-hsuin. *Written on Bamboo and Silk: The Beginnings of Chinese Books and Inscriptions*. Chicago: University of Chicago Press, 1962.

Tu Ching-i. "A Study of Wang Kuo-wei's Literary Criticism." Ph.D. dissertation, University of Washington, 1967.

—— "Conservatism in a Constructive Form: The Case of Wang Kuo-wei 王國維 (1877–1927)." *Monumenta Serica* 28 (1969):188–214.

—— "A Group of Wang Kuo-wei's Tz'u Poems with an Introduction." In *Transition and Permanence: Chinese History and Culture*, edited by David C. Buxbaum and Frederick W. Mote, pp. 379–393. Hong Kong: Cathay Press, 1972.

—— "Some Aspects of the *Jen-chien tz'u-hua*." *Journal of the American Oriental Society* 93, no. 3 (July–September 1973):306–316.

Tung Tso-pin 董作賓. *Chia-ku nien-piao* 甲骨年表 [Oracle Bones: A Chronological Table]. Shanghai: Shang-wu yin-shu kuan, 1937.

—— "Lo Hsueh-t'ang hsien-sheng chuan-lueh" 羅雪堂先生傳畧 [A Biographical Sketch of Mr. Lo Chen-yü]. 1962. Reprint. *LHTCC*, 1st series, 1:i–vi.

—— *Chia-ku-hsueh liu-shih nien* 甲骨學六十年 [Sixty Years of Oracle-Bone Studies]. Taipei: I-wen yin-shu kuan, 1965.

Wang, Chester Chen-I. "Wang Kuo-wei (1877–1927): His Life and His Scholarship." Ph.D. dissertation, University of Chicago, 1962.

Wang Ching-hsien. "Recognition and Anticipation in Wang Kuo-wei's 'Criticism of *Hung-lou meng*.'" *Tsing Hua Journal of Chinese Studies*, n.s. 10, no. 2 (July 1974):91–112.

—— [Yang Mu 楊牧]. "Tsai lun Wang Kuo-wei chih ssu" 再論王國維之死 [Wang Kuo-wei's Death: A Reconsideration]. *Lien-ho pao* 聯合報 [United News], 21–22 November 1982.

Wang Ch'ü-ch'ang 王蘧常. "Chia-hsing Shen Mei-sou hsien-sheng nien-p'u ch'u-kao'' 嘉興沈寐叟先生年譜初稿 [A First Draft of a Chronological Biography of Mr. Shen Tseng-chih of Chia-hsing]. *Tung-fang tsa-chih* 東方雜誌 [The Eastern Miscellany] 26, no. 15 (10 August 1929):59–71; and *Tung-fang tsa-chih* 26, no. 16 (25 August 1929):63–74.

Wang Kao-ming 王高明, Wang Chen-ming 王貞明, Wang Chi-ming 王紀明, Wang Tz'u-ming 王慈明, and Wang Teng-ming 王登明, eds. and comps. *Wang Chung-ch'ueh kung ai-wan lu (AWL)* 王忠慤公哀挽錄 [Wang Chung-ch'ueh kung: A Memorial Volume]. N.p., 1927.

Wang Sen-jan 王森然. *Chin-tai erh-shih chia p'ing-chuan* 近代二十家評傳 [Critical Biographies of Twenty Men of Modern Times]. Peking: Hsing-yen shu-she 杏巖書屋, 1934.

Wang Te-i 王德毅. *Wang Kuo-wei nien-p'u (NP)* 王國維年譜 [A Chronological Biography of Wang Kuo-wei]. Taipei: Chung-kuo hsueh-shu chu-tso chiang-chu wei-yuan hui 中國學術著作獎助委員會, 1967.

Wang Tung-ming 王東明. "Hsien-fu Wang kung Kuo-wei tzu-ch'en ch'ien-hou" 先父王公國維自沈前後 [Information Pertaining to the Suicide of My Late Father, Mr. Wang Kuo-wei]. *Chung-kuo shih-pao* 中國時報 [The China Times], 19 May 1984.

——— "Wei mu-ch'in shuo chi-chü hua" 為母親說幾句話 [A Few Words in Defense of My Mother]. *Chung-kuo shih-pao*, 23 October 1984.

Wang Yi-t'ung. "Biographic Sketches of Twenty-nine Classical Scholars of the Late Manchu and Early Republican Era." Prepared for the Research Project on Men and Politics in Modern China, Columbia University, and distributed by Wang Yi-t'ung, Department of East Asian Languages and Literatures, University of Pittsburgh, 1963.

Weng Tu-chien 翁擱健. "Po-hsi-ho chiao-shou" 伯希和教授 [Professor Pelliot]. *Yen-ching hsueh-pao*, no. 30 (June 1946):329–330.

Windelband, Wilhelm. *A History of Philosophy, with Especial Reference to the Formation and Development of Its Problems and Conceptions.* Translated by James H. Tufts. 1893. Reprint. New York: Macmillan Co., 1926.

Wu Ch'i-ch'ang 吳其昌. "Wang Kuan-t'ang hsien-sheng hsueh-shu" 王觀堂先生學術 [The Scholarship of Mr. Wang Kuan-t'ang]. 1928. Reprint. *WKTCC*, 16: 7265–7282.

Wu Mi 吳宓. "Wan lien" 挽聯 [An Elegiac Couplet]. In *AWL*, p. 26.

Wu P'i-chi 吳丕績. "Sun Ai-k'an nien-p'u ch'u-kao" 孫隘堪年譜初稿 [A First Draft of a Chronological Biography of Sun Te-ch'ien]. *Hsueh-hai* 學海 [Learning] 1, no. 1 (July 1944):86–94; *Hsueh-hai* 1, no. 6 (December 1944):92–96; and *Hsueh-hai* 2, no. 2 (February 1945):54–56.

Yang Ch'eng 楊誠 [Yang Chün-shih 楊君實]. "Wang Kuo-wei tzu-ch'en chih mi (chien lun li-shih jen-wu ti p'ing-chia)" 王國維自沈之謎(兼論歷史人物的評價) [The Mystery of Wang Kuo-wei's Suicide, with a Critical Evaluation of a Historical Figure]. *Ming-pao yueh-k'an* 明報月刊 [Ming Pao Monthly] 19, no. 5 (May 1984):69–76.

Yang Chung-hsi 楊鍾羲. Epitaph for Wang Kuo-wei. 1927. Private manuscript copy prepared from a manuscript copy in the possession of Chiang T'ien-shu; Chiang's copy prepared from a rubbing of the original that Ch'en Yin-k'o evidently made at the time of Wang's death.

Yao Ming-ta 姚名達. "Wang Ching-an hsien-sheng nien-piao" 王靜安先生年表 [A Chronological Table of Mr. Wang Ching-an's (Life, Works, and Times)]. 1927. Reprint. *WKTCC*, 16:7105–7114.

Yeh Chia-ying 葉嘉瑩. "Ts'ung hsing-ko yü shih-tai lun Wang Kuo-wei chih-hsueh t'u-ching chih chuan-pien" 從性格與時代論王國維治學途徑之轉變 [Wang Kuo-wei: His Character and His Scholarship]. *Hsiang-kang Chung-wen ta-hsueh hsueh-pao* 香港中文大學學報 [Journal of the Chinese University of Hong Kong] 1 (1973):61–96.

———— "I-ko hsin-chiu wen-hua chi-pien chung ti pei-chü jen-wu: Wang Kuo-wei ssu-yin chih t'an-t'ao" 一個新舊文化激變中的悲劇人物(王國維死因之探討) [The Tragedy of Wang Kuo-wei]. *Hsiang-kang Chung-wen ta-hsueh hsueh-pao* 3, no. 1 (1975):5–48.

———— "*Jen-chien tz'u-hua* chung p'i-p'ing chih li-lun yü shih-chien" 人間詞話中批評之理論與實踐 [The Theory and Practice of Criticism as Seen in *Remarks on Lyrics in the World of Men*]. *Wen-hsueh p'ing-lun* (Taipei) 文學評論 [Literary Criticism] 1 (May 1975):199–291.

———— "*Jen-chien tz'u-hua* ching-chieh shuo yü Chung-kuo ch'uan-t'ung shih-shuo chih kuan-hsi" 人間詞話境界說與中國傳統詩說之關係 [The Relationship between the Theory of Worlds as Seen in *Remarks on Lyrics in the World of Men* and Traditional Chinese Poetic Theories]. *Tou-sou* 14 (March 1976):1–18.

Yetts, W. Perceval. "The Shang-Yin Dynasty and the An-yang Finds." *Journal of the Royal Asiatic Society*, July 1933, pp. 657–685.

Glossary

Names of persons and books that do not appear below or in the Selected Bibliography may be found either in *Eminent Chinese of the Ch'ing Period (1644–1912)*, 2 vols., ed. Arthur W. Hummel (Washington, D.C.: U.S. Government Printing Office, 1943–44), or in *Biographical Dictionary of Republican China*, 4 vols., ed. Howard L. Boorman (New York: Columbia University Press, 1967–1971).

ai 愛
"Ai Ch'ing fu" 哀清賦
Ai-kuo hsueh-she 愛國學社
Butsuri gakkō 物理學校
cha-chi 札記
Chang An-shih 張安世
Chang Chün-heng 張鈞衡
chang-ts'ao 章草
Chang Yen (Yü-t'ien) 張炎（玉田）
ch'ang-jen chih ching-chieh 常人之境界
Chao shih ku-erh 趙氏孤兒
ch'ao-i ta-fu 朝議大夫
ch'ao-jen 超人
Che-chiang t'ung-chih 浙江通志
che-hsueh 哲學
"Che-ku t'ien" 鷓鴣天
chen-li 真理
Ch'en Ju-chen 陳汝禎
Ch'en Nai-ch'ien 陳乃乾
Ch'en Sheng 陳勝
Ch'en Shou-t'ien 陳壽田
ch'en-tzu (nonmetric words) 襯字
ch'en-tzu (your servant-son) 臣子
Cheng Kuang-tsu 鄭光祖
Cheng meng 正蒙
cheng-ming 証明
Cheng Ssu-hsiao 鄭思肖
ch'eng 誠
Ch'eng I-ch'ou 程易疇
Ch'eng Wei-yuan 程偉元
Chi Chün-hsiang 紀君祥
Ch'i-nien tien 祈年殿
Ch'i Tzu 杞子
chia-chang 甲帳

chia-ku-wen 甲骨文
Chia-kuan 甲觀
chia-ling p'in-chieh 迦陵頻伽
Chiang Ch'un-lin 蔣春霖
Chiang Fu 蔣黼
Chiang Ju-tsao 蔣汝藻
Chiang K'uei 姜夔
chiao-yü-hsueh 教育學
Chiao-yü shih-chieh tsa-chih 教育世界雜誌
Chieh Tzu-t'ui 介子推
chien 檢
chien-hsiu 漸修
chien-sheng 監生
chien-tu 監督
Ch'ien-nü li-hun 倩女離魂
Ch'ien-tzu wen 千字文
chih 志
Chih-hsin mien-ping fa 治心免病法
chih-kuan 直觀
chih po 治亳
chih-yeh ti hsueh-wen chia 職業的學問家
chih-yü 知育
ch'ih 尺
Ch'ih-chang Man-chih 赤章蔓枝
ch'ih-erh shu 尺二書
ch'ih-tzu chih hsin 赤子之心
Chin-ch'üan 金荃
chin-shih 進士
chin-wen 金文
Ch'in Kuan 秦觀
ching (quiescent) 靜
ching (worlds) 境
ching-chieh 境界
ching-she 靜攝

300

ch'ing ching 情景

Ch'ing-shih kuan 清史館

Ch'ing-shih shan-hou wei-yuan hui 清
    室善後委員會

Ch'ing-shu shan-kuan 清舒山館

"Ch'ing yü an" 青玉案

chiu-hsueh 舊學

ch'iu 求

Chou Chi 周濟

Chou Mi 周密

Chou Pang-yen 周邦彥

Chou Te-ch'ing 周德清

Chu Ch'üan 朱權

chu-ju 珠襦

Chu Tz'u 朱泚

Chu Yü-hsun 朱煜勳

chuan 傳

chuan-shu 篆書

ch'uan-ch'i 傳奇

ch'ui-lien t'ing-cheng 垂簾聽政

ch'un ch'en 純臣

"Ch'un-ch'iu" Tung shih hsueh 春秋董氏
    學

ch'un-ts'ui che-hsueh 純粹哲學

ch'un-ts'ui k'o-hsueh 純粹科學

chung 忠

chung ch'ueh 忠愨

Chung-kuo chiao-yü hui 中國教育會

Chung-yung 中庸

chü-jen 舉人

chü-shih 居士

ch'ü 曲

"Ch'ü-tiao yuan-liu piao" 曲調源流表

chüan-yen 倦厭

ch'üan-hsueh so 勸學所

ch'üan-hsueh yuan 勸學員

chueh-chü 絕句

"Ch'ueh-ch'iao hsien" 鵲橋仙

chün 郡

en-k'o 恩科

erh-ch'ih shu 二尺書

Fang-shu 方叔

fei chih-yeh ti hsueh-wen chia 非職業
    的學問家

feng-ai 風埃

Feng Yen-ssu 馮延巳

Fo-hsiang ko 佛香閣

fu-cheng 輔政

fu ch'iang 富強

Fujita Toyohachi (Kempō) 藤田豐八
    (劍峯)

"Genkyoku kenkyū" 元曲研究

Ha-t'ung hua-yuan 哈同花園

Hai-shang san-tzu 海上三子

hai-t'ang 海塘

han-i nung-sun 含飴弄孫

Han kung ch'iu 漢宮秋

Hayashi Taisuke 林泰輔

hou 侯

hou-en 厚恩

"Hou fei chuan" 后妃傳

hou-kung 後宮

hsi 樨

hsi-ch'ü 戲曲

"Hsi-ch'ü k'ao-yuan" 戲曲考源

Hsi Shih 西施

Hsi Shu meng 西蜀夢

hsi-wen 戲文

Hsi-yu chi 西遊記

Hsiang Hung-tso 項鴻祚

hsiang-piao 降表

hsiang-shih 鄉試

Hsiang Yü 項羽

hsiao-hsueh 小學

hsiao tzu 孝子

hsieh 偕

Hsieh Tsan 薛瓚

hsien-kung 先公

hsin-ch'ao 新朝

Hsin Ch'i-chi 辛棄疾

hsin-hai 辛亥

hsin-hsueh 新學

hsin ju-chia 新儒家

hsin ku 信古

hsing 性

hsing-ch'ü 興趣

hsing-hsia 形下

hsiu-yang 修養

hsu 虛

Hsu T'ung-lin 許同藺

hsuan-huo 眩惑

hsueh (knife) 削

hsueh (learning, scholarship) 學

Hsueh-nung she 學農社

Hsueh pu 學部

Hsueh-shu ts'ung-pien 學術叢編

Hsueh-t'ang ts'ung-k'o 雪堂叢刻

hsun-ku 訓詁

Hua-chien chi 花間集

"Huan hsi sha" 浣谿沙

Huan-hua 浣花

Huang-chi ching-shih 皇極經世

Huang-fu Mi 皇甫謐

huang-shang 皇上

Huang Tsung-yang 黃宗仰

hui-shih 會試

hung-chuang 宏壯

hung-hsueh chia 紅學家

i (ideas) 意

i (righteousness) 義

i (technical learning) 藝

i-ch'en 遺臣

i-cheng wang 議正王

i-chih 意志

I-ching 易經

i ku 疑古

i-ku chih kuo 疑古之過

i-ku p'ai 疑古派

i-kuan 一棺

i-shu 藝術

I-shu ts'ung-pien 藝術叢編

i-t'ai 以太

jen 仁

jen-chien 人間

jen-li 人力

ju-tzu 孺子

kai-nien 概念

kan-ching 乾淨

Kao Ming 高明

kao-tsu 高祖

k'ao-cheng 考證

ko 隔

ko-tao 閣道

K'o Ch'ang-chi 柯昌濟

k'o-shih 科試

ku 觚

ku-ch'i-wu hsueh 古器物學

"Ku-chü chiao-se k'ao" 古劇脚色考

ku-ming chih ch'en 顧命之臣

ku-ya 古雅

Ku Yung 谷永

ku-yü 古語

Kuan Han-ch'ing 關漢卿

Kuan-t'ang ping-wu i-ch'ien shih 觀堂丙午以前詩

kung-chü 貢舉

kung-kung chih kan-kuan 公共之感官

K'ung-chiao hui 孔教會

k'ung-hsu ti k'u-t'ung 空虛的苦痛

k'ung-t'an 空談

Kuo Hsien 郭憲

kuo-hsueh 國學

Kuo-hsueh chi-k'an 國學季刊

Kuo-hsueh pao-ts'un hui 國學保存會

Kuo-hsueh yen-chiu yuan 國學研究院

Kuo-ku lun-heng 國故論衡

Lao Tzu 老子

li (pragmatic) 利

li (principle) 理

Li chi 禮記

Li Chih-ch'ang 李志常

li-hsing 理性

Li Huai-kuang 李懷光

li-jen 厲人

li-k'o 理科

Li Sheng (Hsi-p'ing wang) 李晟 (西平王)

li-shu 隸書

Li Yü (Li Hou-chu) 李煜 (李後主)

Liang Chi 梁濟

liang-kung 兩宮

Liao-yuan shih-ch'ao 蓼園詩鈔

lien-ch'ien 連錢

Liu Ta-shen 劉大紳

Liu T'ing-ch'en 劉廷琛

Liu Ts'ang (Tung-p'ing wang) 劉蒼 (東平王)

Liu Tse 劉澤

Lo Chen-ch'ang 羅振常

Lo Fu-ch'ang 羅福萇

Lo Fu-ch'eng 羅福成

Lo Fu-i 羅福頤

Lo Hsiao-ch'un 羅孝純

lou-ch'uan 樓船

Lu Chi 陸機

Lu Chuan-lin 鹿傳霖

Ma Chih-yuan 馬致遠

Mao-ch'in tien hsing-tsou 懋勤殿行走

mei-yü 美育
mi-t'ien 彌天
Mi-yun lou 密韻樓
Miao Chia-hui 繆嘉蕙
Ming-hsueh 名學
ming-t'ang 明堂
Mo Tzu 墨子
Mo Yin-sheng 莫寅生
mu-chien 木簡
mu-yu 幕友
nan-hsi 南戲
Nan shu-fang hsing-tsou 南書房行走
nang 囊
nien-p'u 年譜
Nung-hsueh pao 農學報
Ōtani Kōzui 大谷光瑞
pa-ku wen-chang 八股文章
Pai-yueh t'ing 拜月亭
p'ai-yun ch'i 排雲起
P'ai-yun tien 排雲殿
Pan Ku 班固
P'an Shou-ch'ang 潘綏昌
P'an Tsu-i 潘祖彝
pao-chiao 保教
pao-kuo 保國
pei-chu 北渚
pei-men 北門
pen-ch'ao 本朝
pen-se 本色
Pien-hsueh 辯學
Pien-i t'u-shu chü 編譯圖書局
Pien-ting ming-tz'u kuan 編訂名詞館
p'ien-wen 駢文
Po Ch'in 伯禽
Po-i 伯夷
pu cheng 補正
pu-chih 不智
pu-jen 不仁
pu-ko 不隔
p'u-chi chiao-yü 普及教育
san-ch'ü 散曲
san-kang 三綱
san-wen 散文
Shang shu 尚書
"*Shang shu*" *K'ung chu* 尚書孔注
Shao Hu (Hu of Shao) 召虎
she-cheng 攝政

she-cheng wang 攝政王
shen 神
Shen Chien-shih 沈兼士
Shen Hung 沈紘
Shen Kuan-ying 沈冠英
Shen Te-fu 沈德符
shen yun 神韻
sheng-chuan chih hsin 乘傳之信
sheng-huo chih yü 生活之欲
sheng-yü chih shih-li 餘之勢力
sheng-yuan 生員
Sheng-yun 升允
shih 詩
shih chai 始宅
shih-chien 實踐
shih-hao 嗜好
Shih-hsu 世續
shih-hua 詩話
Shih Hui 施惠
shih-jen chih ching-chieh 詩人之境界
shih-li chih yü 勢力之欲
shih-nien 實念
Shih pen 世本
shih-san ling 十三陵
Shih-shuo hsin-yü 世説新語
shih-ti huang-sun 世嫡皇孫
"*Shih*" *ti-li k'ao* 詩地理考
shou-kao 手槁
Shu-ch'i 叔齊
Shu Hsi 束晳
"Shu Tai chiao '*Shui-ching*' chu hou" 書戴校水經注後
shu-tao 書刀
"Shu tao nan" 蜀道難
shuang-sheng 雙聲
ssu ts'ai-tzu 四才子
su 俗
su-yü 俗語
Sun Te-ch'ien 孫德謙
Sung shih 宋史
"Sung ta-ch'ü k'ao" ("T'ang Sung ta-ch'ü k'ao") 宋大曲考(唐宋大曲考)
ta-i 大邑
Ta-kuan yuan 大觀園
ta-kuei 大歸
ta tao 大道
Ta-yun shu-k'u 大雲書庫

Tachibana Zuichō 橘瑞超
tai-tzu 代字
t'ai-chi 太極
T'ai-chi t'u shuo 太極圖説
t'ai-hsu 太虛
T'ai-hsuan ching 太玄經
tang-hang chia 當行家
tang-p'ai chih jen 黨派之人
tao (knife) 刀
tao (Way) 道
tao-chih tsao 倒枝藻
tao-t'ung 道統
Taoka Sayoji (Reiun) 田岡佐代治（嶺雲）
te-yü 德育
ti (emperor) 帝
ti (a kind of sacrifice) 禘
ti-tzu 帝子
Ti-wang shih-chi 帝王世紀
t'i 體
T'i sha ch'i 替殺妻
t'i-yung 體用
"Tieh lien hua" 蝶戀花
tieh-yun 疊韻
tien-shih 殿試
tien-tao chu-i 顛倒主義
t'ien-kan 天干
t'ien-shou 田狩
t'ien-tao 天道
t'ien-ts'ai 天才
t'ien-yen 天眼
T'ien-yen lun 天眼論
Tomioka Kenzo 富岡謙藏
Tou O yuan 竇娥冤
tsa-chü 雜劇
ts'ai-jen tzu 才人子
Ts'ai Lun 蔡倫
"Ts'ai-sang tzu" 採桑子
tsan-hsiang 贊襄
ts'an-shih 參事
Tsang Mao-hsun 臧懋循
Ts'ang Chieh 倉頡
Ts'ang-sheng ming-chih ta-hsueh 倉聖明智大學
Ts'ao Chih 曹植
Ts'ao Piao 曹彪
Ts'ao Yun-hsiang 曹雲祥
tse 則

tsuan-hsiu 纂修
tsung-li 總理
Tsung-she tang 宗社黨
tsung-tung 總董
Tsung-wu ssu 總務司
tu 牘
tuan-ku ch'e 短轂車
Tun-huang shih-shih i-shu 敦煌石室遺書
tun-wu 頓悟
Tung Cho 董卓
Tung-ming chi 洞冥記
Tung Shih 東施
Tung-wen hsueh-she 東文學社
t'ung-hsin tao-shih 通信導師
t'ung-hsing chih hsin 通行之信
t'ung-shih 童試
t'ung-tao t'ang 同道堂
tzu-ch'iang 自強
tzu-jan 自然
Tzu-kung 子貢
tzu-yü 自娛
tz'u 詞
Tz'u-hsi tuan-yu k'ang-i chao-yü chuang-ch'eng shou-kung ch'in-hsien ch'ung-hsi 慈禧端佑康頤昭豫莊誠壽恭欽獻崇熙
tz'u-hua 詞話
wan-ch'üan chih jen-wu 完全之人物
Wang Chi-te 王驥德
Wang Ch'ien 王謙
Wang Ch'ien-ming 王潛明
Wang Hang 王沆
Wang Hsun 王荀
Wang Hui 王輝
Wang Kuang-tsu 王光祖
Wang Kuei (T'ieh-pien) 王珪（鐵鞭）
Wang Kuo-wei 王國維 (Ching-an 靜安, 靜庵; Po-yü 伯隅; Li-t'ang 禮堂; Kuan-t'ang 觀堂; Yung-kuan 永觀; Chung-ch'ueh kung 忠愨公）
Wang Ming-chu 王明珠
Wang Nai-yü 王乃譽
Wang Pao-hsin 王葆心
Wang Ping 王稟
Wang Shih-chen 王士禛
Wang Shih-fu 王實甫
Wang Shu 王恕

Wang Ssu-tuo 王嗣鐸
Wang Sung-ming 王松明
Wang Tuan-ming 王端明
Wang T'ung-ming 王通明
Wang Yun-yü 王藴玉
wei-chieh 慰藉
Wei Chuang 韋莊
Wei-t'u ti-chi 魏土地記
Wen-feng 文豐
wen-hua shih-yeh 文化事業
Wen T'ing-yun 溫庭筠
wu-chang 武帳
wu-chang ch'i 五丈旗
wu chih tzu-shen 物之自身
Wu Kuang 吳廣
''Wu-shih chih nien, chih ch'ien i-ssu; ching tz'u shih-pien, i wu tsai-ju'' 五十之年，只欠一死；經此世變，義無再辱
Wu Wen-ying (Meng-ch'uang) 吳文英(夢窗)
wu-wo chih ching 無我之境
wu-yung (uncourageous) 無勇
wu-yung (useless) 無用

ya 雅
Yang Liang 楊倞
Yen Chi-tao 晏幾道
Yen-chiu so kuo-hsueh men 研究所國學門
yen-chüan 厭倦
yen-en 延恩
Yen Shu 晏殊
yen-su lun 嚴肅論
Yin-hsu ku-ch'i-wu t'u-lu 殷虛古器物圖錄
Yin-hsu shu-ch'i ching-hua 殷虛書契菁華
Yin-hsu shu-ch'i hou-pien 殷虛書契後編
Yin-hsu shu-ch'i tai-wen pien 殷虛書契待問編
yu-mei 優美
yu-wo chih ching 有我之境
''Yu yü-lu'' 優語錄
yü-chih 玉屁
yü-shang 御賞
yü-shu 御書
Yuan Chin-k'ai 袁金鎧
Yuan Shao (Pen-ch'u) 袁紹(本初)

Index

HARVARD EAST ASIAN SERIES

(Some of these titles may be out of print in a given year. Write to Harvard University Press for information and ordering.)

DATE DUE